Mobile Network Forensics:

Emerging Research and Opportunities

Filipo Sharevski
DePaul University, USA

A volume in the Advances in
Digital Crime, Forensics, and Cyber
Terrorism (ADCFCT) Book Series

Published in the United States of America by
IGI Global
Information Science Reference (an imprint of IGI Global)
701 E. Chocolate Avenue
Hershey PA, USA 17033
Tel: 717-533-8845
Fax: 717-533-8661
E-mail: cust@igi-global.com
Web site: http://www.igi-global.com

Library of Congress Cataloging-in-Publication Data

Names: Sharevski, Filipo, 1985- author.
Title: Mobile network forensics : emerging research and opportunities / by
  Filipo Sharevski.
Description: Hershey, PA : Information Science Reference, [2018]
Identifiers: LCCN 2017057025| ISBN 9781522558552 (hardcover) | ISBN
  9781522558569 (ebook)
Subjects: LCSH: Computer crimes--Investigation. | Computer networks. | Mobile
  communication systems.
Classification: LCC HV8079.C65 S435 2018 | DDC 363.25/968--dc23 LC record available at
https://lccn.loc.gov/2017057025

This book is published in the IGI Global book series Advances in Digital Crime, Forensics, and Cyber Terrorism (ADCFCT) (ISSN: 2327-0381; eISSN: 2327-0373)

British Cataloguing in Publication Data
A Cataloguing in Publication record for this book is available from the British Library.

All work contributed to this book is new, previously-unpublished material.
The views expressed in this book are those of the authors, but not necessarily of the publisher.

For electronic access to this publication, please contact: eresources@igi-global.com.

Advances in Digital Crime, Forensics, and Cyber Terrorism (ADCFCT) Book Series

ISSN:2327-0381
EISSN:2327-0373

Editor-in-Chief: Bryan Christiansen, Global Research Society, LLC, USA & Agnieszka Piekarz, Independent Researcher, Poland

MISSION

The digital revolution has allowed for greater global connectivity and has improved the way we share and present information. With this new ease of communication and access also come many new challenges and threats as cyber crime and digital perpetrators are constantly developing new ways to attack systems and gain access to private information.

The **Advances in Digital Crime, Forensics, and Cyber Terrorism (ADCFCT) Book Series** seeks to publish the latest research in diverse fields pertaining to crime, warfare, terrorism and forensics in the digital sphere. By advancing research available in these fields, the **ADCFCT** aims to present researchers, academicians, and students with the most current available knowledge and assist security and law enforcement professionals with a better understanding of the current tools, applications, and methodologies being implemented and discussed in the field.

COVERAGE

- Vulnerability
- Crime scene imaging
- Hacking
- Malicious codes
- Encryption
- Cyber terrorism
- Mobile Device Forensics
- Telecommunications Fraud
- Cyber Warfare
- Global Threat Intelligence

IGI Global is currently accepting manuscripts for publication within this series. To submit a proposal for a volume in this series, please contact our Acquisition Editors at Acquisitions@igi-global.com or visit: http://www.igi-global.com/publish/.

Titles in this Series

For a list of additional titles in this series, please visit:
https://www.igi-global.com/book-series/advances-digital-crime-forensics-cyber/73676

Psychological and Behavioral Examinations in Cyber Security
John McAlaney (Bournemouth University, UK) Lara A. Frumkin (Open University, UK)
and Vladlena Benson (University of West Lodon, UK)
Information Science Reference • ©2018 • 334pp • H/C (ISBN: 9781522540533) • US $225.00

Combating Internet-Enabled Terrorism Emerging Research and Opportunities
Emily Stacey (Swansea Univerity, UK)
Information Science Reference • ©2017 • 133pp • H/C (ISBN: 9781522521907) • US $115.00

Combating Security Breaches and Criminal Activity in the Digital Sphere
S. Geetha (VIT University, Chennai, India) and Asnath Victy Phamila (VIT University,
Chennai, India)
Information Science Reference • ©2016 • 309pp • H/C (ISBN: 9781522501930) • US $205.00

National Security and Counterintelligence in the Era of Cyber Espionage
Eugenie de Silva (University of Leicester, UK & Virginia Research Institute, USA)
Information Science Reference • ©2016 • 308pp • H/C (ISBN: 9781466696617) • US $200.00

Handbook of Research on Civil Society and National Security in the Era of Cyber Warfare
Metodi Hadji-Janev (Military Academy "General Mihailo Apostolski", Macedonia) and
Mitko Bogdanoski (Military Academy "General Mihailo Apostolski", Macedonia)
Information Science Reference • ©2016 • 548pp • H/C (ISBN: 9781466687936) • US $335.00

Cybersecurity Policies and Strategies for Cyberwarfare Prevention
Jean-Loup Richet (University of Nantes, France)
Information Science Reference • ©2015 • 472pp • H/C (ISBN: 9781466684560) • US $245.00

New Threats and Countermeasures in Digital Crime and Cyber Terrorism
Maurice Dawson (Illinois Institute of Technology, USA) and Marwan Omar (Nawroz
University, Iraq)
Information Science Reference • ©2015 • 368pp • H/C (ISBN: 9781466683457) • US $200.00

For an entire list of titles in this series, please visit:
https://www.igi-global.com/book-series/advances-digital-crime-forensics-cyber/73676

IGI Global
DISSEMINATOR OF KNOWLEDGE

701 East Chocolate Avenue, Hershey, PA 17033, USA
Tel: 717-533-8845 x100 • Fax: 717-533-8661
E-Mail: cust@igi-global.com • www.igi-global.com

Table of Contents

Preface

Digital technologies appeal to cybercriminals because they see powerful tools to support of their malicious actions. The investigation of sources for digital evidence became a forensic practice essential in processing cybercrimes and interrupting unauthorized actions (Palmer, 2001). The field of digital forensics underwent a complex maturation process in its short history as a response to of the technical evolution and creativity of cybercriminals.

Recovering evidence from individual computers and examining basic network traffic were the main tasks in the early years (Harichandran, Breitinger, Baggili, & Marrington, 2016; Pollitt, 2010). By the time the investigative methods and tools matured, cybercriminals had developed new ways to misuse the latest technological advancements. Investigators began to discover instances of complex malicious software developed to exploit previously unknown vulnerabilities in both the desktop and mobile operating systems (Esttom, 2014). Malicious traffic diversified and intensified so quickly that the irregularities in network behavior prompted digital forensics scientists to develop a dedicated field for network forensics (Conlan, Baggili, & Breitinger, 2016). The cyber front also extended to combat the surge in anti-forensics actions - cybercriminals quickly recognized the relative ease of eliminating or hiding the evidence of their activities in the digital domain (Khan, Gani, Wahab, Shiraz, & Ahmad, 2016).

These and many other malicious activities rapidly grew in size and complexity causing unpreceded disturbances in the cyber sphere. More than 7.1 billion confidential data records have been breached or stolen by web application attacks, cyberespionage, and misuse of data access privileges in the past eight years (Verizon, 2017). Around 1.1 billion records were breached 2016 alone, which is more than 50% increase than the number of records breached in the year before. In 2016, cybercriminals developed 357 million new instances of malware and used one in every 131 emails to spread it all over the Internet (Symantec, 2017). The total cost of technology-facilitated crime in United States for 2016 was estimated to $17.36 million, increasing more than 50% over four years (Ponemon Institute, 2017). These numbers are strong indicators that digital forensics professionals will face complex investigations as the digital technology further evolves and cybercriminals' interest with it (Garfinkel, 2010).

Mobile communications as a form of digital networking technology has also witnessed rapid evolution in the last few decades, going through four generations and actively preparing to transition to the fifth in the next few years. This evolution is accelerated by proliferation of mobile devices and the increased demand for wireless broadband speeds. There were 7.8 billion mobile subscriptions registered worldwide in 2016 with a forecast for this number to rise to 8.9 billion in 2023 (Ericsson, 2018). Mobile devices generated 15 Exabytes/month[1] on average per device in the first half of 2018 and forecast to grow 39% by 2023 (Ericsson, 2018). Mobile devices are designed to perform an array of functions including telephony, internet access and computing, global positioning and navigation, or near-field communications (Ayers, Brothers, & Jansen, 2014). Being used more than 4 hours per person per day on average, mobile devices include a trove of artefacts about our daily routines, online behavior, or private communication. It is highly likely that every cybercriminal either possesses a mobile device to facilitate its criminal activities or has an interest in exploiting the mobile communication technology for personal gain. Consequently, forensic practitioners routinely investigate mobile devices for evidence in processing the technology-related crimes and incidents (Barmpatsalou, Damopoulos, Kambourakis, & Katos, 2013).

While investigating mobile devices, forensic practitioners look for potential evidence in many locations, one of which is the subscriber identification module or the external card that is used by the device to establish connection with a mobile network. The information includes labels that uniquely identify the universal SIM card itself, the mobile subscriber, location tags, call history entries, and locally stored short messages in most of the cases. Together with the device label and the mobile phone number, this information is forwarded to the mobile network providers for assistance in obtaining the network records of the device activity, its presence in certain areas, or in some cases the real-time content of communication. The guidelines and best practices for mobile device forensics stop at this stage of "ask the provider" and wait for the network data to complete the investigations. The objective of this book is to extend the knowledge to "what it takes the provider to answer", what actually is included "providers' response", and it shall be analyzed in producing reliable digital forensics evidence.

As we advance from Long Term Evolution (LTE) towards 5G networks, it is critical for the forensic practitioners and researchers to understand the mobile networking environment from an investigative perspective for several reasons. With a 101% global penetration rate[2] mobile broadband users are expected to be connected all the time, at any location, to any device with speeds up to 1 Gbps until 2023 (Vannithamby & Talwar, 2017). The 5G networks will extend the mobile support for Internet-of-Things (IoT) to become the dominant connectivity platform (Nokia, 2017). The next generation is expected to adopt a software-defined architecture to enable "carrier clouds" that give greater flexibility in balancing between service performance, quality-of-experience, and network resilience (Liyanage, Gurtov, & Ylianttila, 2015). In addition to the forecast expansion in traffic, mobile networks inevitably will become, if they are not already, the technology of choice for cyber criminals and with that the most critical place to look for evidence. The investigation trends in mobile device forensics will shift towards examination of IoT devices and applications, in network forensics towards examination of malicious mobile network traffic and traffic irregularities, and in cloud forensics towards examination of the software-defined mobile network backbones.

INTENDED AUDIENCE

This book covers all the aspects of conducting investigations in all generations of mobile networks with an emphasis of the current LTE deployments and future 5G technologies. Forensics practitioners working with mobile devices and networks will find the content helpful in understanding the standardized procedures for identification, collection, acquisition and preservation of mobile network evidence. The analysis, management, and reporting procedures are elaborated in detail, so this book can help investigators utilize the mobile network evidence collected in reference to a given criminal act or incident. Researchers working in digital forensics and network security can use this book as a reference in the latest mobile network and digital forensics standardization and inform themselves of the current trends, vulnerabilities, and anti-forensics techniques relevant for the mobile communication technologies. For legal practitioners, the book discusses the relevant legal framework for mobile network investigations and the probative value of the associated evidence in support of legal theory. The book's content is also useful for all cybersecurity students interested in learning the recent advancements and the emerging research in deriving evidence from mobile network infrastructures.

ORGANIZATION OF THE BOOK

The book contains eight chapters. Chapter 1 reviews the fundamentals of network forensics, and discusses the ISO/IEC SC27 standards for digital forensics investigation together with the role of digital forensics in the legal system. Chapter 2 discusses advances in cloud, software-defined network, and Internet-of-Things (IoT) forensics to identify the opportunities in present and future mobile network forensics investigations. The mobile network system evolution is detailed in Chapter 3 with an emphasis on supported services, connectivity technologies employed and frequency bands, and network performance indicators.

Chapter 4 elaborates the pre-3GPP network architectures (GSM, GPRS, and EDGE) while Chapter 5 the UMTS, LTE, and the candidate technologies for 5G networks as standardized or described by 3GPP. Chapter 6 focuses on mobile network forensics general principles and legal aspects. The mobile network investigative process and procedures are detailed in Chapter 7 in the context of the ISO/IEC SC27 standards with supporting real-world examples of mobile network forensics investigation experiences and evidence. The final chapter presents the emerging challenges and investigative opportunities in all current deployments and 5G including the continuous support for interception, localization, required privacy safeguards, and mobile network anti-forensics.

THE NEED FOR MOBILE NETWORK FORENSICS

The investigation of mobile-facilitated crimes and incidents from a network perspective is a relevant but rarely explored topic. Modern communications are critically dependent on mobile providers for access, turning their infrastructures into treasure troves of forensic information in relation to sophisticated crimes, acts of terrorism acts, and high impact cybersecurity incidents. In keeping pace with the mobile evolution, this book contributes with a comprehensive coverage of technical, legal, and emerging research aspects of conducting investigation in the mobile networking environment. The presented mobile network forensics follow generally accepted digital forensics principles and comprehensiveness of the investigation process so interested practitioners or researchers can easily apply it to their work. The book's topics are organized so readers can combine them with other guidelines, best practices, and digital forensics knowledge to support practical investigations, processing court cases, or yield new scientific information. I hope you will enjoy reading this book and trust that you will use it wisely to benefit from it.

REFERENCES

Androulidakis, I. I. (2016). *Mobile Phone Security and Forensics*. New York, NY: Springer Science and Business Media; doi:10.1007/978-3-319-29742-2

Ayers, R., Brothers, S., & Jansen, W. (2014). Guidelines on mobile device forensics. Gaithersburg, MD: Academic Press. doi:10.6028/NIST.SP.800-101r1

Barmpatsalou, K., Damopoulos, D., Kambourakis, G., & Katos, V. (2013). A critical review of 7 years of Mobile Device Forensics. *Digital Investigation*, *10*(4), 323–349. doi:10.1016/j.diin.2013.10.003

Conlan, K., Baggili, I., & Breitinger, F. (2016). Anti-forensics: Furthering digital forensic science through a new extended, granular taxonomy. *Digital Investigation, 18*, S66–S75. doi:10.1016/j.diin.2016.04.006

Ericsson. (2018). *Ericsson Mobility Report. Ericsson Mobility Report*. Retrieved from https://www.ericsson.com/assets/local/mobility-report/documents/2018/ericsson-mobility-report-june-2018.pdf

Esttom, C. (2014). *System Forensics, Investigation and Response* (2nd ed.). Burlington, MA: Jones & Bartlett Learning.

Garfinkel, S. L. (2010). Digital forensics research: The next 10 years. *Digital Investigation*, *7*(1–2), 64–73. doi:10.1016/j.diin.2010.05.009

Harichandran, V. S., Breitinger, F., Baggili, I., & Marrington, A. (2016). A cyber forensics needs analysis survey: Revisiting the domain's needs a decade later. *Computers & Security*, *57*, 1–13. doi:10.1016/j.cose.2015.10.007

Khan, S., Gani, A., Wahab, A. W. A., Shiraz, M., & Ahmad, I. (2016). Network forensics: Review, taxonomy, and open challenges. *Journal of Network and Computer Applications*, *66*, 214–235. doi:10.1016/j.jnca.2016.03.005

Liyanage, M., Gurtov, A., & Ylianttila, M. (2015). *Software Defined Mobile Networks (SDMN): Beyond LTE Network Architecture* (M. Liyanage, A. Gurtov, & M. Ylianttila, Eds.). West Sussex, UK: Wiley. doi:10.1002/9781118900253

Nokia. (2017). *LTE evolution for IoT connectivity*. Retrieved from www.nokia.com

Palmer, G. (2001). *A Road Map for Digital Forensic Research*. Academic Press.

Pollitt, M. (2010). A History of Digital Forensics. In *IFIP International Conference on Digital Forensics* (pp. 1–11). Springer.

Ponemon Institute. (2017). *2017 Cost of Cyber Crime Study. 2016 Cost of Cyber Crime Study & the Risk of Business Innovation*. Retrieved from http://www.ponemon.org/local/upload/file/2016 HPE CCC GLOBAL REPORT FINAL 3.pdf

Scrivens, N., & Lin, X. (2017). Android Digital Forensics : Data, Extraction and Analysis. *Proceedings of the ACM Turing 50th Celebration Conference – China*. 10.1145/3063955.3063981

Symantec. (2017). *Internet Security Threat Report*. Author.

Vannithamby, R., & Talwar, S. (2017). Towards 5G: Applications, Requirements & Candidate Technologies (R. Vannithamby & S. Talwar, Eds.). West Sussex, UK: Wiley.

Verizon. (2017). *2017 Data Breach Investigations Report*. Retrieved from http://www.verizonenterprise.com/verizon-insights-lab/dbir/2017/

ENDNOTES

[1]   1 Exabyte = 1 Billion Gigabytes.
[2]   A penetration rate of over 100% means that there are more subscriptions than people.

Chapter 1
Network Forensics:
Fundamentals

ABSTRACT

Network forensics investigations aim to uncover evidence about criminal or unauthorized activities facilitated by, or targeted to, a given networking technology. Understanding the fundamental investigative principles is equally important as understanding each of the modern networking technologies for every forensics scientist or practitioner. This chapter provides an overview of the network forensic fundamentals from a contemporary perspective, accenting the formalization of network investigation, various investigative techniques, and how the network forensics support the legal system.

INTRODUCTION

This chapter overviews the fundamentals of the network forensics practice. An updated network forensics definition is provided to reflect the proliferation of new networking solutions including mobile devices, smart objects, industrial controls systems, and cloud computing platforms. The standardized network forensics investigation process recommended by the International Standardization Organization (ISO) is presented throughout the chapter with supporting examples of mobile network investigations. In the same context, the network forensics techniques and their role in the legal system are also discussed. The chapter concludes with a brief review of the current mobile technology to set the accord for the remainder of this book.

DOI: 10.4018/978-1-5225-5855-2.ch001

DEFINITION OF NETWORK FORENSICS

Network forensics is a cross-discipline of digital forensics and communication networks. Digital forensics is the application of scientific methods to investigate evidence from digital sources about security incidents or criminal activities (Palmer, 2001; Ruan *et al.*, 2011). Communication networks refer to any infrastructure used for exchange of information in digital form between two or more network entities. In the early years, the network forensics focused on investigating Internet Protocol (IP) based networks for evidence in relation to malicious traffic packets or irregular traffic flows in violation of the networking policies and principles (Khan *et al.*, 2016).

As both the networks and the malicious behavior evolved, the forensics practice broadened to include mobile networks, cloud computing, Internet-of-Things (IoT), industrial control systems, and software-defined networks. The investigations in these environments follow the common network forensics investigation process with techniques, tools, and procedures tailored specifically for each of them. Modern network forensics thus refer to the *scientific methods for identification, collection, acquisition, and preservation of digital evidence from networking environments for further analysis, interpretation, and presentation in investigating security incidents and criminal activities.*

NETWORK FORENSICS INVESTIGATION PROCESS

Background

The formalization of network forensics is necessary to ensure the soundness and reliability of the investigative process and the veracity of evidence presented in court (Slay *et al.*, 2009). To demonstrate the suitability of the scientific methods for production of network evidence, various formal models have been proposed in the past (Marshall, 2011; Joshi and Pilli, 2016). The ISO recognized that the inconsistency between these models can greatly affect the quality, validity, and credibility of the digital evidence and devised accreditation through the set of interrelated standards depicted in Figure 1. These standards lay down the fundamental set of principles with guidance on how they can be applied in common scenarios. As such, the ISO/IEC SC27 standards are suitable for investigations in various networking environments to ensure the quality of the network forensics products.

Figure 1. ISO/IEC SC27 digital forensics standards

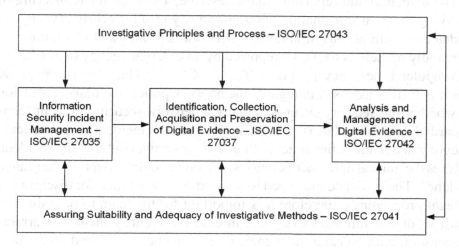

ISO/IEC 27035:2016 - Information Security Incident Management

The production of credible network evidence begins by establishing an *investigative readiness* (International Standardization Organization, 2016). The investigative readiness is a structured approach in handling security incidents and is achieved in five distinct phases:

1. Plan and prepare
2. Detection and reporting
3. Assessment and decision
4. Responses
5. Lessons learned

For network-related security incidents, the plan and preparation phase includes development of *incident management plan* and *investigative capabilities*. The plan encompasses further development of *policies* describing which traffic events are considered malicious or irregular that constitute a network security incident. The plan also requires development of *procedures* describing the steps for responding to an incident. The *network protection controls* such as firewalls, intrusion detection and prevention, or unified threat management systems are recommended as incident response capabilities together with an *incident response team* and a relationship with one or several Law Enforcement Agencies (LEA)s.

3

The detection and reporting phase describes the steps for registering or receiving external information about a security event. Security events can be detected with alarms of abnormal network activities and recognition of potentially malicious traffic or reported by an external agency (e.g. LEA or a Computer Emergency Response Team – CERT). This alarm or external report is further assessed in regards the network policies to make a decision on whether the security event is actually a network security incident (or is discarded as a false alarm). If it is an incident, the incident response team categorizes and classifies it according to its severity, contains the incident, restores the normal network operations, and proceeds in collecting the related evidence. The evidence may need to be used at a future time for disciplinary or legal proceedings, therefore it is important for the team to be trained in handling digital forensics evidence. In case the security incident warrants cooperation with an external agency, there must be established procedures and handover interfaces for evidence delivery. Once the incident is resolved, the investigation is reviewed so the policies, procedures, and network security controls are further improved for other emerging threats.

ISO/IEC 27037:2012 - Identification, Collection and Acquisition, and Preservation of Digital Evidence

With ISO/IEC 27035:2016 in place, the investigation follows the ISO/IEC 27037:2012 guidelines for identification, collection, acquisition and preservation of network evidence (International Standardization Organization, 2012). The initial phases of the network forensics investigation process are: *identification*, *collection & acquisition*, and *preservation* of digital evidence.

Identification

The identification is the search for, recognition, and documentation of potential network evidence. Consider a lawful interception of mobile traffic including calls and texts for a prepaid user during a period of 30 days. The mobile network investigators need to be able to uniquely recognize the traffic based on the user's phone numbers or other network identifiers that the investigators were able to obtain. Further, investigators need to search for the meta-data corresponding to the user activity in these days, e.g. prepaid account activity, or network registrations. For both types of potential mobile network evidence, investigators need to document the evidence, the network elements and persons involved, and the identifier(s) used to search for the subjects of the investigation. Chapter 4 and Chapter 5 provide further details on mobile network evidence identification.

Collection and Acquisition

ISO/IEC 27037:2012 distinguishes between collection and acquisition of digital evidence to remain general enough for all digital forensics investigations. The collection is the process of gathering data that contain potential digital evidence, while acquisition happens when investigators create a copy of the data to maintain the original condition of the potential digital evidence. In most investigations, the collection and acquisition is essentially one step because the network infrastructure is distributed in nature so it is infeasible to physically access the network elements (e.g. routers, security appliances, or servers) to make a copy of the stored data. In the interception example above, the investigators are making copies of the call and text contents in real-time as they are realized over the mobile network, i.e. they acquire the *content-of-communication* (CC) to bring it as a potential digital evidence under forensic custody. They also acquire the meta-data for the targeted subjects immediately after the interception is concluded as the *interception-related information* (IRI) to ensure its original condition when in forensic custody. Both the CC and IRI data are delivered over standardized and secured handover interfaces between the mobile operators and the LEAs rather than sending the network equipment for local analysis. Chapter 6 through Chapter 8 discuss the lawful interception as an investigative practice and the handling of CC and IRI as mobile network evidence.

Preservation

Once the potential evidence is in forensic custody, the preservation takes place to protect its integrity so to ensure its usefulness for the investigation. The preservation method is dependent on the type of network evidence. If the evidence is volatile, i.e. acquired in real-time as the CC during a lawful interception, investigators need to stored it in a safe place, with integrity checks in place, and at least one back-up copy. The back-up is important because if the evidence is tampered or lost, it will be impossible to be recreated or re-acquired again. This holds also for the meta-data, although there is a possibility for the investigators to request a copy for some of the information like the prepaid account history because most mobile operators are obliged by law to keep copies of aggregated meta-data for three or more years. The chain-of-custody also plays a critical role in the potential evidence preservation, especially for privacy sensitive data like the intercepted calls or texts. Investigators need to ensure that only authorized parties have access to the data and limit the disclosure of the CC. Chapter 6 and Chapter 7 elaborate on the preservation of mobile network evidence to safeguard the privacy of the involved parties.

ISO/IEC 27042:2015 - Analysis and Interpretation of Digital Evidence

ISO/IEC 27042:2015 guidelines describe the methodology for extracting the probative value out of the potential digital evidence (International Standardization Organization, 2014a). The analysis can be carried out in two modes: *static analysis* and *live analysis*. The static analysis is the inspection of raw consequential data (e.g. packet captures, logs files, or traces) and meta-data (e.g. file permissions and timestamps) in *non-real* time. Static analysis should normally be carried out on a copy of the original potential digital evidence (as described in ISO/IEC 27037:2012) to avoid accidental spoliation or obfuscation. The live analysis is inspection of the live version of the systems and is carried out in *real-time* while the network traffic is actually in transit. In these circumstances, great care must be taken to minimize the risk of damaging and losing the potential network evidence with a full and detailed record of all forensic processes performed. In both cases, the forensic analysis can be facilitated with forensic tools adequate for examination of the potential network evidence (as described in ISO/IEC 207041:2015). The product of the network forensic analysis is the segment of the data selected as the actual network forensics evidence that is next subjected to interpretation.

The objective of interpretation is to evaluate the network forensics evidence based on its contents and context including key patterns, topics, relevant people, etc., to derive meaning in respect to the investigated security incident or criminal activity. The interpretation involves fact finding and validation/ verification of results. In searching for facts, it is important to distinguish between facts that have been found in the evidence, and facts inferred from additional data or information provided. For example, a lawfully intercepted CC from a mobile network is a fact. If combined with the meta-data of the call, the conversation can be placed in time and the broad location of the calling and/or called party can determined. This distinction is important when reporting these facts so the logical process of inference can be validated. The interpretation of the network evidence is dependent on its context of creation, that is, the investigators need to consider information about the network operation itself.

In our example, this information can include call handling configurations (e.g. active call forwarding rules, prepaid balance), geographical mapping of the cell towers used to realize the call, etc. This is important so that the investigators ensure the quality of the network evidence (completeness, source and original purpose, prevention of evidence obfuscation). If the contextual information changes, the interpretation may also have to change to reflect this. The network forensics interpretation is delivered as a formal report that contains the information about the competence of the investigators, the nature of the investigation, the factual details, the contextual information, any analytical and interpretative limitations, list of processes and tools used, the final interpretation and conclusion, and if needed, a recommendation for further investigative work. Chapter 7 and Chapter 8 detail the analysis and interpretation of mobile network evidence including specific tools, techniques, and procedures.

ISO/IEC 27043:2015 - Incident Investigation Principles and Processes

ISO/IEC 27043:2015 guidelines describe a harmonized digital investigation model for various operational scenarios involving digital evidence (International Standardization Organization, 2014b). This model is shown in Figure 2 and provides a succinct guidance on the exact logical steps to be followed during any kind of investigation in such a way that, if challenged in any court of law, no doubt should exist as to the accuracy of the investigation and the quality of the evidence. ISO/IEC 27403:2015 outlines four classes of investigative processes: *readiness, initialization, acquisitive,* and *interpretative.* In parallel, there is a set of concurrent actions: authorization, documentation, information flow management, chain-of-custody, digital evidence preservation, and interaction with the physical crime scene.

Readiness Processes

The readiness processes help the pre-incident preparation and include planning, implementation and assessment phases. This class of processes is optional to the network investigation processes and is effectuated by an organization rather than the investigator(s). However, for networks that are subject to regulation or are categorized as critical infrastructures (e.g. mobile networks or industrial control systems), the readiness is required to ensure that the forensic investigation will yield digital evidence without negative consequences to the involved parties (i.e. privacy intrusion or environmental pollution). The planning phases includes identification of all sources of potential network evidence and the necessary policies and processes for this evidence to be handed over for further analysis or to the external LEAs. If for example, a mobile operator has to implement lawful interception capabilities, follow the regulatory requirements for wiretapping invocation, establish the lawful interception architecture, and create the handover interfaces with LEAs for evidence delivery. The implementation phase includes the procurement of the required equipment, testing of the handover interfaces for security, and appointment of responsible entities on both sides. The assessment phase is set in place to ensure that all the regulatory and technical requirements are met prior to instantiating any network investigation. The readiness process and the legal framework for mobile network investigations is discussed in Chapter 6.

Initialization Processes

The initialization processes deal with incident detection, first response, planning, and preparation of the network investigation. The incident detection and first response phases correspond with the detection and reporting phases from the ISO/IEC 27035:2016 guidelines. In these phases the investigation is initialized by registering or receiving external information about a security event. Assuming lawful interception capabilities in place, the investigation is initialized by receiving a request for target subjects of lawful interception (identified by a list of phone numbers, for example) by a LEA. The planning and preparation phases follow to determine the period, format and type of interception (e.g. only calls and text messages in the next 30 days), the registration status (e.g. currently active prepaid subscriber registered in the Chicago metropolitan area), and the transfer of the intercepted material in real-time over the handover interface to the LEA. Chapter 6 provides the initialization mechanics for mobile network investigations.

Acquisitive Processes

The acquisitive processes are concerned with the acquisition of network evidence following the steps described in ISO/IEC 27035:2012. In the interception example, the identification and acquisition corresponds to activation of the lawful interception feature for the target subjects on the network side for all the calls and text messages they will eventually send/ receive in the next 30 days. The network evidence in this case is the content of the calls and the text messages together with the associated network meta-data. During the acquisition, investigators need to document the registration status and if there are any changes to the user profile on the network side during the lawful interception period (e.g. the subject has roamed in Canada in the last 7 days of the investigation period and cannot initiate originating calls due to insufficient balance on the prepaid account). Investigators can decide to include historical information from the targets' prepaid accounts to form the context of evidence creation as discussed in ISO/IEC 27042:2015. During the acquisition, the intercepted material is transferred in real-time over the handover interfaces to the LEA, where it is securely stored for further analysis. Chapter 6 through 8 elaborate the acquisition of digital evidence from the second generation (2G) up to the forthcoming fifth (5G) of mobile networks.

Investigative Processes

The investigative processes closely follow the ISO/IEC 27042:2015 guidelines for analysis and interpretation of digital evidence. The potential digital evidence – the content of the calls and the text messages with the associated meta-data - is analyzed together with the prepaid balance history of the targeted subject of investigation. The overall information is interpreted to create the mobile activity profile of the subjects for the period of the investigation. The profile includes the list of other parties contacted in this period and subject's coarse movement pattern (e.g. traveled to New York and after two days roamed in the Montreal area for the last 7 days of the investigation period). The investigators detail the profiling to reflect the subject's inability to initiate calls due to an insufficient balance while in roaming, i.e. supporting the fact that the subject

Figure 2. Common Network Investigation Model

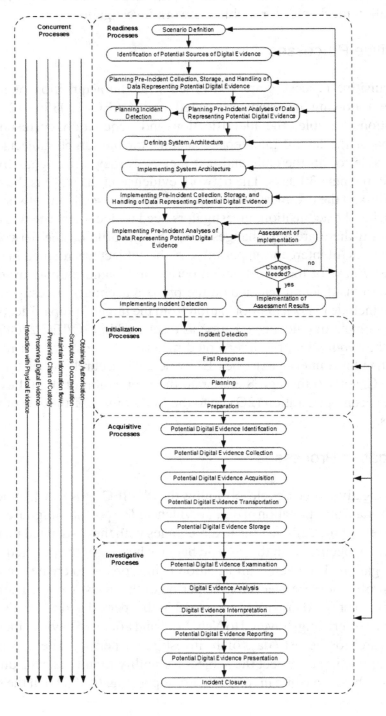

has only sent two and received three text messages, but made no calls. The profile is then presented in the court of law to support the hypothesis for the implicated criminal activities of the subject. The investigation concludes with the closure phase where the investigators decide whether to reiterate the investigation, reject or accept the hypothesis, and safely store the intercepted evidence for the period required by the interception regulation and local laws. Chapter 6 through 8 elaborate the analysis, interpretation, and presentation of mobile network evidence in practice.

Concurrent Processes

The concurrent processes are a set of actions that should be followed throughout the network investigation include: authorization, documentation, information flow definition, chain-of-custody preservation, network evidence preservation, and interaction with the physical investigation. Prior to any lawful interception, mobile operators need to formally accept an interception request and authorize the investigation. The information flow definition and the realization of the interception are also required together with the documentation to reflect every change in subjects' mobile network activity or changes in the network configuration that can affect the context of evidence creation. The preservation of the chain-of-custody and the network evidence is critical during the investigation to ensure that no one has tampered (both digitally and physically) with the intercepted material and any other related evidence to ensure proper analysis, interpretation, and presentation in court.

ISO/IEC 27041:2015 - Assuring Suitability and Adequacy of Investigative Methods

The ISO/IEC 27041:2015 provides guidance for assuring suitability and adequacy of investigative methods. To assure the suitability of the lawful interception as a form of mobile network forensics investigation in real-time, the regulators, LEAs, and the mobile operators need to define and analyze the requirements for its realization. Following an agreement on the requirements, the lawful interception needs to be designed, implemented, verified, and validated in accordance with the local regulatory directives and laws, as well as with the global mobile technology standardization. If this is confirmed by all stakeholders, the interception architecture is deployed and regularly reviewed and maintained as needed. Chapter 6 elaborates on the suitability and adequacy of the lawful interception in greater detail.

TAXONOMY OF NETWORK FORENSICS TECHNIQUES

The ISO/IEC SC27 guidelines detail the network investigations to maximize the probative value of the network evidence, but say little about how to operationalize the investigations depending on the criminal activity or the nature of the security incident. Table 1 shows the taxonomy of network forensics techniques based on the various parameters used to identify the type of crimes or security incidents investigated (Joshi and Pilli, 2016; Khan *et al.*, 2016).

Table 1. Types of network forensics techniques

Category	Parameter	Description
Mechanism	Logging	Recording of network flows and patterns
	Packet Marking	Marking of network packets and flows (e.g. e.g. source destination IP/port, number of packets, etc.)
	Heuristic Base	Network topology analysis (e.g. nodes distances, traffic load, traffic distribution, etc.)
Data Source	Traffic	User network traffic
	Meta-data	Signaling (network control) traffic
	Traffic and meta-data	Combination of raw/signaling traffic
Data Instance	Packet header	Investigation based only on packet header information
	Packet payload	Investigation based only on packet payload information
	Packet flow	Investigation based on both the traffic header and the payload, e.g. the traffic flow
	Network node	Analysis of the network infrastructure
Forensic Processing	Centralized	Processing of potential network evidence centralized forensics server
	Decentralized	Processing of potential network evidence Distributed forensics servers
Time of Investigation	Real-time	The identification and acquisition of the potential network evidence at the time of its flow, e.g. in transit
	Non-real-time	Ex-post-facto or identification and acquisition of the potential network evidence after the attack
Purpose of Investigation	Attribution	Investigating the origin of security incidents
	Crime Reconstruction	Investigating the network events corresponding to criminal activities
	Evidence Validation	Validating evidence resulting from other investigations

These techniques need to be adapted to the specific technologies for each networking environment. The taxonomy mostly relates to Internet networks, but it can be modified for investigations in mobile networks, cloud computing, internet-of-things, industrial control systems, software-defined networks, or any other digital networks. Mobile network investigations use the same techniques with the addition of a *circuit marking* parameter for intercepting circuit-switched calls. The data sources in mobile networks typically include voice, messaging, packet services, localization information, charging records, and signaling traffic (the IRI or the network meta-data)

The forensics processing can be centralized, i.e. with one LEA working on evidence from one or multiple national mobile operators; or decentralized, i.e. coordinated forensic processing of different mobile network data by different LEAs. Decentralized processing is useful for handling evidence coming from different jurisdictions and international mobile carriers. The time of investigation corresponds with the interception of real-time traffic (CC) or non-real-time data (IRI or meta-data) that can be retrieved *ex-post-facto* (after the fact). The forensics investigations in mobile networks deal with *mobile network facilitated crimes* or *mobile network targeted attacks*. When investigating mobile network facilitated crimes, the objective of the investigation is to collect potential evidence that can later be used in crime reconstructions in the court of law. In some cases, the localization information about the whereabouts of the perpetrators at the time of the crime can be challenged. A forensic radio survey can be devised to investigate the network coverage to validate the localization evidence provided by the network as an independent on-site investigation. The mobile networks like every network can become a target for an attack on its services so any related incident also needs to be forensically investigated to determine the origin of attack and the vulnerabilities exploited. The objective is to provide the evidence of the mobile network targeted attack so that the mobile operators, equipment vendors, and standardization bodies can work on improving the security of the network infrastructure.

NETWORK FORENSICS IN THE LEGAL SYSTEM

The legal processing of network facilitated crimes is critically dependent on the quality of the network evidence, its pertinence to the criminal activity, and the trustworthiness of its interpretation (Casey, 2011; Daniel and Daniel, 2011).

Evidence Admissibility

Before any network evidence is admitted in courtroom, it must meet certain standards, that is, courts need to test its:

1. Relevance
2. Authenticity
3. Not hearsay or admissible hearsay
4. Best evidence
5. Not unduly prejudicial

It is critically important for any type of network evidence to be obtained with court authorization – or warrant – otherwise it will not be admitted in court. This is especially important when conducting lawful interceptions in mobile networks. In order to invoke an interception as "lawful", the investigators need to convince the court authorities the mobile traffic indeed is a source of potential evidence for a given crime. The main exceptions allowing warrantless investigations (or searches) in the US are plain view, consent, and exigency. Evidence can be obtained without a warrant if the investigators see the evidence in plain view, they have a valid consent from the network users, for emergency life threatening situations or threat of an immediate evidence destruction. Mobile localization data is often used to pinpoint the geographical position of a target user in the case of an emergency following a 911 call, for example.

To demonstrate authenticity of the network evidence, investigators provide proofs that it was obtained from a network infrastructure and that the chain-of-custody and integrity checks show the evidence was preserved while in forensic custody. Investigators also need to provide proofs for the reliability of the evidence or to show that the network infrastructure was functioning normally during the time the evidence was created. The original data acquired during the investigation is always considered the best evidence for the crime. Copies of the evidence can also be submitted as best evidence if investigators can demonstrate they are the exact duplicate of the original digital data. Network evidence might not be admitted if it contains hearsay because the speaker or the author of the evidence is not present in court to verify the truthfulness (Casey, 2011). For example, the CC needs to be verified to prove that the speakers in the phone conversations are actually the target subjects of the lawful interception.

Expert Reports and Testimony

Communicating the results of a network investigation in court is highly important in understanding the pertinence of the evidence to the criminal act. The investigators' report or testimony can easily become hard to follow if rendered in too many technical terms because very few are familiar with the specific language of the technologies investigated. When writing a report, investigators need to build a solid interpretation based on the facts and inferences with detailed entries of every stage of investigation so another competent investigator or expert can evaluate the evidence and associated conclusions. Investigative reports need to include the steps taken to prepare for the investigation, summarize the sources of potential digital evidence, the techniques, tools, and procedures used for examination, the forensics analysis and interpretation, the findings, and an elaborate conclusion. In reporting an investigation including a lawful interception, LEA's requests shall be included with the subjects' identifiers, mobile services of interest, the period of investigation, and any input information from a related mobile device forensics report. The CC needs to be accompanied with transcripts of the conversations or the messages together with the IRI or network meta-data. The techniques and tools used for analysis of the mobile data have to be documented so the courts can test the scientific process used for interpretation (known as the Daubert test). Investigators need to clearly indicate their level of confidence in their interpretations and conclusions. In case further assistance is needed in verifying the evidence, investigators need to clearly indicate the need for additional forensics help (e.g. forensics speech recognition for the speakers included in the CC evidence).

CONCLUSION

Mobile technology is a dominant networking platform with 390 million users in North America in 2017 more than 80% of them being 4G Long Term Evolution (LTE) subscriptions. This means that there are more subscriptions than people on the continent; at least 8% of these subscriptions are either used for connecting smart objects, people have two or more mobile devices, or are inactive but registered with the mobile operators. In terms of traffic, an active smartphone in North America realized on average 6 GB/month and is expected to generate around 50 GB/Month in 2023 (Ericsson, 2018).

From a legal perspective, a mobile penetration of more than a 100% implies that almost all crimes are facilitated by mobile devices, directly or indirectly. Consequently, evidence about mobile device network activity is becoming more prevalent in various court proceedings. From a forensics perspective, the millions of gigabytes of mobile data require understanding of the different mobile networking technologies, how the forensics principles apply respectively, the operationalization of the investigation process, and the applicable techniques in the production of mobile network evidence. Bringing this knowledge closer to the investigators, forensic practitioners, or researchers is the main goal of this book. The subsequent chapters elaborate on all of these topics to help interested readers understand the forensics context of the mobile networks, the role of mobile network evidence in the legal system, and the emerging challenges and opportunities in the ubiquitous mobile communications.

REFERENCES

Casey, E. (2011). *Digital Evidence and Computer Crime* (3rd ed.). Waltham, MA: Elsevier.

Daniel, L. E., & Daniel, L. E. (2011). *Digital Forensics for Legal Professionals: Understanding Digital Evidence From the Warrant to the Courtroom*. Waltham, MA: Syngress.

Ericsson. (2018). *Ericsson Mobility Report, Ericsson Mobility Report*. Available at: https://www.ericsson.com/en/mobility-report/reports/june-2018

International Standardization Organization. (2012). *ISO/IEC 27037:2012 guidelines for identification, collection, acquisition and preservation of digital evidence*. Available at: https://www.iso.org/standard/44381.html

International Standardization Organization. (2014a). *ISO/IEC 27042 -- Guidelines for the analysis and interpretation of digital evidence*. Available at: https://www.iso.org/standard/44406.html

International Standardization Organization. (2014b). *ISO/IEC 27043 -- Incident investigation principles and processes*. Available at: https://www.iso.org/standard/44407.html

International Standardization Organization. (2016). *ISO/IEC 27035:2011 -- Information security incident management*. Available at: https://www.iso.org/standard/62071.html

Joshi, R. C., & Pilli, E. S. (2016). *Fundamentals of Network Forensics* (1st ed.). London, UK: Springer; doi:10.1007/978-1-4471-7299-4

Khan, S., Gani, A., Wahab, A. W. A., Shiraz, M., & Ahmad, I. (2016). Network forensics: Review, taxonomy, and open challenges. *Journal of Network and Computer Applications. Elsevier*, *66*, 214–235. doi:10.1016/j.jnca.2016.03.005

Marshall, A. M. (2011). Standards, regulation & quality in digital investigations: The state we are in. *Digital Investigation. Elsevier Ltd*, *8*(2), 141–144. doi:10.1016/j.diin.2011.11.001

Palmer, G. (2001) *A Road Map for Digital Forensic Research*. Academic Press.

Ruan, K., Carthy, J., Kechadi, T., & Crosbie, M. (2011). Cloud forensics. *Advances in Digital Forensics 7th IFIP WG 11.9 International Conference on Digital Forensics*, 35–46. 10.1007/978-3-642-24212-0_3

Slay, J., Lin, Y.-C., Turnbull, B., Beckett, J., & Lin, P. (2009). Towards a Formalization of Digital Forensics. In Advances in Digital Forensics V. New York: Springer. doi:10.1007/978-3-642-04155-6_3

KEY TERMS AND DEFINITIONS

2G: 2nd generation of mobile networks. The most dominant technology is the global system for mobility (GSM).

3G: 3rd generation of mobile networks. The most dominant technology is universal mobile telecommunication system (UMTS).

3GPP: 3rd generation partnership project.

4G: 4th generation of mobile networks. The 4G technologies are long term evolution (LTE) and the advanced version, LTE-advanced. Colloquially, the terms LTE/LTE-A are used as a synonym for 4G as they are the only global standard for mobile communication from the fourth generation.

5G: 5th generation of mobile networks. Still in standardization phase, the first 5G deployments are envisioned for 2020.

CERT: Computer emergency response team.

CC: Content-of-communication.

Exabytes: 10^{18} bytes or 1 billion gigabytes.

Gigabytes: 1 billion bytes. Bytes are units of digital information consisting of eight bits – zeroes or ones.

IoT: Internet of things.

IP: Internet protocol.

ISO/IEC: International Standardization Organization/International Electrotechnical Commission.

LEA: Law enforcement agency.

LTE: Long term evolution.

TCP/IP: Transmission control protocol/internet protocol.

Chapter 2
Network Forensics:
Practice

ABSTRACT

In the last few decades, networks have grown to accommodate evolved technologies on every open system for interconnection (OSI) level. On the physical and data link layers, numerous wireless innovations introduced the mobile networks and the interconnection of smart objects. The innovations in network abstraction introduced the cloud- and software-defined networking environments. The high rate and diversity of networking innovations requires adaptations in the forensics approach, so the practice remains capable of uncovering evidence. This chapter explores the operational aspect of both the traditional and the evolved network forensics.

INTRODUCTION

This chapter overviews the evolved network forensics practice. The common tools for sensing, traffic capturing, meta-data acquisition, and forensics analysis are presented as the parts of every network forensics investigation. The advances in cloud, software-defined network, and Internet-of-Things (IoT) forensics are presented as of their specific investigative adaptations and associated challenges. Each of these subfields is discussed to identify the practical similarities that practitioners can find useful for the respective investigations. The chapter concludes by summarizing the unique role of

DOI: 10.4018/978-1-5225-5855-2.ch002

the mobile network forensics for the present investigations and the overall evolution of the forensics field.

TRADITIONAL NETWORK FORENSICS

Network forensics in its traditional form aims to uncover evidence from Internet based communication networks. To do so, investigators collect and examine the data-in-transit itself, the logs of the supporting systems such as routers or servers, and the management data of the network. Chapter 1 outlines the techniques for forensics processing but it does not inform how they are operationalized in investigations in different networking environments. For Internet-based networks, this section details the procedures, tools, and forensics investigation challenges.

Network Sensing

Nmap

When preparing and initiating investigations, practitioners need to map the infrastructure to identify the potential sources of evidence. The most popular tool network enumeration is *nmap* (Lyon, 2017). Designed as a network mapping utility, *nmap* can be used to discover hosts (ping sweep), scan for known services and ports (Transmission Control Protocol – TCP SYN/ACK, Unsolicited Datagram Protocol - UDP or Streaming Control Transport Protocol - SCTP on a given port) or trace paths to hosts of interest (traceroute). Various scanning techniques can be specified with different TCP flags, ports for known services (e.g. 22 for Secure Shell-SSH or 53 for Domain Name Service - DNS) or a range of ports (1-65535 for all ports). The information about the active Internet Protocol (IP) addresses, associated Medium Access Control (MAC) addresses and the open ports can be complemented with the information about the version of the operating systems and the services running on the hosts. Figure 1 provides an example scan command: **nmap -p 1-65535 -sV -O -sS -T4 192.168.56.0/24**. The command scans all hosts on a local network (192.168.56.0/24), for all ports (-p 1-65535), checks their service version info (-sV), the operating system (-O) and the scan is executed using a TCP SYN packets (-sS) in a faster mode (-T4). The scan shows two active hosts: 192.168.56.1 (the network gateway) and the host

Figure 1. Example output results from network sensing with nmap

```
nmap -p 1-65535 -sV -O -sS -T4 192.168.56.0/24

Starting Nmap 7.01 ( https://nmap.org ) at 2017-06-05 11:21 EDT
Nmap scan report for 192.168.56.1
Host is up (0.00051s latency).
Not shown: 65531 closed ports
PORT      STATE SERVICE        VERSION
22/tcp        open  ssh               OpenSSH 7.4 (protocol 2.0)
88/tcp    open  kerberos-sec  Heimdal Kerberos (server time: 2017-06-05 15:33:34Z)
3283/tcp open  netassistant?
5900/tcp open  vnc             Apple remote desktop vnc
MAC Address: 0A:00:27:00:00:00 (Unknown)
OS details: Apple Mac OS X 10.7.0 (Lion) - 10.10 (Yosemite) or iOS 4.1 - 8.3 (Darwin 10.0.0 -
14.5.0)
Network Distance: 1 hop
Service Info: OS: Mac OS X; CPE: cpe:/o:apple:mac_os_x

Nmap scan report for 192.168.56.101
Host is up (0.0011s latency).
Not shown: 65527 closed ports
PORT      STATE SERVICE      VERSION
21/tcp    open  ftp          vsftpd 2.3.5
22/tcp    open  ssh          OpenSSH 5.9p1 Debian 5ubuntu1.1 (Ubuntu Linux; protocol 2.0)
23/tcp    open  telnet       Linux telnetd
53/tcp    open  domain       ISC BIND 9.8.1-P1
80/tcp    open  http         Apache httpd 2.2.22 ((Ubuntu))
443/tcp   open  ssl/http     Apache httpd 2.2.22 ((Ubuntu))
3128/tcp open  http-proxy   Squid http proxy 3.1.19
8080/tcp open  http         Apache httpd 2.2.22 ((Ubuntu))
MAC Address: 08:00:27:53:6F:E6 (Oracle VirtualBox virtual NIC)
Device type: general purpose
Running: Linux 2.6.X|3.X
OS CPE: cpe:/o:linux:linux_kernel:2.6 cpe:/o:linux:linux_kernel:3
OS details: Linux 2.6.32 - 3.10
Network Distance: 1 hop
Service Info: OSs: Unix, Linux; CPE: cpe:/o:linux:linux_kernel
```

192.168.56.101, running Linux 2.6.32 - 3.10 with open TCP ports for SSH, kereberos-sec, netassistant, and VNC services (TCP ports 22, 88, 3283, and 5900, respectively).

The *nmap* tool can also be used for probing firewalls and Intrusion Detection Systems (IDS)/Intrusion Prevention Systems (IPS). This is important for the investigators to test potential hypothesis about a security incident. For example, probing can be performed with fragmented or variable length packets (-f and -mtu flags), packets with random payload (--data-length) decoy or fake IP addresses (-D and –S), spoofed source ports (-g --source-port), proxies (-proxies), random packets' time-to-live values (-ttl) or spoofed MAC address (--spoof-mac).

Wireless Spectrum Scanners

From a forensics perspective, the information on the physical layer can also be of use in sensing the network together with its logical *nmap* enumeration. This is particularly the case when WiFi networks are investigated, for example for spatial localization of network hosts or analysis of wireless-related security events. WiFi networks are based on the IEEE 802.11 standards and are deployed in the 2.4GHz and 5GHz unlicensed frequency bands, with options for deployment in the 900 MHz, 45 GHz and 60 GHz from 2017 onwards (IEEE, 2017). Investigators can passively scan the unlicensed wireless bands with various tools to determine the number of active WiFi networks, signal strength, occupied channels, mode of communication, throughput, and security protocols are used. An example of a wireless network scan performed with the *WiFi Explorer* tool is shown in Figure 2 (Granados, 2017). For a list of other network survey tools, interested readers can refer to (Forero, 2017).

The information on the wireless access point MAC address is listed under the Basic Service Set ID (BSSID) column next to the network name (commonly referred as Service Set ID - SSID). The received signal strength is shown in percentage relative to the maximum output power that the access point can emit. These three parameters can help investigators segment and analyze networks with information about the attached hosts that can be obtained from the access point logs. This information can be paired with the geographical coordinates and placement of the access points to determine the security incident or the criminal event of interest in place and time. The channel number depends on the band the WiFi is deployed with channels 1-14 in the 2.4 GHz band (known as the Industry, Science, and Medicine - ISM) and channels 36-165 in the 5 GHz band (known as Unlicensed National Information Infrastructure - U-NII).

Figure 2. Example output results from WLAN sensing with WiFi Explorer

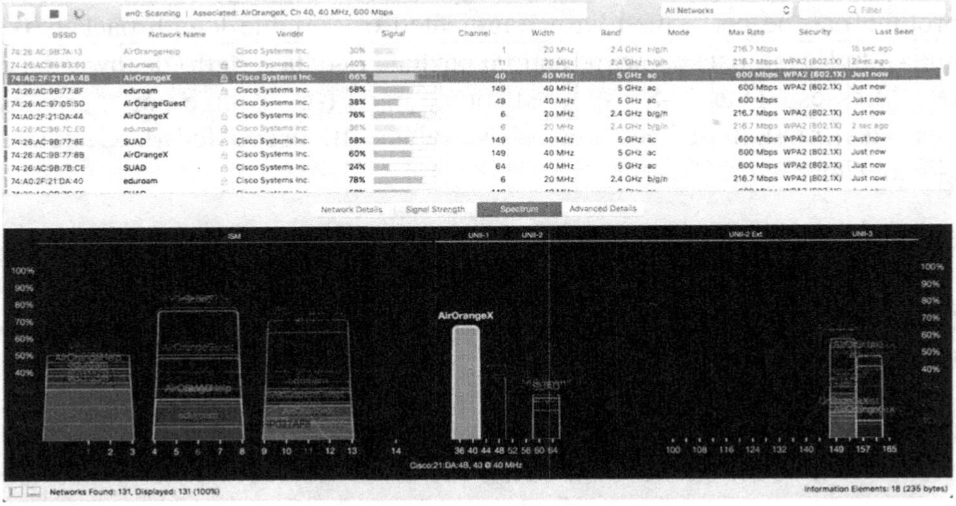

The early 802.11b/g modes allow 20 MHz channel width, with the option for bundling two or more channels in the later 802.11n and 802.11ac to allow 40 MHz channels to increase the throughput. This can inform the investigators on the maximum data throughput for investigating intensive traffic events like denial of service attacks. The security protocols are depicted so the investigators can learn whether the networks use Wired Equivalent Privacy (WEP), WiFi Protected Access (WPA), or WPA2 for personal or enterprise use (together with 802.1X). This information is important if the forensics analysis warrants obtaining the wireless key to decipher any potential evidence communicated over the wireless network.

Traffic Capturing

Once the network is mapped for potential evidence sources, investigators proceed to record the live network data (and obtain the associated network meta-data) to search for potential network evidence. The most common software tools for traffic capturing are *tcpdump* and *Wireshark*, based on the *libpcap* library (Ham and Davidoff, 2012). This library enables data capturing and filtering based on value comparisons on the network, session, and application layers. The filtering is specified using the Berkley Packet Filtering (BFL) syntax (Lillard, 2010).

Tcpdump

The early option for traffic capturing was provided by *tcpdmp* for UNIX architectures (with later adoption of the *WinDump* tool for Windows systems). As a command line tool, *tcpdump* is of forensics interest for mainly two reasons: (1) brief on-the-fly analysis, and (2) prolonged traffic capturing for non-real time analysis. The on-the-fly analysis is facilitated because *tcpdump* enables command line specification of capturing, filtering and analyzing flags and outputs quick results of the state of the network. Capturing and storing voluminous network traffic for a prolong time can be easily set on a dedicated forensics host using *tcpdump* (Ham and Davidoff, 2012). Figure 3 shows an example of a brief *tcpdump* analysis for investigating web traffic. The command tcpdump -n -i eth13 dst port 80 captures any packets on the eth13 interface where the destination port is 80 and displays the IP addresses and port numbers. Figure 4 shows an example command tcpdump -i eth13 -v -w capture.pcap, used to capture and store the entire traffic on the erth13

Figure 3. Example packet capturing, filtering, and displaying in real-time with tcpdump

```
# sudo tcpdump -n -i eth13 dst port 80
tcpdump: verbose output suppressed, use -v or -vv for full protocol decode
listening on eth13, link-type EN10MB (Ethernet), capture size 262144 bytes
15:07:46.935682 IP 10.0.2.4.55811 > 66.147.240.174.80: Flags [S], seq 4051360338, win 14600,
options [mss 1460,sackOK,TS val 73382 ecr 0,nop,wscale 7], length 0
15:07:47.004806 IP 10.0.2.4.55811 > 66.147.240.174.80: Flags [.], ack 89830, win 14600, length 0
15:07:47.192786 IP 10.0.2.4.55811 > 66.147.240.174.80: Flags [P.], seq 0:319, ack 1, win 14600,
length 319: HTTP: GET /program/c/echoserv.php HTTP/1.1
15:07:47.349086 IP 10.0.2.4.55811 > 66.147.240.174.80: Flags [.], ack 1239, win 17332, length 0
15:07:47.349364 IP 10.0.2.4.55811 > 66.147.240.174.80: Flags [.], ack 2699, win 20440, length 0
15:07:47.351448 IP 10.0.2.4.55811 > 66.147.240.174.80: Flags [.], ack 3411, win 23360, length 0
15:07:47.389795 IP 10.0.2.4.45574 > 216.58.217.164.80: Flags [S], seq 887556295, win 14600, options
[mss 1460,sackOK,TS val 73495 ecr 0,nop,wscale 7], length 0
15:07:47.391160 IP 10.0.2.4.54950 > 172.217.10.226.80: Flags [S], seq 2177043150, win 14600,
options [mss 1460,sackOK,TS val 73495 ecr 0,nop,wscale 7], length 0
15:07:47.406592 IP 10.0.2.4.54950 > 172.217.10.226.80: Flags [.], ack 92132, win 14600, length 0
15:07:47.411687 IP 10.0.2.4.45574 > 216.58.217.164.80: Flags [.], ack 90981, win 14600, length 0
15:07:48.363689 IP 10.0.2.4.37094 > 172.217.10.110.80: Flags [S], seq 689395251, win 14600, options
[mss 1460,sackOK,TS val 73738 ecr 0,nop,wscale 7], length 0
15:07:48.364783 IP 10.0.2.4.37095 > 172.217.10.110.80: Flags [S], seq 2044785352, win 14600,
options [mss 1460,sackOK,TS val 73739 ecr 0,nop,wscale 7], length 0
15:07:48.378426 IP 10.0.2.4.37094 > 172.217.10.110.80: Flags [.], ack 102508, win 14600, length 0
15:07:48.379640 IP 10.0.2.4.37095 > 172.217.10.110.80: Flags [.], ack 103661, win 14600, length 0
15:07:48.383885 IP 10.0.2.4.37094 > 172.217.10.110.80: Flags [P.], seq 0:468, ack 1, win 14600,
length 468: HTTP: POST /ocsp HTTP/1.1
15:07:48.419128 IP 10.0.2.4.37094 > 172.217.10.110.80: Flags [.], ack 747, win 15666, length 0
15:07:48.653583 IP 10.0.2.4.55811 > 66.147.240.174.80: Flags [P.], seq 319:717, ack 3411, win
23360, length 398: HTTP: GET /program/c/echoclnt.php HTTP/1.1
```

interface in the file named "capture.pcap". Investigators can use the command tcpdump –r capture.cap to read the network trace saved in the capture.pcap file.

Wireshark

Wireshark is the leading open source tool used for capturing, filtering, and analyzing different types of network traffic. *Wireshark* greatly extends the capabilities of *tcpdump* providing a graphical user interface where protocols from data link to application layer can be dissected and analyzed both for real-time traffic and saved packet captures. It supports more than 28 network protocol families, with TCP/IP being only one of them. For mobile network forensics analysis, *Wireshark* supports most of the mobile network protocol suites from 2G to 4G Long Term Evolution (LTE), including legacy telephony

Figure 4. Example packet capturing for later analysis with tcpdump

```
#tcpdump -i eth13 -v -w capture.pcap
tcpdump: listening on eth13, link-type EN10MB (Ethernet), capture size 262144 bytes
5924 packets captured
```

signaling protocols. Chapters 7 provides several examples for using Wireshark in mobile network forensic analysis and interpretation. A sample network capture with *Wireshark* is shown in Figure 5. Interested readers can look for excellent examples on using Wireshark for security and forensics traffic capturing, filtering, and analysis in (Bullock and Parker, 2017).

Network Meta-Data Acquisition

The captured traffic is not always sufficient in containing security incidents or reconstructing criminal events. For a complete overview of the network states and operation, the forensics processing requires acquisition of network meta-data, that is, logging or configuration data from network nodes (switches, routers, firewalls, wireless access points, etc.), servers (web, mail, Dynamic Host Configuration Protocol – DHCP, DNS, proxies, etc.), or network hosts (Linux or Windows logs). The network logging architecture can be local, centralized, or remote-distributed, therefore investigators need to collect meta-data with different acquisition methods. This is important for the later aggregation and analysis so the captured traffic and logged events can be ordered in time and preserved under forensic custody (Ham and Davidoff, 2012). From a mobile network forensics perspective, the traditional network meta-data are useful to a certain degree, however, there are other mobile specific meta-data discussed later in Chapter 6.

Figure 5. Sample packet capture with Wireshark

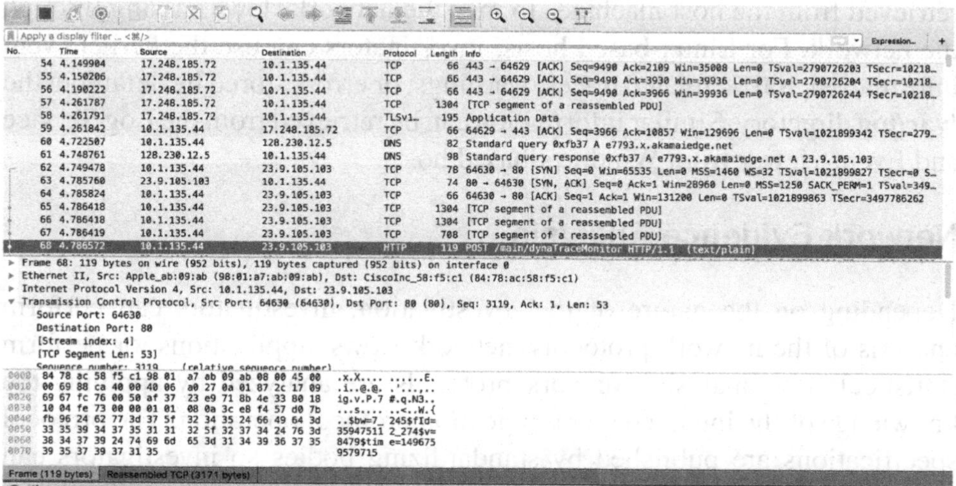

The configuration data contained on the switches includes mapping between physical ports and the associated MAC addresses (or Content Addressable Memory CAM tables that can help with physical tracking of hosts), mapping between MAC and IP addresses (or Address Resolution Protocol - ARP tables that can help with logical tracking of hosts), access control lists, running configuration, or traffic statistics. Routers are critical network exchanges in IP-based networks, so the configuration data contains routing tables, network address translations, stored packets before they are forwarded, packet counts and statistics, DHCP lease assignments, and all the switch-level information (Casey, 2010; Ham and Davidoff, 2012). Firewalls also contain a rich set of potential forensics evidence such as access control lists, firewall rules mapping security policies, tunnels and tunnel state, routing tables and ARP cache, traffic statistics, DHCP logs, or system running data.

Application server logs are also of interest for network investigation because they can inform on both the traffic and the related meta-data. For example, web servers log the client authentication, client IP addresses, browser and Operating System (OS) type, type and time of the Hyper Text Transfer Protocol (HTTP) request, the HTTP response returned by the server, or the system level configuration. Mail servers log data on the exchanged emails, Internet Protocol (IP) addresses of the intermediary mail servers, mail and traffic statistics, or error messages related to mail deliver notifications. IDS/IPS systems log the type of traffic flow passing or attempting to pass through the network and inform on the malicious pattern (i.e. unusual-client-port-connection, denial-of-service, information-leakage-detected, attempted-user/admin-privilege-gain, etc.). This information can be combined with the logs retrieved from the host machines to map the network flows passing through the network. For Linux-based hosts, investigators can use the kernel event information, traffic related traces, warnings, or errors stored by default in the **/var/log** directory. Similar information can be retrieved from the Log Service and Event viewer from Windows-based hosts.

Network Evidence Analysis

Depending on the nature of the investigation, investigators can perform analysis of the network protocols, network flows, applications, or perform statistical flow analysis. Network protocols are analyzed by applying the knowledge of the intended communication protocol operation. The protocol specifications are published by standardizing bodies so investigators can learn how the protocols are designed to work. It must be noted that there is a difference between "designed to work" and "implemented to work" because the implementation differs between vendors and logical inconsistencies can be encountered when processing potential network evidence. The analysis of the acquired network traffic can be performed with *Wireshark* or *tshark*. Investigators can use these tools together with *ngrep* (regular expression search for particular strings, binary sequences, or patterns anywhere in the packets) to look for specific TCP/UDP ports, portions of protocol headers (0x4500 for IP or 0x06 for TCP) or follow protocol streams. Network flows can be inspected for traffic exchanged between a pair of IP hosts, traffic associated with a host of interest, or application traffic like DNS, Simple Mail Transfer Protocol (SMTP), or HTTP. The information can be coupled with meta-data including logs and configuration files, usually aggregated in a centralized database such as *Splunk*. Network investigations often need to deal with a large volume of acquired data. By segmenting the data into *network flow records* that include source and destination IP address, ports, date, time, and the data volume transmitted, investigators can perform large-scale analysis of the network state. This can yield information about compromised or malicious hosts or malicious traffic patterns in the network.

There is a significant academic work to facilitate the traditional network forensics analysis by interpreting mostly the Internet Engineering Task Force (IETF) and International Telecommunication Union (ITU) standards (Lillard, 2010; Ham and Davidoff, 2012; Joshi and Pilli, 2016; Bullock and Parker, 2017). However, there are very few references helping forensic investigators understand the 3rd Generation Partnership Project (3GPP) standardization for conducting investigations in mobile networks. That is the main goal of this book, so Chapter 3, Chapter 4, and Chapter 5 delve into detail to explain the design and implementation of mobile networks, as well as interpret the 3GPP standards from a forensics perspective.

Investigative Challenges

High Speed Network Access

Although the higher networking layers have not changed much, the physical and data link layers witnessed tremendous expansion in transmission techniques and speeds. Standard fixed connections nowadays enable network access with tens or hundreds of Gigabits per second (Gb/s) and wireless networks are approaching 1 Gb/s rates with the last IEEE 802.11ac standards. This development has direct implications on the network forensics investigations in every phase. Acquisition of high speed data requires abundant processing power that not all the capturing devices have, which may not capture every bit of the targeted traffic. The incomplete traffic captures will be inconsistent with the logging or configuration data, affecting the analysis and interpretation phases (Khan, Gani, Wahab, *et al.*, 2016). High speed data directly requires vast storage space, making the evidence custody, examination and preservation challenging for investigative facilities without large evidence archiving centers.

Network Evidence Diversity

While the traffic captures are consistent due to the protocol and network interoperability, the diversity and heterogeneity of network meta-data increases the complexity of the evidence analysis and interpretation. Without standardized techniques for meta-data creation and correlation with the captured traffic, investigators may omit critical facts when analyzing multiple evidence sources. Network forensics analysis tools are designed to look for fragments of data, but can rarely assist in large scale investigations or mobile network interceptions. In addition, the inability to consolidate the overall network evidence makes its sharing between collaborating law enforcement agencies difficult (Scanlon and Kechadi, 2014).

Time Synchronization

Synchronization divergent evidence often arises as an issue during evidence analysis. Multiple sources can present different time zone references and there might be system clock skew/drift issues that investigators have no knowledge of. Moreover, timestamps are written in different formats and representations by different network elements, imposing a preprocessing burden for the investigators to unify the time before any meaningful fact finding and interpretation can take place (Lillis *et al.*, 2016).

Privacy

In practice, it is hard to contain the traffic capturing process to only select and acquire those instances of interest in the investigation. Captured traffic traces always contain records with uniquely identifiable information about other users or confidential internal transactions. Without proper safeguards, companies may be reluctant to enable investigators to even capture data at all. The same problem arises for large-scale and real-time traffic acquisition involving Internet Service Provider (ISPs). Even if a court authorizes such a network traffic acquisition, ISPs may require close monitoring so the investigators are not violating users' privacies and organizational policies (Khan, Gani, Wahab, *et al.*, 2016).

Anti-Forensics

Perpetrators are aware that forensics investigators will attempt to trace their actions and uncover the associated evidence. To avoid being detected, they employ methods to thwart the legitimate investigation process, actions collectively known as *anti-forensics*. Common anti-forensics techniques include encryption of both data in transit and stored data on the host, steganography, filesystem manipulation, artifact wiping, trail obfuscations, and attacks against the forensic processing tools (Conlan, Baggili and Breitinger, 2016). Perpetrators use anonymization and encryption software like Tor, I2P, Virtual Private Networks (VPNs), or operating systems like Tails or Whonix to eliminate any potential evidence that can unequivocally implicate them behind the criminal or unauthorized network activities.

Implications for Mobile Network Forensics Investigations

The same challenges may arise when investigating mobile networks, especially with the 5G network rollout. Targeting speeds beyond 1 Gb/s in downlink and capacity of 15 Tb/s per km^2 (3rd Generation Partnership Project, 2017) will require high end evidence acquiring and analysis capabilities that can hardly be met with the current forensics equipment and archiving centers. The forecasted surge in the number of users and smart devices together with the heterogeneous network nature of the 5G networks will add to the network evidence diversity, especially for the network meta-data (Ericsson, 2017). Networks will need to support all ratio access types from the past generations (2G, 3G, LTE) that certainly will complicate the evidence and meta-data correlation, time synchronization, examination, and interpretation. Mobile network evidence is extremely sensitive when it comes to privacy. Both the intercepted communication contents and the meta-data contain uniquely identifiable elements that reveal private information about the investigated users. The global surveillance disclosures in 2013 showed the technical capabilities for acquiring mobile content-of-communication and intercept-related-information on a large scale. On the anti-forensics side, the increasing use of applications for end-to-end encryption and evasion of the investigative analysis is making the analysis of the intercepted traffic increasingly challenging. Special attention to each of these challenges is devoted in Chapter 8.

CLOUD FORENSICS

Practice

Cloud computing is a model that enables convenient on-demand network access to a shared pool of computing resources, e.g. networks, servers, storage, applications, and services (Mell and Grance, 2011). The convenience and cost effectiveness makes the cloud computing attractive for perpetrators thus demanding specialized forensics investigative methods. Cloud forensics extend the network forensics practice to address distributed and elastic storage of data, multi-tenancy and virtualization, and legal challenges for evidence gathering. There are three dimensions defining the practice of cloud forensics: *technical, organizational*, and *legal* (Ruan *et al.*, 2011). The technical dimension includes data acquisition in real and non-real time, traffic capturing, traffic and evidence segregation, and investigation of virtualized environments. The cloud environment by design is elastic – resources are provisioned and deprovisioned on demand – so the forensics tools need to account for capturing and recovery of ephemeral data containing potential evidence (Roussev *et al.*, 2016).

The resource polling entails data segregation between users that subject to investigation and other cloud users, so the tools and procedures need to account for this too. As part of the investigative readiness, cloud forensics investigators need to account for the Cloud Service Provider (CSPs) next to the ISPs and external agencies where the potential cloud evidence may reside. Organization of a cloud investigation can be a daunting process because there are CSPs or cloud applications dependent on other CSPs, making it hard for the investigators to identify and acquire the potential evidence or maintain a chain-of-custody. On the legal side, investigators need to deal with local regulations where the CSPs store the data as well as the service level agreements that they have with their tenants. This requires the investigation to be structured to prevent violation of local laws, regulations, and customer confidentiality and privacy policies.

Investigative Challenges

The multidimensional nature of the cloud forensics imposes numerous challenges in every phase of the investigative process (NIST, 2014; Alqahtany *et al.*, 2016). In the identification and acquisition phase, access to the cloud data of interest can be an issue because the cloud nodes are distributed and investigators have no way of locating the ones needed for the investigation. Even if they are able to come with the investigative map, acquiring potential cloud evidence from another jurisdiction or international provider might be impossible. The CSP dependency and the lack of transparency provides little options for the investigators to ensure the provenance of the data because the acquisition goes though centralized interface on the CSP side. This directly affects the integrity preservation and chain-of-custody without which the evidence might not be admitted in court. In the analysis phase, investigators have difficulties to correlate and time synchronize the captured and meta-data cloud evidence due to different cloud technologies and the tendency for cloud data encryption on CSPs side (Ryder and Le-Khac, 2017). It is noteworthy that the analysis phase by itself can be challenging for the investigators trained only in network investigations because it requires knowledge about virtualization technology, distributed storage, service provisioning, and relevant laws and regulations.

Relation to Mobile Network Forensics

Many cloud services provide mobile users the convenience of always-on access for personal data, offloaded computation, or rapid information sharing. When these cloud services are maliciously or illegally used, a mobile cloud investigation is initiated to uncover the associated evidence on the cloud and the devices involved (Faheem, Kechadi and Le-Khac, 2015). Acting as a proxy for cloud access, the mobile network can facilitate this investigation with information about users' service activity (current and historical), registration status, charging records, and in certain instances, real-time location as seen by the network. This can be important when investigating social networking or other interactive services. Investigations could warrant real-time localization for users posting messages about suicides, terrorist attacks, or other life-threatening situations. Mobile networks can also help with attribution in investigating denial-of-service attacks targeting mobile cloud applications, providing with the mapping between the IP addresses and users' phone numbers or other network identifiers.

On the other side, there is an active research for cloudificaition of different mobile network functions. (Chen *et al.*, 2015; Wang *et al.*, 2015; Simeone *et al.*, 2016). In the radio segment, cloud computing is introduced as Cloud-based Radio Access Network (C-RAN) and Mobile Edge Computing (MEC). C-RAN offers more flexible allocation of radio resources, efficient implementation of coordinated and cooperative transmission and reception schemes, and simplifies the maintenance (Simeone *et al.*, 2016). The idea of MEC is to offload some of the resource-demanding functions that mobile devices need to perform (Mach *et al.*, 2017). In the core segment, the Network Functional Virtualization (NFVs) enables running Evolved Packet Core (EPC) functions (i.e. Mobility Management Entity - MME, Serving/Packet Gateway – S/P-GW, Home Subscriber Server - HSS) in virtual machines instead of a dedicated hardware. The ultimate goal of virtualized mobile network core is to provide EPC-as-a-service (EPCaaS) so operators can utilize their infrastructure in a cost and resource effective way (Taleb *et al.*, 2015).

The future cloud-native mobile networks are prone to both mobile- and cloud-related attacks. The distributed denial-of-service attacks against C-RAN and EPCaaS can be initiated as a coordinated jamming or signaling storm to saturate the mobile network elements (Gorbil *et al.*, 2015; Vassilakis *et al.*, 2016). Privacy violation, rogue gateways, service manipulation, and misuse of resources are plausible attacks for the MEC and for the virtualized core (Roman, Lopez and Mambo, 2016). Investigating similar security incident requires both cloud and mobile network forensics expertise. The cloud investigations are suitable for identification and acquisition of potential evidence on the infrastructure level while the mobile forensics are suitable for investigation on the network level. The collaborative techniques for cloud-based mobile network investigations are further elaborated in Chapter 9.

SOFTWARE-DEFINED NETWORK FORENSICS

Practice

The separation between the logical functions and dedicated hardware as in the cloud computing has also been explored in the networking domain. The Software-Defined Networking (SDN) provides such a functionality where a centralized controller defines and implements network forwarding policies in a multipurpose forwarding hardware (e.g. bare metal routers, switches, firewalls, or load balancers). This networking paradigm contrasts the decentralized and tightly coupled IP infrastructure where the control plane and user data plane are implemented in the same networking devices and require separate configuration (Kreutz and Ramos, 2015).

In SDN, the networking infrastructure is composed of simple forwarding hardware that can be reconfigured to perform the functions of a router, switch, load balancer, or a firewall depending on the network conditions and needs. The network brain, or the SDN controller, dynamically reprograms these devices using SDN protocols (i.e. OpenFlow) that specify the traffic forwarding rules. The rules map the physical communication ports of the equipment (i.e. Open vSwitch) with the network logic expressed in terms of *flows* so to enable actions as ingress/egress traffic forwarding, encapsulation and return to the controller, drop packets, or per packet/flow statistics (Nguyen, Do and Kim, 2016). In practice, this means that there can be many overlay networks existing concurrently over the same physical infrastructure.

The SDN forensics have the benefit of identifying and acquiring both the traffic and network meta-data directly from the forwarding devices because of the centralized architecture. The information about the flow tables together with the statistics and a copy of the forwarded traffic can be obtained at once for real-time or after the fact forensics analysis. The SDN architecture thus implies changes in the network forensics approach as summarized in Table 1 (Khan, Gani, Wahid, *et al.*, 2016).

The potential SDN evidence resides either in the SDN forwarding configuration (infrastructure layer), SDN controller logic (control layer) or the overlay network applications (application layer). To process this data, investigators need to examine the SDN flow graphs or the finite state machines of the controller/application together with the captured flow traffic. Having forensics modules such as forwarding device selector, integrity checker, and SDN interpreter as proposed in (Khan, Gani, Wahid, *et al.*, 2016), investigators can conduct investigations while adhering to the prescribed network forensics investigation process elaborated in Chapter 1. This SDN approach can be operationalized using the *ForCon* tool developed by (Spiekermann, Eggendorfer and Keller, 2017). *ForCon* supports the capturing of SDN traffic, extraction of flow-related information, and automated evidence analysis and interrelation.

Investigative Challenges

As a novel networking paradigm, SDN poses several challenges for conducting forensics investigations. The programmable network logic limits the investigators to verify the trustworthiness and integrity of the SDN configuration or protocol data. Perpetrators able to gain access to the SDN controller can eliminate or modify any trace for an authorized activity by interfering with the flow configuration or network service abstraction. Real-time investigations can suffer from high-speed flow access because the centralized forensics processing can overburden the SDN controller leading to incomplete flow capturing. Consolidation of evidence can be a challenging task in cases where SDN data is collected from multiple SDN controllers. The proprietary formats or SDN protocols require additional effort to eliminate any potential misinterpretation of evidence. A possibility for SDN anti-forensics also exists because of the lack of authentication between the SDN controller and the infrastructure nodes. In such a scenario, investigators have no reliable information about the origination/termination of a flow of interest and cannot attribute the source of the security incident.

Relation to Mobile Network Forensics

The simplified network management, automated configuration, and the cost-effectiveness made SDN an attractive extension of the traditional mobile networks, leading to the so-called Software-Defined Mobile Networks (SDMN). Conceptually, SDMNs are one possible application that uses the SDN abstraction, having the infrastructure and controller layers supporting the mobile functions as overlaying applications implemented using Network Functional Virtualization (NFV). However, SDMNs require adaptation in the lower SDN layers – flow graphs and mobile-specific finite state machines – to meet the strict requirements for service quality and support of user mobility (Liyanage, Gurtov and Ylianttila, 2015). This repurposing of the

Table 1. Comparison between traditional network forensics and SDN forensics

Category	Traditional Network Forensics		SDN Forensics
Mechanism	Logging		SDN forwarding configuration – flow graphs, SDN controller/application logic – finite state machines
	Packet Marking		
	Heuristic Base		
Data Source	Traffic		SDN protocol traffic (i.e. OpenFlow) and SDN flows (i.e. encapsulated IP traffic)
	Meta-data		
	Traffic and meta-data		
Data Instance	Packet header		Investigation based on SDN forwarding rules, network flows, and flow statistics
	Packet payload		
	Packet flow		
	Network node		SDN forwarding devices, SDN Controller
Scalability	Less scalable		Highly scalable
Real-time analysis	Difficult, resource-demanding		Easy, centralized infrastructure
Data Privacy	Less		High

SDN environment requires a layered forensic approach to account for the SDN-related forensics steps, but also for understanding the mobile network application logic.

Eventually, mobile network forensics will evolve to SDMN forensics in the future, where the lawful interception and acquisition of interception-related information need to be performed in the SDN environment. This transition poses a unique set of challenges in meeting the legal and forensics obligations of the mobile network operators (European Telecommunications Standards Institute, 2016). Traditionally, operators and the Law Enforcement Agencies (LEAs) are in the same jurisdiction so the interception and evidence acquisition need to be performed on the traffic that is routed or handled in the same country (in case the traffic is encrypted, the entity responsible for key management ensures it can be decrypted by the operator or the LEA). Due to the nomadic access to NFV platforms and SDN networks, no infrastructure provider will be capable of dealing with all the lawful interception requests. The potential evidence identification and acquisition in the traditional mobile networks can be either network-centric (based on network related identifiers, i.e. a phone number or an IP address) or service-centric (based on service or application related identifiers, i.e. email address). This functionality needs to remain as a legal obligation with certain adaptations for the SDMNs:

1. **Access Based:** SDMNs need to provide access to potential mobile network evidence along the SDN access path for the targeted users or services.
2. **Inter NFV/SDN Based:** SDMNs need to provide access to potential mobile network evidence routed or residing on NFV/SDN infrastructure used by the SDMNs but not in the same jurisdiction (for example, the SDMN is routing traffic using "foreign" forwarding devices).
3. **Intra NFV/SDN Based:** SDMNs need to provide access to potential mobile network evidence residing on their NFV/SDN infrastructure, except for "foreign" NFV/SDN usage and stored information (for example, if the SDMN is providing EPCaaS for a provider not in the same jurisdiction).

However, these adaptions are hard to implement due to several challenges. The SDMN traffic and meta-data can be encrypted by many parties so the provision of the decryption capability can be impossible to be met, especially for real-time traffic interception. Due to the heterogeneous access opportunities, segments of communications as part of the same target session need to be consolidated and integrated, which might be difficult if the NFV/SDN traffic is routed or stored outside the target jurisdiction. The infrastructural separation also affects the evidence provenance with no mechanism to preserve its integrity on a logical SDMN level. These challenges and the implementation of the SDMN lawful interception functions are further discussed in Chapter 8.

There is also a need to investigate security incidents related to the SDN/NFV nature of the future mobile networks. The multi-tenancy nature of the SDN/NFV introduces the possibility for malicious applications to tamper with the SDN controller, insert fraudulent flow rules, or flood the underlying network (Bates *et al.*, 2014). The irregular and malicious SDN flow patterns can affect the availability of the SDMNs in a similar way as the traditional traffic and signaling storms (or mobile network denial-of-service attacks). Therefore, the proper understanding of the SDN/NFV operations is critical for the future mobile network forensics investigation. As with the lawful interception, the investigations for SDMN security incidents face the same challenges, however, the nature and the scope of the SDMN forensics is yet to be defined with proper understanding of the SDMN operations from real deployments envisioned to rollout with the introduction of 5G networks.

INTERNET-OF-THINGS FORENSICS

Practice

Internet-of-Things (IoT) extends the traditional networking to include "things" other than computers or mobile devices: home appliances, utility meters, medical devices, wearables, cars, and any other machines capable of sending/receiving network traffic. The basic idea of the IoT is to allow autonomous, machine-to-machine (M2M) communication between these smart devices and applications typically hosted on a cloud (Zawoad and Hasan, 2015). The M2M communication and remote coordination requires a slightly different network forensic approach as summarized in Table 2.

The traffic capturing and collection of network meta-data requires decomposition of the IoT application logic and understanding of the embedded device structure. IoT devices often communicate over WiFi, but other wireless protocols (i.e. ZigBee or LTE) are used for resource-constrained IoT scenarios like medical body monitoring. For a complete forensics investigation, the wireless spectrum scanning in the IoT domain plays an important role in looking for potential evidence about malicious application or irregular traffic patterns. With the large number of IoT devices, the forensics processing can be time consuming and challenging even with the presence of a centralized IoT gateway. These devices generate large data volume that could easily reveal private information or the characteristics of the physical environment.

To address the complexity, the IoT forensics investigation process is divided in three logical parts: *device-level forensics*, *network forensics*, and *cloud forensics* (Zawoad and Hasan, 2015; Kebande and Ray, 2016). The device-level forensics are concerned with identification and acquisition of evidence residing internally on the devices, i.e. communication logs, locally stored credentials, or data in their memory. The network forensics encompasses traditional network investigation including investigation of the IoT specific wireless protocols. Similarly, the cloud forensics complete the IoT investigations in acquiring and processing evidence from the central IoT applications hosted on a remote cloud platforms. This logical segmentation of the forensics process is intuitive; however, each part brings specific challenges affecting the overall quality of the integrated IoT evidence.

Table 2. Comparison between traditional network forensics and IoT forensics

Category	Traditional Network Forensics	IoT Forensics
Mechanism	Logging	IoT application and internal devices' logic – finite state machines
	Packet Marking	
	Heuristic Base	
Data Source	Traffic	Non-traditional physical and data link communication protocols (i.e. ZigBee, NFC, LTE); device-specific meta-data (embedded logs and traces); IoT cloud application meta-data
	Meta-data	
	Traffic and meta-data	
Data Instance	Packet header	Physical, data link, and IP level analysis of packet headers, payloads, and flows
	Packet payload	
	Packet flow	
	Network node	IoT Gateways
Scalability	Small number of network elements and/or hosts; potential evidence of several Terabytes of data	Large number of devices; potential evidence of several Exabytes of data
Real-time analysis	Difficult, resource-demanding	Difficult, demands IoT logical decomposition and physical presence
Data Privacy	Less	Little to no privacy

Investigative Challenges

The device-level forensics make little use of the present forensics tools and techniques because the IoT devices embed a customized computing structure. A typical IoT deployment scenario involves a large number of distributed IoT devices that generate potential evidence (traffic and meta-data) in the order of several Exabytes requiring extra capturing and storage capacity, beyond the one for a standalone network forensics processing. The heterogeneity of IoT devices and applications entails integrity preservation mechanisms applicable to the entire corpora of device-level, network, and cloud evidence data. Such mechanisms and forensics processing tools are currently not available or are very expensive to be created.

Relation to Mobile Network Forensics

Most of the IoT deployments are managed by a remote application communicating over an IoT gateway with the locally connected devices. This IoT scenario requires WiFi connection in the local segment and additional internet connection to the central application server. Alternatively, the IoT devices can have dedicated mobile connection where the implementation of the gateway is inconvenient or not possible at all. Such IoT scenarios include smart tracking (cars, trucks, shipment containers), vehicle telematics (traffic control), agriculture (irrigation control, environmental sensing, animal tracking), smart cities (parking, lightning, infrastructure monitoring), or industrial monitoring (equipment status, air pollution, early disaster warning sensors). An extended network coverage is critically important for these applications so the communication part is usually realized over a mobile network. The first implementations used a standard 2G/3G/LTE connection, but the computational and power consumption was too high for the restricted resources of the IoT devices.

The need for optimized IoT mobile network connection was realized and the latest 3GPP requirements include narrowband cellular IoT connectivity option (Nokia, 2017). The cellular IoT is envisioned to dominate the market in the future with additional connectivity evolution in the 5G networks under the broad connectivity concept of massive Machine Type Communications (mMTC). From an IoT forensics point of view, part of the device-level and the entire network forensics can be processed with mobile network forensics techniques and tools. The cellular IoT investigations will then benefit from reliable mobile network evidence, centralized data acquisition and delivery, opportunity to conduct real-time forensics, and verifiable privacy safeguards.

CONCLUSION

The evolved network forensics practice requires specialized knowledge about cloud computing, software-defined networking, IoT, as well as understanding of mobile networks. Although all of these fields share the fundamental aspect of IP connectivity, they differ in all other OSI layers. In forensic terms, this means that an the traditional techniques, tools, and procedures need to be adapted for each networking domain to ensure efficient investigation and reliable evidence. The investigative practice with the challenges characteristic for the cloud, SDN, and IoT forensics was briefly reviewed in this chapter to facilitate this adaptation. Each of these network forensics subfields was approached from a mobile network forensics perspective to create the broader context for the subsequent chapters and emphasize the importance for the overall evolution of the field. The network cloudificaition together with the software defined networking are envisioned as key enablers for the future 5G networks, clearly indicating that the cloud, SDN, and mobile network forensics practice will critically depend on each other in near future. Similarly, such an interdependence is inevitable for conducting effective investigations in cellular IoT environments.

REFERENCES

3rd Generation Partnership Project. (2017). *5G Service Requirements, 5G Service Requirements.* Available at: http://www.3gpp.org/news-events/3gpp-news/1831-sa1_5g

Alqahtany, S., Clarke, N., Furnell, S., & Reich, C. (2016). A forensic acquisition and analysis system for IaaS. *Cluster Computing, 19*(1), 439–453. doi:10.100710586-015-0509-x

Bates, A., Butler, K., Haeberlen, A., Sherr, M., & Zhou, W. (2014). Let SDN Be Your Eyes: Secure Forensics in Data Center Networks. *Proceedings 2014 Workshop on Security of Emerging Networking Technologies*, 1–11. 10.14722ent.2014.23002

Bullock, J., & Parker, J. T. (2017). *Wireshark for Security Professionals: Using Wireshark and the Metasploit Framework* (1st ed.). Indianapolis, IN: Wiley. doi:10.1002/9781119183457

Casey, E. (2010). *Handbook of Digital Forensics Investigations.* San Diego, CA: Elsevier Academic Press.

Chen, M., Zhang, Y., Hu, L., Taleb, T., & Sheng, Z. (2015). Cloud-based Wireless Network: Virtualized, Reconfigurable, Smart Wireless Network to Enable 5G Technologies. *Mobile Networks and Applications.*

Conlan, K., Baggili, I., & Breitinger, F. (2016). Anti-forensics: Furthering digital forensic science through a new extended, granular taxonomy. *Digital Investigation*, *18*, S66–S75. doi:10.1016/j.diin.2016.04.006

Ericsson. (2017). *Ericsson Mobility Report, Ericsson Mobility Report*. Available at: https://www.ericsson.com/assets/local/mobility-report/ documents/2016/ericsson-mobility-report-november-2016.pdf

European Telecommunications Standards Institute. (2016). *Lawful Interception (LI); Cloud/Virtual Services for Lawful Interception (LI) and Retained Data (RD)*. Author.

Faheem, M., Kechadi, T., & Le-Khac, N. A. (2015). The State of the Art Forensic Techniques in Mobile Cloud Environment. *International Journal of Digital Crime and Forensics*, *7*(2), 1–19. doi:10.4018/ijdcf.2015040101

Forero, E. (2017). *The Bad-Fi, Tools*. Available at: https://badfi.com/toolroll/

Gorbil, G., Abdelrahman, O., Pavloski, M., & Gelenbe, E. (2015). Modeling and Analysis of RRC-Based Signalling Storms in 3G Networks. *IEEE Transactions on Emerging Topics in Computing*, *XX*(X), 1–1.

Granados, A. (2017). *WiFi Explorer, About*. Available at: https://www. adriangranados.com

Ham, J., & Davidoff, S. (2012). *Network Forensics: Tracing Hackers Thorugh Cyberspace*. Upper Saddle River, NJ: Prentice Hall.

IEEE. (2017). *IEEE 802.11 Working Group, Stanards Timeline*. Available at: http://grouper.ieee.org/groups/802/11/Reports/802.11_Timelines.htm

Joshi, R. C., & Pilli, E. S. (2016). *Fundamentals of Network Forensics* (1st ed.). London, UK: Springer. doi:10.1007/978-1-4471-7299-4

Kebande, V. R., & Ray, I. (2016). A Generic Digital Forensic Investigation Framework for Internet of Things (IoT). A Generic Digital Forensic Investigation Framework for Internet of Things (IoT), 356–362. doi:10.1109/ FiCloud.2016.57

Khan, S., Gani, A., Wahab, A. W. A., Shiraz, M., & Ahmad, I. (2016). Network forensics: Review, taxonomy, and open challenges. *Journal of Network and Computer Applications. Elsevier*, *66*, 214–235. doi:10.1016/j. jnca.2016.03.005

Khan, S., Gani, A., Wahid, A., Wahab, A., Abdelaziz, A., Ko, K., ... Guizani, M. (2016). Software-Defined Network Forensics : Motivation, Potential Locations, Requirements, and Challenges. *IEEE Network, 30*(December), 6–13. doi:10.1109/MNET.2016.1600051NM

Kreutz, D., Ramos, F., Esteves Verissimo, P., Esteve Rothenberg, C., Azodolmolky, S., & Uhlig, S. (2015). Software-Defined Networking: A Comprehensive Survey. *Proceedings of the IEEE, 103*(1), 1–61. doi:10.1109/JPROC.2014.2371999

Lillard, T. V. (2010). *Digital Forensics for Network, Internet, and Cloud Computing: A Forensic Evidence Guide for Moving Targets and Data.* Burlington, MA: Syngress.

Lillis, D., Becker, B., O'Sullivan, T., & Scanlon, M. (2016). Current Challenges and Future Research Areas for Digital Forensic Investigation. *Proceedings of the 11th Annual ADFSL Conference on Digital Forensics, Security and Law (CDFSL 2016)*, 9–20. doi: 10.13140/RG.2.2.34898.76489

Liyanage, M., Gurtov, A., & Ylianttila, M. (2015). *Software Defined Mobile Networks (SDMN): Beyond LTE Network Architecture* (M. Liyanage, A. Gurtov, & M. Ylianttila, Eds.). West Sussex, UK: Wiley. doi:10.1002/9781118900253

Lyon, G. (2017). *NMAP, Nmap Newtwork Scanning.* Available at: https://nmap.org

Mach, P., Member, I., Becvar, Z., & Member, I. (2017). Mobile Edge Computing: A Survey on Architecture and Computation Offloading. *IEEE Communications Surveys and Tutorials, 20*(3), 1–29.

Mell, P., & Grance, T. (2011). The NIST Definition of Cloud Computing Recommendations of the National Institute of Standards and Technology. Gaithersburg, MD: Academic Press.

Nguyen, V., Do, T., & Kim, Y. (2016). SDN and Virtualization-Based LTE Mobile Network Architectures : A Comprehensive Survey. *Wireless Personal Communications, 86*(3), 1401–1438. doi:10.100711277-015-2997-7

NIST. (2014). *NIST Cloud Computing Forensic Science Challenges.* NIST.

Nokia. (2017). *LTE evolution for IoT connectivity.* Available at: www.nokia.com

Roman, R., Lopez, J., & Mambo, M. (2016). Mobile edge computing. In *A survey and analysis of security threats and challenges*. Elsevier B.V. doi:10.1016/j.future.2016.11.009

Roussev, V., Ahmed, I., Barreto, A., McCulley, S., & Shanmughan, V. (2016). Cloud forensics -Tool development studies & future outlook. *Digital Investigation. Elsevier Ltd*, *18*(June), 79–95. doi:10.1016/j.diin.2016.05.001

Ruan, K., Carthy, J., Kechadi, T., & Crosbie, M. (2011). Cloud forensics. *Advances in Digital Forensics 7th IFIP WG 11.9 International Conference on Digital Forensics,* 35–46. 10.1007/978-3-642-24212-0_3

Ryder, S., & Le-Khac, N. A. (2017). The end of effective law enforcement in the cloud? - To encypt, or not to encrypt. *IEEE International Conference on Cloud Computing, CLOUD*, 904–907. doi: 10.1109/CLOUD.2016.131

Scanlon, M., & Kechadi, T. (2014). Digital evidence bag selection for P2P network investigation. Lecture Notes in Electrical Engineering, 307–314. doi:10.1007/978-3-642-40861-8_44

Simeone, O., Maeder, A., Peng, M., Sahin, O., & Yu, W. (2016). Cloud Radio Access Network : Virtualizing Wireless Access for Dense Heterogeneous Systems. *Journal of Communications and Networks (Seoul)*, *18*(2), 135–149.

Spiekermann, D., Eggendorfer, T., & Keller, J. (2017). Network forensic investigation in OpenFlow networks with ForCon. DFRWS Europe, 66–74. doi:10.1016/j.diin.2017.01.007

Taleb, T., Corici, M., Parada, C., Jamakovic, A., Ruffino, S., Karagiannis, G., & Magedanz, T. (2015). EASE: EPC as a service to ease mobile core network deployment over cloud. *IEEE Network*, *29*(2), 78–88. doi:10.1109/MNET.2015.7064907

Vassilakis, V. G., Moscholios, I. D., Alzahrani, B. A., & Logothetis, M. D. (2016). On the Security of Software-Defined Next-Generation Cellular Networks. *IEICE Information and Communication Technology Forum (ICTF)*, 1–5.

Wang, H., Chen, S., Xu, H., Ai, M., & Shi, Y. (2015). *SoftNet: A Software Defined Decentralized Mobile Network Architecture toward 5G*. Academic Press.

Zawoad, S., & Hasan, R. (2015). FAIoT: Towards Building a Forensics Aware Eco System for the Internet of Things. *Proceedings - 2015 IEEE International Conference on Services Computing, SCC 2015*, 279–284. 10.1109/SCC.2015.46

KEY TERMS AND DEFINITIONS

2G: 2nd generation of mobile networks. The most dominant technology is the global system for mobility (GSM).

3G: 3rd generation of mobile networks. The most dominant technology is universal mobile telecommunication system (UMTS).

3GPP: 3rd generation partnership project.

4G: 4th generation of mobile networks. The 4G technologies are long term evolution (LTE) and the advanced version, LTE-advanced. Colloquially, the terms LTE/LTE-A are used as a synonym for 4G as they are the only global standard for mobile communication from the fourth generation.

5G: 5th generation of mobile networks. Still in standardization phase, the first 5G deployments are envisioned for 2020.

ARP: Address resolution protocol.

BPF: Berkeley packet filtering syntax for captured network packets.

C-RAN: Cloud-based radio access network.

CAM: Content addressable memory.

CSP: Cloud service provider.

DHCP: Dynamic host configuration protocol.

DNS: Domain name system.

EPC: Evolved packet core.

EPCaaS: Evolved packet core as a service.

HSS: Home subscriber server.

HTTP: Hypertext transfer protocol.:

IDS/IPS: Intrusion detection system/intrusion protection system.

IETF: Internet engineering task force.

IoT: Internet-of-things.

IP: Internet protocol.

ISM: Industry, science, and medicine spectrum in the 2.4 GHz frequency segment.

ISO/IEC: International Standardization Organization/International Electrotechnical Commission.

ISP: Internet service provider.
ITU: International Telecommunication Union.
LEA: Law enforcement agency.
LI: Lawful interception.
LTE: Long term evolution.
M2M: Machine-to-machine communication.
MAC: Medium access control.
MEC: Mobile edge computing.
MME: Mobility management entity.
mMTC: Massive machine type communications.
NFC: Near field communications.
NFV: Network functional virtualization (NFVs).
OS: Operating system.
OSI: Open system for interconnection.
RAN: Radio access network.
S/P-GW: Serving/packet gateway.
SCTP: Session control transport protocol.
SDMN: Software-defined mobile network.
SDN: Software-defined networks.
SMTP: Simple mail transport protocol.
SSH: Secure shell.
SSID/BSSID: Service set ID/basic SSID.
TCP SYN/ACK: TCP synchronization/acknowledgment protocol messages.
TCP/IP: Transmission control protocol/internet protocol.
U-NII: Unlicensed national information infrastructure spectrum in the 5 GHz frequency segment.
UDP: Unsolicited datagram protocol.
VPN: Virtual private network.
WEP: Wired equivalent privacy.
WLAN: Wireless local area network.
WPA/WPA2: Wireless protected access/wireless protected access 2.

Chapter 3

Mobile Network Systems:
Fundamental Generations

ABSTRACT

Mobile communication systems were initially designed to carry voice traffic with limited support for packet and messaging services. The constant increase in demand for packet traffic evolved the mobile networks to ultimately become data pipes with support for mobility. While the mobile applications changed dramatically over time, the fundamental principles for mobile service delivery remain the same to a large extend in every network generation. These principles are important to form the investigative context and identify the sources of network evidence with the highest probative value. This chapter details the mobile service delivery fundamentals together with the key features implemented in each mobile network generation. In practice, the sources of mobile network evidence belong to network segments from different generations; therefore, the fundamentals are necessary to establish an effective forensics plan and maximize the investigative outcome.

INTRODUCTION

This chapter details the mobile service evolution from the first (1G) up to the latest, fifth generation (5G). The main features of each generation are outlined in terms of the supported services, connectivity technologies employed, and network performance indicators as bitrate and latency. The standardized architectural specifications and frequency bands are presented as a common

DOI: 10.4018/978-1-5225-5855-2.ch003

reference for the operations, functions, and the main elements of every mobile network deployment. Fundamental to understanding of these aspects are the principles of wireless communications, therefore, this chapter overviews the radio transmission and reception, propagation, error management, duplex communication, and the multiple access techniques. A high-level overview of a generic network architecture is also provided.

THE EVOLUTION OF MOBILE NETWORK SYSTEMS

Mobile networks have so far evolved through four generations of networking technologies with the fifth one envisioned for commercial rollout from 2020 onwards. Wireless telephony systems from the first generation needed to support mobility and large user capacity with a limited frequency bandwidth. To overcome this problem, the network service area was organized into smaller logical units called *cells* (the network coverage map resembles the organization of biological cells). This concept, introduced in the 1970s by Bell Laboratories, was used to develop and deploy the 1G cellular networks[1] based on different radio transmission and mobility management technologies, with no support for international roaming. Examples of 1G systems are AMPS in the United States, NMT in Scandinavia, and TACS in the UK.

The widespread adoption of the 1G networks was limited by the unreliability of the analogue wireless interface, modest mobility management, and lack of security and roaming support. The second generation of mobile systems or 2G addressed these issues with a digital network implementation supporting encryption in the radio interface, extended user capacity, new mobility management techniques and support for global roaming. Examples of 2G systems are Global System for Mobile (GSM) in Europe, IS-95 Code Division Multiple Access (CDMA) and IS-136 Time Division Multiple Access (TDMA) in the United States. GSM is by far the most widely deployed of these systems and became the global *de-facto* standard for 2G mobile network infrastructures.

Both the 1G and 2G systems were design to support voice services, with 2G systems providing limited support for instant messaging and packet data access. In response to the demand for packet data access as a result of the World Wide Web (WWW) proliferation, GSM networks were enhanced to 2.5G and 2.75G with the General Packet Radio Service (GPRS) and Enhanced Data rates for GSM Evolution (EDGE), respectively. Compared to the 76.8

Kb/s rates of GSM, GPRS provided theoretical maximum bitrate of 160 Kb/s and EDGE of 473.6 Kb/s. These speeds were insufficient to provide an acceptable browsing experience or use of multimedia applications that were already supported in the wired broadband networks. The demand for higher data rates on a global level impelled the International Telecommunication Union (ITU) to start working on a third generation or 3G with harmonized specifications for mobile communications for global interoperability (Ghosh *et al.*, 2010). The data requirements for the 3G systems (known as IMT 2000) were 2 Mb/s for fixed or in-building environments, 384 Kb/s for pedestrian or in urban environments, and 144 Kb/s for wide area or vehicular environments. In addition, 3G systems were required to provide better Quality-of-Service (QoS) for conversational (voice services), streaming (video, multimedia), interactive (web browsing), and background (telemetry, emails) classes of services.

ITU accepted the following technologies as 3G candidates: Universal Mobile Telephone System (UMTS) as evolution to GSM in Europe and Japan, CDMA2000 as evolution to IS-95 in United States, and Time Division-Synchronous CDMA (TD-SCDMA) in China (variant of UMTS). The standardizing body responsible for maintenance and evolution of the UMTS and TD-CSDMA is the 3rd Generation Partnership Project (3GPP) and the same role for CDMA2000 has the 3rd Generation Partnership Project 2 (3GPP2). The first 3G UMTS networks supported peak bitrates between the 384 – 2048 Kb/s and the typical user bitrates were around 150 – 300 Kb/s. CDMA2000 peak bitrate was 307 Kb/s and the users were able to achieve bitrates up to 200 Kb/s. To fully meet the IMT-2000 requirements, both UMTS and CDMA2000 were upgraded to 3.5G and adapted to then largely asymmetric nature of the Internet (most applications in the early 2000s were demanding higher data throughput on the downlink than on the uplink to the users). UMTS was upgraded in two steps with High Speed Downlink Packet Access (HSDPA) providing peak downlink bitrates between 3.6 – 14.4 Mb/s in the first step and High Speed Uplink Packet Access (HSUPA) providing peak uplink bitrates between 2.3 – 5 Mb/s (the typical user experienced bitrate was up to 700 Kb/s). CDMA2000 was evolved with the EVolution-Data Only (EV-DO) to support 2.4-4.9 Mb/s downlink and 800 – 1800 Kb/s uplink bitrates. The UMTS High Speed Packet Access (HSPA or both the HSDPA/HSUPA) was further evolved to 3.75G with the HSPA+ with peak bitrates up to 42 Mb/s.

Even with all of the improvements, the 3G speeds lagged behind the wired broadband access which typically supported several hundred Mb/s and few Gb/s in the late 2000s. The imperative of ITU was to match the fixed broadband experience, so it set the following requirements for the fourth generation of mobile networks or 4G (known as IMT-Advanced): nominal data rate of 1 Gb/s for stationary clients, 100 Mb/s for highly mobile users, improved infrastructural efficiency, and further enhanced QoS. There were two competing technologies for the 4G architecture: Long Term Evolution (LTE) as a further evolution of the GSM/UMTS family; and Mobile WiMAX created as a wide area version of WiFi with added mobility support (Hoy, 2015). 3GPP2 also made an effort to evolve the CDMA2000/EV-DO to a technology known as Ultra-Wide Band (UWB), but the development efforts were abandoned in favor of the LTE as the proffered 4G technology.

Neither of the candidate technologies initially met the initial IMT-Advanced requirements, however, LTE later became the global standard for 4G mobile networks. The key features that made LTE the ultimate 4G technology were the peak downlink/uplink bitrate of 100/50 Mb/s, lowest latency (5-15 milliseconds) and call set up time (50 milliseconds), flat IP architecture, built-in interoperability with the GSM/UMTS protocols, and flexible deployment scenarios. The "true 4G" network came with the LTE-Advanced that extended the LTE to support downlink/uplink bitrates of 3/1.5 Gb/s. Further enhancement of the 4G networks were made with the LTE-Advanced-Pro to account for a machine type of communication (for Internet-of-Things - IoT devices), use of LTE in unlicensed bands (Unlicensed National Information Infrastructure -U-NII), and support for mission critical applications (push-to-talk public safety service).

For the fifth generation of mobile networks, ITU and 3GPP are continuously working on the key performance requirements of 5G technologies for IMT-2020. The future 5G networks need to support minimum of 20 Gb/s downlink and 10 Gb/s uplink bitrates, while the user experience bitrates must be minimum of 100 Mb/s in downlink and 50 Mb/s in uplink (International Telecommunication Union, 2017). In addition, the enhanced Mobile BroadBand (eMBB) service in 5G must be delivered with a maximum of 4 milliseconds latency (1 millisecond for Ultra-Reliable and Low-Latency Communications - URLLC), providing minimum connection density of 1 million users per km^2 (International Telecommunication Union, 2017). Table 1 and Table 2 summarize the evolution of mobile communications systems. A systematic overview of each of the generations is provided in Chapter 4, Chapter 5, and Chapter 8.

Table 1. Mobile communications systems evolution: pre 3GPP

	1G	2G	2.5/2.75G
Requirements	None		
Technologies	AMPS, NMT, TACS	GSM, IS-95, IS-136	GPRS/EDGE
Peak Data Rates (DL – downlink; UL - uplink)	N/A	GSM: 76.8 Kb/s IS-95: 115 Kb/s IS-136:	GPRS: 160 Kb/s EDGE: 473.6 Kb/s
User Experienced Data Rates (maximum)	N/A	GSM: 9.6 Kb/s IS-95: <64 Kb/s IS-136: 9.6 Kb/s	GPRS: 40 Kb/s EDGE: 120 Kb/s
Latency	>700 ms	600-700 ms	
Mobility	Stationary (0 km/h) Pedestrian (0-10 km/h) Vehicular (0-60km/h)	Stationary (0 km/h) Pedestrian (0-10 km/h) Vehicular (0-120 km/h) High Speed Vehicular (120-250 km/h)	
Services	Voice only	Voice, limited messaging and data	Voice, messaging, basic Internet access

MOBILE NETWORK SPECIFICATIONS

Standards

For the first two generations, the standardization of the mobile networks was the responsibility of the local governing bodies with a limited ITU involvement. In the United States, the Telecommunications Industry Association (TIA) specified the architecture of AMPS, IS-95, IS-136. In Europe, GSM was designed and developed by the European Telecommunications Standardization Institute (ETSI). The regional standardization limited the global interoperability, network scaling, equipment development, and optimization of mobile operators' deployment costs. Starting with IMT-2000, the mobile network standardization was consolidated in two main bodies: 3GPP responsible for evolving the GSM/GPRS/EDGE to UMTS and beyond; and 3GPP2 responsible for evolving the IS-95/IS-136 to CDMA2000 and beyond (IEEE as a separate standardization body designed and developed the WiMAX standard in the IEEE 802.16e/m specifications). From the IMT-Advanced onwards, the 3GPP took the leading role for the global standardization of the mobile network infrastructures from the 4G and beyond. As of 2017, there are 591 commercially launched LTE, LTE-Advanced or LTE-Advanced Pro networks in 186 countries with 1.9 billion subscriptions worldwide (Ericsson, 2017; Global Mobile Suppliers Association, 2017). The second and third generation

Table 2. Mobile communications systems evolution: 3GPP onwards

	3G	3.5/3.75G	4G	4.5G/4.75G	5G
Requirements	IMT-2000		IMT-Advanced		IMT-2020
Technologies	UMTS (W-CDMA, TD-SCDMA), CDMA2000	EV-DO, HSPA, HSPA+	LTE, WiMAX	LTE-Advanced, LTE-Advanced-Pro	TBD
Peak Data Rates (DL – downlink; UL - uplink)	UMTS: 384 – 2048 Kb/s CDMA2000: 307 Kb/s	EV-DO: 4.9/1.8 Mb/s (DL/UL) HSPA: 14.4/5 Mb/s (DL/UL) HSPA+: 42/11.5 Mb/s (DL/UL)	LTE: 100/50 Mb/s (DL/UL) WiMAX: 46/7 Mb/s (DL/UL)	DL: 3 Gb/s UL: 1.5 Gb/s	DL: 20 Gb/s UL: 10 Gb/s
User Experienced Data Rates (maximum)	UMTS: 300 Kb/s CDMA2000: 200 Kb/s	EV-DO: 600 Kb/s HSPA: 700 Kb/s HSPA+: 1 Mb/s	LTE: 20 Mb/s WiMAX: 4 Mb/s	46 Mb/s	DL: 100 Mb/s UL: 50 Mb/s
Latency	UMTS: 200 ms CDMA2000: 600 ms	EV-DO: 50-200 ms HSPA: 70-90 ms HSPA+: 10-40 ms	LTE: 5-15 ms WiMAX: 15-40 ms	10 ms	eMBB: 4 ms URLLC: 1 ms
Mobility	Stationary (0 km/h); Pedestrian (0-10 km/h); Vehicular (0-120 km/h); High Speed Vehicular (120-500 km/h)				
Services	Voice, streaming video, multimedia, web browsing, email		3G services + Web 2.0, Video/Music on Demand, interactive gaming	LTE services + machine-to-machine, mission critical services interoperability with WiFi	LTE-Advanced/ Pro + high definition multimedia, Internet-of-Things

3GPP-based infrastructures are also prevalent across the world, setting the 3GPP specifications as the de-facto global standard for mobile networks.

The 3GPP specifications are organized in releases, each of which contains a stable and detailed set of features (Cox, 2014). Within each release, the specifications progress through a number of different versions adding new functionality with each new version until the release is frozen for final publication. Table 3 lists the 3GPP releases corresponding to the technologies developed from UMTS to LTE-Advanced-Pro, as well as the planned 5G releases.

Table 3. 3GPP Specification Releases

Release	Functional Freeze Date	Features
R99	March 2000	UMTS (W-CDMA) Radio Access Networks – UTRAN
Rel-4	March 2001	TD-SCDMA Air interface, QoS Architecture for UMTS
Rel-5	June 2002	HSDPA, IP Multimedia Subsystem (IMS)
Rel-6	March 2005	HSUPA, IMS phase 2
Rel-7	December 2007	HSPA+ with support for spatial multiplexing (Multiple-In Multiple-Out antennas - MIMO)
Rel-8	December 2008	System Architectural Evolution (SAE), LTE and Evolved UTRAN – E-UTRAN
Rel-9	December 2009	Enhancements to LTE/SAE: security, Multimedia Broadcast Multicast Services (MBMS), Self-Organizing Networks (SOA)
Rel-10	March 2011	LTE-Advanced: Carrier Aggregation (CA), Relay Nodes (RN), enhanced Inter-Cell Interference Coordination (eICIC)
Rel-11	September 2012	Enhancements to LTE-Advanced: Coordinated Multi Point operation (CoMP)
Rel-12	March 2015	Enhancements to LTE-Advanced: Small cells and Network densification, Security Assurance Methodology (SECAM), integration of WiFi
Rel-13	March 2016	LTE-Advanced-Pro: Machine Type Communications (MTC), indoor positioning, latency reduction
Rel-14	June 2017	Enhancement to LTE-Advanced-Pro: 5G requirements, Control and User Plane Separation of EPC nodes (Software Defined Networks - SDMN)
Rel-15	September 2018	First set of 5G standards

3GPP organizes the technical specifications into several series that detail specific components of the overall mobile network infrastructure. Table 4 summarizes the subjects of the series that specify the mobile networks from R99 and later (series 21 to 38), 2G only from Rel-4 and later (41 - 55), and 2G before Rel-4 (01-11). The technical specifications are formatted as TS *[Series number].[Specification Number]* V*[Release Number].[Technical Version Number].[Editorial Number]*. For example, the technical specification for Lawful Interception (LI) in LTE-Advanced-Pro is TS 33.106 v13.4.0. Here, 33 indicates that the LI functionality is specified under the security aspects of the LTE-Advanced-Pro, 106 is the specification number for the LI requirements, 13 refers to the Release 13, 4 for the technical version, and 0 for the editorial version. In Table 3 there are references to "stages" for different specifications used for logical grouping of the technical specifications. Stage 1 specifications define the service from the user's point of view, stage 2 specifications define the system's high-level architecture and operation, and stage 3 specifications define all the functional details. All the 3GPP series are open for access to the public from the 3GPP website (3rd Generation Partnership Project, 2017a).

Frequency Bands

Mobile networks operate in licensed frequency bands allocated by the regulatory bodies of each country (International Telecommunication Union, 2016). On a global level, ITU harmonizes the radio regulations in three regions: Region 1 (Europe, Africa, Russia and the ex-Soviet Union, Middle East, and Mongolia); Region 2 (Americas); and Region 3 (Iran, Asia Pacific and Oceania). All the 3GPP specifications are developed in alignment with the ITU Radio Regulation to support worldwide deployment, interoperability, and user roaming.

2G Frequency Bands (GSM)

2G GSM networks operate into frequency bands specified in the TS 45.005 technical specifications (3rd Generation Partnership Project, 2017c). The allocation of these bands as of the latest Rel-14 (v.14.0.0) is shown in Table 5. Most of the commercial GSM networks are deployed in the GSM-850, P-GSM-900, E-GSM-900, DCS-18000, and PCS-1900. With evolution towards the LTE, 2G networks will be phased out so eventually the operating bands will be free to be used by LTE or other 5G deployments. Therefore, some of the bands are also allocated as equivalent bands for LTE in Table 5 (see Appendix).

3G Frequency Bands (UMTS)

3G UMTS networks operate into frequency bands specified in the TS 25.104 technical specifications (3rd Generation Partnership Project, 2017b). The allocation of these bands as of the latest Rel-14 (v.14.1.0) is shown in Table 6 for a Frequency Division Duplex mode of communication (FDD). There is also a Time Division Duplex (TDD) frequency allocation for the

Table 4. 3GPP Specification Series

3G and beyond / GSM (R99 and later)	2G only (Rel-4 and later)	2G only (before Rel-4)	Subject of Specification Series
21 series	41 series	01 series	Requirements
22 series	42 series	02 series	Service aspects ("stage 1")
23 series	43 series	03 series	Technical realization ("stage 2")
24 series	44 series	04 series	Signaling protocols ("stage 3") - user equipment to network (Non-Access Stratum - NAS)
25 series	45 series	05 series	Radio aspects (W-CDMA and TD-SCDMA)
26 series	46 series	06 series	CODECs
27 series	n/a	07 series	Data terminal equipment
28 series	48 series	08 series	Signaling protocols ("stage 3") - (RSS-CN) and Operations, administration, maintenance, provisioning (OAM&P) and Charging (overflow from 32.-range)
29 series	49 series	09 series	Signaling protocols ("stage 3") – Core Network
30 series	50 series	10 series	Programme management
31 series	51 series	12 series	Subscriber Identity Module (SIM / USIM), IC Cards.
32 series	52 series	13 series	OAM&P and Charging
33 series	Spread throughout 3G and beyond series	Spread throughout 3G and beyond series	Security aspects
34 series	Spread throughout 3G and beyond series	11 series	UE and (U)SIM test specifications
35 series	55 series	GSMA specified, not open	Security algorithms
36 series	n/a	n/a	LTE (Evolved UTRA), LTE-Advanced, LTE-Advanced Pro radio technology
37 series	n/a	n/a	Multiple radio access technology aspects
38 series	n/a	n/a	Radio technology beyond LTE

TD-SCDMA in China specified in TS 25.105 technical specifications (the concept of duplex communication is explained in the following section of this chapter). Most of the commercial UMTS networks are deployed in the bands I, IV, V and VIII (band VIII occupies the same frequency spectrum as P/E-GSM so the UMTS networks deployment need to consider previous 2G networks operating in these bands). Some of the bands are also allocated as equivalent bands for LTE in Table 6 for the eventual phase out of the 3G deployments (see Appendix).

4G Frequency Bands (LTE, LTE-Advanced, LTE-Advanced-Pro)

LTE, LTE-Advanced, and LTE-Advanced-Pro networks operate into frequency bands specified in the TS 36.104 technical specifications (3rd Generation Partnership Project, 2017f). The allocation of these bands as of the latest Rel-14 (v.14.3.0) is shown in Table 7 for both the FDD and TDD modes of communication (see Appendix).

PRINCIPLES OF MOBILE COMMUNICATION

Digital Wireless Transmission and Reception

Every digital wireless communication system consists of several key elements as depicted in Figure 1: transmitter, wireless channel, and receiver. The transmitter accepts a bitstream for the upper communication layers and encodes the bitstream to add redundancy so that receiver can correct any errors introduced to the signal by the wireless channel. The modulator takes the encoded stream and maps it to a transmitting *symbol* according to a modulation scheme. The modulation scheme represents all the possible combinations of amplitudes and phases of the transmitted waveform to which the group of bits are modulated. For example, a Binary Phase Shift Keying (BPSK) represents two possible waveforms with a difference in phase of 180 degrees, and is used to map 1 bit per symbol. Mobile systems like LTE use additional modulation schemes that map 2 bits per symbol or Quadrature Phase Shift Keying (QPSK), 4 bits per symbol or 16 Quadrature Amplitude Modulation (16-QAM), and 6 bits per symbol or 64-QAM. Figure 2 shows the constellations of these modulation schemes. The modulated signal is then converted into a representative analog waveform by the Digital-to-Analog (D/A) converter and passed to the Radio Frequency (RF) module. Up to this step, all the operations by the transmitter are performed on the baseband signal. The RF module takes the baseband signal and upconverts it to one of the desired frequency bands listed in Tables 6, 7 or 8 as electromagnetic waves emitted through the wireless channel.

The receiver performs the reverse of these operations. The downconverted signal from the RF module is passed though the Analog-to-Digital converter (A/D) to get the received symbols. Due to the inconstant nature of the wireless channel, the received symbols are distorted so the receiver needs to estimate them to be able to demodulate the transmitted bitstream. As a result of potential errors during the estimation, the demodulated signal is passed through the decoder that tries to recover the original bitstream and passes it to the upper communication layers for further processing.

Figure 1. Wireless digital communication system

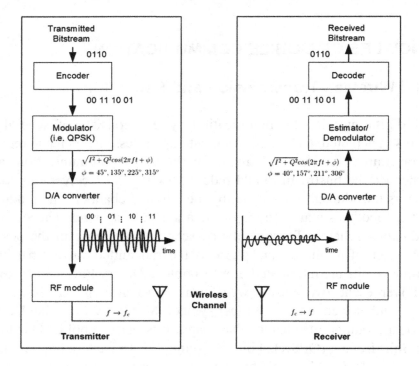

Wireless Channel and Propagation

The electromagnetic waves of the transmitted signal have finite power that dissipates as they traverse to reach the receiver. Assuming the RF module uses an isotropic antenna (radiates its power uniformly in all directions), the propagated signal occupies a spherical surface with an area of $4\pi d^2$ where d is the distance between the transmitter and the receiver. Due to the dissipation in all directions of the sphere, the power of the received signal is inversely proportional to the d^2, an effect known as *path loss* or *propagation loss*. However, the terrestrial propagation environment is not a free space so the waves reflect from Earth or are diffracted/absorbed from other objects between the transmitter and the receiver. These alternating effects further exacerbate the path loss making the actual received signal in mobile networks inversely proportional to d^m where m typically lies between 3.5 and 4 (Ghosh *et al.*, 2010; Cox, 2014).

Figure 2. Modulation schemes used by mobile communication systems

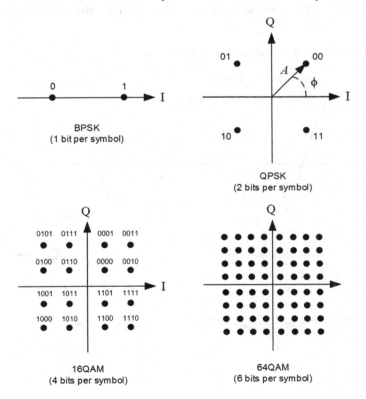

The reflection, diffraction (bending), or scattering of the electromagnetic waves causes components of the transmitted signal to travel along different propagation paths before reaching the receiver. This phenomenon is known as *multipath*. If the multiple components coincide at nearly the same time and are not significantly phase shifted, the combined effect reinforces the received signal and is known as a *constructive interference*. If the phase shift is such that the components cancel each other as shown in Figure 3, the received signal suffers from a *destructive interference*. The case when the destructive interference causes severe degradation of the received signal is known as *fading*.

In a mobile networking scenario, the relative distance between the receiver and the transmitter (being that the mobile device and the network base station) changes with the mobility speed, which in turn changes the nature of the wireless channel. The time-varying nature of the channel is described with two parameters, *Doppler spread* and *coherence time*. Doppler spread is the power distribution of the multiple signal components over a range of frequencies that is non-zero, i.e. not all the components will arrive on the exact same frequency that they were transmitted. The coherence time is the inverse of the Doppler spread and characterizes the time varying nature

Figure 3. Constructive and destructive interference

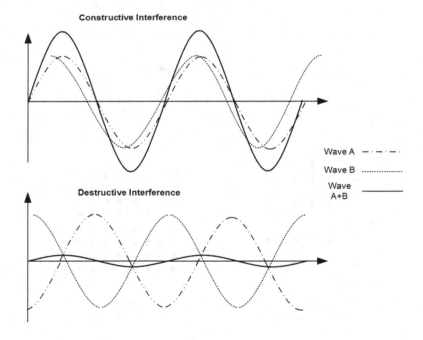

of the frequency dispersiveness of the channel in the time domain (Sklar, 2001). Essentially, the coherence time indicates the period over which the amplitude and the phase of different signal components are roughly constant. If the Doppler spread is much smaller than the bandwidth of the baseband signal, its effect at the receiver is negligible so the wireless channel in this case is referred to as a *slow fading* channel. In other words, the coherence time is much larger than the time used by the RF module to transmit one symbol. This helps for successful estimation of the transmitted symbols on the receiver side – the receiver may assume constant channel properties and will need no channel estimation to combat the fading. If the Doppler spread is larger than the baseband bandwidth of the transmitted signal – the coherence time is smaller than the symbol time – the channel is referred to as a *fast fading* channel.

The time-dispersive nature of the channel is described with two other parameters, *delay spread* and *coherence bandwidth*. The delay spread indicates the time difference of arrival between the first and the last non-negligible signal components at the receiver. The coherence bandwidth is the inverse of the delay spread and refers to the range of frequencies over which two signal components have roughly constant amplitude and phase. If the coherence bandwidth is larger than the baseband bandwidth of the transmitted signal – or the symbol time is larger than the delay spread – the channel is characterized as a *flat fading* channel. In the opposite case, the channel fading is characterized as a *frequency selective*.

These parameters have different impacts on mobile communication systems design. The delay spread determines the symbol rate – the larger the delay time is compared to the symbol time, the more severe the Inter-Symbol Interference (ISI) is. ISI is the effect of symbol overlapping from signal components arriving at different times at the receiver. The more severe the ISI is, the higher the probability for incorrect estimation of the symbol at the receiver, which ultimately results in a decrease of the throughput or the overall bitrate. The coherence time determines how often a channel needs to be estimated to cancel the fast fading effect. The smaller the coherence time, the more channel estimations are needed, which again, raises the probability for incorrect symbol estimation at the receiver.

Error Management

After the symbols are estimated and demodulated, the receiver needs to make the final decision on the transmitted bits at the decoder. Various types of fading may affect the symbol estimation and with that result in an incorrect decision on the transmitted bitstream. In addition, the symbol estimation is affected with the noise and external interference that are detected together with the received signal components at the receivers' RF module. Errors in the bitstream are damaging to the mobile network applications (i.e. voice calls, web pages, streaming services, or interactive messaging) and are inevitable in every wireless system. There are two main techniques for managing wireless transmission errors: use of *forward error correction codes* when the bitstream is encoded/decoded at the transmitter/receiver (handled on the physical level) and Automatic Repeat reQuest or ARQ (handled on the data link level).

The forward error correction codes add redundancy to the bitstream passed from the upper communication layers by representing essentially every bit with a *codeword* that is two or three bits in size. For example, if two-bit codewords are used, the encoding rate or the robustness is said to be 1/2 or the number of information bits divided by the number of encoded bits. Mobile communication systems use *convolutional* or *turbo* codes for forward error correction. If the channel conditions are good, the robustness of the error correction codes can be relaxed by dropping some of the encoded bits in a process known as *puncturing*. If for example a puncturing factor of 1/4 is used, the transmitter drops one out of four encoded bits making a 1/2 encoding rate effectively a 2/3 encoding rate.

Another technique for dealing with errors is to employ an ARQ technique on the data link layer that enables quick retransmission of erroneous packets. Here the transmitter computes extra bits, known as Cyclic Redundancy Check (CRC) and appends them at the end of each data link packet before it transmits it. The receiver separates the original CRC bits from the packet bits, computes an expected CRC bits and compares with the original ones. If they match, the receiver sends an acknowledgment to the receiver and passes the packet to the network layer. If the CRC bits differ, the receiver sends negative acknowledgment and demands retransmission of the entire packet. Since a single wrongly transmitted bit requires entire packet retransmission, the scheme can be very ineffective. Mobile communication systems use scheme known as Hybrid ARQ (HARQ) where the CRC error detection bits are added before the encoding so to take advantage of the error correction scheme provided on the physical level.

Duplexing

The first mobile network infrastructures were designed to support telephony traffic. The telephony service requires the conversational parties to have the ability to speak and listen simultaneously. This requirement can be met by implementing two communication channels in a so-called *duplex* connection. The downlink channel is the one where the base station is the transmitter and the mobile device is the receiver, and vice versa, the uplink channel is the one where the mobile device is the transmitter and the base station is the receiver. The duplex connection can be configured in two ways: Frequency Division Duplex (FDD) or Time Division Duplex (TDD), both shown in Figure 4.

Figure 4. FDD and TDD duplexing techniques

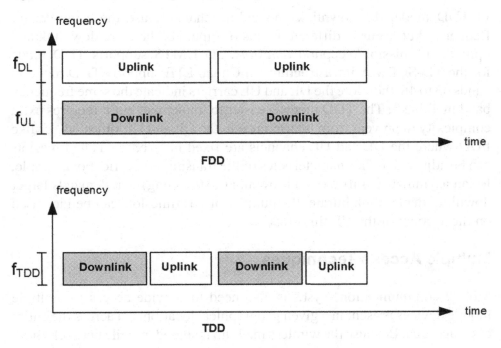

Frequency Division Duplex (FDD)

In FDD mode, the downlink and uplink channels use different frequency bands i.e. frequency carriers. 2G GSM, 3G UMTS, and LTE networks mainly employ a FDD mode of transmission, hence each of the operating bands in Table 5 and Table 6 have distinct pairs of DL and UL frequency carriers and Table 7 indicates the FDD duplex mode for each band. The DL and UL frequency carriers are not adjusted to one another; instead a duplex spacing is introduced so the simultaneously transmitted signals do not interfere and impair the receiver. This is particularly important for the mobile devices that have limited signal processing capabilities due to cost constraints. There is an option for a so-called *half duplex FDD* where the base station can transmit and receive simultaneously on the DL and UL carriers, but the mobile device either transmits or either receives in a given point of time.

Time Division Duplex (TDD)

In TDD mode, the downlink and uplink channels use the same carrier frequency but occur in different points of time, i.e. there are downlink and uplink transmission/reception *timeslots*. 3G UMTS supports TDD mode for the TD-SCDMA infrastructures in China. LTE supports TDD mode in bands 33 to 48, therefore the DL and UL carriers indicate the same frequency band in Table 7. The TDD mode is easier to implement but it requires extra complexity to prevent from interference in the DL and UL timeslots. Unlike FDD where the DL and UL channels are fixed in size, the TDD timeslots can be adjusted to the characteristics of the transmitted traffic. For example, for an asymmetric traffic (web browsing or streaming) that demands larger downlink than uplink bitrate, the number of DL timeslots can be increased on the account of the UL timeslots.

Multiple Access Techniques

Mobile communications systems also need to provide access to multiple mobile devices present in a given geographical location and across the entire coverage area. Because the wireless medium is shared, mobile networks have to use multiple access techniques to enable simultaneous communication with each mobile device at any point in time. The multiple access can be organized by time, code, frequency, or a combination of these properties.

Each multiple access technique is applicable in both downlink and uplink directions: the duplexing separates the communication directions, while the multiple access coordinates the individual communication streams in each direction (therefore it is also referred to as *multiplexing*).

As a property, the multiple access is the most salient discriminator between different network technologies and different generations. 2G GSM employed a combination of Time Division Multiple Access (TDMA) and Frequency Division Multiple Access (FDMA), while IS-95 used Code Division Multiple Access (CDMA). Both 3G UMTS and CDMA2000 employed CDMA and UMTS combined it with TDMA for the 3G TD-SCDMA variant. The 4G LTE family (LTE, LTE-Advanced, and LTE-Advanced-Pro) employs an evolved version of FDMA called Orthogonal FDMA or OFDMA. These multiple access techniques are shown in Figure 5.

Generally, TDMA uses different timeslots to communicate with multiple mobile devices that share the same frequency carrier. FDMA uses different frequencies instead, so the mobile devices can communicate at the same time without interference. In GSM, a group of geographically collocated users communicate with the base station at different time slots (TDMA), but different mobile stations can use different frequency carriers (or are divided

Figure 5. TDMA, CDMA, FDMA, and OFDMA multiple access techniques

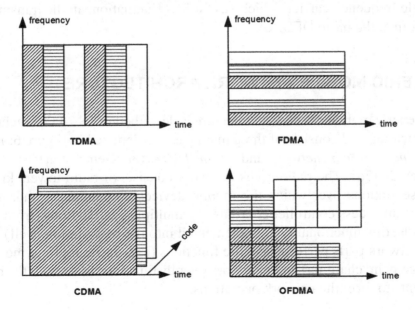

by frequency, therefore FDMA). CDMA organizes the multiple access by assigning different codes to different users that share the same frequency carrier and communicate in the same time. To prevent from interference, CDMA bitstreams are "scrambled" with different codes to produce a wireless signal with distinct and distinguishable characteristics so the users or the base stations can "unscramble" it among a set of other CDMA signals (Hoy, 2015).

OFDMA evolves the FDMA by organizing the communication in parallel, low bandwidth subcarriers, each of which is part of the main frequency carrier. The subcarriers are selected to be *orthogonal* (the peak response of one subcarrier coincides with zeros of all the others in the frequency domain), a property that helps systems like LTE effectively combat the varying and dispersive nature of the wireless channel. A variable number of subcarriers can be dedicated for different users for variable portion of time with OFDMA, enabling more flexible organization of the multiple access in LTE. However, this robustness and flexibility come at a cost: the power of the output signal from the RF module fluctuates to large variations. These variations can only be accounted for with expensive, non-linear power amplifiers for normal operations. Instead of driving the price and complexity of the mobile devices by using advanced RF modules, OFDMA in LTE is employed only for the downlink channel. For the uplink, LTE employs a pre-coded OFMDA technique called Single Carrier-FDMA (SC-FDMA). SC-FDMA preprocess the different substreams so the resulting transmitted signal is effectively transmitted on a single frequency carrier, which has far less fluctuations in the transmitted power than the basic OFDMA.

GENERIC MOBILE NETWORK ARCHITECTURE

The generic mobile network architecture is described in TS 23.002 technical specification and consists of three main parts as depicted in Figure 6: *radio access network*, *core network*, and *mobile devices* (3rd Generation Partnership Project, 2017d). The radio access network consists of radio towers known as base stations over which the mobile devices communicate and, up to the 3G, an access controller coordinating multiple base stations (from LTE onwards, this functionality is implemented into the base station itself). The core network parts perform specific functions (e.g. traffic routing, mobility management, charging) and interwork over distinct interfaces with the radio elements to form the network operations.

Depending on the traffic type, the elements can handle telephony-related traffic (circuit switched nodes) or packet traffic (packet switched nodes). Some deployments like LTE for example have only packet switched domain nodes because they handle packet traffic only (including the voice telephony service). In addition, the core network includes administrative nodes that handle the user and network management functions and provide external access to the Internet or other telephony or corporate networks. All the network operations are organized in protocols that either realize the mobile device traffic (user plane) or control the state of the mobile device in the network (control or signaling plane). Each generation has a specific implementation of the network architecture, further elaborated in Chapter 4 and Chapter 5.

Radio Access Network

The Radio Access Network (RAN) is the wireless or the *air interface* between the users and the mobile network. Common for all RANs is the logical organization of the service area coverage or the *cellular* concept. In a cellular system, the service area is divided into smaller geographical areas called *cells* that are each served by their own base station as shown in Figure 7. Such a division is possible due to the nature of the wireless medium. As a result of the propagation loss, signals can traverse a limited distance at which they can be successfully detected. This allows for spatial isolation of different cells and operators' can reuse the frequency carriers in the same time for sufficiently separated cells (in distance) without causing any interference

Figure 6. Generic mobile network architecture

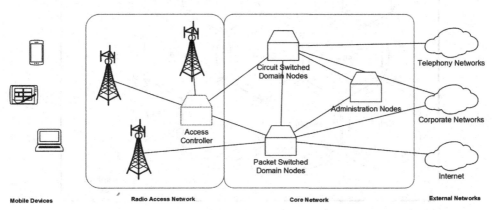

(that is why Tables 5, 6, and 7 have a limited number of operating bands for national and worldwide use).

The cellular coverage is realized using variable power levels, which allow cells to be sized according to the user density and traffic demand of a given area. The typical cell sizes deployed in practice are depicted in Figure 8 and include:

1. **Macrocell:** Radius of 1-30 km, used for wide area outdoor coverage
2. **Microcell:** Radius of 200 m - 1 km, used for urban area coverage
3. **Picocell:** Radius than up to 500 m if deployed outdoor or 20-200 m if deployed indoor, mostly used for extended coverage
4. **Femtocell:** Radius less 30 meters, used for mainly indoor coverage for homes or small business

Figure 7. Service area coverage with cells

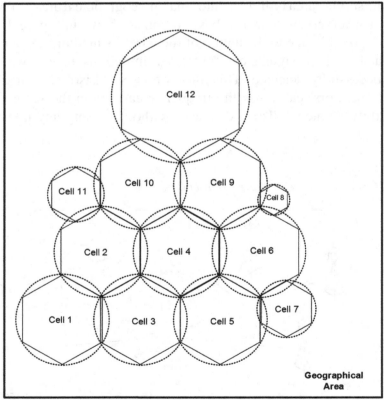

Figure 8. Various cell sizes

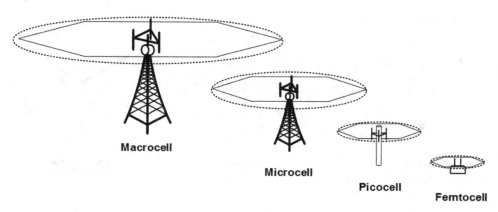

There are three common configurations of a cell as shown in Figure 9: *omnidirectional*, *sectorized*, and *hybrid*. The omnidirectional configuration uses a single operating band within the entire cell coverage for both uplink and downlink communication and the base station implements RF module with an antenna emitting in 360 degrees. The sectorized transmission and reception divides the cell coverage in sectors, usually 2, 3 or 6 sectors. Within each sector, the mobile operator has the flexibility to reuse different carrier frequencies to extend the cell capacity, cover weak reception spots, or improve the overall throughput. Sectorized cells use RF modules with directional antennas emitting in either 180 (2 sectors), 120 degrees (3 sectors) or 60 degrees (6 sectors). If an operator needs further flexibility for balancing the downlink and uplink traffic, for example responding to crowded cells, the hybrid option can be used where the downlink transmission is realized in an omnidirectional fashion and the uplink one is sectorized. In this case, the base station's transmitting antenna is omnidirectional while the receiving antennas are directional.

The key feature of the cellular concept is the support for mobility. Users can have continuous service while moving with different speeds (up to 350 km/h as indicated in Table 1 and Table 2) from cell to cell. The RAN in coordination with the core network manages users' mobility through the handover (service for active users) and *cell reselection* procedures (service for idle users). The mobility management procedures are elaborated in Chapter 4 and Chapter 5.

The RAN deployments are different for each generation:

Figure 9. Various cell configurations

1. **2G RAN - GSM/EDGE RAN (GERAN):** Consists of Base Transceiver Stations (BTS) and Base Station Controllers (BSC). BTSs are the base stations managing the cell and handling the radio communication. BSCs control groups of BTSs, handle radio resource management, and interface with the core network. The overall description of the GERAN is provided in the TS 03.02 technical specification (3rd Generation Partnership Project, 2000).
2. **3G RAN - UMTS RAN (UTRAN):** Consists of NodeBs and Radio Network Controllers (RNC). The NodeBs perform the base station role While the RNCs perform the radio resource management, traffic routing, and interface with both the 2G and 3G core network elements. The UTRAN overall description is provided in the TS 25.401 technical specification (3rd Generation Partnership Project, 2017e).
3. **4G RAN - Evolved UTRAN (E-UTRAN):** The main element is the evolved Node B (eNB). The eNB is responsible for all the radio segment operations and it merges the base station and the access network controller functionalities into one RAN element. As such, it simplifies the network architecture, reduces the network latency, and enables for flexible radio resource management. The overall description of the E-UTRAN is provided in the TS 36.300 technical specification (3rd Generation Partnership Project, 2017g).

Core Network

The core network is responsible for the mobile service delivery beyond the radio interface. The core network controls the traffic routing, provides access to other mobile networks or Internet, performs the mobility and user security management, handles the user charging, and enables lawful interception. The 2G networks were designed to support mostly telephony traffic so the GSM core elements were developed to handle *Circuit Switched* (CS) data. With the introduction of the GPRS/EDGE and the evolution to 3G, core networks were upgraded to support packet switched services, therefore, the UMTS core also has a *Packet Switched* (PS) domain next to the legacy CS domain. The 4G networks support mainly packet services, therefore the core is evolved to provide flat access to Internet or other packet networks. Although the mobile traffic is handled differently in every generation, core networks can share common elements like databases of users, billing systems, application servers, or prepaid platforms. To understand the structure and core network functioning, Chapters 4 and 5 explain the interfaces, protocols, and main core functions of every mobile generation.

Mobile Devices

A "mobile device" is the general term representing the mobile users from a network point of view and the terminology differs from generation to generation – 2G networks refer to the mobile device as the *Mobile Station* (MS) while the 3G UMTS and 4G LTE as the *User Equipment* (UE). In any case, the mobile device has two logical elements: A Subscriber Identification Module (SIM) card and a terminal equipment. The SIM card contains details of the user account (i.e. network identificators, encryption keys, etc.) while the terminal equipment is a device capable of communicating with any standardized mobile network (e.g. mobile phones, smartphones, tablets, computers, IoT devices, etc.). The structure and network control of the mobile devices are further overviewed in Chapter 4 and Chapter 5.

CONCLUSION

Understanding the fundamental principles of mobile communications is essential in producing high quality mobile network evidence. The evolution of mobile infrastructure helps creating a general investigative context because most operators have heterogeneous network deployments with elements from different generations. Investigators familiar with mobile communication concepts can reference the mobile network standardization to inform on particular network parts, elements, functions, and protocols of interest. To help the investigation execution, the next two chapters discuss the mobile network systems from a detailed operational perspective.

NOTE

The term *cellular network* as introduced in this chapter is a synonym for *mobile network* and is used interchangeably throughout the book.

REFERENCES

3rd Generation Partnership Project. (2000). *TS 25.401 V14.0.0 - Technical Specification Group Radio Access Network; UTRAN overall description.* Sophia Antipolis Cedex: 3GPP.

3rd Generation Partnership Project. (2017a). *3GPP Specifications Numbering, Technical Specifications.* Available at: http://www.3gpp.org/specifications/79-specification-numbering

3rd Generation Partnership Project. (2017b). *3GPP TS 25.104 V14.1.0 -Technical Specification Group Radio Access Network; Base Station (BS) radio transmission and reception (FDD).* Sophia Antipolis Cedex: 3GPP.

3rd Generation Partnership Project. (2017c). *3GPP TS 45.005 V14.0.0 - Technical Specification Group Radio Access Network; GSM/EDGE Radio transmission and reception.* Sophia Antipolis Cedex: 3GPP.

3rd Generation Partnership Project. (2017d). *TS 23.002 V14.1.0 - Technical Specification Group Services and System Aspects; Network architecture.* Sophia Antipolis Cedex: 3GPP.

3rd Generation Partnership Project. (2017e). *TS 25.401 V14.0.0 - Technical Specification Group Radio Access Network; UTRAN overall description.* Sophia Antipolis, France: 3GPP.

3rd Generation Partnership Project. (2017f). *TS 36.104 V14.3.0 - Technical Specification Group Radio Access Network; Evolved Universal Terrestrial Radio Access (E-UTRA); Base Station (BS) radio transmission and reception.* Sophia Antipolis Cedex: 3GPP.

3rd Generation PARTNERSHIP Project. (2017g). *TS 36.300 V14.2.0 - Technical Specification Group Radio Access Network; Evolved Universal Terrestrial Radio Access (E-UTRA) and Evolved Universal Terrestrial Radio Access Network (E-UTRAN); Overall description; Stage 2.* Sophia Antipolis, France: 3GPP.

Cox, C. (2014). *An Introduction to LTE: LTE, LTE-Advanced, SAE and 4G Mobile Communications (2nd ed.).* New York, NY: Wiley. doi:10.1002/9781118818046

Ericsson. (2017). *Ericsson Mobility Report, Ericsson Mobility Report.* Available at: https://www.ericsson.com/assets/local/mobility-report/documents/2016/ericsson-mobility-report-november-2016.pdf

Ghosh, A., Zhang, J., Andrews, J., & Muhamed, R. (2010). *The Fundamentals of LTE* (1st ed.). Boston, MA: Prentice Hall.

Global Mobile Suppliers Association. (2017). *Evolution from LTE to 5G.* Author.

Hoy, J. (2015). *Forensic Radio Survey Techniques for Cell Site Analysis.* West Sussex, UK: Wiley. doi:10.1002/9781118925768

International Telecommunication Union. (2016). *Radio Regulations.* Available at: http://search.itu.int/history/HistoryDigitalCollectionDocLibrary/1.43.48.en.101.pdf

International Telecommunication Union. (2017). *Minimum requirements related to technical performance for IMT-2020 radio interface(s).* Available at: https://www.itu.int/md/R15-SG05-C-0040/en

Sklar, B. (2001). *Digital Communications: Fundamentals and Applications* (2nd ed.). Upper Saddle River, NJ: Prentice Hall.

KEY TERMS AND DEFINITIONS

1G: 1st generation of mobile networks.

2G: 2nd generation of mobile networks. The most dominant technology is the global system for mobility (GSM).

3G: 3rd generation of mobile networks. The most dominant technology is universal mobile telecommunication system (UMTS).

3GPP: 3rd generation partnership project.

4G: 4th generation of mobile networks. The 4G technologies are long term evolution (LTE) and the advanced version, LTE-advanced. Colloquially, the terms LTE/LTE-A are used as a synonym for 4G as they are the only global standard for mobile communication from the fourth generation.

5G: 5th generation of mobile networks. Still in standardization phase, the first 5G deployments are envisioned for 2020.

A/D: Analog to digital conversion.

AMPS: Advanced mobile phone system.

ARQ: Automatic repeat request.

BPSK: Binary phase shift keying.

CA: Carrier aggregation.

CDMA: Code division multiple access.

CoMP: Coordinated multi-point operation.

CRC: Cyclic redundancy check.

D/A: Digital to analog conversion.

DL: Downlink.

EDGE: Enhanced data rates for global evolution.

eICIC: Enhanced inter-cell interference coordination.

eMBB: Enhanced mobile broad band.

EPC: Evolved packet core.

E-UTRA: Evolved-universal terrestrial radio access.

E-UTRAN: Evolved UTRAN.

EV-DO: Evolution data only.

FDD: Frequency division duplex.

FDMA: Frequency division multiple access.

GERAN: GPRS/EDGE RAN.

GPRS: General packet radio service.

GSM: Global system for mobile.

HARQ: Hybrid ARQ.

HSDPA: High speed downlink packet access.

HSPA: High speed packet access.

HSPA+: HSPA advanced.
HSS: Home subscriber server.
HSUPA: High uplink packet access.
IEEE: Institute of Electrical and Electronics Engineers.
IMS: Internet multimedia subsystem.
IMT Advanced: International mobile telecommunications advanced (ITU's name for the family of 4G standards).
IMT-2000: International mobile telecommunications 2000 (ITU's name for the family of 3G standards).
IMT-2020: International mobile telecommunications 2000 (ITU's name for the family of 5G standards).
IoT: Internet-of-things.
ISI: Inter symbol interference.
ITU: International Telecommunication Union.
MBMS: Multimedia broadcast multicast services.
MIMO: Multiple in multiple out.
MME: Mobility management entity.
MS: Mobile station.
MTC: Machine type communications (MTC).
NMT: Nordic mobile telephony.
OFDMA: Orthogonal FDMA.
OSI: Open system for interconnection.
QAM: Quadrature amplitude modulation.
QPSK: Quadrature phase shift keying.
RAN: Radio access network.
RF: Radio frequency.
RN: Relay nodes.
S/P-GW: Serving/packet gateway.
SAE: System architectural evolution.
SC-FDMA: Single carrier FDMA.
SDMN: Software-defined mobile network.
SECAM: Security assurance methodology.
SIM: Subscriber identification module.
SOA: Self-organizing networks.
TACS: Total access communication system.
TD-SCDMA: Time division synchronous CDMA.
TDD: Time division duplex.
TDMA: Time division multiple access.
TIA: Telecommunication Industry Association.

U-NII: Unlicensed national information infrastructure spectrum in the 5 GHz frequency segment.

UE: User equipment.

UL: Uplink.

UMTS: Universal mobile telephone system.

URLLC: Ultra reliable and low latency communication.

USIM: Universal SIM.

UTRAN: UMTS RAN.

UWB: Ultra-wide band.

W-CDMA: Widespread CDMA.

WWW: Worldwide web.

APPENDIX

2G Frequency Bands (GSM)

Table 5. 2G GSM Frequency bands

Operating Band	Uplink (UL): mobiles transmit, base station receives (MHz)	Downlink (DL): mobiles receive, base station transmits (MHz)	Deployment
	$f_{UL\_low} - f_{UL\_high}$	$f_{DL\_low} - f_{DL\_high}$	
T-GSM 380	380.2 – 389.8	390.2 – 399.8	Not used
T-GSM-410	410.2 – 419.8	420.2 – 429.8	Not used
T-GSM-450	450.4 – 457.6	460.4 – 467.6	Allocated as an equivalent LTE band 31 (see Table 7)
GSM-480	478.8 – 486.0	488.8 – 496.0	Not used
GSM-710	698 – 716	728 – 746	Allocated as an equivalent LTE band 12 (see Table 7)
GSM-750	747 – 763	777 – 792	Not used
T-GSM-810	806 – 821	851 – 866	Allocated as an equivalent LTE band 27 (see Table 7)
GSM-850	824 – 849	869 – 894	Americas (equivalent LTE band 5)
P-GSM-900	890.0 – 915.0	935.0 – 960.0	Global
E-GSM-900	880.0 – 915.0	925.0 – 960.0	Global; (equivalent LTE band 8)
R-GSM-900	876.0 – 915.0	921.0 – 960.0	GSM for Railways
DCS-1800	1710 – 1785	1805 – 1880	Global (equivalent LTE band 3)
PCS-1900	1850 – 1909.8	1930 – 1990	Americas (equivalent LTE band 2)

3G Frequency Bands (UMTS)

Table 6. 3G UMTS Frequency bands

Operating Band	Uplink (UL): mobiles transmit, base station receives (MHz)	Downlink (DL): mobiles receive, base station transmits (MHz)	Deployment
	$f_{UL\_low} - f_{UL\_high}$	$f_{DL\_low} - f_{DL\_high}$	
I	1920 – 1980	2110 – 2170	Global
II	1850 – 1910	1930 – 1990	Americas
III	1710 – 1785	1805–1880	Not Used
IV	1710 – 1755	2110 – 2155	Americas
V	824 – 849	869 – 894	Global
VI	830 – 840	875 – 885	Japan
VII	2500 – 2570	2620 – 2690	Global (equivalent LTE Band 7)
VIII	880 – 915	925 – 960	Global
IX	1749.9 – 1784.9	1844.9 – 1879.9	Japan
X	1710 – 1770	2110 – 2170	Americas
XI	1427.9 – 1447.9	1475.9 – 1495.9	Japan
XII	699 – 716	729 – 746	Americas
XIII	777 – 787	746 – 756	Americas
XIV	788 – 798	758 – 768	Americas
XV	Reserved	Reserved	Reserved
XVI	Reserved	Reserved	Reserved
XVII	Reserved	Reserved	Reserved
XVIII	Reserved	Reserved	Reserved
XIX	830 – 845	875 – 890	Japan
XX	832 – 862	791 – 821	Europe (equivalent LTE Band 20)
XXI	1447.9 – 1462.9	1495.9 – 1510.9	Japan (equivalent LTE Band 21)
XXII	3410 – 3490	3510 – 3590	Not Used
XXV	1850 –1915	1930 – 1995	Not Used
XXVI	814 – 849	859 – 894	Not Used
XXXII	n/a	1452 – 1496	Not Used

4G Frequency Bands (LTE, LTE-Advanced, LTE-Advanced-Pro)

Table 7. LTE, LTE-Advanced, LTE-Advanced-Pro frequency bands

Operating Band	Uplink (UL): mobiles transmit, base station receives (MHz)	Downlink (DL): mobiles receive, base station transmits (MHz)	Duplex Mode	Deployment
	$f_{UL\_low} - f_{UL\_high}$	$f_{DL\_low} - f_{DL\_high}$		
1	1920 - 1980	2110 – 2170	FDD	Global
2	1850 - 1910	1930 - 1990	FDD	Americas
3	1710 - 1785	1805 – 1880	FDD	Global
4	1710 – 1755	2110 - 2115	FDD	Americas
5	824 - 849	869 – 894	FDD	Americas, Africa, Asia Pacific
6	830 – 840	875 – 880	FDD	Japan
7	2500 – 2570	2620 – 2690	FDD	Global, not United States
8	880 – 915	925 – 960	FDD	Global, not United States
9	1749.9 – 1784.9	1844.9 – 1879.9	FDD	Japan
10	1710 – 1700	2110 - 2170	FDD	Americas, Asia Pacific
11	1427.9 – 1447.9	1475.9 – 1495.9	FDD	Japan
12	699 – 716	729 - 746	FDD	Americas, Asia Pacific
13	777 – 787	746 – 756	FDD	Americas
14	788 - 798	758 - 768	FDD	Americas
15	Reserved	Reserved	FDD	Reserved
16	Reserved	Reserved	FDD	Reserved
17	704 - 716	734 - 746	FDD	Americas
18	815 - 830	860 - 875	FDD	Global, not Europe
19	830 – 845	875 – 890	FDD	Global, not Europe
20	832 – 862	791 – 821	FDD	Eastern Europe, Africa, Middle East
21	1447.9 – 1462.9	1495.9 – 1510.9	FDD	Japan
22	3410 – 3490	3510 – 3590	FDD	Global
23	2000 – 2020	2180 – 2200	FDD	Global S-Band
24	1626.5 – 1660.5	1525 – 1559	FDD	Global L-Band
25	1850 - 1915	1930 – 1995	FDD	Americas
26	814 – 849	859 – 894	FDD	Americas
27	807 – 824	852 – 869	FDD	Americas
28	703 – 748	758 – 803	FDD	Asia Pacific
29	n/a	717 - 728	FDD	Americas
30	2305 - 2315	2350 – 2360	FDD	Global

continued on following page

Table 7. Continued

Operating Band	Uplink (UL): mobiles transmit, base station receives (MHz)	Downlink (DL): mobiles receive, base station transmits (MHz)	Duplex Mode	Deployment
	$f_{UL\_low} - f_{UL\_high}$	$f_{DL\_low} - f_{DL\_high}$		
31	452.5 – 457.5	462.5 – 467.5	FDD	Americas, Eastern Europe, Asia
32	n/a	1452 - 1496	FDD	Restricted for LTE-A Carrier Aggregation
33	1900 - 1920	1900 - 1920	TDD	Global
34	2010 - 2025	2010 – 2025	TDD	Global
35	1850 - 1910	1850 - 1910	TDD	Americas
36	1930 - 1990	1930 - 1990	TDD	Americas
37	1910 - 1930	1910 - 1930	TDD	Americas
38	2570 - 2620	2570 – 2620	TDD	Global
39	1880 - 1920	1880 – 1920	TDD	China
40	2300 – 2400	2300 – 2400	TDD	Global
41	2496 - 2690	2496 – 2690	TDD	Americas
42	3400 – 3600	3400 – 3600	TDD	Global
43	3600 - 3800	3600 – 3800	TDD	Americas
44	703 - 803	703 – 803	TDD	Asia Pacific
45	1447 - 1467	1447 – 1467	TDD	Global
46	5150 - 5925	5150 – 5925	TDD	Unlicensed band (U-NII)
47	5855 - 5925	5855 – 5925	TDD	Global
48	3550 – 3700	3550 – 3700	TDD	Global
65	1920 – 2010	2110 – 2200	FDD	Global
66	1710 – 1780	2110 – 2200	FDD	Restricted for LTE-A Carrier Aggregation
67	n/a	738 – 758	FDD	Restricted for LTE-A Carrier Aggregation
68	698 – 728	753 - 783	FDD	Global
69	n/a	2570 – 2620	FDD	Restricted for LTE-A Carrier Aggregation
70	1695 – 1710	1995 – 2020	FDD	Restricted for LTE-A Carrier Aggregation

Chapter 4
Mobile Network Architecture:
Pre–3GPP Generations (GSM, GPRS, and EDGE)

ABSTRACT

Critical for identification of the potential sources of evidence in every network forensics investigation is the definition of the system architecture. The mobile network architecture has two main definitions, one concerning the network deployments before the 3GPP consolidated the mobile standardization, and one for the 3GPP networks onwards. Forensic investigators need to know both of them; the real-world network deployments include elements from different generations, so the uncovering of mobile network evidence requires knowledge of how every generation operates in practice. This chapter provides a detailed overview of the pre-3GPP network architecture, defining the critical elements for recognizing, acquiring, analyzing, and interpreting potential mobile network evidence.

INTRODUCTION

This chapter introduces the basic elements and protocols from the pre-3GPP networks. The Global System for Mobile (GSM) as the de-facto second generation (2G) standard is described in terms of the reference network architecture, user and network identifiers, wireless radio interface, security aspects, and protocols supporting mobile telephony delivery. The enhancement

DOI: 10.4018/978-1-5225-5855-2.ch004

introduced for GSM to support packet data in form of a 2.5G evolution with the General Packet Radio Service (GPRS) and 2.75G with Enhanced Data rates for Global Evolution (EDGE) are also described. The resulting architecture provides useful insights into the mobile network operations that retained to a great extent in the later 3GPP generations. Both GSM and GPRS/EDGE are of significant forensics importance because they layout the fundamental principles of mobile service operations.

2G: GLOBAL SYSTEM FOR MOBILE COMMUNICATION (GSM)

Reference Network Architecture

The GSM system was design as an extension of the fixed landline networks so the early network deployments are referenced as Public Land Mobile Networks or PLMNs. Figure 1 shows the GSM reference network architecture specified in TS 23.003 V4.3.0 technical specification, Section 5 (3rd Generation Partnership Project, 2002). GSM has three subsystems: Base Station Subsystem (BSS), the Network Subsystem (NSS), and the Intelligent Network Subsystem (IN). The BSS in fact is the Radio Access Network (RAN) while the NSS and IN together form the core network (3rd Generation Partnership Project, 2005). Each element in the network performs certain functions and is logically connected over an *interface* with the other network elements. The interfaces are reference points that implement certain types of protocols for either control or user traffic realization.

The BSS consist of Base Station Transceivers (BTS) and Base Station Controllers (BSC) that communicate over the *Abis* interface with each other. In the radio segment, BTSs represent the network cells and communicate over the *Um* interface with the mobile stations. The BSCs on the other side communicate with the NSS over the *A* interface. The mobile station represents a mobile user that in the GSM is referenced as a *subscriber* to indicate the need for a subscription (in the form of a Subscriber Identity Module - SIM card) for using the mobile service. Throughout this book, the terms "subscriber" and "user" will be used interchangeably, with both referring to the same entity as seen from the network, that is, the mobile user.

The NSS consists of the following elements:

Figure 1. GSM PLMN reference network architecture

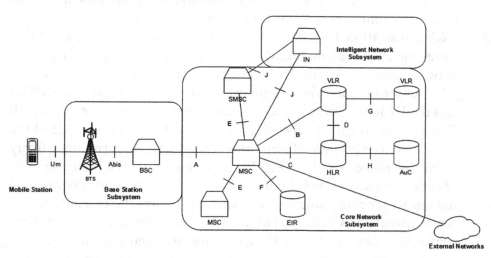

1. **Mobile Switching Centers (MSC):** In a classic circuit switched network, the MSC is implemented as a typical telephone exchange with a switching matrix for call realization. Modern MSCs support virtual circuit switching and are implemented in two parts: a MSC-Server (MSCS) handling the call control and mobility management; and a Media Gateway (MGW) handling the call realization. The call control responsibilities of the MSC include: registration of mobile subscribers, call establishment and call routing between two or more subscribers, and forwarding of Short Message Service (SMS) traffic. MSC's mobility management responsibilities are: authentication of subscribers, location update, and handover. MSCs are also responsible for interconnection with other mobile networks to enable *roaming* (use of mobile service in a visiting network or VPLMN) or calling fixed landline numbers. As the MSC only has a limited switching capacity and processing power, a GSM PLMN is usually composed of dozens of independent MSCs. Each MSC thus covers only a certain area of the network (segment of the BSS). MSCs communicate with other MSCs and SMS Centers (SMSC) over the *E* interface, VLRs over the *B* interface, HLR over the *C* interface, and EIR over the *F* interface.

2. **Home Location Register (HLR):** This is the main user database in GSM and has entries for every subscriber that has her or his "home" in the respective PLMN network (HPLMN). It stores the service subscriptions and permissions for every user (discussed in following subsection) as

well as its current (or last registered) location of the mobile station. The HLR communicates with the VLR over the *D* interface.

3. **Visitor Location Registers (VLR):** This is the visitor database that stores the data of all mobile stations which are currently staying in the network segment serviced by one MSCs. These data are copies of the HLR subscriber data to reduce any excessive signaling between the MSCs and the HLR for the purpose of subscriber verification for every call. The database is called "visitor" to reflect the temporal presence of the mobile stations in one MSC service area – subscribers are roaming freely within the home or visiting PLMN, therefore, VLRs holds the user data of only a portion of mobile subscribers in the associated geographical region. VLRs communicate with other VLRs over the *G* interface.

4. **Authentication Center (AuC):** AuC hold the same secret keys subscribers have on their SIM cards that are used for authentication and traffic encryption. The air interface is a shared wireless medium so subscribers' traffic can be easily eavesdropped and modified. Therefore, GSM designers made an effort to provide a built-in security protection on a subscriber level. AuC communicates with the HLR over the *H* interface. The associated authentication and encryption procedures are discussed further in this chapter.

5. **Equipment Identity Register (EIR):** As noted in the previous chapter, mobile networks distinguish between the SIM card and the mobile terminal, i.e. the user equipment. The EIR contains information about all the devices that are permitted (white-listed), forbidden (black-listed) or monitored by the network (gray-listed). This information is used for call evaluation together with the service subscriptions and permissions.

6. **Short Message Switching Center (SMSC):** Implemented four years after the first GSM deployment, the SMSC provides the functionality for the users to send short text messages. The SMSC is responsible for exchanging these messages in conjunction with the MSCs.

The Intelligent Network Subsystem (IN) supports prepaid and value added services for the GSM subscribers. By default, all subscribers in a GSM network are postpaid and billed after they use the mobile service (using aggregated call record details from the MSCs). The *prepaid mobile service* for real-time charging and billing is enabled with the introduction of the Customized Applications for Mobile Network Enhanced Logic (CAMEL) protocol (3rd Generation Partnership Project, 2017c). The IN subsystem consists of gsmSCF, gsmSSF, and gsmSRF implementing the control plane, user plane, and management functionalities, respectively. CAMEL was developed in four different phases and enables PLMN operators to offer Operator Specific Services (OSS) like prepaid calls, roaming SMS messages, or Unstructured Supplementary Service Data (USSD) roaming call-back in both the Home PLMN (HPLMN) and Visiting PLMN (VPLMN). CAMEL also supports convergent GPRS/EDGE services like prepaid packet data charging and Voice-over-IP (VoIP) calls. The IN communicates with the serving MSC over the *J* interface and with the HLR over the *C* interface in the reference GSM architecture.

Addressing and Network Identifiers

Mobile devices in GSM are represented with two logical entities: mobile station and mobile equipment. Every mobile station is associated with a Subscriber Identity Module (SIM) card and can be used with different mobile equipment, and vice versa, a mobile equipment can be used with different SIM cards at a given point of time. This concept is introduced to enable both user and equipment mobility (Jorg Eberspacher, Hans-Jorg Vogel, 2001). Both the SIM and the mobile equipment have their own internationally unique identifiers. Because the SIM is associated with a single subscriber at a time, GSM distinguishes between the SIM card identifier and a user telephone number. This flexibility enables operators to reuse SIM cards of inactive users or change telephone numbers of users without changing the SIM. It also enables users to port to other operators and keep their telephone number while receiving a new SIM card. GSM specifies each of these identifiers in the TS 23.003 V.4.3.0 technical specifications together with several other network identifiers necessary for user mobility management and addressing between network elements (3rd Generation Partnership Project, 2001b).

International Mobile Equipment Identity (IMEI)

The IMEI uniquely identifies every mobile equipment on a global level. It is allocated by the equipment manufacturer and stored in the EIR database on the network side. GSM uses the IMEI to distinguish between permitted, forbidden/suspended, and mobile equipment under monitoring by the network. For this purpose, the EIR stores three lists, respectively. The white list is a register of all devices successfully communicating with the network; The black list is a register of devices that are forbidden to access the network and cannot be used with any SIM card; The gray list is a register for devices that are permitted access, but are closely monitored by the operator to ensure they do not affect the normal network operation. The IMEI is usually registered in the network when the devices with a valid SIM card are powered up (in a procedure called *network attach*). The network can also explicitly request the mobile device to report its currently associated IMEI. It is 15 digits long and is composed as shown in Figure 2:

1. **Type Approval Code (TAC) [6 Digits]:** Issued by the GSM Association (GSMA) (GSMA, 2017)
2. **Final Assembly Code (FAC) [2 Digits]:** Assigned by the manufacturer
3. **Serial Number (SN) [6 Digits]:** Assigned by the manufacturer in a serial order
4. **Spare Digit [1 Digit]:** Check digit, assigned by the manufacturer (calculated using the Lunn formula described in the TS 23.003 V.4.3.0 technical specification, Appendix B)

There is a variation of the IMEI called IMESV (16 digits long) where the spare digit is replaced with two digits indicating the Software Version Number (SVN).

International Mobile Subscriber Identity (IMSI)

The IMSI uniquely identifies every mobile station on a global level and is stored on the SIM card. For a subscriber to successfully register with the network, she or he has to possess a valid IMSI and valid IMEI. The IMSI is 15 digits long and is composed as shown in Figure 3:

1. **Mobile Country Code (MCC) [3 Digits]:** Uniquely identifies the country of domicile of the mobile subscriber

Figure 2. IMEI structure

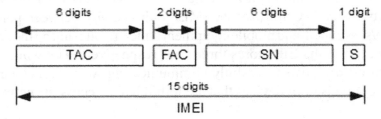

2. **Mobile Network Code (MNC) [2 Digits]:** Uniquely identifies the HPLMN within the country
3. **Mobile Subscriber Identification Number (MSIN) [Maximum 10 Digits]:** Uniquely identifies the subscriber within the HPLMN

For example, MCC=262 identifies Germany, MNC=01 is for T-Mobile, and so on.

Mobile Subscriber ISDN Number (MSISDN)

The telephone number of the user is referred to as the MSISDN and it is allocated by the ITU-T Recommendation E.164 numbering plan (ITU, 2017). E.164 defines the number in an Integrated Services Digital Network (ISDN) format for all telecommunication networks, therefore it is also used for addressing in mobile networks. The network maps the MSISDN with the IMSI in the HLR and uses this mapping anytime a call is realized to/from the subscriber. Another reason for this mapping is to minimize the use of the IMSI in the network operations so to protect from unauthorized IMSI replication and use of mobile services. The structure of the MSISDN is shown in Figure 4 and is composed as:

1. **Country Code (CC) [up to 3 Digits]:** Uniquely identifies the country according to E.164
2. **National Destination Code (NDC) [2-3 Digits]:** HPLMN E.164 code
3. Mobile Subscriber Number (MSN) [Maximum 10 Digits]

For example, the CC for Germany is 49 and for US is 1. The NDC are assigned locally according to the geographical distribution designated by the local regulation authority.

Figure 3. IMSI structure

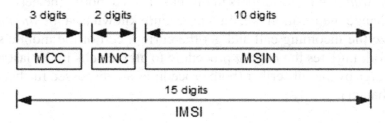

Figure 4. MSISDN structure

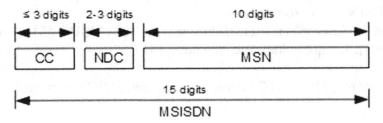

Mobile Subscriber Roaming Number (MSRN)

The MSRN is used to route calls directed to the mobile station in the network. It has the same structure as the MSISDN but does not always equal to the dialed MSISDN of the called mobile station (VPLMNs may have other configuration for MSRNs assigned to roaming users, for example). MSRNs are allocated by the VLR in two ways: (1) when the mobile station enters the area served by the corresponding MSC/VLR; and (2) each time the HLR requests it for setting up a connection for incoming calls to the mobile station. In the first case, the MSRN is passed from the VLR to the HLR (the mobile station is idle state). In the second case, instead of the MSRN the HLR stores the address of the VLR and asks the VLR to assign an MSRN at the time of the call (the mobile station transitions from idle to active state).

Location Area Identity (LAI)

To realize incoming calls to users, the network needs to know the subscriber location. GSM implements the cellular coverage concept where the subscribers are associated with a given cell at one point in time, so the network can pinpoint a subscriber on a cell level. When subscribers move from cell to cell, they need to notify the network about their new cell, but this introduces a huge signaling load in the radio network if their mobile stations are in idle mode. To reduce this signaling load, the network groups several cells into a *Location Area* (LA). Subscribers in this case need to notify the network only if they change the location area in a procedure known as a *location update*. To realize the incoming call and get the current cell of the mobile station, the network initiates the *paging* procedure to all the cells in the last register location area by the subscriber (both procedures are discussed further bellow in this chapter).

Each LA has an internationally unique identifier called Location Area Identifier (LAI), shown in Figure 5 and is composed as:

1. **Mobile Country Code (MCC) [3 Digits]:** Identifies the country in which the PLMN is located
2. **Mobile Network Code (MNC) [2 Digits]:** The network code of the PLMN
3. **Location Area Code (LAC) [Maximum 5 Digits or 2 Octets (16 Bits)]:** Identifies a location area within a GSM PLMN. It can be coded using a full hexadecimal representation except for the following reserved hexadecimal values: 0000 and FFFE (to indicate a non-existent LAI)

Temporary Mobile Subscriber Identity (TMSI)

The VLR in which the subscriber currently resides can assign a TMSI instead of the IMSI to realize the identification and addressing with the mobile station. Because the TMSI has only a local and temporal significance, it is infeasible to determine the real IMSI of the subscriber by an intruder in the wireless channel. On the subscriber side, the TMSI is stored on the SIM card while on the network side is stored on the VLR and not passed to the HLR. A TMSI may therefore be assigned in an operator-specific way and consists of up to 4 octets (8 bits) except the hexadecimal value of FFFF FFFF (this is because the TMSI must be stored in the SIM, and the SIM uses 4 octets with all bits equal to 1 for indicating that no valid TMSI is available). Together with the LAI, a TMSI allows for a mobile station to be uniquely identified at any point of time by replacing the IMSI with the tuple (TMSI, LAI) (Jorg Eberspacher, Hans-Jorg Vogel, 2001).

Figure 5. LAI structure

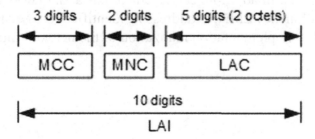

Local Mobile Subscriber Identity (LMSI)

The VLR can also assign a LMSI as a search key that enables for fast phone interrogation in establishing incoming calls and sent it to HLR. The LMSI is only used when the MSRN is newly assigned with each call. The structure of the LMSI is similar to the TMSI and consists of up to 4 octets assigned in an operator-specific way.

Cell Identity (CI) and Cell Global Identification (CGI)

The BTSs with their corresponding cells are identified within a location area by adding a Cell Identity (CI). CI is 2 octets long, assigned in an operator specific way, and must be unique within a location area. Together with the LAC (LAC + CI) it forms the Cell Global Identification (CGI). CGI thus uniquely identifies a given cell on an international level.

BTS Identity Code (BSIC)

GSM allows for faster cell discrimination on a physical level between different BTSs. This is important so the mobile stations can quickly distinguish between neighboring cells (so to select the best serving one). For this purpose, GSM assigns the BSIC as the physical cell identifier. BSIC consists of two parts:

1. **Network Color Code (NCC) [3 Bits]:** Color code of the PLMN
2. **Base Transceiver Station Color Code (BCC) [3 Bits]:** Different for neighboring cells

Identification of Network Elements

NSS and IN elements are addressed with ISDN E.164 numbers different than the one used for the mobile stations (i.e. starting from lower numbers and in a sequential order). In addition, each element has a unique Signaling Point Code (SPC) within the PLMN, an addressing identification used for Signaling System 7 (SS#7) implementation realization of the network interfaces.

User Data in GSM

There are two types of data associated with every user in a GSM network: address data and service-specific data. Address data serve to identify, authenticate, and localize users. Service-specific data are used to parametrize and personalize the mobile services offered to the users (interested readers can find good overview of the GSM supplementary services in (Jorg Eberspacher, Hans-Jorg Vogel, 2001)). Figure 6 depicts the association of the address data and their storage locations.

In addition to the IMSI, TMSI, MSISDN, and MSRN (stored also in the VLR with the LAI), the SIM card contains the secret key *Ki* that is used for authentication and generation of the ciphering key *Kc*. The same secret key is stored in the AuC together with the parameters used in the authentication procedure, RAND and SRES. The SIM also stores the number of the SMSC so it can include it any time it is sending a SMS. The SIM card implementation is specified in 31 series of the 3GPP technical specification (3rd Generation Partnership Project, 2017a). The HLR maps the IMSI and MSISDN of the users and stores their temporal address data (MSRN, VLR address, or LMSI). It also stores the service-specific data including service restrictions (i.e. roaming restrictions or use SMS only) and service subscriptions (i.e. data fax, call barring, call forwarding, or calling information restriction). All these data are used by the MSC/SMSC for call control and mobility management and is logged in the Call Data Records (CDRs), generated every time a mobile service is realized over the network.

Figure 6. User data in GSM

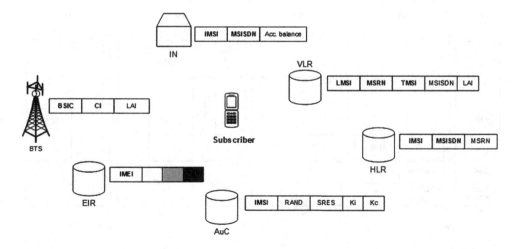

Control Plane

Voice Signaling

Figure 7 shows the control plane protocols used in GSM for the transport of voice traffic. The voice traffic in GSM is circuit-switched, so the role of the signaling is to establish, maintain, and tear down "circuits" or connections between the calling and called party. In the same time, the signaling handles the user mobility and realizes the SMS and supplementary service traffic from and to the user.

The *Um* interface on the physical layer is implemented using the combination of TDMA/FDMA. GSM uses the Link Adaptation Protocol developed for the *Um* interface (LAPDm) on the data link layer between the BTS and the mobile station. On the network layer, the BTS communicates with the MS using the Radio Resource (RR) protocol. The BTS uses the RR for the administration of the operating bands and definition of physical layer channel parameters. The mobile station implements two other protocols on the network for Mobility Management (MM) and Connection Management (CM). The *Abis* interface is implemented on the physical layer using the Synchronous Data Hierarchy (SDH) and on the data link layer using the LAPD protocol. On the network layer, the communication is realized using the RR and the Base Transceiving Station Management (BTSM) protocol. The BTSM protocol is used for coordination and administration of the BTSs for functions like

Figure 7. GSM control plane

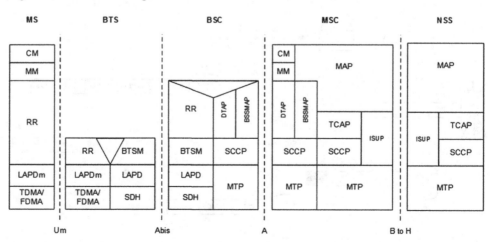

paging or establishing an enciphered channel between the network and the mobile station.

The BSC also maps the BSS Mobile Application Part (BSSMAP) and Direct Transfer Application Part (DTAP) protocols over the RR. The BSSMAP implements the MM functionality while the DTAP implements the CM functionality between the mobile station and the MSC, respectively. Essentially, they are used to set up, maintain, and terminate network connections with the mobile station. These protocols are exchanged over the *A* interface with the Signaling Connection Control Part (SCCP) on the network layer and the Message Transfer Part (MTP) protocol on the data link and physical layer. The MM in the NSS is realized using the Mobile Application Part (MAP) protocol that is transferred over the Transaction Capabilities Protocol (TCAP), SSCP and MTP on the remaining NSS interfaces. On the *E* interface, the MM is realized using the ISDN User Part (ISUP) that is directly transferred over the MTP protocol. On the *J* interface, the MSC and the IN communicate over the CAMEL Application Part (CAP) protocol.

GSM is not a traditional IP network so Figure 8 shows a comparison between the SS7-based GSM stack and the TCP/IP stack respective to the seven levels of the Open System for Interconnection (OSI).

Modern networks implement a combination of SS7 and IP for transport of GSM signaling in a configuration known as SIGTRAN. In the SS7 over IP configuration, MTP-1 and MTP-2 are replaced with Ethernet, while the MTP-3 with IP. Instead of Transmission Control Protocol (TCP) or User Datagram Protocol (UDP), SIGTRAN on the transport layer uses a newly specified protocol referred to as the Stream Control Transmission Protocol (SCTP). On the session layer, SCTP is followed by the MTP-3 User Adaptation Layer (M3UA) protocol that provides mapping between the upper protocol layers like SCCP and the SCTP/IP transport implementation. SIGTRAN adapts the ISUP protocol so the voice traffic can be realized as VoIP by modifying the ISUP signaling to a new protocol called Bearer Independent Call Control (BICC) that enables transport of the GSM voice in a packet fashion. GSM support translation between the VoIP switched traffic and circuit-switched traffic by implementing the MSC with MSCS and MGW components. This comparison between the standard GSM SS7 and SIGTRAN with the corresponding interfaces is shown in Figure 9.

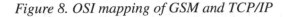

Figure 8. OSI mapping of GSM and TCP/IP

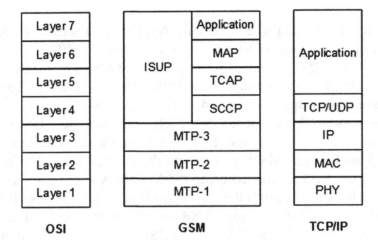

SMS Signaling

The control plane in GSM is also used for the transportation of SMS traffic. SMS messages are transmitted in a store-and-forward mode though the SMSC and are up to 160 characters long as specified in TS 23.040 technical specification. Between the mobile station and the SMSC, SMSs are transmitted using the Short Message Transport Protocol (SM-TP) which is a CM protocol very similar to the DTAP. As such, the SMS is sent as a DTAP message that contains a text, a destination MSISDN and the address of the SMSC (this is needed so users can send messages while in roaming). According to the destination MSISDN, the SMSC retrieves the registered MSC for the user from the HLR and forwards the SMS to the corresponding MSC using the MAP protocol. If the user is active, the MSC forwards the message, otherwise it sets a message waiting flag in the VLR and the SMS is stored in the SMSC. The SMS service is specified in the TS 23.040 technical specification (3rd Generation Partnership Project, 2017d)

Supplementary Services Signaling

In addition to the telephony and SMS traffic, GSM provides a set of supplementary services to the user, including: call forwarding (unconditional, busy, no reply, not reachable), call barring (outgoing and incoming calls), call waiting/hold, Calling Line Identification Presentation/Restriction (CLIP/

Figure 9. GSM and SIGTRAN

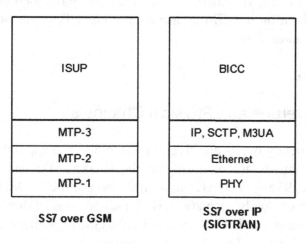

CLIR), and multiparty calling. These services can be activated either by the network or by the user in which case the Unstructured Supplementary Service Data (USSD) protocol is used. Users activate/deactivate a supplementary service by a number string starting with the "*" character. These codes are identical for all networks and are listed in the TS 22.030 technical specification. This string is transferred over a circuit-switched data connection to the MSC and forwarded as a MAP message to the HLR. The HLR analyzes the string and activates/deactivates the requested service. The USSD service is specified in the TS 23.090 technical specification (3rd Generation Partnership Project, 2017e).

User Plane

The basic services in GSM are realized over *connections*, resembling the telephony service delivery in fixed mobile networks. Connections can be used to transfer speech traffic or circuit-switched data and are realized as shown in Figure 10. The connections are established on the networking level and have two parts: one realized over the Um interface with GSM specific signaling; and one over the A interface realized with ISDN specific signaling. On the Um interface, the GSM-coded speech with a13 Kb/s rate is codded for error protection and encryption and transferred over the TDMA/FDMA physical layer. At the BTS side, the GSM signal is decrypted, checked for errors and transcoded into a ISDN speech signal of 64 Kb/s that is further transferred to the MSC. GSM also enables transfer of data with a 9.6 Kb/s for proprietary circuit-switched data services. More detailed description on the speech realization in GSM is provided in (Jorg Eberspacher, Hans-Jorg Vogel, 2001; Sauter, 2010)

Air Interface

Wireless Coverage and Physical Channels

The GSM frequency bands are given in Table 5 in the appendix of Chapter 3. Most deployments are operating in the P-GSM-900 band (890 – 915 MHz in uplink; 935 – 960 MHz downlink) where the 35 MHz wide band is split into 125 channels with 200 KHz bandwidth and a duplex separation of 45 MHz between the UL/DL channel pair. GSM specifies channel index for each channel pair (referred also as a carrier) in the TS 45.005 technical specification called the Absolute Radio Frequency Channel Numbers (ARFCN) (3rd Generation Partnership Project, 2017h). The ARFCN range from 0 to 1023 for the P-GSM band and are calculated as $ARFCN = 5(f_{UL} - 890)$. For example, for $f_{UL} = 913.2$ MHz, the ARFCN is 116.

The number of channels are not sufficient to cover an entire country or a larger geographical region because far more than 125 cells will be needed. Therefore, operators need to reuse the frequency channels for the distant cells to be able to cover the entire service area. This is possible by grouping multiple cells in clusters and assigning a set of different channels for each of the cell in the cluster as shown in Figure 11. The cluster pattern and the associated frequency set is then replicated to cover the entire service area and is applicable for all cell sizes noted in Chapter 3. Figure 11 shows examples

Figure 10. GSM data plane

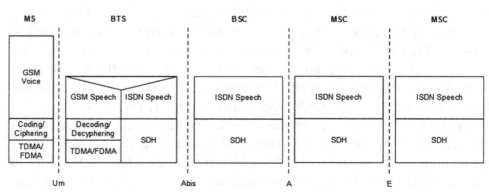

with frequency reuse factors 3 and 7 for clusters of 3 and 7 micro cells, respectively. It is important for the planners to select the reuse set of channels so the adjusted cells on the cluster borders experience minimum interference.

For each channel pair, GSM employs TDMA for simultaneous access (therefore the hybrid TDMA/FDMA access). Users are time multiplexed by dividing the carrier into frames with durations of 4.615 milliseconds. The frame is further divided in eight timeslots that are assigned to a given user (known as bursts) and carry 144 bits each. For modulation, GSM uses Gaussian Minimum Shift Keying (GMSK) that transmits one bit per symbol. For encoding, a ½ convolution code is used to add an error correction redundancy to the user data.

Logical Channels

The TDMA/FDMA channels on the physical level are used to transport both the signaling and user data. For this purpose, GSM arranges the channels in two logical groups: *traffic* channels and *signaling* channels. The first two timeslots in a cell are usually used for the signaling channels while the remaining six are used for the traffic channels. As indicated below, there are more than two signaling channels so GSM needs to use multiple frames to realize each of them. GSM defines a structure called a *multiframe* consisting of 51 frames

Figure 11. Frequency reuse in GSM

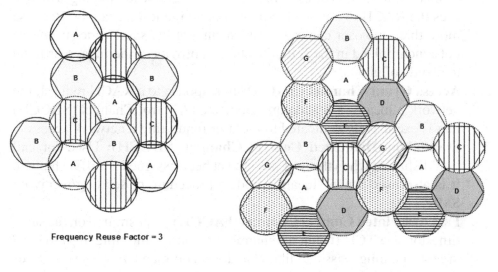

Frequency Reuse Factor = 3

Frequency Reuse Factor = 7

and specifies which logical channels are transmitted in which timeslots on a given frame. The multiframe used for traffic channels is similarly organized, but groups 26 timeframes instead. The multiframe structure is specified in the TS 45.002 technical specification (3rd Generation Partnership Project, 2017g).

The traffic channels (TCH) is a user data channel for transmission of circuit-switch voice or data of up to 14.4 Kb/s (the GSM speech is 13 Kb/s, the remaining bits in the timeslot are used for traffic encoding and encryption). GSM defines the following signaling channels (Sauter, 2010):

1. **Synchronization Channel (SCH):** Used by the mobile devices during network and cell searches; It broadcasts the BSIC code of the BTS and the relative frame numbers for frame synchronization
2. **Frequency Correction Channel (FCCH):** Used by the mobile devices to calibrate their transceiver units and detect the beginning of a multiframe
3. **Broadcast Common Control Channel (BCCH):** The main information channel of a cell and is monitored by all mobile devices (both idle and active). It broadcasts the LAI, CI, and the frequency configurations of the neighboring cells so the mobile devices need not to scan the entire frequency band in case the need to associate with another cell
4. **Paging Channel (PCH):** Used to inform idle users of incoming calls or SMSs. The network knows the user's LA so it pages all the cells in it including the TMSI assigned by the VLR
5. **Random Access Channel (RACH):** This channel is an uplink common channel shared by all devices in the cell. In response to a paging, a device uses the RACH to contact the network and request a channel. Because more than one user can request a channel at the same time (users are not synchronized in the cell), the channel provides random access logic to avoid collisions
6. **Access Grant Channel (AGCH):** In response to a RACH request, the network allocates a Standalone Dedicated Control Channel (SDCCH) that is exclusively dedicated to the user requesting a network access
7. **Standalone Dedicated Control Channel (SDCCH):** Used for call establishment when the user has not yet been assigned a traffic channel. It is also used for the location update procedure or sending/receiving SMSs
8. **Fast Associated Control Channel (FACCH):** Transmitted on the same timeslot as a TCH (using a dynamic preemptive multiplexing) to send urgent signaling messages like a handover command. As these messages do not have to be sent very often, no dedicated physical timeslots are

allocated to the FACCH; instead user data are removed from a TCH channel (there are bit indicators in each timeslot to indicate weather TCH or FACCH is used)

9. **Slow Associated Control Channel (SACCH):** Used in the uplink report signal quality measurements of the serving and neighboring cells to the network for mobility management purposes. In downlink is used for timing advance and power control commands issued by the network to the mobile devices

Examples of connection set up for an incoming call is shown in Figure 12. Similar procedure is followed for an ongoing call establishment where the mobile device instead initiates the random access by itself.

Radio Measurements

GSM requires mobile stations to perform regular measurements of the signal quality they receive from the network. Idle stations periodically measure the signal level of the BCCH channels, while active stations with assigned TCH or SDCCH measure the power of the respective channel and communicate it over an SACCH as a measurement info to the BTS. The measurement results in both cases are used as inputs for either the cell selection/reselection, handover, or power control procedures. A list of neighboring cells called BCCH Allocation (BA) is broadcasted on the BCCH to enable measurements for the candidate cells for handover.

GSM uses two parameters to describe the quality of a channel: Received Signal Level (RXLEV) and Received Signal Quality Level (RXQUAL). RXLEV is measured in dBm and can take values between 48 dBm (very strong) and -110 dBm (very weak). RXQUAL is measured as bit error ratio as a percentage before error correction and is reported using values from RXQUAL_0 (highest quality, <0.2% errored bits) to RXQUAL_7 (lowest quality, >12.8% errored bits).

Security

Security Functions

To prevent from wireless eavesdropping, user impersonation, or traffic modification, GSM introduces several security related functions related to:

Figure 12. Connection setup for an incoming call in the air interface

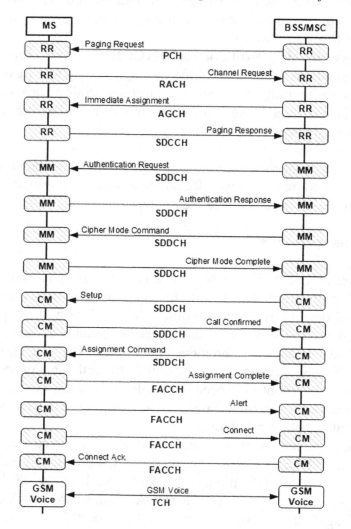

(1) subscriber identity confidentiality, (2) subscriber identity authentication; and (3) data confidentiality for physical connections. These functions are specified in the TS 03.20 technical specifications (3rd Generation Partnership Project, 2001a). The cryptographic algorithms used for authentication (A3), key generation (A8), and physical connection encryption (A5) are specified in the TS 55 technical series (3rd Generation Partnership Project, 2017b).

The intent of the subscriber identity protection is to prevent disclosing which subscriber is using which network resources to perpetrators able to listen to the signaling traffic in the air interface. Because the signaling is mostly sent in plain text, there is a threat that perpetrators might localize, track, or impersonate a mobile station simply by obtaining the IMSI number associated with it. As indicated earlier, GSM instead uses the TMSI when communicating with mobile stations which is temporarily assigned by the serving VLR and has only a local significance. When the user moves to another location area, it reports the old LAI and old TMSI to the new MSC/ VLR. The MSC/VLR sets up an encrypted connection with the mobile station, assigns the new TMSI, and sends it in encrypted form. However, this procedure works assuming the user has already been assigned a TMSI and the network knows its IMSI. During an initial network registration, the network has no information on users' IMSI nor has it assigned any TMSI. Therefore, the network requests the mobile station to send the IMSI in a plain text. Once the IMSI is received on the network side, the MSC/VLR verifies it with the HLR, sets up an encrypted channel and sends a new TMSI in an encrypted form (Jorg Eberspacher, Hans-Jorg Vogel, 2001).

To verify the subscriber identity, GSM uses the A3 algorithm with the private key *Ki* stored on the SIM card on the user side and the AuC on the network side. The AuC prepares a random, non-predictable number RAND for each verification invocation and inputs it together with the *Ki* and the subscriber IMSI into the A3 algorithm to calculate a value called Signature Response (SRES). The RAND is also communicated with the user, which calculates a SRES value independently using its Ki and sends it back to the AuC. The AuC compares the computed and received values of SRES and authenticates the user if they match, otherwise it restarts the procedure with a new RAND number. This challenge-response authentication is implemented to prevent from replaying potentially recorded messages by a perpetrator on the air interface. The verification procedure is shown in Figure 13.

GSM realizes the data confidentiality on the physical lever by ciphering (encrypting) the transmitting bitstream after the data is encoded and before is modulated (deciphering follows after the demodulation). A ciphering key *Kc* is generated both at the mobile station and the network using the generator algorithm A8, the *Ki*, and the RAND number of the authentication process as shown in Figure 14. The computed *Kc* key is then used in the encryption algorithm A5/1; A5/2; A5/3; or A5/4 for symmetric encryption of the user data. On the network side, the keys are computed and stored together with the RAND and SRES values in the HLR and forwarded to the serving VLR/ BSC/BTS. Signaling and user data are then encrypted together (TCH/SACCH/ FACCH).

Figure 13. GSM subscriber identity verification procedure

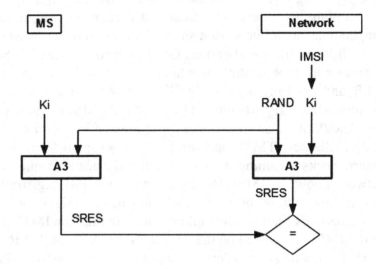

Figure 14. GSM key generation and ciphering procedure

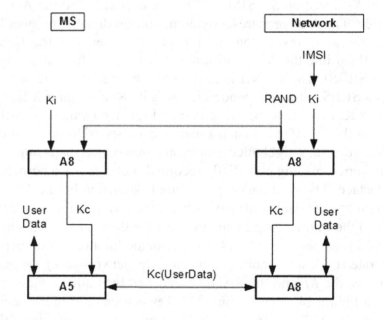

Known Attacks

Each of the security functions in GSM has an inherent vulnerability that has been exploited so far. In the subscriber identity confidentiality procedures, the mobile station at least once is sending the IMSI in clear, so a rouge base station can broadcast a BCCH with a stronger signal of the legitimate networks around, force the mobile station to attach to it, and reveal the IMSI in the registration procedure. In the subscriber identity authentication procedure, the network verifies the authenticity of the mobile station, but that is not the case in the reverse direction. Because the mobile station cannot verify the mobile network, there is a possibility for a man-in-the middle attack where a rogue base station intercepts and forwards the signaling messages between the mobile station and the network, posing as the "legitimate" network to the mobile station on one side, and like the "legitimate" user to the network on the other (Meyer and Wetzel, 2004). Furthermore, GSM enables for a fail-safe mode where the network and the mobile station can agree not to use encryption (indicated as an open lock symbol on the screen of the phone), making it trivial for the perpetrators to listen to the user traffic.

For data confidentiality, the initial A5 algorithms were developed secretly, violating the well-known security principle "security through obscurity does not work". The algorithms were also developed with shorter keys to enable export of GSM systems to countries with strict restrictions on the use of encryption as technology (A5/2 algorithm). It has been shown that is possible to retrieve the ciphering key Kc within seconds with only little ciphering data collected (Barkan, Biham and Keller, 2008; Sauter, 2010). A5/1 and A5/3 can also be exploited by recording the respective encrypted data, instructing the device to use the same key Kc, and switch to the A5/2 encryption. A5/1 can be brute-forced with a rainbow table and a 4 TB recorded encrypted data, too. It is worth mentioning that no practical methods exist except a physical access to the SIM card to get the stored key Ki. Even if a perpetrator is able to retrieve the Kc, it will be still infeasible to authenticate during the challenge/response authentication procedure (assuming the perpetrator is not performing a man-in-the-middle attack and is trying to impersonate the SIM card only by traffic analysis).

Mobility and Connection Management

Location Registration

First time users in GSM need to register or IMSI *attach* with the network. This is usually the HPLMN with which the user has subscribed to, but it can be any VPLMN if there exists a roaming agreement between the two operators. Registration is also required when changing networks because the new network has not issued any TMSI yet to the user. In these cases, users invoke the *Location Registration* procedure shown in Figure 15. After the user sends a *location update request* with the their IMSI and LAI (obtained by monitoring the BCCH of the camping cell), the network responses with an authentication request prior to inserting the new user in the serving VLR. Following the successful verification of user's identity, the VLR updates the user location in the HLR with its IMSI and MSRN, assigns a new TMSI, and sends it to user in an encrypted form. The registration is completed once the user acknowledges the reallocation of the TMSI. The TMSI is stored in a nonvolatile memory in the SIM card so the user can reuse it in case the mobile station powers down. To deregister or IMSI *detach*, the user sends explicit deregistration requests including the TMSI to which the VLR and HLR respond by clearing all the registered information (TMSI, MSRN, LAI) about the user.

Cell Selection and Location Update

Following a successful registration, users can generally be in two modes: (1) *Idle mode* – no active connection, but available for initiating/receiving user traffic; and (2) *Connected mode* – active connection with radio and network resources assigned and the ability to exchange user traffic (3rd Generation Partnership Project, 2017f). Users in idle mode search for and select a local cell with the best signal quality to "camp on" (their serving cell). Periodically, users perform radio measurements of the neighboring cells to see if any of them offer better signal than the serving cell. If that is the case, they reselect the stronger cell as their serving cell and camp on it instead. The *cell selection procedure* in GSM is performed according to the C1 algorithm, while the *cell reselection procedures* according to the C2 algorithm, both specified in the TS 45.008 technical specifications (3rd Generation Partnership Project, 2017h). Essentially, the C1 and C2 algorithm use the RXLEV parameters to select the strongest available cell or to move to a stronger cell if the camping cell signal is degraded for a period of 1-5 seconds.

Users' availability in the idle mode also needs to be maintained on the network side in terms of their locations so the network can realize the originating and terminating user traffic. The network can keep information on their current camping cell, but that can generate unnecessary signaling traffic every time a user reselects a cell. Instead, the network groups multiple cells in location areas (LAs) and users need to inform the network only if they reselect a cell belonging to a different LA than the LA of the camping cell. For this purpose, users invoke the *location update procedure* that is very similar to the registration procedure, but instead using the IMSI, the procedure is initiated with users' old TMSI and the LAI of the new location area.

Figure 15. Location registration (IMSI Attach) procedure

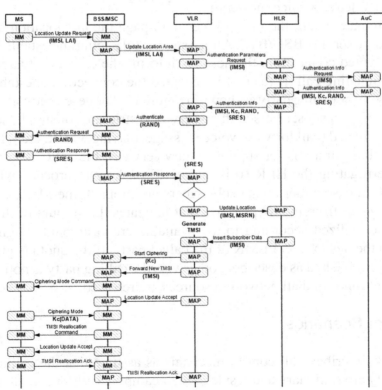

Call Control

Any time a user needs to initiate or receive traffic, she or he has to transition from idle to connected mode. The transition is initiated as a response to a PCH or a RACH request as described in the previous subsection. The connected mode provides dedicated radio resources (TCH, SACCH, FACCH) used for originating or terminating calls, SMSs and/or circuit-switched data. Figure 16 shows the setup for an originating call in GSM. After the setup is indicated and the encrypted tunnel is established between the user and the network, the user reports the called party's MSISDN as the information for the originating call. The MSC assigns a dedicated channel for user's mobile station, proceeds to receive routing information (MSRN) of the called party from the HLR, and contacts the respective serving MSC (note, this is a terminating call for the called party). Once the serving MSC answers the request, the calling party is alerted and connected if the called party answers the call (otherwise the network informs that the called party is unreachable or busy, and is optionally forwarded to leave a voice message).

To terminate a call, the network needs to page the last location area to determine the serving BSC/BTS. After a successful paging and establishment of an encrypted connection, the network informs the called party about an active terminating call. If the call is accepted the connection is established between with the calling party as shown in Figure 17. The described call control assumes postpaid subscribers with no service restrictions or supplementary services activated (call forward, voice message, barring, CLIR, etc.). In case there are configurations for supplementary services, the MSC is informed when interrogating the HLR so is instructed on how to proceed with the call setup. In case either of the subscribers are prepaid, the MSC requests a serving *quota* from the IN platform that indicates the amount of time the call can be realized according to the available credit amount, originating VLR, and the destination PLMN of the called party. If the quota is granted, the call is established as described, otherwise the calling party is notified of insufficient funds and all network resources are released.

Handover Scenarios

Previously described call control mechanisms assume that the calling and called party are stationary and reside in their camping cells during the entire call. The network also needs to maintain any active call if the users move

Figure 16. GSM signaling for a mobile originating call

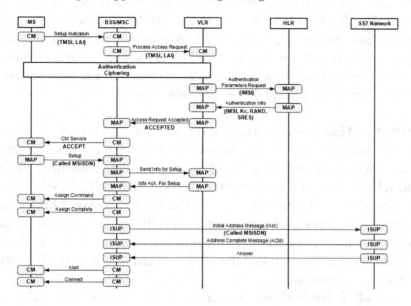

Figure 17. GSM signaling for a mobile terminating call

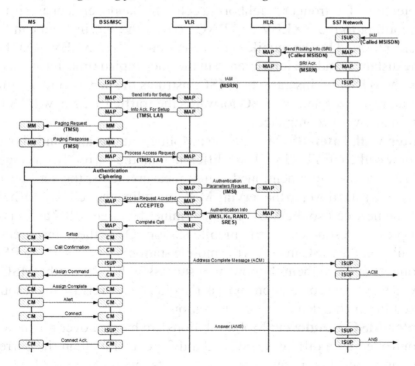

to other cells, the radio conditions deteriorate, or there are changes in the network traffic load without breaking the established connection. GSM realizes this functionality with so-called *handover procedures* (known also as *handoff procedures*). The network in GSM has the control of all handovers, i.e. all handovers are *network-initiated* (as opposed to the *mobile-initiated* handovers). There are several different types of handovers:

1. **Intra-Cell Handover:** Mobile stations are handed over to another channel in the same cell due to deterioration of the channel signal or channel selective interference. It is based on the radio measurements RXLEV and RXQUAL that are reported to the BSS and MSC. MSC makes the decision for handover and instructs the BSS to assign a new physical channel. The BSS then coordinates with the mobile station to release the old channel and connect to the new one. During this procedure, the service is uninterrupted and the BTS forwards the user traffic once the handover is completed.

2. **Inter-Cell, Intra-BSC Handover:** Mobile stations are handed over to a new cell controlled by the same BSC of the serving cell. This handover results as a deterioration of the signal quality in the serving cell and detection of a stronger neighboring cell. The handover decision is made according to the RXLEV and RXQUAL of the serving and candidate cells reported by the mobile station, as well as the RXLEV, RXQUAL, the distance, and the interference in the unoccupied timeslots measured by the BTSs. In this case, the MSC instructs the new cell to assign the radio resources and the BSC forwards the traffic to the new BTS once the handover is completed.

3. **Inter-Cell, Inter-BSC Handover:** Mobile stations are handed over to a new cell controlled by a BSC different than the currently serving one. Based on the aforementioned signal measurements, the serving BSC requests a handover to the serving MSC including the cell ID and the LAI of the new cell so the MSC can determine the target BSC and instruct to prepare resources for the mobile station. Once these resources are available, the MSC instructs the mobile station over the serving BSC to connect and use them. Following a successful handover, the MSC can switch over the connection and ask the old BSC to release the resources used for the handed over mobile station.

4. **Inter-MSC Handover:** Mobile stations are handed over to a new cell controlled by a different BSC and a different MSC than the currently serving ones. In this case, the MSC detects that the reported LAI is not

part of its coverage area and proceeds to find the MSC that is responsible for it. The serving MSC requests establishment of resources from the target MSC and once it gets confirmation, it instructs the mobile station to connect to the new cell. Following a successful handover, the serving MSC switches the connection to the new MSC and asks to release all resources for the handed over mobile station.

The detailed description of all handover procedures with the associated parameters is specified in the TS 03.09 and TS 23.009 technical specifications (3rd Generation Partnership Project, 1999, 2014).

2.5G AND 2.75G: GENERAL PACKET RADIO SERVICE (GPRS) AND ENHANCED DATA RATES FOR GLOBAL EVOLUTION (EDGE)

Reference Network Architecture

The telephony traffic required GSM to support dedicated end-to-end channels for every call, even if the calling and called party are not continuously transmitting data (in most of the conversations one of the speakers remains silent while the other talks). In the fixed line networks vocabulary, such a traffic realization is known as *circuit switching*, referring to the dedicated channels as the circuits. Unlike the telephony, the Internet traffic is packetized and requires *packet switching*. This means routing of the user traffic based on source and destination in the packet headers without the need for a pre-established connection between the users and a web server, for example. To support *packet switching*, the General Packet Radio Service (GPRS) was developed as the 2.5G evolutionary upgrade of the GSM networks.

In order to integrate the GPRS into the existing GSM architecture, the BSS subsystem is upgraded with the Packet Control Unit (PCU), while the Serving GPRS Supporting Node (SGSN) and the Gateway GPRS Supporting Node (GGSN) elements are introduced in the core network. Figure 18 illustrates the upgraded GSM/GPRS architecture from the TS 23.002 technical specification (3rd Generation Partnership Project, 2008).

The PCU adds the functionality for packet switching at the BSC between the users on one side (BTS transparently passes both the circuit- and packet-switched traffic), and the SGSN on the network side, over the *Gb* interface.

Because there are no changes in the TDMA/FDMA architecture of the Um interface, the PCU deals with the assignment of both control and traffic timeslots to subscribers in uplink and downlink, subscriber paging, and retransmission of lost or faulty received traffic. For coexistence, the BSC switching matrix redirects certain traffic timeslots from the GSM pool to the PCU to be used exclusively for the GPRS signaling and user traffic.

The SGSN is the packet-switching counterpart of the MSC and is responsible for realization of both the control and user data. The SGSN is also responsible for mobility management and ciphering. This is because the handovers in GPRS are mobile-initiated and as such the data confidentiality protection has to be moved from BTS-level to the core network (the GSM types of handovers are also available in GPRS). The SGSN communicates with the home/other GGSNs over the *Gn/Gp* interface (both the signaling and user traffic), with the HLR over the *Gr* interface (signaling traffic), and with the EIR over the *Gf* interface (signaling traffic). The GGSN on the other side connects the GRPS network with the external packet networks (Internet) over the *Gi* interface (user traffic) and is responsible for the IP management of the mobile user. For that purpose, it also communicates with the HLR over the *Gc* interface (signaling traffic). and with the IN platform over the *Gy* interface to enable online packet data charging.

Figure 18. GPRS reference network architecture

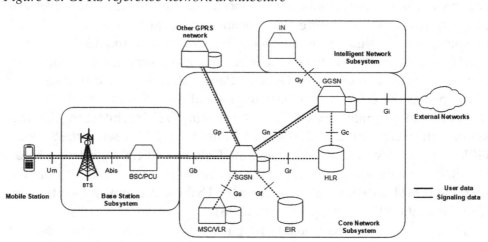

Addressing and Network Identifiers

In addition to the GSM network addresses and network identifiers, GPRS defines a set of IP-related addressing to support the delivery of Internet and packet services to the mobile users in the TS 23.003 and 29.060 technical specifications (3rd Generation Partnership Project, 2001b).

GSN Address/Number

To support routing of user traffic within the core and with the external networks, the SGSN and GGSN are assigned GSN addresses composed as:

1. **Address Type (2 Bits):** Identifying the type of address that is used in the Address field
2. **Address Length (6 Bits):** Identifying the length of the Address field
3. **Address (Variable Length):** Either IPv4 or IPv6 IP address

Address Type 0 and Address Length 4 are used when Address is an IPv4 address, while Address Type 1 and Address Length 16 are used when Address is an IPv6 address. The IPv4 address structure is defined in RFC 791 and the IPv6 address structure is defined in RFC 2373. For exchanging signaling messages with the other GSM nodes, the SGSN and GGSN have assigned SCP numbers.

Access Point Name (APN)

For routing purposes, the Access Point Name (APN) is a reference to the HPLMN's GGSN. The APN is a fully qualified domain name like "Internet" or "Corporate_Network" and the mobile users are using it to indicated the external network to which they want to get packet access. The SSGN has internal Domain Name System (DNS) functionality to resolve this name to the GSN address of the GGSN that provides connection to the desired network to be able to forward the user packets. This works both when the user is in the HPLMN and VPLMN so to enable GPRS roaming. To resolve potential conflicts between same APNs for home and visiting subscribers, i.e. an APN named "Internet", the APN has two segments: the network identifier or the fully qualified network domain name, and the operator identifier formatted as "mnc<MNC>.mcc<MCC>.gprs" where the MNC and MCC correspond to the home subscriber network.

Packet Data Protocol (PDP) Information Element

The user sessions in GPRS are realized over the Packet Data Protocol (PDP), essentially resulting with an assignment of an IP address to the user. The information transferred in the PDP information element include the mobile station PDP identifier, APN, reference GGSN, the Quality-of-Service (QoS) type for the packet traffic requested by the user, and the PDP address (the assigned IP address). Users in GPRS can have more than one PDP address to simultaneously connect to different packet networks. These addresses are distinguished with the Network Service Access Point Identifier (NSAPI) reference which essentially is the PDP identifier for the requesting user. For the routing of the packet traffic, the NSAPI is combined with the user's IMSI (using the TLLI identifier explained bellow) to form the Tunnel Identifier (TID) for the user packet session on the network side.

Packet TMSI (P-TMSI)

A Packet Temporary Mobile Subscriber Identity (P-TMSI) is assigned to every mobile station during the GPRS network registration (or *GPRS attach*). The P-TMSI serves the same purpose as the TMSI over the air interface and is four octets long. GPRS allows for inclusion of so-called Network Routing Identifier (NRI) in the P-TMSI to be able to distinguish the GSN address of the SGSN that has assigned it. Similarly, the P-TMSI is of local significance and if the mobile station moves to another SGSN service area, the new SGSN assigns a new P-TMSI. In addition to the P-TMSI, the SGSN can also assign a so-called P-TMSI signature (three octets long) to enable optimized authentication and mobile station identification for the subsequent network procedures.

Temporal Logical Link Identity (TLLI)

The GPRS mobile station on the air interface is identified with the Temporal Logical Link Identity (TLLI) which is also four octets long. The TLLI is generated by the mobile station and there is one-to-one mapping between the IMSI and the TLLI. During the initial registration when no P-TMSI is assigned to the mobile station, a random TLLI is generated to identify the logical GPRS link between the mobile station and the network. When the network has already assigned a P-TMSI to the mobile station and the mobile station is not updating its location, a *local* TLLI is derived from the assigned P-TMSI. During a location update procedure in which the mobile station moves into a service are of another SGSN, a *foreign* TLLI is derived from the P-TMSI assigned by the new SGSN.

Routing Area Identity (RAI)

GPRS mobility is supported with Routing Areas (RA) that serve the same purpose as the LAs in GSM. Each RA has an internationally unique identifier called Routing Area Identifier (RAI) that consists of the GSM LAI (MCC+MNC+LAC) plus the Routing Area Code (RAC) as shown in Figure 19. The RAI is also a network-defined parameter with a fixed length of 15 digits.

Control Plane

GRPS control plane handles the GPRS user mobility and session management, i.e. implements procedures like GPRS attach/detach, PDP context activation, routing, and handover. Figure 20 shows the GPRS control plane between the mobile station and the SGSN; Figure 21 shows the control plane between the SGSN and HLR (or EIR), SGSN and MSC/VLR; and Figure 22 shows the control plane between the SGSN and the GGSN.

While the physical layer remains the same as in GSM, the data layer on the *Um* interface implements Medium Access Control (MAC) and Radio Link Control (RLC) for packet transmission between the mobile station and the BTS/PCU. On the *Gb* interface, the BSS GRPS Protocol (BSSGP) handles the user flow control between the PCU and the SGSN, acting as a relay between the mobile station and the SGSN. This is needed to prevent from overflowing the SGSN with data from the BSS. The Logical Link Control (LLC) on top of the RLC/MAC handles the ciphering, retransmission, and

Figure 19. RAI structure

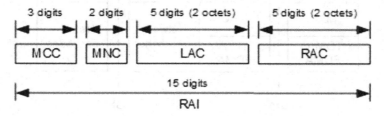

packet reordering. Since both GPRS signaling and data traffic are sent through one dedicated GSM traffic channel, the LLC handles the multiplexing of both traffic streams on the GSM RF multiframe. The GPRS Mobility Management Session Management (GMM/SM) protocol implement the mobility and session management functions.

On the *Gr* or *Gf* interfaces, GPRS implements the GSM protocol stack for exchanging MAP messages. The interaction between SGSN and the HLR is important for retrieving the authentication information, activating/deactivating GPRS-related user settings (i.e. roaming packet traffic restrictions), and the PDP information about every user. The SGSN communicates with the EIR for IMEI management purposes. On the *Gs* interface, the BSSAP+ extends the BSSAP protocol from GSM to support functions like combined GSM/ GPRS attach, GSM/GPRS IMSI detach, location update, or paging of mobile stations.

On the *Gn* or *Gp* interface, GPRS implements the GPRS Tunneling Protocol-Control (GTP-C) layer. The GTP-C protocol is used to establish, maintain, and terminate GTP tunnels between the SGSN and the GGSN to route the user traffic the SGSN received from the PCU towards the external networks such as Internet. GTP-C is also used for location and mobility management if the *Gc* interface is not present, so the SGSN can assist with the retrieval of the user information HLR or exchange PDP information. A GTP tunnel is established/modified/terminated during the PDP context activation/

Figure 20. GPRS control plane: Mobile station-SGSN

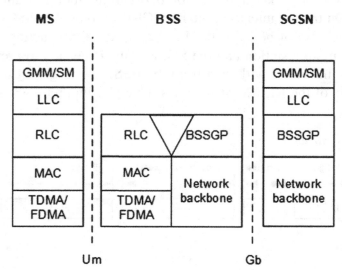

Figure 21. GPRS control plane: SGSN-HLR (or EIR); SGSN-MSC/VLR

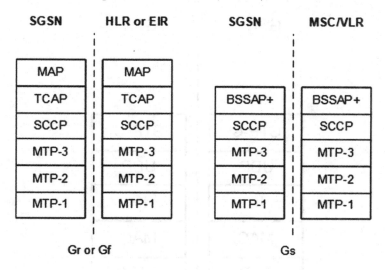

modification/removal procedures and is identified in each GPRS node by a TID an IP address (of the SGSN/GGSN node), and a UDP port number. The GTP-C transfer all the signaling messages that are part of these procedures.

User Plane

Protocols

GRPS User plane is shown in Figure 23. The same underlying protocol architecture on the lower layers with the control plane enables transport of the upper protocols such as the Subnetwork Dependent Convergence Protocol (SNDCP) over the *Um* and *Gb* interfaces. The SNDCP is used to transfer packets from the user network layer, i.e. IP packets between the mobile station and the SGSN. SNDCP functionalities include multiplexing of several PDP contexts into one virtual local connection on the underlying LLC layer, segmentation/reassembly of user IP packets, and compression and decompression of TCP/IP headers of user traffic. The LLC handles the in-order delivery of the user traffic and defining reliable links between the mobile station and the SGSN (identified with the TLLI). The user traffic that arrives at the SGSN on the SNDCP layer is further routed towards the GGSN over a GTP-User (GTP-U) tunnel. The GGSN extracts the GTP-U IP packets and routes them to the final destination indicated by the mobile station.

Figure 22. GPRS control plane: SGSN-GGSN

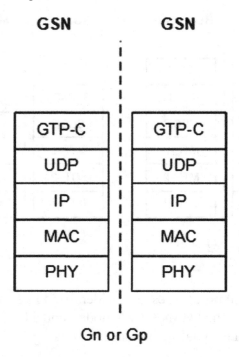

Figure 23. GPRS user plane

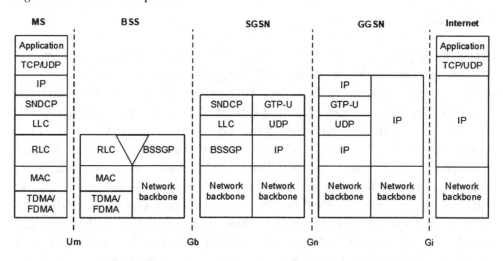

Routing

Figure 24 provides an example of downlink packet routing towards and from the mobile station, respectively. When an IP packet arrives at the GGSN with the destination address of the mobile station, the GGSN uses the PDP context information to determine the TID (TLLI+NASAPI) and the IP address of the serving SGSN so it can forward it for further delivery. The SGSN derives the associated TLLI (NASAPI/IMSI) to identify the serving PCU and the last reported RAI so the PCU can page the mobile station and delver the IP packet. Similarly, the mobile station in the uplink sends its IP traffic towards the SNDCP endpoint in the SGSN where through the GTP-U tunnel it reaches the GGSN and is routed to its final IP destination.

Air Interface

Logical Channels

GPRS uses the TDMA/FDMA organization on the physical layer as in the GSM, but enables a far more flexible resource allocation for packet transmission. The mobile station can transmit on several of the 8 timeslots instead of one at a time (multislot operation). The timeslots for uplink and downlink are allocated separately to accommodate asymmetric traffic, for example web browsing traffic. Because the same BTSs are used for both GSM and GPRS, a cell must allocate physical channels for GPRS traffic referred to as Packet Data Channels (PDCH). PCU coordinates the allocation of PDCH to different mobile stations in both downlink and uplink. The packet data

Figure 24. Routing and address conversion for delivery of IP traffic

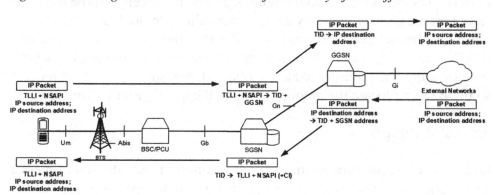

channel can be either used for traffic purposes or for signaling purposes, so GPRS distinguishes between the following logical channels:

1. **Packet Data Traffic Channel (PDTCH):** Used for user data transmission; one mobile station can use several PDTCH simultaneously to increase the data throughput (minimum of four, called a *block*)
2. **Packet Broadcast Control Channel (PBCCH):** Used by BSS to signal the organization of GPRS resources in a cell, as well as the basic cell configuration that was also signaled on the BCCH in GSM so the stations can perform the necessary network procedures and radio measurements
3. **Packet Random Access Control Channel (PRACH):** A common signaling channel used by the mobile stations to request one or more PDTCH channels
4. **Packet Access Grant Control Channel (PAGCH):** Used to allocate one or more PDTCH to the requesting mobile stations
5. **Packet Paging Channel (PPCH):** Used by the BSS to locate the mobile station prior to downlink packet transmission
6. **Packet Associated Control Channel (PACCH):** Always allocated with one or more PDTCH for dedicated control of the mobile station's transmission
7. **Packet Timing Advanced Control Channel (PTCCH):** Used for adaptive time synchronization of the transmission in the uplink and downlink on the TDMA frame

Figures 25 show examples of uplink and downlink packet transfer on the air interface. On the mobile station's request for packet channel in uplink, the BSS responds with an immediate response and establishes so called Temporary Block Flow (TBF) with the station (one or more PDTCH and buffers). BSS also signals to the other stations in the cell that the assigned resources are already in use by a parameter called Uplink State Flag (USF). Once the channel is established, the PACCH is used between the BSS and mobile station to periodically signal the successful reception of the packets. For downlink, the same procedure is followed, preceded by a paging request so the BSS can locate the mobile station in the last register routing area.

Timeslot Usage

GPRS uses a 52 multiframe structure for its timeslot and allows for timeslot aggregation so a user can further increase the transmission speed. GPRS

Figure 25. GPRS uplink and downlink channel allocation

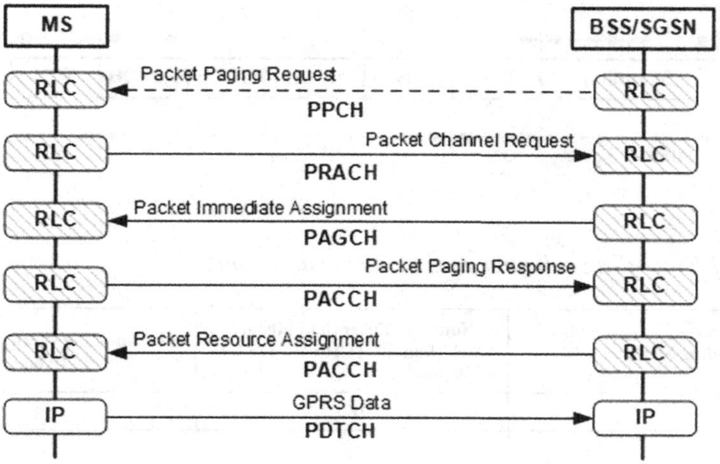

defines multislot classes with three, four, and five slots combined in downlink or uplink. Since the TDMA/FDMA organization allows for a maximum of eight timeslots per frequency carrier, the BSS needs to balance between the timeslots used for signaling, for GSM traffic, and GPRS traffic, depending on the aggregate user demand. Figure 26 shows an example of resource allocation for GSM/GPRS co-existence on the *Um* interface.

Another way to increase the data transfer speeds in GPRS is to use different coding schemes. GPRS uses four coding schemes shown in Table 1. The codding schemes differ on the error correction speed, i.e. for CS-1, CS-2, and CS-3 the GSM 1/2 convolutional coder is used (some of the bits are punctured for increasing the speed in CS-2 and CS-3, respectively). CS-4 does not add error correction redundancy and it is used only in cases with a good signal quality on the air interface.

EDGE

GPRS was evolved to 2.75G to support Enhanced Data rates for Global Evolution (EDGE). EDGE introduces new coding schemes and adds the 8-symbol Phase Shift Keying (8PSK) modulation option next to the GMSK used for GPRS. Given that 8PSK transmits three user bits per symbol, the EDGE speeds are considered to be three times faster than the one introduced with GPRS. EDGE also adds the possibility of using a 1/3 convolutional coder with puncturing to allow for more efficient coding rates as summarized in Table

Figure 26. Timeslot distribution on the Um interface for GSM/GPRS transmission

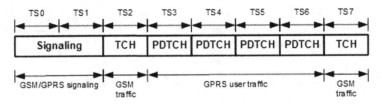

Table 1. GPRS coding schemes and transmission speeds

Coding Scheme	Number of user data bits per block (four PDTCH with 114 bits each)	Transmission speed per timeslot (Kb/s)
CS-1	160	8
CS-2	240	12
CS-3	288	14.4
CS-4	400	20

2. With small modifications on the BSS side to support these transmission improvements, EDGE is fully backward compatible with GPRS and GSM.

Security

The security functions in GPRS are almost equivalent to the ones in GSM. GPRS uses updated versions of the A3 algorithm for authentication, A8 algorithm

Table 2. EDGE coding and modulation schemes and transmission speeds

Coding Scheme	Modulation	Transmission speed per timeslot (Kb/s)	Coding Rate
MCS-1	GMSK	8.8	0.53
MCS-2	GMSK	11.2	0.66
MCS-3	GMSK	14.8	0.85
MCS-4	GMSK	17.6	1.00
MCS-5	8PSK	22.4	0.37
MCS-6	8PSK	29.6	0.49
MCS-7	8PSK	44.8	0.76
MCS-8	8PSK	54.4	0.92
MCS-9	8PSK	59.2	1.00

for key generation, and A5 (A5\3 and A5\4) for packet data transmissions. As noted earlier, the SGSN is responsible for handling the authentication, key generation and ciphering, so the triplet (RAND, SRES, Kc) is requested from the HLR for every user. It must be noted that the SGSN triplet is different and independently assigned from the one in the MSC for same users who simultaneously are using the GSM and GPRS services.

GPRS Mobility Management and Session Management (GMM/SM)

GPRS Attach/Detach

As in GSM, first time GPRS users need to register or IMSI *attach* with the network. The location registration procedure is similar as the one shown in Figure 14 for the GSM registration. It is initiated by the mobile station sending a location update request with its IMSI and the RAI (obtained from monitoring the PBCCH) and further orchestrated by the SGSN. Instead of the TMSI, GPRS users are assigned P-TMSIs by every serving SGSN to be used for the subsequent signaling with the GPRS core network. The detach procedure follows the similar logic to remove all network resources assigned to the user.

Session Management and PDP Context

To exchange packet data traffic after a successful GPRS attach, the user needs to acquire an IP address, referred in GPRS as a PDP address. For each session, a PDP context needs to be created with an information element that contains the type of IP address requested, the QoS class of the traffic, the adders of the GGSN serving the APN, and the APN itself. Figure 27 shows the PDP activation procedure. The user sends a PDP context activation request to the GGSN for the APN "Internet" to the SGSN. the SGSN queries the network DNS element to retrieve the IP address of the associated GGSN to which it forwards the activation request. The GGSN responds with a Dynamic Host Configuration Protocol (DHCP) allocated IP address for the user and establishes tunnel with the SGSN for the subsequent user data transmission. the SGSN confirms the PDP activation by creating logical connection and assigning the IP address to the user. Similar logic is followed for modification (i.e. routing area update, change in QoS class) or PDP context deactivation (termination of the user session) to update the tunneling parameters or to release the tunnel and the assigned IP address, respectively.

GPRS State Model

As in GSM, GPRS users may not be active or registered with the network all of the time. For that reason, GPRS defines a state model shown in Figure 28. GPRS users in IDLE state are not reachable so they have to perform GPRS attach to transition to READY state. In READY state, the users have already activated a PDP context, the SGSN is aware of their location and serving cell, and can transmit and receive data. An activity timer is started in the READY state to enable transitioning of an inactive user to a STANDBY state. Every user in the STANDBY state needs to perform random access or response to a paging if it wants to transmit data, which is not necessary for a user already in READY state.

Users in GPRS perform cell reselections, handovers and routing area updates, too. For routing area updates, there are two possible scenarios: intra-SGSN and inter-SGSN routing area update, shown in Figure 29 and Figure 30, respectively. In the case of intra-SGSN, the user has moved to a RA that is under control of the same SGSN serving the user, therefore only the P-TMSI and the P-TMSI signatures are updated. In the case of inter-SGSN cell reselection, the new RA is under the control of another SGSN, so the

Figure 27. PDP context activation procedure

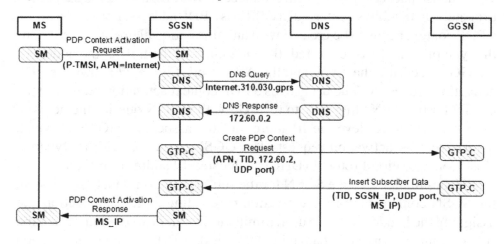

Figure 28. GPRS state model

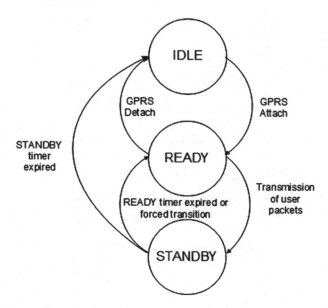

new SGSN requests the PDP contexts from the old SGSN to reestablish a new tunnel with the GGSN and update the location of the user in the HLR. There is a possibility for a combined RA/LA update, where the user indicates that she or he also performs a GSM location update so the SGSN can contact the serving MSC/VLR.

Figure 29. Intra SGSN routing area update

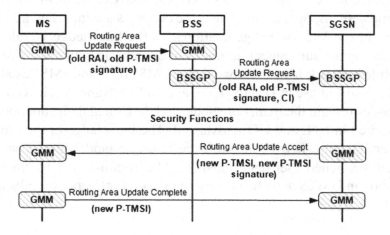

Figure 30. Inter SGSN routing area update

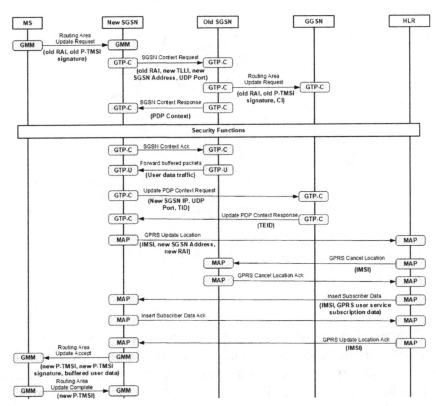

CONCLUSION

The fundamental concepts in GSM, GPRS, and EDGE form the basis of the mobile network operations. The same concepts are inherited and further enhanced in the later 3GPP generations, so the knowledge is valuable in understanding the subsequent upgrades in the mobile network architecture. The mobile network identificators such as MSISDN and IMSI established in GSM are still in use in UMTS, LTE, and LTE-Advanced. The GGSN and SGSN nodes remain the main core nodes in UMTS and their functionality is also inherited in LTE and LTE-Advanced. The knowledge of the pre-3GPP mobile architecture helps forensic experts understand complex scenarios like circuit-switched user data transport. The circuit-switched voice is the main option in UMTS and one of the two options for telephony calls in LTE.

Although the security algorithms have proven weak in GSM and GPRS, the concept of built-in security on a system level was kept and enhanced in the later 3GPP generations to eliminate most of the weaknesses. The next chapter explains how these concepts have evolved in the generations of networks developed as part of the 3rd generation partnership project.

REFERENCES

3rd Generation Partnership Project. (1999). *TS 03.09 V.7.0.0 - Handover procedures; (Release 1998)*. Sophia Antipolis, France: 3GPP.

3rd Generation Partnership Project. (2001a). *TS 03.20 V9.0.0 - Digital cellular telecommunications system (Phase 2+); Security related network functions (Release 2000)*. Sophia Antipolis, France: 3GPP.

3rd Generation Partnership Project. (2001b). *TS 23.003 V4.3.0 - Technical Specification Group Core Network; Numbering, addressing and identification (Release 4)*. Sophia Antipolis, France: 3GPP.

3rd Generation Partnership Project. (2002). *3GPP TS 23.002 V4.3.0 - Technical Specification Group Services and Systems Aspects; Network architecture (Release 4)*. Sophia Antipolis, France: 3GPP. Available at: http://www.3gpp.org/

3rd Generation Partnership Project. (2005). *3GPP TS 23.060 V5.10.0 - Technical Specification Group Services and System Aspects; General Packet Radio Service (GPRS); Service description; Stage 2*. Sophia Antipolis, France: 3GPP.

3rd Generation Partnership Project. (2008). *3GPP TS 23.002 V7.6.0 -- Technical Specification Group Services and Systems Aspects -- Network architecture (Release 7)*. 3rd Generation Partnership Project. Available at: http://www.3gpp.org/

3rd Generation Partnership Project. (2014). *TS 23.009 - V12.0.0 - Technical Specification Group Core Network and Terminals; Handover procedures (Release 12)*. Sophia Antipolis, France: 3GPP.

3rd Generation Partnership Project. (2017a). *3GPP Specifications Numbering, Technical Specifications*. Available at: http://www.3gpp.org/specifications/79-specification-numbering

3rd Generation Partnership Project. (2017b). *55 Series - Security Algorithms, Standards*. Available at: http://www.3gpp.org/DynaReport/55-series.htm

3rd Generation Partnership Project. (2017c). *TS 22.078 V14.0.0 - Technical Specification Group Services and System Aspects; Customised Applications for Mobile network Enhanced Logic (CAMEL); Service description; Stage 1*. Sophia Antipolis, France: 3GPP.

3rd Generation Partnership Project. (2017d). *TS 23.040 V 14.0.0 - Technical Specification Group Core Network and Terminals; Technical realization of the Short Message Service (SMS) (Release 14)*. Sophia Antipolis, France: 3GPP.

3rd Generation Partnership Project. (2017e). *TS 23.090 - 14.0.0 - Technical Specification Group Core Network and Terminals; Unstructured Supplementary Service Data (USSD); Stage 2 (Release 14)*. Sophia Antipolis, France: 3GPP.

3rd Generation Partnership Project. (2017f). *TS 23.122 14.3.0 - Technical Specification Group Core Network and Terminals; Non-Access-Stratum (NAS) functions related to Mobile Station (MS) in idle mode (Release 14)*. Sophia Antipolis, France: 3GPP.

3rd Generation Partnership Project. (2017g). *TS 45.002 V 14.2.0 - Technical Specification Group Radio Access Network; GSM/EDGE Multiplexing and multiple access on the radio path (Release 14)*. Sophia Antipolis, France: 3GPP.

3rd Generation Partnership Project. (2017h). *TS 45.008 V.14.0.0 - Technical Specification Group Radio Access Network; GSM/EDGE Radio subsystem link control (Release 14)*. Sophia Antipolis, France: 3GPP.

Barkan, E., Biham, E., & Keller, N. (2008). Instant Ciphertext-Only Cryptanalysis of GSM Encrypted Communication. *Journal of Cryptology*, *21*(3), 392–429. doi:10.100700145-007-9001-y

Eberspacher, J., & Vogel, H.-J. C. B. (2001). GSM switching, Service and Protocol. Munich, Germany: Wiley.

GSMA. (2017). *IMEI Type Allocation Codes, Type Allocaiton Codes*. Available at: https://www.gsma.com/managedservices/mobile-equipment-identity/type-allocation-codes/

ITU. (2017). *The International Telecommunicaiton Numbering Plan, Numbering Plans*. Available at: https://www.itu.int/rec/T-REC-E.164/en

Meyer, U., & Wetzel, S. (2004). On the impact of gsm encryption and man-in-the-middle attacks on the security of interoperating gsm/umts networks. *IEEE International Symposium on Personal, Indoor and Mobile Radio Communications*, 2876–2883. 10.1109/PIMRC.2004.1368846

Sauter, M. (2010). *From GSM to LTE, An Introduction to Mobile Networks and Mobile Broadband.* Wiley. doi:10.1002/9780470978238

KEY TERMS AND DEFINITIONS

2G: 2nd generation of mobile networks. The most dominant technology is the global system for mobility (GSM).

2.5G: Enhancement of the GSM architecture to handle packet data traffic. Introduction of the general packet radio service (GPRS).

2.75G: Further enhancement of the GPRS in the radio segment with the enhanced data rates for global evolution (EDGE) network update.

3G: 3rd generation of mobile networks. The most dominant technology is universal mobile telecommunication system (UMTS)

3GPP: 3rd generation partnership project.

4G: 4th generation of mobile networks. The 4G technologies are long term evolution (LTE) and the advanced version, LTE-advanced. Colloquially, the terms LTE/LTE-A are used as a synonym for 4G as they are the only global standard for mobile communication from the fourth generation.

8PSK: 8-symbol phase shift keying.

A3: Algorithm 3; used for authentication with a secret key Ki.

A5: Algorithm 5; used for ciphering with a ciphering key Kc. There are four versions referred to as A5/1-A5/4, respectively.

A8: Algorithm 8; used for Kc derivation with a secret key Ki.

AGCH: Access granting channel.

APN: Access point name.

ARFCN: Absolute radio frequency channel numbers.

AuC: Authentication center.

BA: BCCH allocation list.

BCC: BTS color code.

BCCH: Broadcast common control channel.

BICC: Bearer independent call control.

BSC: Base station controllers.

BSIC: Base station identity code.

BSS: Base station subsystem.

BSSAP+: Enhanced BSSAP.

BSSGP: BSS GRPS protocol.

BSSMAP: BSS mobile application part.

BTS: Base station transceiver.

BTSM: BTS management.

C1: Cell selection algorithm 1.

C2: Cell selection algorithm 2.

CAMEL: Customized applications for mobile network enhanced logic.

CAP: CMAMEL application part.

CC: Country code.

CDR: Call data records.

CGI: Cell global identification.

CI: Cell identity.

CLIP: Calling line identification presentation.

CLIR: Calling line identification restriction.

CM: Call management.

CRC: Cyclic redundancy check.

CS: Coding scheme. There are four coding schemes defined in GPRS, referred to as CS-1 to CS-4, respectively.

DL: Downlink.

DNS: Domain name system.

DTAP: Direct transfer application part.

EDGE: Enhanced data rates for global evolution.

EIR: Equipment identity register.

FAC: Final assembly code.

FACCH: Fast associated control channel.

FCCH: Frequency correction channel.

FDD: Frequency division duplex.

FDMA: Frequency division multiple access.

GGSN: Gateway GPRS supporting node.

GMM: GPRS mobility management.

GMSK: Gaussian mean shift keying.

GPRS: General packet radio service.

GSM: Global system for mobile communication.

GSMA: GSM association.

GSN: GPRS supporting node.

GTP-C: GPRS tunneling protocol-control.

GTP-U: GPRS tunneling protocol-user.

HLR: Home location register.

HPLMN: Home public land mobile network.

IMEI: International mobile equipment identity.

IMESV: IMEI software version.

IMSI: International mobile subscriber identity.

IN: Intelligent network subsystem.

IP: Internet protocol.

ISDN: Integrated services digital network.

ISI: Inter symbol interference.

ISO/IEC: International Standardization Organization/International Electrotechnical Commission.

ISUP: ISDN user part.

ITU: International Telecommunication Union.

Kc: The main ciphering key in GSM/GPRS/EDGE.

Ki: Secret key used for derivation of the Kc ciphering key used between the MS and the BTS for data confidentiality protection.

LA: Location area.

LAC: Location area code.

LAI: Location area identity.

LAPD: Link adaptation protocol D.

LAPDm: Link adaptation protocol D for the Um interface.

LLC: Logical link control.

LMSI: Local mobile subscriber identity.

M3UA: MTP-3 user adaptation layer.

MAC: Medium access control.

MAP: Mobile application part.

MCC: Mobile country code.

MGW: Media gateway.

MM: Mobility management.

MNC: Mobile network code.

MS: Mobile station.

MSC: Mobile switching center.

MSCS: MSC server.

MSIN: Mobile subscriber identification number.

MSISDN: Mobile subscriber ISDN number.

MSN: Mobile subscriber number.

MSRN: Mobile subscriber routing number.

MTP: Message transfer part. It has 3 layers referred to as MTP-1, MTP-2, and MTP-3, respectively.

NCC: Network color code.

NDC: National destination code.

NSAPI: Network service access point identifier.

NSS: Network subsystem.

OSI: Open system for interconnection.

OSS: Operator specific services.

P-TMSI: Packet temporary mobile subscriber identity.

PACCH: Packet associated control channel.

PAGCH: Packet access grant control channel.

PBCCH: Packet broadcast control channel.

PCH: Paging channel.

PCU: Packet control unit.

PDCH: Packet data channels.

PDP: Packet data protocol.

PDTCH: Packet data transfer channel.

PHY: Physical layer.

PLMN: Public land mobile networks.

PPCH: Packet paging channel.

PRACH: Packet random access control channel.

PTCCH: Packet timing advanced control channel.

QAM: Quadrature amplitude modulation.

QoS: Quality-of-service.

QPSK: Quadrature phase shift keying.

RA: Routing area.

RAC: Routing area code.

RACH: Random access channel.

RAI: Routing area identity.

RAN: Radio access network.

RAND: Random number.

RF: Radio frequency.

RLC: Radio link control.

RR: Radio resource.

RXLEV: Received signal level.

RXQUAL: Received signal quality level.

SACCH: Slow associated control channel.

SCCP: Signaling connection control part.

SCH: Synchronization channel.

SCTP: Streaming control transmission protocol.

SDCCH: Standalone dedicated control channel.

SDH: Synchronous data hierarchy.
SGSN: Serving GPRS supporting node.
SIGTRAN: Signaling transport of SS7 over IP.
SIM: Subscriber identification module.
SM: Session management.
SM-TP: Short message transport protocol.
SMS: Short message service.
SMSC: SMS center.
SN: Serial number.
SNDCP: Subnetwork dependent convergence protocol.
SPC: Signaling point codes.
SRES: Signature response.
SS#7: Signaling system no. 7.
SVN: Software version number.
TAC: Type approval code.
TBF: Temporary block flow.
TCAP: Transaction capabilities protocol.
TCH: Traffic channel.
TCP: Transmission control protocol.
TDD: Time division duplex.
TDMA: Time division multiple access.
TID: Tunnel identifier.
TLLI: Temporal logical link identity.
TMSI: Temporal mobile subscriber identity.
UDP: User datagram protocol.
UL: Uplink.
UMTS: Universal mobile telecommunication system.
USF: Uplink state flag.
USSD: Unstructured supplementary service data.
VLR: Visitor location register.
VoIP: Voice-over-IP.
VPLMN: Visited public land mobile networks.
WWW: Worldwide web.

Chapter 5
Mobile Network Architecture:
3GPP Generations (UMTS, LTE, and Pre–5G)

ABSTRACT

The mobile service was globally popularized with the ease of internet access enabled with the 3rd generation of networks and the broadband wireless speeds enabled with the 4th generation known as the long-term evolution (LTE). LTE became the most popular architecture with around 600 commercially launched networks worldwide. This prompted further advancements for hundreds of gigabits per second speeds and connect tens of billions of devices worldwide. The LTE-advanced and LTE-advanced-pro were introduced as intermediary network enhancements towards the future 5th network generation. For the first time, the 3rd generation partnership project (3GPP) architectures included built-in features for conducting mobile network forensics so investigators can structure and coordinate the investigation with maximum safeguards for the quality of the evidence, users' privacy, and network performance. To fully capitalize on the forensics features, this chapter details all the infrastructural, security, and forensics-related aspects of the modern 3GPP networks.

DOI: 10.4018/978-1-5225-5855-2.ch005

INTRODUCTION

This chapter introduces the basic elements and protocols of the existing 3GPP networks, from UMTS to LTE-Advanced-Pro. The 3G Universal Mobile Telecommunication System (UMTS) architecture overview covers the improvements brought both into the radio and core network subsystems, the security functions including lawful interception, and protocols supporting packet data delivery. Similarly, the novel architectural aspects of the 4G LTE are elaborated in detail, including the LTE-Advanced and LTE-Advanced pro network upgrades. Both architectures serve more than 5 billion subscribers worldwide, with each subscriber generating on average 3.4 gigabytes per month. From a forensic perspective, the 3GPP networks possess an enormous amount of potential evidence not just in terms of traffic, but also of the associated meta-data. Knowing how these networks operate is instrumental in collecting, analyzing, interpreting, and delivering highly-quality mobile network evidence in a timely and safely manner.

3G: UNIVERSAL MOBILE TELECOMMUNICATION SYSTEM (UMTS) AND HIGH SPEED PACKET ACCESS (HSPA)

Reference Network Architecture

The third generation of mobile networks resulted from the global effort for unification of the mobile architecture and service delivery. In response to the International Telecommunication Union (ITU) request for IMT-2000, the 3GPP was formed in 1998 to produce the technical specifications for the UMTS. UMTS has evolved the Global System for Mobile (GSM)/General Packet Radio Service (GPRS) architecture to introduce a completely new radio network subsystem, called UMTS Terrestrial Radio Access Network (UTRAN). The Release 99 architecture retained the circuit and packet switched domains from the GSM/GPRS with incremental improvements in response to the demand for increased speeds on the air interface. Release 4 introduced a so-called "bearer independent circuit switched domain" where the Mobile Switching Center (MSC) functions are split between a MSC-Server (MSCS) and Media Gateway (MGW). In GSM, the MSC controls both the signaling and user traffic so the radio access capacity is dependent on the MSC circuit-switching capacity. This limits the network scalability, so UMTS delegates the main control functions to the MSC while the traffic handling is delegated to the MGW, which in turn, can be easily scaled depending on the traffic load. Also, the legacy radio access network is referred to as the GPRS/EDGE Radio Access Network (GERAN) from Release 4 onwards.

Both the UTRAN and the core network were further enhanced with the Release 5. On the air interface, the downlink speeds were enhanced with a reorganization of the radio resource management called High-Speed Packet Downlink Access (HSDPA). In the core, the Home Location Register (HLR) and the Authentication Center (AuC) were merged into the Home Subscriber Server (HSS) and a new subsystem - called IP Multimedia Subsystem (IMS) - was introduced so the packet-switched core domain can support real-time voice and multimedia services (i.e. Voice-over-IP - VoIP). Release 6 enhanced the uplink speeds with the High-Speed Uplink Packet Access (HSUPA) upgrade to complement the HSDPA speeds. Release 7 introduced a joint HSPA+ upgrade to ultimately enhance the peak downlink speeds to 42.2 Mbit/s and peak uplink speeds to 22 Mbit/s.

Figure 1 shows the UMTS architecture from Release 7 (3rd Generation Partnership Project, 2008). The newly introduced elements in the UTRAN are the NodeB, acting as a base station, and the Radio Network Controller (RNC), replacing the Base Station Controller (BSC) and Packet Control Unit (PCU) functionality. The NodeBs communicates with the users over the *Uu* interface on one side, and with the RNCs over the *Iub* interface on the other side. The RNCs communicate over the *Iur* interface to support so-called *soft handovers* where a user is allowed to receive data simultaneously from multiple NodeBs, so this communication is needed for inter RNC handover scenarios. The other newly introduced interfaces are: *Iu-CS* for circuit switched user and signaling data between the CS domain and the GERAN, *Iu-PS* for packet switched user and signaling data between the PS domain and UTRAN, *Mc* interface between the MSCS and the MGW, and the *Go* interface between the GPRS Gateway Support Node (GGSN) and the Internet Multimedia Subsystem (IMS).

Addressing and Network Identifiers

UMTS keeps most of the user and network identifiers introduced in GSM and GRPS, with the main updates on the UTRAN and IMS side. The Temporary Logical Link Identifier (TLLI) used in GPRS is now replaced with the Radio

Network Temporary Identifier (RNTI). The main purpose of the RNTI is to identify one or several UMTS users on the air interface and is four octets long (usually it includes the number of the serving RNC). UTRAN distinguishes between different RNTI designations depending on the interaction between the user and the network, which are discussed throughout the remainder of this section. Because UTRAN also handles part of the user mobility (in GSM/GPTS the mobility management was a sole responsibility of the core network), the routing areas inherited from GPRS are further organized into UTRAN Registration Areas (URA).

URAs allow for logical organization of the cells in the Serving GPRS Support Node (SGSN) to be able to distinguish between GERAN and UTRAN packet traffic or to handle different types of users, i.e. fast moving and stationary users. UTRAN also updates the Location Area Identity (LAI) to match the Routing Area Identity (RAI) in structure and renames it as the Service Area Identity (SAI). The SAI is formatted as Mobile Country Code (MCC) + Mobile Network Code (MNC) + Location Area Code (LAC) + Service Area Code (SAC), where the SAC stands for the Service Area Codes for different segments in the Circuit Switched (CS) domain.

To provide real-time packet services over the network, the IMS identification follows the Internet identification as of *username@realm.* Usually, the username is the user's IMSI and the realm is "ims.mnc<MNC>. mcc<MCC>.3gppnetwork.org". For a public reachability, the *firstname.*

Figure 1. UMTS reference network architecture

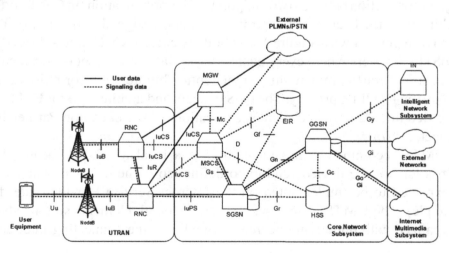

133

lastname@operator.com IMS identifiers are mapped to the users' MSIDSN numbers.

UMTS User Management

UMTS Users

UMTS refers to the mobile stations as User Equipment (UE) that consists of Mobile Equipment (ME) and Universal Integrated Circuit Card (UICC). The mobile equipment can be either a single phone that integrates both the functions of 3G mobile termination and terminal equipment, or can be an external card (e.g. USB) that handles the 3G mobile termination for another terminal equipment like a laptop or a personal computer. The UICC is the physical card or the hardware that is integrated with the Universal Subscriber Identity Module (USIM) software. Both perform similar storage and calculation functions as the SIM card in the GSM/GPRS, although with different addressing and security parameters. Because the USIM is actually a software, the operators can access it and modify its structure, unlike the SIM in GSM that was preprogrammed on the underlying card. The UICC and USIM implementations are specified in TS 31.101 and TS 31.102 technical specification (3rd Generation Partnership Project, 2011b, 2012).

Bearers and QoS Classes

UMTS distinguishes between different bearers throughout the system as a logical connection between two endpoints of communication (in GSM/GPRS architecture, the bearers are the traffic channels assigned to the users). The UMTS bearers shown in Figure 2 provide different types of Quality-of-Service (QoS) to the users where every bearer is associated with a set of parameters like class of traffic, maximum and guarantied bitrate, bit error ratio, delay, and traffic handling priority. The QoS concept and architecture for UMTS is specified in TS 23.107 technical specifications (3rd Generation Partnership Project, 2007a).

UMTS recommends implementation of a local ME-UICC bearer, but that is left for the device vendors to define (so is the external bearer that is expected to be implemented on the Internet Service Provider side, for example). The UMTS bearer spans several network elements so it needs to be realized with underlying bearers defined over the connecting interfaces between these elements. The core network bearer handles the traffic path over the core network, while the Radio Access Bearer (RAB) handles the traffic path between the user and the UTRAN. Further, the RAB is broken down into an Iu bearer between the core network and the RNC, and a radio bearer between the RNC and the user. The physical level bearers correspond to the physical connections between the elements of the network. UMTS also defines five Signaling Radio Bearers (SRB) for different types of signaling, for example signaling in the access stratum (the lower level protocols between the user and UTRAN) or signaling in the non-access stratum (the higher-level protocols between the user and the core network).

UMTS supports four end-to-end QoS classes with the following attributes:

1. **Conversational Class:** Real-time applications with short predictable response times. Symmetric transmission without buffering of data and with a guaranteed data rate (i.e. voice or video calls)
2. **Streaming Class:** Real-time applications with short predictable response times. Asymmetric transmission with possible buffering of data and with a guaranteed data rate (i.e. gaming or streaming service)
3. **Interactive Class:** Non-real-time applications with acceptable variable response times. Asymmetric transmission with possible buffering of data but without guaranteed data rate (i.e. browsing a web page)

Figure 2. UMTS bearer/QoS architecture

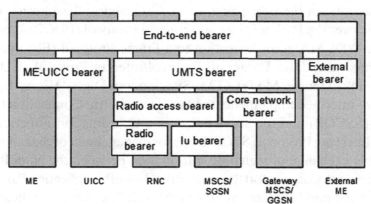

4. **Background Class:** Non-real-time applications with long response times. Asymmetric transmission with possible buffering of data but without a guaranteed data rate (i.e. best effort)

UMTS Protocol Architecture

UMTS organizes the protocol architecture on three logical layers: the transport network layer (operator specific implementation), radio network layer (or the access stratum between the UTRAN and the UE), and system network layer (or the non-access stratum between the core network and the UE). Each of these layers implement their own set of control and user plane protocols, specified in TS 24 and TS 29 series of specifications (3rd Generation Partnership Project, 2017a).

Packet Switched Protocol Architecture

The packet switched protocol architecture on all layers for both the control and user plane is shown in Figure 3. On the *Uu* interface, the UE implements a Wideband Code Division Multiple Access (WCDMA) based physical layer. The data-link layer is implemented using cellular specific Medium Access Control (MAC) and Radio Link Control (RLC) protocols. These layers are shared between the control and user plane. In the control plane, the UE transports the signaling using the Radio Resource Control (RRC), Packet-switched Mobility Management (PMM) and Session Management (SM) protocols. In the user plane, the UE transports the Internet Protocol (IP) traffic over the Packet Data Convergence Protocol (PDCP). The NodeB relays the WDCMA communication to a Frame Protocol (FP) than can be implemented over User Datagram Protocol/Internet Protocol (UDP/IP) or Asynchronous Transfer Mode (ATM)/Synchronous Digital Hierarchy (SDH).

The *Iub* interface implements the Service Specific Connection Oriented Protocol (SSCOP) and the service Specific Coordination Function - User Network Interface Protocol (SSCF-UNI) for management of the radio bearers and reliable exchange of signaling information between the NodeB and the RNC. These protocols support the transport of NodeB Application Part (NBAP) protocol in the control plane and the Access Link Control Application Part (ALCAP) over the Signaling Transport Converter (STC) in the user plane. In the control plane, the RNC relays the RRC messages carrying the SM and PMM signaling over the Radio Access Network Application Part (RANAP)

Figure 3. UMTS protocol architecture – packet switched

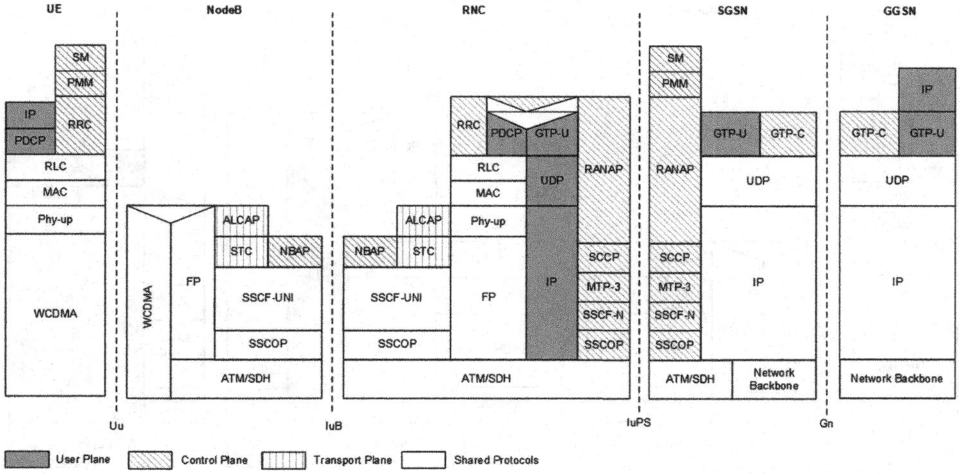

to the SGSN. In the user plane, the PDCP traffic carrying the user IP traffic is relayed over the Gateway Tunneling Protocol – User part (GTP-U) to the Serving GPRS Support Node (SGSN). The *Gn* interface remains unchanged as implemented in GPRS.

Circuit Switched Protocol Architecture

A similar implementation is followed for both the control and user plane on the circuit switched as shown in Figure 4. In this case, the control plane transfers the Connection Management (CM) and Mobility Management (MM) protocols introduced in GSM for realization of telephony traffic between the UE and the MSCS/MGW. The user plane in UMTS transport the voice calls over the Iu User Part (Iu UP) protocol, which are encoded with a new standard for speech coding, called Adaptive Multi Rate (AMR) or G.722.2 ITU speech code. AMR is introduced in UMTS in two variants, one that supports narrowband channels in GERAN and another that supports wideband channels in UTRAN as specified in the TS 26 series of specifications (3rd Generation Partnership Project, 2017a). The MSCS/MGW interaction is realized over the MEGACO protocol (not depicted on Figure 4) which enables coordination for both the call control and mobility management.

Figure 4. UMTS protocol architecture – circuit switched

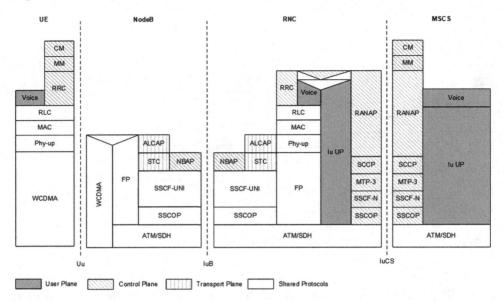

Air Interface

Wireless Communication

The UMTS frequency bands are listed in Table 6 in the appendix of Chapter 3. Most UMTS deployments are realized in a Frequency Division Duplex (FDD) mode as in GSM, except for the Time Division Synchronous Code Division Multiple Access (TD-SCDMA) in China which is realized in a Time Division Duplex (TDD) mode. UMTS introduces completely a new multiple access scheme in the air interface, WCDMA to overcome the limitations of Time Division Multiple Access (TDMA)/Frequency Division Multiple Access (FDMA) in GSM to support packet traffic and higher access speeds, as well as to accommodate larger numbers of mobile users. The implementation of the air interface is specified in the TS 25.101 and TS 25.104 technical specifications (3rd Generation Partnership Project, 2010, 2017c).

WCDMA principle of operation is known as Direct Sequence Spread Spectrum (DSSS) and is shown in Figure 5 and Figure 6. At the transmitter (i.e. the UE), the baseband bitstream of rate R is "spread" by combining it with a wideband spreading signal, creating a "spread signal" with bandwidth W. The term "spread" indicates that each of the baseband bits are replaced with sequences of bits with smaller duration, called *chips*, that in the frequency domain occupy wider bandwidth than the one needed to transmit the original bitstream (hence the wideband characteristic).

These chips sequences are unique for each user in a cell and are referred to as the user *codes* (hence the CDMA multiple access). At the receiver (i.e. NodeB), the spread signal is multiplied with the corresponding code to retrieve the sending bitstream. If there are multiple signals at the receiver, they are distinguished by different codes so the receiver only sees the effect of each other sharing the same time and frequency bandwidth as a noise-level interference. The chip rate in UMTS is usually 3.84 Mega chips per second, resulting in a 3.84 MHz wide bandwidth. UMTS includes guard bands to protect from inter carrier interference, so a typical UMTS carrier is 5 MHz wide (Kaaranen *et al.*, 2007).

The WCDMA system uses several codes, shown in Table 1. The scrambling codes provide user separation in uplink and cell/sector separation in downlink (also referred to as *Gold* codes). The channelization codes are used to separate the user and control streams from the users, given that both types of traffic occupy the entire frequency band of the carrier. The scrambling and channelization code form the spreading code, or the unique "channel key" that UMTS uses to distinguish and manage multiple concurrent communication links.

Figure 5. WCDMA principle of operation – system level overview

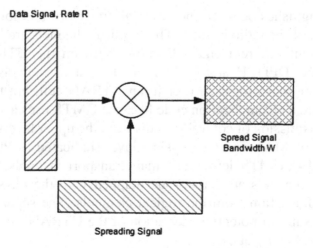

Data Signal, Rate R

Spread Signal
Bandwidth W

Spreading Signal

Figure 6. WCDMA principle of operation – bitstream level overview

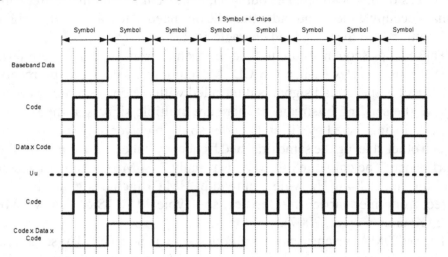

Table 1. WCDMA codes used in UMTS

Code Type	Uplink (UL)	Downlink (DL)
Scrambling codes	User separation	Cell/sector separation
Channelization codes	User and control channels from the same terminal	Users within one cell
Spreading codes	Channelization code X scrambling code	

Physical, Transport, and Logical Channels

UMTS distinguishes between the physical, transport, and logical channels in realization of the radio bearers. The physical channels are listed in Table 2 and represent different channelization codes on the UTRAN physical layer interface. DPDCH and DPCCH as dedicated channels with unique channelization codes for each user in an UTRAN cell, but the remaining ones can share a channelization code because UMTS uses a 10ms frame to schedule transmission of control streams from the upper layers (Cox, 2008).

Between the MAC and the physical layer (indicated as Phy-up layer in Figures 3 and 4), UMTS defines five main transport channels, listed in Table 3. Transport channels are one-to-one mapped with the physical channels and carry information from the logical channels. The separation is made in UMTS to support potential adaptation of the UTRAN interface to other multiple access techniques.

Table 2. Physical Channels in UMTS

Channel	Name	Direction	Upper Layers' Information Flow
PCCPCH	Primary Common Control Physical Channel	DL	BCH
SCCPCH	Secondary Common Control Physical Channel	DL	PCH and FACH
PRACH	Physical Random Access Channel	UL	RACH
DPDCH	Dedicated Physical Data Channel	UL, DL	DCH
PICH	Paging Indicator Channel	DL	Control signals to support the PCH
AICH	Acquisition Indicator Channel	DL	Control signals to support the RACH
DPCCH	Dedicated Physical Control Channel	UL, DL	Control signals to support the DCH
SCH	Synchronization Channel	DL	Control signals to support acquisition
CPICH	Common Pilot Channel	DL	Pilot signal to assist the UE receiver

Table 3. Transport Channels in UMTS

Channel	Name	Direction	Upper Layers' Information Flow
BCH	Broadcast channel	DL	BCCH
PCH	Paging Channel	DL	PCCH
FACH	Forward Access channel	DL	User and control traffic on a common canalization code
RACH	Random Access channel	UL	User and control traffic on a common canalization code
DCH	Dedicated Channel	UL, DL	User and control traffic on a common canalization code

Table 4. Logical Channels in UMTS

Channel	Name	Direction	Upper Layers' Information Flow
BCCH	Broadcast Control Channel	DL	System information messages
PCCH	Paging Control Channel	DL	Paging messages
CCCH	Common Control Channel	UL, DL	Signaling to/from a UE in RRC Idle mode
DCCH	Dedicated Control Channel	UL, DL	Signaling to/from a UE in RRC Connected mode
CTCH	Common Traffic Channel	DL	Broadcast/multicast traffic

Figure 7. Mapping of UMTS physical, transport, and logical channels

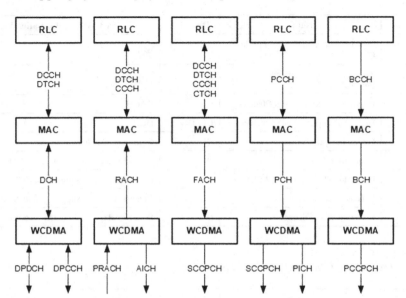

Between the MAC and RLC, UMTS defines six main logical channels, listed in Table 4. DTCH is a dedicated traffic channel that carries user traffic (voice or packet data) and is accompanied with a dedicated control channel (DTCH) for each user in a UTRAN cell. The remaining channels are shared between multiple UEs in a cell for the purpose of paging, random access, and broadcast/multicast traffic. The mapping between the physical, transport, and logical channels is depicted in Figure 7.

UTRA Coverage and Radio Measurements

UMTS preserves the cellular coverage concept introduced in GSM. Each of the cells uses the same pair of 5 MHz carrier in uplink/downlink directions with WCDMA separating users on the same carrier in the same time by different codes. An interesting phenomenon, called *cell breathing*, is observed in the WCDMA cellular coverage depending on the number of serving users in a given cell and their traffic demands. The uplink signals from different users are created with different scrambling codes so that the NodeB can distinguish each of the users. For this "code division" to work, the NodeB need to receive each of the user signals at roughly the same power level so that it can decode them without minimal interference from the other users (seen as background noise).

The NodeB controls the maximum transmit power, so in crowded cells where the background noise is high (piled up from different users), a user might find oneself outside a cell because the NodeB needs to transmit with a higher power than the maximum permitted. In this case, it is said that the cell has *contracted* (breathing in). Conversely, when there are a few users in a cell, users can transmit with the maximum power from further distances due to the low background noise, having the cell *expanding* (breathing out). This means that the cell sizes, network capacity, and user speeds vary with the network load and traffic demand (Hoy, 2015).

UMTS also preserves the Absolute Radio Frequency Channel Number (ARFCN) logic for physical channel numbering in the air interface introduced in GSM. ARFCN are used only for UL/DL pairs and have no logical significance beyond distinctions of sectors or layers of different carriers in deployments with more than one frequency carrier in conjunction with the cell identifier and the Primary Scrambling Code (PSC) in downlink (maximum 512 possible values). For example, several three-sector cells in a given geographical area can share the same ARFCN = 10562 but will use unique PSCs to avoid co-code interference between different sectors and different cells, 203, 204, and 205 for the first cell, 206, 207, and 208 for the second, and so on.

UMTS UEs also need to perform regular measurements of the signal quality they receive from the network for transmission and handover purposes. In the case of UMTS they measure the level of the CPICH instead of the BCCH as in GSM. UMTS uses three radio measurement parameters:

1. **Received Signal Code Power (RSCP):** This is the "wanted" signal level or the received energy of the CPICH code and is measured in dBm. Typical ranges of RSCP are around -80 dBm (very strong) to -120 dBm (very weak)
2. **Received Signal Strength Indicator (RSSI):** This is the overall background noise in a cell and is measured in dBm. Typical ranges of RSSI are -75 dBm (low background noise) to -100 dBm (high background noise).
3. **Ec/No (Energy [of wanted signal] over Noise):** This is the primary measurement in UMTS and it compares the energy on the RSCP with

the RSSI. It is measured in dB (comparative value). Typical ranges of Ec/No are from -3 dB (very strong) to -24 dB (very weak).

High Speed Packet Access: HSPA

Release 5 (HSDPA) and Release 6 (HSUPA) have introduced new techniques in the UTRAN air interface to increase the downlink and uplink throughput for users with variable demands for packet data (Holma and Toskala, 2007; Kaaranen *et al.*, 2007; Cox, 2008). These techniques are:

1. **Hybrid ARQ With Soft Combining:** This technique is an improved Automatic Reply ReQuest (ARQ) error correction where not all RLC blocks are discarded due to an error. Instead, the transmitter has a buffer of blocks for fast retransmission if needed. In the receiver, the erroneously detected blocks are not discarded but softly combined with the retransmitted blocks to infer the correct sequence of bits. In addition, the basic ARQ procedure which is a stop-and-wait procedure is changed to a hybrid one where multiple ARQ processes are initiated in parallel between the transmitter and the receiver to eliminate the waiting gaps in transmission.

2. **Fast Scheduling:** In Release 99, the user traffic scheduling was managed by the RRC which made the scheduling process inefficient: the signaling messages for creation, termination, and increase in rate exchanged between the UE and the RRC usually took hundreds of milliseconds, a time where no other user could utilize the difference in radio resources. In HSPA, the scheduling is shifted down to the NodeB to eliminate the unnecessary delays and increase the efficiency in radio resource usage (and with that the user throughput).

3. **Adaptive Modulation and Coding (Only in HSDPA):** To optimize the maximum downlink throughput for the serving users, the NodeB varies its transmitted data rate in two ways. In adaptive coding, it transmits with a constant spreading factor, but varies the amount of puncturing or repetition in the error correction. In adaptive modulation, it uses not only QPSK but also a 16-QAM (Quadrature Amplitude Modulation).

HSDPA introduces the High-Speed Downlink Shared Channel (HS-DSCH) as a new transport channel and three new physical channels. Users receive packet traffic on the High-Speed Physical Downlink Shared Channel (HS-PDSCH), signaling traffic on the High Speed Shared Control Channel (HS-

144

SCCH), and send acknowledgments on the High Speed Dedicated Physical Control Channel (HS-DPCCH).

HSUPA introduces the Enhanced Dedicated Channel (E-DCH) as a new transport channel and as five new physical channels. The E-DCH Absolute Grant Channel (E-AGCH) and the E-DCH Relative Grant Channel (E-RGCH) are used to indicate the maximum transmission rate for each. Users transmit packet traffic on the E-DCH Dedicated Physical Data Channel (E-DPDCH), while the signaling traffic is transmitted on the E-DCH Dedicated Physical Control Channel (E-DPCCH). Each NodeB sends an acknowledgement on the E-DCH Hybrid ARQ Indicator Channel (E-HICH).

HSPA Evolution - HSPA+

Release 7 (HSPA+) evolved the HSPA by adding an additional transmission technique using multiple input and multiple output antennas, referred to as MIMO transmission, to further increase the throughput in the UTRAN (Holma and Toskala, 2007; Kaaranen *et al.*, 2007; Cox, 2008). HSPA+ also introduces the possibility for 64-QAM modulation in downlink, improved power management for idle UEs, and decreased signaling delay below 100 milliseconds so the UMTS networks can accommodate real-time voice or video traffic.

The basic MIMO operation is shown in Figure 8. UMTS supports a maximum of two antennas at the transmitter and two antennas at the receiver. The transmitter divides the increased bitstream in two, and sends half the bits to each antenna. The receiver is configured as a beamforming system, which adds together the signals that arrive at the two receiver antennas so that they interfere. Signals can arrive from different directions and can interfere destructively or constructively (recall the constructive and destructive interference from Chapter 3) with each other.

To eliminate the destructive and capture the constructive signals on each of the antennas, the receiver applies phase shifts so that the receiver beam 2 appears in a destructive mode while receiver beam 1 appears in a constructive mode at antenna 1 (and vice versa on antenna 2). In that way, there are two nearly independent bit streams at the antennas 1 and 2 in receiver, resulting in nearly double the bit rate that can be achieved by using only one set of transmitting and receiving antennas (this is highly simplified explanation, the actual operation and implementation is far more complex).

Figure 8. Simplified MIMO transmission

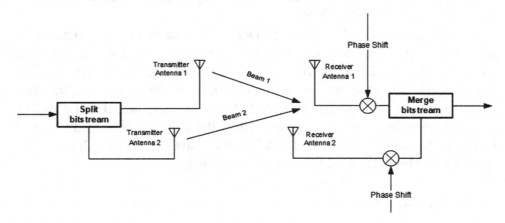

Security

Security Architecture

UMTS makes marked improvements in the security of mobile network communication. While it retains most of the security features from GSM (i.e. subscriber identity confidentiality, subscriber identity authentication, and data confidentiality for physical connections), UMTS introduces mutual authentication between the user and the network to eliminate the possibility for a man-in-the-middle attack, as well as new ciphering algorithms. The overall UMTS security architecture is specified in the TS 33 specification series (3rd Generation Partnership Project, 2017a).

Figure 9. UMTS security Architecture

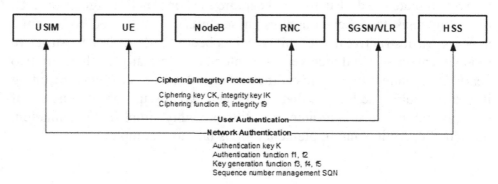

The UMTS security architecture is shown in Figure 9. On a system level, UMTS shifts the ciphering capabilities to the RNC from the NodeB (in GSM, the Base Transceiver Station - BTS was responsible for ciphering) and introduces new ciphering and integrity protection functions. Supporting authentication and confidently/integrity protection in both the Home Public Land Mobile Network (HPLMN) and Visiting PLMN (VPLMN), UMTS distinguishes between the Serving Network (SN) where the user currently resides, and the Home Environment (HE) where the user's home HSS resides.

The UE and the USIM share a permanent 128-bit master key K that is stored in the HSS. During the authentication procedure, both the 128-bit ciphering key CK and the 128-bit integrity key IK are derived from the K. The CK and IK are temporary valid, i.e. new pair of keys is generated every time the authentication procedure is invoked. The joint procedure in UMTS is referred to as Authentication and Key Agreement (AKA) and is shown in Figure 10.

Authentication and Key Agreement

The AKA is invoked when the HSS receives a trigger event, for example an *IMSI attach request* from the user. Upon receiving the event, the serving MSC/VLR or SGSN sends an authentication request to the UE HSS for the respective IMSI of the user. The HSS then starts the authentication generation procedure shown in Figure 11 to generate the authentication vector for the user. The inputs used by the HSS are the master key K, a Sequence Number (SQN) used for keeping track of user's authentication requests, a random value RAND, and an Authenticated Management Field (AMF) used for defining operators-specific versions of the authentication procedure.

Using the f1 one-way algorithm, HSS generates the Message Authentication Code (MAC) from all of these input parameters. The remaining algorithm from f2 to f5 use only the master K and the RAND to generate the XRES, CK, IK, and the AK (the 128-bit authentication key). HSS then responds with an authentication vector containing two values: AUTH = SQN $\oplus$ AK || AMF || MAC and AV = RAND || XRES || CK || IK || AUTH. The one-way functions are part of the authentication and key generation set referred to as MILEAGE in 3GPP and specified in the TS 35.205 technical specification (3rd Generation Partnership Project, 2014e).

Upon receiving these values, the serving MSC/VLR or SGSN sends an authentication request to the UE containing the RAND and AUTH values. The

Figure 10. UMTS AKA procedure

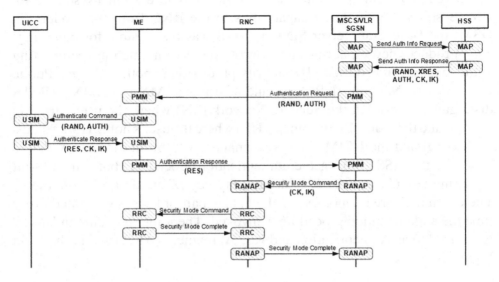

Figure 11. Authentication procedure in the HSS

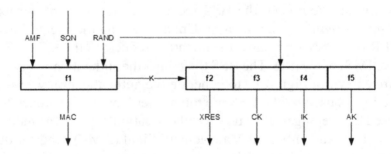

Figure 12. Authentication procedure in the USIM

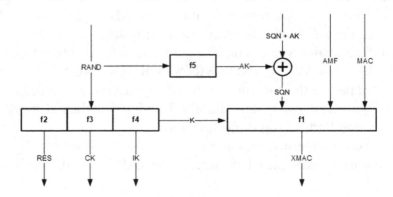

UE uses the functions shown in Figure 12 to check the validity of the MAC using the f1 algorithm, calculate a response value RES using the f2 algorithm, and derive the *CK* and *IK* with the f3 and f4 algorithms respectively. With these algorithms and values, the UE is able to verify that the network is valid and it can further proceed with the remaining security procedures (this is the step missing in GSM for authenticating the network towards the user, together with the integrity protection described bellow). If the MAC is valid, the UE sends the RES back to the MSC/Visitor Location Register (VLR) or SGSN and the SGSN validates by comparing with the XRES value. Assuming they match (the UE is a valid network subscriber), the user is instructed to start the ciphering and integrity protection from this point onwards with the RNC.

Ciphering and Integrity Protection

The ciphering procedure is shown in Figure 13. It is a stream cipher that takes the *CK* as an input together with a counter value received from the upper layers (depending on whether the MAC or the RLC is handling the encryption), the type of radio bearer, the direction (UL/DL), and the length of the plaintext block into a f8 function to create the keystream block. The f8 function is the KASUMI block cipher algorithm specified in the TS 35.201 technical specification (3rd Generation Partnership Project, 2014d). The ciphertext is generated using the exclusive-OR operation between the plaintext block and

Figure 13. Ciphering procedure in UMTS

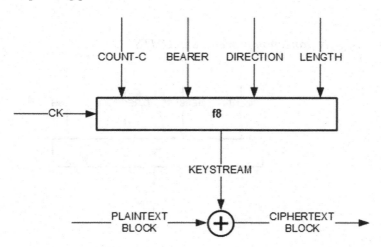

the keystream block, sent over the air interface, and accordingly deciphered on the RNC side.

The purpose of integrity protection is to authenticate individual control messages so that if there is a man-in-the-middle attacker that is successful in relaying the messages between the UE and the RNC, at least she/he will not be able to modify the signaling traffic. Figure 14 shows the integrity protection procedure used in UMTS. Each RRC message is included as an input into the f9 algorithm together with the indicator of direction, the *IK*, the count value for the RRC message, and a random number FRESH (to protect from replay attacks). The f9 algorithm is a special implementation of the KASUMI block cipher specified in the TS 35.202 technical specification (3rd Generation Partnership Project, 2014). The output value is a 32-bit message authentication code MAC-I that the sender is appending together with the RRC message. This value is verified on the receiving by comparing with the XMAC-I calculated upon the receiving the RRC + MAC-I message following the same procedure.

Known Attacks

The AKA procedure together with the ciphering and integrity protection works well in an UMTS-only environment. There are several attacks on the KASUMI cipher for recovering the *K*, but require chosen user messages and related keys which makes them impractical to the actual ciphering and integrity protection in UMTS (Dunkelman, Keller and Shamir, 2014). However, the real-world deployments need to support both UTRAN and GERAN capable subscribers meaning that the UTMS networks need to be

Figure 14. Integrity protection procedure in UMTS

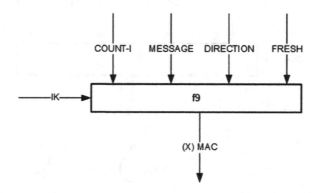

backward compatible with the GSM security functions. It was shown that the backward compatibility still suffers from man-in-the-middle attack similarly as in the native GSM implementations (Meyer and Wetzel, 2004).

Although the security architecture in UMTS achieves the desired protection on a user level, it has no incorporated protections for any network-level attacks. The advent of open-source mobile operating systems and the increase in mobile subscriptions yielded the UMTS deployments susceptible to Denial-of-Service (DoS) attacks by abusing both the control and user plane protocols. Several works have shown the plausibility of mounting a so-called signaling storms where a malicious group of users sends overwhelming number of requests for dedicated radio resources or authentication with the core network elements, depleting the available radio bandwidth and signaling capacity (Ricciato, Coluccia and D'Alconzo, 2010; Kambourakis *et al.*, 2011; Gorbil *et al.*, 2015). Similarly, the so-called mobile botnets can be orchestrated to target given network element (i.e. SGSN, RNC, or HSS) with large traffic in a short period of time to render it irresponsive (Traynor *et al.*, 2009).

Lawful Interception and Lawful Access Location Services

UMTS is the first mobile network to incorporate the Lawful Interception (LI) and Lawful Access Location Services (LALS) network features in the initial network architecture. Such an arrangement was also made for GSM, but as a later add-on to the existing system architecture. With the increased popularity of the mobile service, national regulators recognized the need for accessing sensitive information and localizing subscribers, so 3GPP responded by developing these network feature to assist Law Enforcement Agencies (LEAs) in a structured way. The realization of the LI and LALS

Figure 15. UMTS LI Architecture

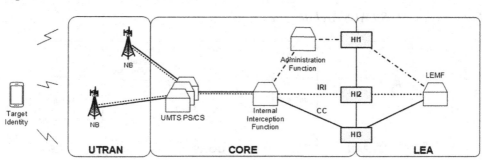

151

functions is specified in the TS 33.106, TS 33.107, and TS 33.108 technical specifications (3rd Generation Partnership Project, 2014c, 2015a, 2015b).

Figure 15 shows a high-level overview of the UMTS LI architecture. LEAs' interception requests are sent over a Handover Interface 1 (HI1) (not to be confused with the handover feature for user mobility in the air interface) between the LEA and the operators specialized Internal Interception Function (IIF). The LI option for the targeted subscribers is activated on this equipment (connected with the MSC/MGW and/or SGSN/GGSN). The intercepted information is delivered over the HI2 (signaling traffic) and the HI3 (user traffic) back to the Law Enforcement Monitoring Facility (LEMF).

UMTS provides the ability for the LEA to intercept the Content-of-Communication (CC) and Interception-Related-Information (IRI) of users that are subject to an investigation. The investigated users are referred to as *targets* and may have several identities, for example Mobile Subscriber ISDN Number (MSISDN), International Mobile Subscriber Identity (IMSI), or International Mobile Equipment (IMEI). The CC corresponds to the user plane traffic (i.e. the actual phone calls, text messages, or the packet traffic) and the IRI corresponds to the associated signaling traffic.

UMTS provides the ability for the LEA to localize any attached user (in response to a 911 emergency call, for example) in a defined geographical zone referred to as an *interception area* with the LALS feature. The LALS architecture is shown in Figure 16 and is a part of the Location Services (LCS) or the UMTS network. There are Location Measurement Units (LMU) placed on each NodeB/BTS and a separate Serving Mobile Location Center (SMLC) that request and assist users to estimate their approximate geographical coordinates. These coordinates are reported to the Gateway Mobile Location Center (GMLC), which transfers them to the LEMF as an external LCS client. The localization architecture and the positioning algorithms in UMTS are

Figure 16. UMTS LALS Architecture

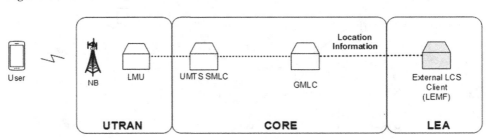

specified in the TS 23.271, TS 25.305, and TS 25.111 technical specifications (3rd Generation Partnership Project, 2007b, 2007c, 2009a).

The LI and LALS functions are the essential component of the mobile network forensics. Therefore, the next three chapters are entirely devoted on the technical implementation of the LI and LALS as standardized mobile network forensics mechanisms for all mobile architectures.

Mobility and Session Management

UMTS State Models

UMTS defines three types of state models for the users, depending on the logical part of the network handling the user connection. Figure 17 shows the state model for user connections with endpoints in the CS domain and PS domain as specified in the TS 23.060 technical specification (3rd Generation Partnership Project, 2005). UMTS users in CS-CONNECTED state have already been registered with the network and have active UMTS and radio bearers. The serving VLR has assigned them with a valid Temporary IMSI (TMSI) and keeps track of their serving RNC/BSC. CS-CONNECTED users can initiate/receive calls or text messages readily over the network.

UMTS users in CS-IDLE state are also registered with the network, but without any active bearers assigned to them. Usually most of the CS-CONNECTED users transition into the CS-IDLE state after a period of time of inactivity. In this state, the VLR knows the last register LA of the user so it can page it for any incoming CS traffic using the already assigned TMSI. Users transition back from CS-IDLE to CS-CONNECTED every

Figure 17. UMTS state model for the CS and PS network domains

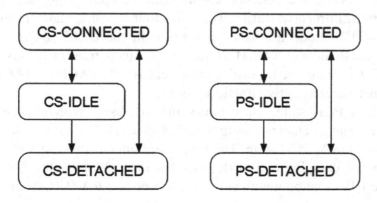

153

time they need to initiate a call or send a text message. Users that are in CS-DETACHED state cannot be reached by the CS domain either because they are switched off or they are outside the coverage areas of UTRAN/GERAN. They can transition back to CS-CONNECTED after they register with the network. The CS state diagram is managed by the MM and CM protocols in the UMTS CS control plane shown in Figure 4.

UMTS applies a similar logic for the users with connections to the PS domain, though the network can force a user into a PS-DETACHED state to save radio and network resources. This is possible because the packet traffic is asymmetric in nature and does not require a dedicated two-way connection with the network. The network can also force a user into PS-IDLE state if the packet traffic is bursty in nature, i.e. web browsing where there is a long period of inactivity after a web page is downloaded and presented on the user device (the time the user is viewing the website). In both PS-CONNECTED and PS-IDLE states the network has assigned a Packet TMSI (P-TMSI) to the user and keeps track of their currently registered RAs. The PS state diagram is managed by the PMM and SM protocols in the UMTS PS control plane shown in Figure 3.

UMTS also defines a state diagram for the UTRAN domain, shown in Figure 18. The UTRAN state diagram is managed by the RRC protocol present both in the CS and the PS control planes as specified in the TS 25.331 technical specification (3rd Generation Partnership Project, 2014f). Users can be in two main modes, RRC-IDLE and RRC-CONNECTED. In RRC-IDLE mode, users do not have an active radio bearer (no RNTI is assigned) and the network knows only their last registered RA. RRC-IDLE users can transition to RRC-CONNECTED anytime the network pages them for incoming traffic or they initiate a RRC Connection request.

In RRC-CONNECTED mode, users have an active RRC connection (assigned RNTI), the network knows their camping cell, and they can readily transmit/receive traffic. There are four possible states in the RRC-CONNECTED mode the users can be in. In the CELL_DCH state, the network has dedicated a DCH to the user for its active traffic sessions. In CELL_FACH state, the network has dedicated only FACH or RACH to the user for periodically active traffic sessions.

In CELL_PCH state, the network informs users with inactive packet sessions about any changes using the PCH channel. The same holds true for the users in URA_PCH state. The main difference is that the network does not know the camping cell of the user but instead knows the URA of the user. The URA can be identical to or a subset of a RA (URAs are used for

Figure 18. UMTS state model for the UTRAN domain

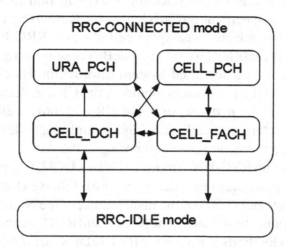

Table 4. Relationships between the UMTS radio and core state models

	CS-DETACHED	CS-IDLE	CS-CONNECTED
PS-DETACHED	RRC-IDLE		RRC-CONNECTED (CELL_DCH or CELL_FACH)
PS-IDLE			
PS-CONNECTED	RRC-CONNECTED (any state)		

fast moving users that perform large number of cell reselection/RA updates to decrease the signaling load in the radio network each time they initiate these procedures). The relationships between the CS, PS, and the UTRAN state models is given in Table 4 (Cox, 2008).

Cell Selection and RRC Connection Setup

To register with the network, UMTS users first select a camping cell and establish a RRC connection as shown in Figure 19 and specified in the TS 25.931 technical specification (3rd Generation Partnership Project, 2007e). The UE listens to the P-SCH/S-SCH and the CPICH to identify the scrambling codes for each of the nearby NodeBs and measures the quality of the signal. The cell selection is based on the S1 algorithm which uses the RSCP and RSSI measurements to select the cell with the best signal quality (as in GSM, there is an accompanying algorithm S2 for reselecting a cell with a better signal quality). The procedures for cell selection and reselection are specified in the TS 23.304 technical specification (3rd Generation Partnership Project, 2009b).

Once the UE has selected a camping cell, it enters RRC-IDLE mode and listens to the BCH messages from the NodeB. These messages include RRC related information in a so-called System Information Block (SIB). Using these messages and the parameters included, the UE can determine the LAI/RAI, PLMN-ID of the network, optional URA identity, cell selection and reselection parameters, channelization and scrambling codes for the control channels of the camping and the neighboring cells.

To transition from RRC-IDLE mode to CELL_DCH, UE invokes the RRC connection setup procedure (a similar procedure is followed for transitioning to CELL_FACH state only without the involvement of the NodeB). In response to the UE RRC connection request, the NodeB and RNC exchange messages to reserve resources for the user. Following the UL/DL synchronization, the RNC instructs the UE with a connection set up message to enter the CELL_DCH state, assigns a RNTI, and assigns a DCH (a unique channelization code). The UE uses DCH to proceed with the UMTS attach procedure described below.

Figure 19. UMTS RRC connection setup procedure

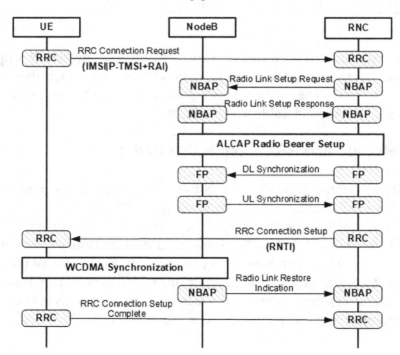

UMTS Attach/Detach and Location/Routing Area Update

The UMTS attach procedure is a joint procedure of the IMSI and GPRS attached procedures described in Chapter 3 and detailed in the TS 23.060 specification (3rd Generation Partnership Project, 2005). As shown in Figure 20, the US initiates the procedure with the PS domain, then the PS domain registers the user in the CS domain. The UE sends an attach request to the SGSN including the last assigned Packet TMSI or P-TMSI (IMSI if this is a first-time registration) and the serving SGSN initiates the AKA procedure from Figure 9.

After the AKA is completed, the serving SGSN updates the location of the user in the HSS, the HSS releases the last serving SGSN information, and updates the new SGSN for the user (these steps are not required if the serving SGSN has stayed the same). The SGSN then sends a location update request to the corresponding MSC/VLR on behalf of the user. Once the user is inserted and registered for CS services, the serving SGSN optionally assigns a new P-TMSI and a new routing area identity. The UE is now attached to both core network domains and transitions to PS-CONNECTED state for the PS services and CS-IDLE for the CS services.

Figure 20. UMTS Attach procedure

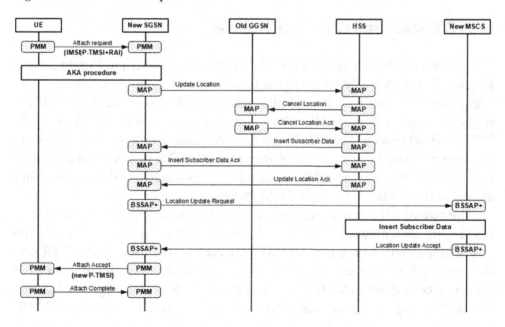

Figure 21. UMTS packet-switched data transfer

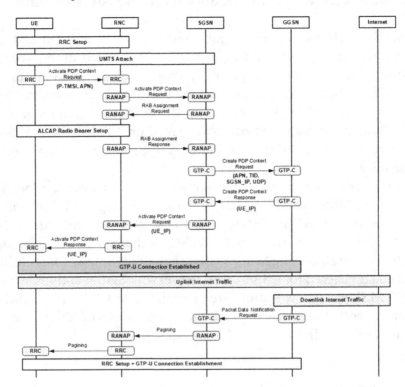

UMTS Packet and Call Data Transfer

The procedures for PS and CS user data transfer are shown in Figure 21 and Figure 22, respectively (3rd Generation Partnership Project, 2007e). The packet data transfer follows a similar logic to the one introduced in GPRS in the core network part. The UE is assumed to be in RRC-IDLE and PS-DETACHED modes. The SGSN and GGSN create user tunnels and allocate the core network bearer as part of the overall UMTS bearer for the user. In the UTRAN, the serving RNC creates a RRC connection with the user and allocates the RAB part from the UMTS bearer.

The circuit data transfer follows a similar logic to the one introduced in GSM in the core network part. The MSCS creates the circuit and allocates the CN bearer as part of the overall UMTS bearer for the user. In the UTRAN, the serving RNC creates a RRC connection with the user and allocates the Radio Access Bearer (RAB) part from the UMTS bearer. Figure 22 shows the mobile originating call scenario realized over the CS domain in UMTS.

Figure 22. UMTS circuit-switched data transfer

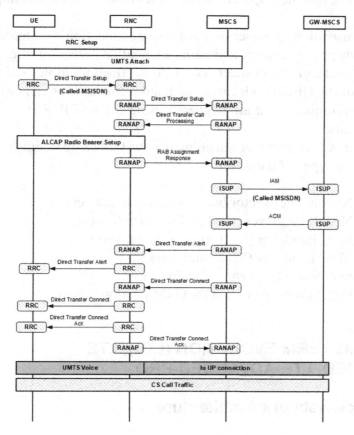

The mobile terminating call is realized in a similar way, preceded by the paging procedure shown in Figure 17 in Chapter 4.

UMTS Handovers

UMTS distinguishes between two logical types of handovers in the UTRAN: (1) hard handover (break before make); and (2) soft handover (make before break). When the UE performs a hard handover, it releases the old connection with the serving NodeB before making a new connection with the new NodeB (3rd Generation Partnership Project, 2007e). UMTS usually uses the same frequency on all NodeBs so it is possible for a user to make a new connection with the new NodeB before it releases the old one, i.e. to perform a *soft handover*. The complete management of the soft handover is described in the TS 25.922 technical specifications (3rd Generation Partnership Project, 2007d).

UMTS also allows for users to have active connection with more than two NodeBs, where the network maintains a so-called *active set* of connections for the UE and can add or delete connections from multiple NodeBs in the proximity of the UE. In both cases, the handover decisions can be both user- and network-initiated and are triggered using the RSCP, RSSI, and Ec/No measurements.

From the system architectural point of view, UMTS distinguishes between the following types of handover:

1. Intra-NodeB/inter-sector handover (soft handover)
2. Inter-NodeB handover (hard and soft handovers)
3. Inter-RNC handover (hard and soft handovers)
4. Inter-MSC handover (hard handover)
5. Inter-SGSN handover (hard handover)
6. Inter-system handover (UMTS-GSM handover, hard)

4G: LONG TERM EVOLUTION (LTE), LTE-ADVANCED, LTE-ADVANCED-PRO

Reference Network Architecture

The fourth generation of mobile networks come as an effort from 3GPP to evolve the entire mobile network architecture from Release 8 onwards. The objective was to evolve the radio segment an Evolved-UTRAN (EUTRAN) and deliver higher bitrates and low latencies for mobile users. In the core segment, the objective was to move towards an Evolved Packet Core (EPC) and provide flat, all-IP access to enable fast network deployment, scalability, and immediate Internet access. 3GPP designed the new evolved architecture, called Evolved Packet System (EPS) in two separate parts: Long Term Evolution (LTE) for the radio segment, and System Architecture Evolution (SAE) for the core segment. Despite this logical organization, the LTE became the synonym for the EPS and is used colloquially to refer to any mobile network deployment specified in Releases 8 to 14.

In practical terms, the future LTE systems were required to support peak data rate of 100 Mbit/s in the downlink, 50 Mbit/s in the uplink, and less than

5 milliseconds of latency for user traffic to reach any external network. LTE systems were allowed to operate on variable size carrier bandwidth, including 1.4 MHz, 3MHz, 5MHz, 10MHz, 15MHz, and a maximum of 20MHz. On the SAE side, the EPC eliminated the CS domain of the UMTS core network and enhanced the PS domain for IPv4 and/or IPv6 based network operation. EPC systems were required to provide *always-on* connectivity for the users, i.e. dedicated IP connection from the moment the user switches on her or his device to the moment the device is switched off (in UMTS and GPRS/EDGE, the IP connection was created on the user's demand). The main idea for the LTE and EPC was to provide an IP data pipe for mobile users without any network involvement in the realization of the user-level services.

LTE-Advanced was introduced with Release 10 in response to the IMT-Advanced requirements from ITU for 1 Gbit/s peak data rate in the downlink and 500 Mbit/s in the uplink. LTE-Advanced enhanced the basic LTE architecture to support up to 3 Gbit/s in the downlink and 1.5 Gbit/s in the uplink peak data rates. LTE-Advanced-Pro was introduced with Release 13 to extend the air interface and support a machine type of communication (Internet-of-Things - IoT devices) and use of LTE in unlicensed bands (Unlicensed National Information Infrastructure - U-NII).

Figure 23 shows the main LTE architecture from Release 8. LTE has removed the intermediary controllers from the previous generations, the RNC and BSC, and merged the entire radio access control into the *evolved NodeB* (eNB). The internal communication in the EUTRAN is realized over the *X2* interface while the eNBs communicate over the *Uu* interface with the mobile users (different protocol implementation than the *Uu* interface in UMTS). The architectural aspects of the EUTRAN are given in the TS 36.300 and TS 36.401 technical specifications (3rd Generation Partnership Project, 2011c, 2017g)

As shown in Figure 23, the EPC retained only one element from the previous generation, that is the HSS as the central repository of network subscribers. Because the core is all-IP based, the mobility and user traffic related functions are divided between a Mobility Management Entity (MME) and a Serving and Packet Gateways (S-GW and P-GW), respectively. The MME is responsible for signaling, mobility management, and security control in the network and communicates over the *S1-MME* interface with the eNBs, *S6a* interface with the HSS, *S11* with the S-GW, and *S10* with other MMEs.

The S-GW acts as a router handling the internal delivery of user traffic from the UE to the P-GW over the *S5/S8* interface(s). The PG-W is the gateway router interfacing towards the external packet data network and the Internet

Figure 23. LTE reference network architecture

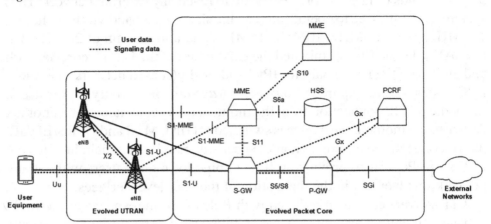

through the *SGi* interface. The Intelligent Network (IN) is replaced by the Policy Charging Rules Function (PCRF) element that communicates with the S-GW/P-GW over the *Gx* interface. The architectural aspects of the EPC are given in the TS 23.002 technical specification versions from 8 onwards (3rd Generation Partnership Project, 2014a).

Compared with the UMTS and GSM architectures, the P-GW performs the GGSN functions, while the SGSN functions are split between the MME and the S-GW. This allows for a more flexible network management: operators can add additional S-GWs in response to an increased traffic demand, and additional MMEs in response to an increased number of subscribers. It has to be noted that LTE is backward compatible with USIMs only from Release 99 onwards, but not with the SIMs used in the pre-3GPP networks (Cox, 2014).

LTE defines three types of geographical areas for logical network separation. In the EPC, there are the *MME pool area* and the *S-GW service area*. Both areas are controlled by one or more MMEs/S-GWs in a pool that is connected through the same S1-MME interface with the EUTRAN. Both areas cover smaller geographical areas in the EUTRAN consisting of multiple cells, known as *Tracking Areas* (TA), which are similar to the Routing Areas (RA) and Location Area (LA) from UMTS and GSM, respectively.

Addressing and Network Identifiers

Global Unique Temporal Identity (GUTI)

LTE retains the IMEI, IMSI, and the MSISDN as the network-level user identifiers as specified in the TS 23.003 technical specification (3rd Generation Partnership Project, 2014b). However, to protect from communicating the IMSI through the entire network, LTE defines a Globally Unique Temporal Identity (GUTI) as shown in Figure 24. The GUTI is 80 bits long and consists of:

1. **M-TMSI (32-Bits):** Uniquely identifies a user within the MME
2. **MME Code (MMEC) (8 Bits):** Uniquely identifies a MME in a MME pool
3. S-TMSI (40 bits) = MMEC + M-TMSI – uniquely identifies a user within the MME pool
4. MME Group ID (MMEGI) (16 Bits) – Uniquely identifies a MME pool
5. PLMN_ID (24 bits) = MCC + MNC of the operator
6. PLMN_ID + MMEGI + S-TMSI (80 bits) = GUTI – uniquely identifies a user within a LTE network

Figure 24. GUTI structure

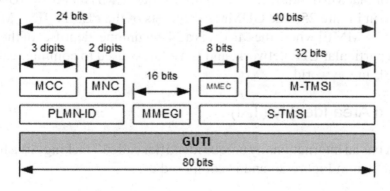

Figure 25. GUMMEI structure

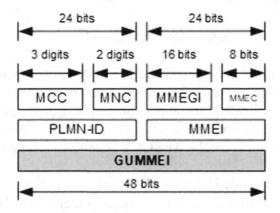

Figure 26. TAI structure

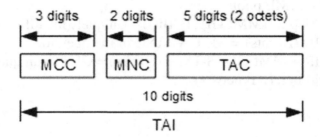

Global Unique MME Identity (GUMMEI)

The GUTI is allocated by the serving MME and is always associated with the address of that MME, known as Globally Unique MME Identity (GUMMEI) as shown in Figure 25. The GUMMEI consists of the PLMN_ID + MMEGI + MMEC + MMEI where the MMEI is a 24-bit unique identifier of the MME within a particular LTE network, and is a address used to communicate with any MME in the world.

Tracking Area Identity (TAI)

Each TA has an internationally unique identifier called Tracking Area Identity (TAI), shown in Figure 26 and is composed as:

1.   PLMN_ID (24 bits) = MCC + MNC of the operator

2. Tracking Area Code (TAC) (16 bits) - identifies tracking area within a LTE network. It can be coded using a full hexadecimal representation except for the following reserved hexadecimal values: 0000 and FFFE

EUTRAN Cell Identity (ECI) and E-UTRAN Cell Global Identifier (ECGI)

The eNBs with their corresponding cells are globally identified with the EUTRAN Global Cell Identity (EGCI) that consists of PLMN_ID + EUTRAN Cell Identity (ECI). The ECI identifies a cell within a LTE network and is a 28-bits long identifier assigned by the operator.

Physical Cell Identity (PCI)

LTE allows for faster cell discrimination on a physical level between different eNB, so UEs can quickly distinguish between neighboring cell. Each cell is assigned a Physical Cell Identity (PCI) that consists of Physical Layer Group ID (number from 0 to 168) and Physical Cell ID (three per group). There are 0 to 503 possible PCI so LTE operators reuse them for cells belonging to different TAs.

LTE User Management

LTE Users

LTE retains the same UE reference architecture from UMTS with ME and the UICC (USIM). To support the flexible air interface with variable bandwidth and in the same time remain backwards compatible with UMTS, LTE defines several UE *categories* with different UE *capabilities*. The capabilities are defined in the TS 36.306 technical specification and define the maximum UL/DL bitrate, number of receiver antennas required, number of downlink MIMO layers required, support for higher modulation schemes (LTE introduces 64-Qudarature Amplitude Modulation), and required memory capacity. As of Release 14, there are twelve UE categories specified in section 4.1. in the TS 36.306 (3rd Generation Partnership Project, 2017h).

Figure 27. LTE bearer/QoS Architecture

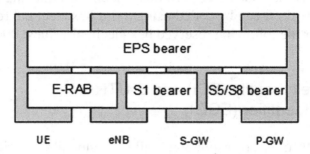

Table 5. LTE QoS Classes

QCI	Resource Type	Packet error	Packet Delay (ms)	Priority	Example Services
1	GBR	10^{-2}	100	2	VoIP
2		10^{-3}	150	4	Video Conferencing
3		10^{-3}	50	3	Gaming
4		10^{-6}	300	5	Streaming
5	Non-GBR	10^{-6}	100	1	Signaling
6		10^{-6}	300	6	Streaming, Web browsing
7		10^{-6}	100	7	VoIP, Conferencing
8		10^{-3}	300	8	Streaming, Web browsing
9		10^{-6}	300	9	Streaming, Web browsing

LTE Bearers and QoS Classes

LTE implements a simplified bearer architecture as shown in Figure 27. The *EPS bearer* is a system-wide, bi-directional data pipe that transfers user traffic to and from the UE with a specific QoS as defined by the network. It is established whenever a UE to the network and provides always-on connectivity with a dedicated IP address for the user. The EPC bearer can support either Guarantied Bit Rate (GBR) for real-time services like VoIP, or non-GBR for non-real time services like web browsing (3rd Generation Partnership Project, 2011a).

For practical implementation, the EPC bearer is broken down into three other bearers: *radio bearer* implemented on the air interface between the UE and the eNB (known as Evolved RAB or E-RAB); *S1 bearer* implemented between the eNB and the S-GW; and the *S5/S8 bearer* between the S-GW and the P-GW. The radio and the S1 bearers are also referred to as the Evolved Radio Access Bearer (E-RAB). LTE supports nine end-to-end QoS classes identified with a QoS Class Identifier (QCI), shown in Table 5.

LTE Protocol Architecture

Control Plane

The signaling protocols used in LTE are shown in Figure 28 and are specified in the TS 24.301, TS 36.331, TS 36.413, TS 29.272, and TS 29.274 technical specifications (3rd Generation Partnership Project, 2017a). For the Non-Access Stratum (NAS) user management, MME communicates with the UE using the Evolved Mobility Management (EMM) and Evolved Session Management Protocols (ESM) protocols. On the Uu interface, the eNB communicates with UE using the RRC protocol that is implemented on top of the Packet Data Convergence Protocol (PDCP). On the X2 interface, eNBs communicate using the X2-Application Protocol (X2-AP). On the S1-MME interface, MME communicates with the eNBs using the S1 Application Protocol (S1-

Figure 28. LTE control plane

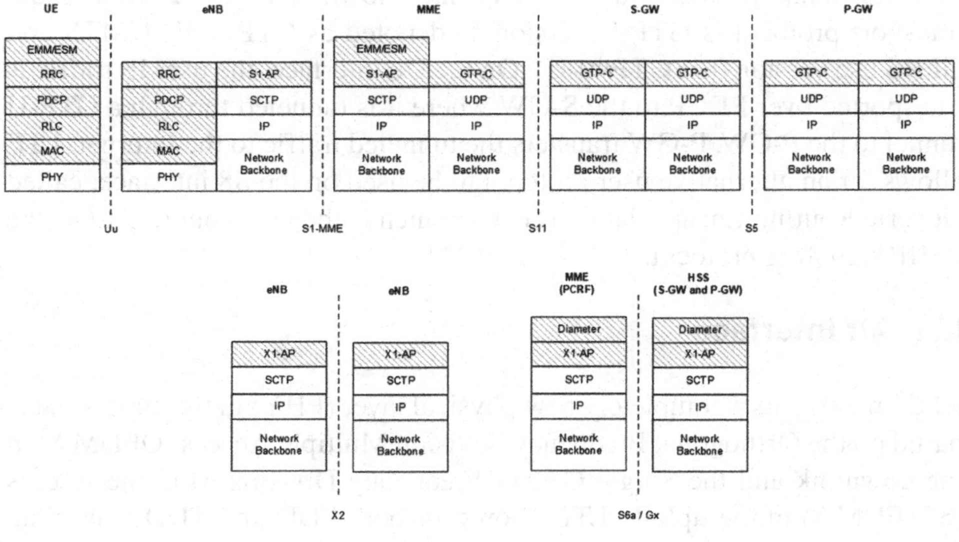

Figure 29. LTE user plane

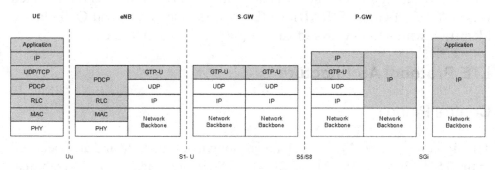

AP). Both X2-AP and S1-AP are implemented on top of the Stream Control Transmission Protocol (SCTP).

Inside the EPC, interfaces S11 and S5 are realized over GTP-C protocol (S8 over Proxy Mobile IP - PMIP) and interfaces S6a and Gx are realized over Diameter protocol (IETF protocol for Authentication, Authorization, and Accounting - AAA). LTE Uses version 2 of the GTP-C protocol (sometimes denoted as GTPv2-C) while UMTS and GPRS use version 1 (denoted as GTPv1-C).

User Plane

The user plane protocols used in LTE are shown in Figure 29. The main transport protocol is GTP-U version 1 (denoted as GTPv1-U; UMTS and GPRS use version 0 or GTPv0-U). On the Uu interface, the user IP traffic is transported over PDCP to the S-GW where it is tunneled through a GTP-U tunnel to the P-GW. P-GW transfers the tunneled traffic to the Internet. LTE allows for an alternative user protocol to be used on the S8 interface, called Generic Routing Encapsulation (GRE), which is the user counterpart of the PMIP signaling protocol.

LTE Air Interface

LTE implements a completely new physical layer (PHY) in the air interface, based on the Orthogonal Frequency Division Multiple Access (OFDMA) in the downlink and the Single Carrier Frequency Division Multiple Access (SC-FDMA) in the uplink. LTE allows for both FDD and TDD operation, however, the FDD dominates in the practical LTE deployments across the world (Global Mobile Suppliers Association, 2017).

OFDMA

The OFDMA is realized with a technique called Orthogonal Frequency Division Multiplexing (OFDM) where the multiplexed frequency resources are dynamically shared over time by multiple users. The basic principle of the OFDM operation is shown in Figure 30 with an example modulation of Quadrature Phase Shift Keying (QPSK) (Sesia, 2009; Ghosh *et al.*, 2010; Cox, 2014; Dahlman, Parkvall and Skold, 2014). LTE allows for three modulation schemes: QPSK (2 bits per symbol), 16-QAM (4 bits per symbol), and 64-QAM (8 bits per symbol).

The bitstream from the upper layers is mapped to four symbols with different amplitudes and phase shifted. These symbols are serial following the bitstream, but they are converted for a parallel transmission on different subcarriers with a 15KHz spacing. If the subcarrier spacing is inversely proportional to the symbol duration, then the peak amplitudes of each of the subcarrier signals in the frequency domain coincides with the zero amplitudes of all the others. Such subcarrier parallelization is said to be *orthogonal*. In LTE, the symbol duration is 66.7 microseconds, accounting for the effects of Doppler shift and inter symbol interference for users traveling to a maximum speed of 350 km/h and a maximum carrier frequency of 3.5 GHz. LTE supports 72, 180, 300, 600, 900, and 1200 subcarriers in the 1.4 MHz, 3MHz, 5MHz, 10MHz, 15MHz, and 20MHz bandwidths, respectively.

The main idea in OFDM is to transmit multiple low-rate streams that when added up, will result in a high-rate bitrate. Therefore, the OFDM transmitter implements the serial-to-parallel conversion and stream addition using a well-known mathematical operation called Inverse Fast Fourier Transformation (IFFT). IFFT is used to convert the frequency domain processed signal to a time domain RF transmission signal. At the receiver, the Radio Frequency (RF) transmission signal is processed using Fast Fourier Transformation (FFT) so it can be processed in the frequency domain to extract the transmitted bitstream. OFDMA uses this principle to communicate multiple UE in the same time using different subcarriers and time slots for different users in frequency and time. An example of the OFDMA operation is shown in Figure 31 where the eNB communicates with 3 UEs.

Figure 30. Basic OFDM operation

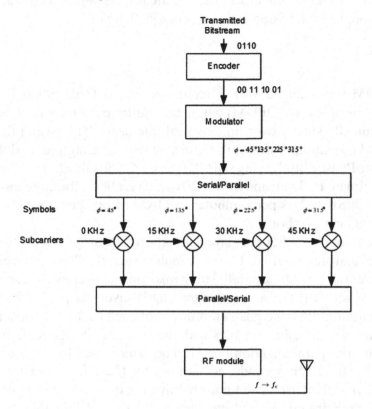

Figure 31. Basic OFDMA operation

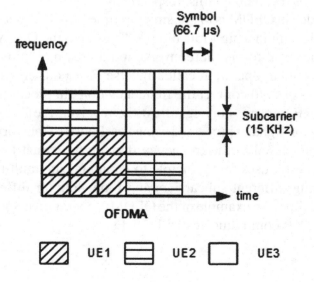

SC-FDMA

OFDMA benefits come at a cost: the RF transmission signal has large fluctuations in the amplitude of the signal, requiring expensive power amplifiers. Mobile terminals have basic amplifiers and the implementation of an OFDM amplifier will drive their price very high, so LTE implements OFDMA only in the downlink direction. For the uplink, LTE uses modified version of the OFDMA, called SC-FDMA.

SC-FDMA includes an extra FFT step before the signal is parallelized with the IFFT in UE and prior to the transmission (similarly, an IFFT step is added to the FFT processing in the eNB). This is useful because it translates combinations of the transmitting symbols on different subcarriers in the frequency domain instead of directly mapping one symbol to one subcarrier. These combinations result in an amplitude of the SC-FDMA transmission signal that varies much less compared to the OFDMA transmission signal. Such a manipulation of the symbols and subcarriers is possible because the UE transmits on a continuous set of subcarriers, which due to the FFT is "serialized" and looks like a *single carrier* transmission (sum of the carriers in the continuous set). Multiple UEs use non-overlapping sets of subcarriers in the same time, therefore, the uplink transmission in LTE is called Single Carrier FDMA.

Physical, Transport, and Logical Channels

LTE keeps the organization of the air interface with physical, transport, and logical channels. The physical channels are listed in Table 6 and represented

Table 6. Physical Channels in LTE

Channel	Name	Direction	Upper Layers' Information Flow
PUSCH	Physical Uplink Shared Channel	UL	UL-SCH and or Uplink Control Information (UCI)
PRACH	Physical Random Access Channel	UL	RACH
PDSCH	Physical Downlink Shared Channel	DL	DL-SCH and PCH
PBCH	Physical broadcast channel	DL	BCH
PMCH	Physical multicast channel	DL	MCH

Table 7. Physical Control Channels in LTE

Channel	Name	Direction	Upper Layers' Information Flow
PUCCH	Physical Uplink Control Channel	UL	UCI
PCFICH	Physical Control Format Indicator Channel	UL	Control Format Indicator (CFI)
PHICH	Physical Hybrid ARQ Indicator Channel	UL	Hybrid ARQ Indicator (HI)
PDCCH	Physical Downlink Control Channel	DL	Downlink Control Information (DCI)
R-PDCCH	Relay Physical Downlink Control Channel	DL	DCI

Table 8. Physical Signals in LTE

Signal	Name	Direction	Use
DRS	Demodulation Reference Signal	UL	Channel estimation
SRS	Sounding Reference Signal	UL	Scheduling
PSS	Primary Synchronization Signal	DL	Cell acquisition
SSS	Secondary Synchronization Signal	DL	Cell acquisition
Radio Signals	Cell specific reference signal	DL	Channel estimation and scheduling
	UE specific reference signal	DL	Channel estimation
	MBMS reference signal	DL	Channel estimation
	Positioning reference signal	DL	Localization services
	Channel State Information (CSI) reference signal	DL	Scheduling

Table 9. Transport Channels in LTE

Channel	Name	Direction	Upper Layers' Information Flow
UL-SCH	Uplink Shared Channel	UL	User and control traffic
RACH	Random Access Channel	UL	Random access requests
DL-SCH	Downlink Shared Channel	DL	User and control traffic
PCH	Paging Channel	DL	Paging Messages
BCH	Broadcast Channel	DL	MIB
MCH	Multicast Channel	DL	MBMS

Table 10. Logical Channels in LTE

Channel	Name	Direction	Upper Layers' Information Flow
DTCH	Dedicated Traffic Channel	UL, DL	User traffic
DCCH	Dedicated Control Channel	UL, DL	Signaling
CCCH	Common Control Channel	UL, DL	Signaling
PCCH	Paging Control Channel	DL	Paging messages
BCCH	Broadcast Control Channel	DL	System information
MTCH	Multicast Traffic Channel	DL	MBMS user traffic
MCCH	Multicast Control Channel	DL	MBMS signaling

Figure 32. Mapping of LTE physical, transport, and logical channels in downlink

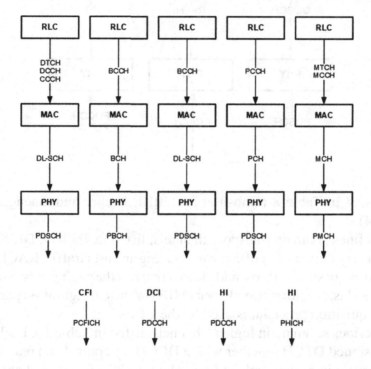

different combinations of symbols and subcarriers. PUSCH and PDSCH carry shared information from the transport layers in uplink and downlink, respectively. PRACH is used for random access, while the PBCH and PMCH are used for broadcasting/multicasting information on a cell level. LTE also defines physical control channels used specifically for realization of the OFDMA access. These channels are listed in Table 7 and carry the physical

Figure 33. Mapping of LTE physical, transport, and logical channels in uplink

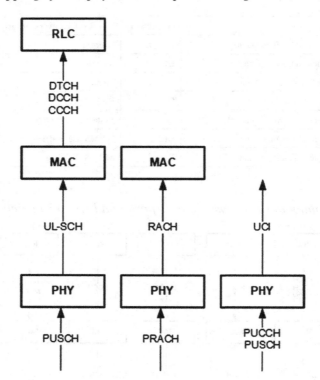

signals listed in Table 8 (Ghosh *et al.*, 2010; Kreher and Gaenger, 2010; Cox, 2014).

LTE defines six main transport channels, listed in Table 9. DL-SCH and UL-SCH carry the majority of control signaling and user traffic, RACH carries the random requests from UEs, and the PCH carries the paging messages. BCH carries the Master Information Block (MIB) or the configuration parameters for cell acquisition procedures used by the UE.

LTE defines seven main logical channels, listed in Table 10. Each user in LTE is assigned DTCH together with a DCCH for control and realization of the user traffic in both uplink and downlink. CCCH is a shared channel for mobility and user management signaling. PCCH carries the paging messages in downlink, BCCH the system information needed for cell acquisition, and MTCH/MCCH carry the MBMS user/control traffic.

The mapping between the physical, transport, and logical channels in depicted in Figure 32 for the downlink direction and Figure 33 for the uplink direction (Ghosh *et al.*, 2010; Kreher and Gaenger, 2010; Cox, 2014).

Figure 34. LTE resource grid

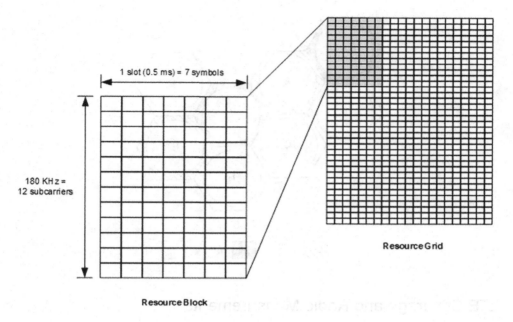

LTE resource grid labels: 1 slot (0.5 ms) = 7 symbols; 180 KHz = 12 subcarriers; Resource Block; Resource Grid

LTE Resource Grid

LTE organizes the OFDMA/SC-FDMA as a function of time and frequency in a so-called *resource grid*, shown in Figure 34. The basic unit is the resource element which spans one symbol duration of 66.7 microseconds transmitted over one subcarrier of 15KHz. Each resource element transmits either 2 bits (QPSK), 4 bits (16 QAM), or 8 bits (64 QAM). Resource elements are grouped into resource blocks spanning 7 symbol durations (0.5 milliseconds) and 12 subcarriers (180 KHz).

The duration of the resource block forms the basic timeslot in LTE. LTE groups the slots into subframes (two resource blocks, 1 millisecond) and frames (twenty resource blocks, 10 milliseconds). Each of the physical channels are mapped in resources blocks, subframes, and frames as specified in the TS 36.211, TS 36.212, and TS 36.213 technical specifications (3rd Generation Partnership Project, 2017d, 2017e, 2017f).

Figure 35. LTE fractional frequency reuse

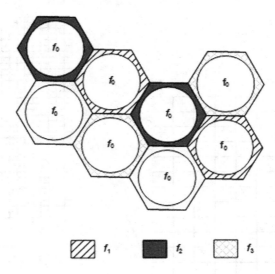

LTE Coverage and Radio Measurements

The frequency bands used for LTE are listed in Table 7 in Chapter 3. In theory, every evolved NodeB (eNB) can transmit in the same frequency band as in UMTS. However, because of the OFDM implementation of subcarriers, operators can deploy a so-called *fractional frequency reuse* type of cellular coverage, borrowing the frequency reuse concept from GSM. The fractional frequency reuse cellular organization is shown in Figure 35. In this type of coverage, every eNB is transmitting to nearby UEs using the same set of subcarriers, denoted f_0. For the distant UEs on the edges of the cell, eNBs transmit with different sets of subcarriers. denoted f_1, f_2, and f_3 to minimize the interference the UEs experience from the neighboring cells.

LTE uses Evolved ARFCN (EARFCN) numbering of the carrier frequencies in each of the frequency bands. The EARFCN range from 0 to 65535 and are calculated as EARFCN $= 10(f_c + f_{DL_LOW}) + $ DL_OFFSET for downlink and EARFCN $= 10(f_c + f_{UL_LOW}) + $ UL_OFFSET for uplink. The values for the offsets and the mapping between the carriers and EARFCNs is specified in the TS 36.101 technical specification (3rd Generation Partnership Project, 2017b).

UEs in LTE perform regular measurements of the signal quality they receive from the network for transmission and handover purposes. The measurements in LTE are performed using the physical signals described in Table 8. LTE uses several radio measurement parameters (Hoy, 2015):

1. **Received Signal Received Power (RSRP):** This is the average power per resource element and it is measured in dBm. Typical ranges of RSRP are around -80 dBm (very strong) to – 140 dBm (very weak)
2. **Received Signal Strength Indicator (RSSI):** This is total power received across all subcarriers that is accounted as background noise to the subcarriers used by the eNB. RSSI is measured in dBm. Typical ranges of RSSI are -60 dBm (low background noise) to -110 dBm (high background noise).
3. **Reference Signal Receive Quality (RSRQ):** This is the ratio between the RSRP and the RSSI and it is measured in dB. Typical ranges of Ec/No are from -3 dB (very strong) to -30 dB (very weak).

LTE Multiple Antenna Transmission

To increase the data rates in the air interface, LTE also uses the MIMO transmission technique introduced in HSPA+ and shown in Figure 7. This technique assumes that the multiple antennas are used for transmitting to and from a single user and is denoted as SU-MIMO (also referred to as spatial multiplexing). LTE implements a variation of this technique called Multi User MIMO (MU-MIMO) where the antennas are on two different UEs instead of a one. Initially, LTE supported MU-MIMO only in the uplink direction in Release 8. The downlink MU-MIMO was fully supported from Release 10 onwards with the introduction of LTE-Advanced. Further description on the multiple antenna transmission supported in LTE can be found in (Ghosh *et al.*, 2010; Sesia, Toufik and Baker, 2011; Dahlman, Parkvall and Skold, 2014).

LTE-Advanced

Releases 8 and 9 LTE features were not fully compliant with the IMT-Advanced requirements set by ITU (International Telecommunication Union, 2017). To meet these requirements, 3GPP introduced the *LTE Advanced* in Release 10, 11, and 12 with the following enhancements (Wannstrom, 2013):

1. Increased peak data rates: 3 Gbit/s in DL and 1.5 Gbits/s in UL
2. Higher spectral efficiency, from a maximum of 16 b/s/Hz in LTE to 30 b/s/Hz in LTE-Advanced

Figure 36. LTE-Advanced carrier aggregation

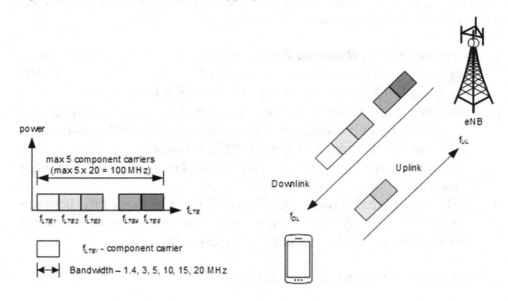

3. Increased number of simultaneously active subscribers
4. Enhanced MIMO transmission and support for heterogeneous network deployments

LTE-Advanced realizes these improvements with three new network functionalities: (1) Carrier Aggregation (CA); (2) Enhanced use of multi-antenna techniques and coordinated transmission; and (3) Relay Nodes (RN). All of these features are backward compatible with the Release 8 and 9 LTE architecture. To increase the peak data rates, CA aggregates multiple frequency carriers for simultaneous transmissions. LTE-Advanced allows aggregation of up to five carriers from each of the LTE component carriers (1.4 MHz, 3 MHz, 5 MHz, 10 MHz, 15 MHz or 20 MHz) from same or different LTE bands. An example of the CA with three component carriers in uplink and downlink is shown in Figure 36.

LTE-Advanced enhanced the transmission to a higher spectral efficiency with a support for 4x4 MIMO in the uplink and 8x8 in the downlink (the basic MIMO in LTE is 2x2). In addition, LTE-Advanced introduced a transmission scheme called Coordinated MultiPoint (CoMP) that enables for multiple eNBs to coordinate the transmission to reduce the interference in the cell edges and increase the user throughput. There are two CoMP variants: Joint Transmission (JT), where the UE traffic can be transmitted

Figure 37. LTE-Advanced CoMP transmission

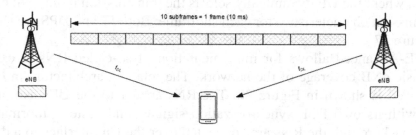

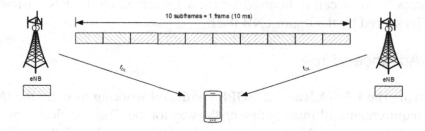

Figure 38. LTE-Advanced relay architecture

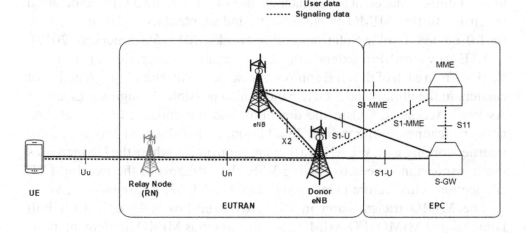

on two transmission points (different eNBs or different sectors) on the same frequency carriers and in the same subframe; and Dynamic Point Selection (DPS), where the UE dynamically selects the transmission point with better transmission characteristics for each subframe. Both JT and DPS are shown in Figure 37.

LTE-Advanced allows for implementation of so-called RNs to extend the basic eNB coverage of the network. The relaying architecture in LTE-Advanced is shown in Figure 38. The RNs appear to the UEs as normal eNB with its own PCI, synchronization signals, and system information. In the background, the RNs are connected over the Un interface to a donor eNB (modified Uu interface). The donor eNB allows a portion of the radio resources from its cell to be used for the UEs served by the RN, instead of the UEs served by the donor eNB itself.

LTE-Advanced-Pro

Following the LTE-Advanced, 3GPP continued working to meet the IMT-2020 requirements, ultimately paving the way for the 5th generation of mobile networks (International Telecommunication Union, 2017). 3GPP introduces a series of network enhancements in Release 13 and 14 as part of the *LTE-Advanced-Pro* step in the long-term evolution, with peak data rates greater than 3 Gbit/s, reduced network latency, use of LTE in the 5 GHz unlicensed spectrum, further MIMO enhancements, and adaptations of the air interface for IoT devices (Nokia Solutions and Networks, 2015; 5G Americas, 2017).

LTE-Advanced-Pro extends the CA to enable aggregation of up to 32 carriers from each of the LTE component carriers. Alternative aggregation of carriers in the unlicensed 5 GHz band is also possible through the Licensed Assisted Access (LAA) in the downlink and the enhanced LLA (eLAA) network features in the uplink. In addition, LTE-Advanced-Pro allows for internetworking with WLAN in a transmission option where the UE increases the transmission speeds by adding WiFi data streams to the existing LTE connection. This feature is referred to as LTE-WLAN Aggregation (LWA).

The MIMO transmission in LTE-Advanced-Pro is brought to a Full Dimensional MIMO (FD-MIMO). All the previous MIMO implementations were realized in a horizontal transmission plane of the wireless channel (2-Dimensional MIMO); LTE-Advanced-Pro adds additional dimension in the MIMO transmission (3D-MIMO) to further increase the spectral efficiency in the air interface. FD-MIMO enables for larger number of antennas at the eNB, supporting multi user MIMO with 8, 16, and up to 64 simultaneous users.

Figure 39. LTE security architecture

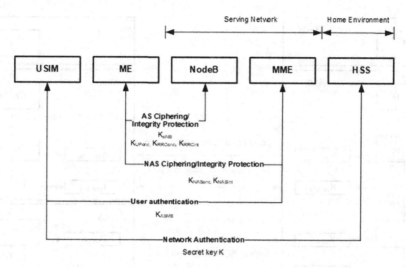

LTE-Advanced-Pro adapts the air interface so low-power, low-bandwidth devices can transmit over LTE networks. This is enabled through the massive Machine Type Communication (mMTC) feature which allows for operating frequency of 200 KHz, transmission in one resource block, large periods of discontinuous transmission (for saving battery life up to 10 years), and improved signaling and network capacity so the LTE networks can serve tens of billions of IoT devices. The adaptation in the air interface is also referred to as Narrowband-IoT (NB-IoT) and includes new set of narrowband physical, transport, and logical channels, increased cell coverage, and peak data rates of 250 Kbit/s (Nokia, 2017).

Security

Security Architecture

LTE enhances the UMTS security architecture to extend the user data confidentiality from the radio access network to the core network as shown in Figure 39. In addition, it introduces an updated key hierarchy organization, new ciphering and integrity protection algorithms, and network domain security. On a system level, LTE distinguishes between Access Stratum (AS) security (in the radio network subsystem) and Non-Access Stratum Security (NAS) security (in the core network subsystem) as specified in the TS 33.401 (3rd

Figure 40. LTE key hierarchy

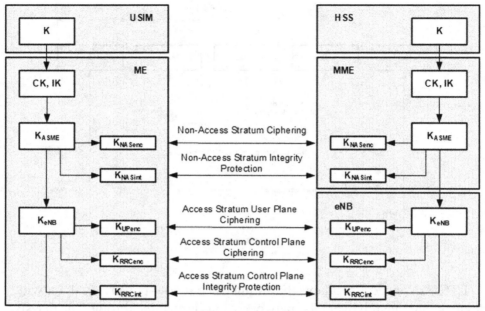

Generation Partnership Project, 2015c). This is reflected in the updated key hierarchy organization shown in Figure 40.

Instead of using the *IK* and *CK* directly for ciphering and integrity protection, LTE uses these keys to derive an Access Security Management Entity (ASME) key, denoted K_{ASME}. This key is 256 bits long and it is the output of the HMAC-SHA-256 algorithm with concatenated *CK* and *IK* and a modified *AK* as inputs. From K_{ASME}, MME and UE derive three other keys: K_{NASenc}, K_{NASint} and K_{eNB}. The first two keys are used for NAS ciphering and integrity protection of both the user and signaling traffic, while the last key is passed to the eNB.

The eNB and the UE use the K_{eNB} to derive three additional keys for the AS security: K_{UPenc}, K_{RRCenc}, and K_{RRCint}. The first AS key is used for ciphering of the user traffic in the air interface and the last two are used for ciphering and integrity protection of the signaling traffic between the UE and the eNB. All of the keys are derived using the HMAC-SHA-256 algorithm with different inputs as specified in the TS 33.401 technical specification (3rd Generation Partnership Project, 2015c).

Figure 41. Authentication procedure in LTE

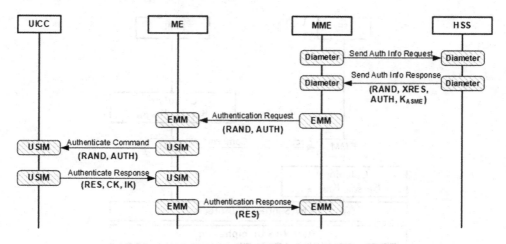

Figure 42. AS security activation in LTE

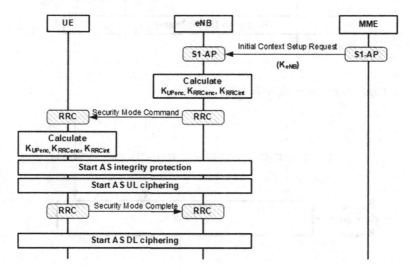

AKA and Security Activation

The AKA procedure is modified in LTE as shown in Figure 41. Essentially, the process remains the same as in UMTS, except that the HSS generates the K_{ASME} and sends it to the MME, instead of communicating the *CK* and *IK* directly. Once the UE is authenticated with the network, it can proceed

Figure 43. NAS security activation in LTE

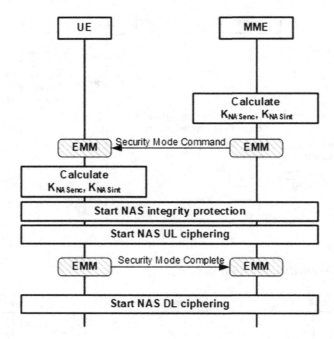

Figure 44. Ciphering procedure in LTE

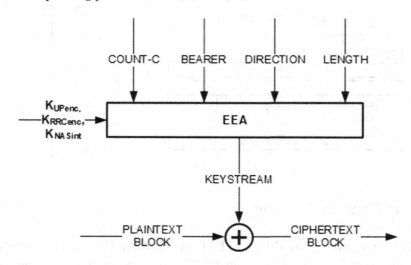

Figure 45. Integrity protection procedure in LTE

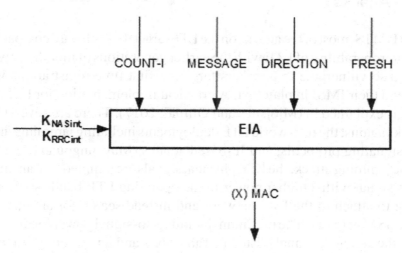

to activate both the AS and NAS security as shown in Figure 42 and Figure 43, respectively.

Ciphering and Integrity Protection

The ciphering procedure used in LTE is shown in Figure 44. LTE replaces the f8 algorithm used in UMTS with the EPS Encryption Algorithm (EEA), which can be either the SNOW 3G or Advanced Encryption Standard (AES) algorithm. For the AS security, this procedure is invoked with the K_{UPenc} for user traffic ciphering and with K_{RRCenc} for signaling traffic ciphering. Similarly, the procedure is invoked using the K_{NASenc} for the NAS ciphering for both the user and signaling traffic.

The integrity protection procedure used in LTE is shown in Figure 45. LTE uses an updated version of the f9, called EPS Integrity Algorithm (EIA). This procedure is invoked with the K_{RRCint} and K_{NASint} for integrity protection of all signaling messages and user traffic packets as part of the AS and NAS security. The ciphering and the integrity protection algorithms are specified in the TS 35.216 and TS 35.221 technical specifications (3rd Generation Partnership Project, 2016a, 2016b).

Known Attacks

As with UMTS, most of the attacks on the LTE target the backward compatibility or the interoperability of LTE with the earlier generations of mobile networks. LTE is also vulnerable to attackers targeting first time registrations where users send their IMSI in plaintext. A practical implementation for LTE IMSI catcher is explained in (Mjølsnes and Olimid, 2017). There are several types of attacks against the real-world LTE deployments including jamming, attacks on the signaling protocols, and IP-based attacks (Mavoungou *et al.*, 2016)

In the jamming attack, the LTE physical signals are jammed by transmitting a bogus signal with a higher power in the operating LTE bands so users are not able to attach to the LTE network and instead search for an alternative UMTS/GSM network. The minimum jamming-to-signal power for disrupting each of the signals/channels listed in Tables 6, 7 and 8 is given in (Lichtman *et al.*, 2016). A practical attack has been demonstrated where LTE users are lured into an attacker-controlled GSM network by jamming the LTE signal (Golde, Redon and Borgaonkar, 2012; Lin, 2016). Once attached to GSM, the attackers were able eavesdrop on the user traffic as described in Chapter 3.

The attacks on the signaling protocols target the control plane in LTE to either cause a DoS or reveal users' location (Shaik *et al.*, 2016). DoS can be caused by repetitive requests for TA update, activation of dedicated E-RAB

Figure 46. LTE EPS mobility management state diagram

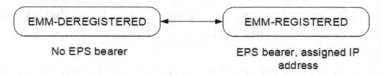

Figure 47. LTE EPS connection management state diagram

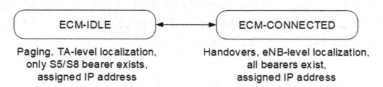

S1, or S5/S8 bearers, or VoIP signaling flooding. It has been practically demonstrated that users can be tracked by their GUTI in networks where the GUTI is not regularly refreshed during the network attach or TA updates. Attackers in possession of a rogue eNB can also sniff and reveal users' RNTI and match it with the assigned P-TMSI to determine their presence in a targeted cell or force their UEs to send measurements reports that potentially include their GPS coordinates. Users' location can also be revealed by analyzing the LTE internetworking function, based on legacy and non-encrypted SS#7 signaling traffic (Holtmanns and Oliver, 2016).

LTE Mobility and Session Management

LTE State Models

The procedures for mobility and session management are specified in the TS 23.122, TS 24.301, TS 23.401 TS 36.304, and TS 36.331 technical specifications (3rd Generation Partnership Project, 2017a). LTE defines three types of state models for the users: EPS mobility management (Figure 46), EPS connection management (Figure 47), and RRC management (Figure 48). From a mobility perspective, users can be in two states: EMM-DEREGISTERED and EMM-REGISTERED. In the first state, the user is out of network coverage and no IP address or EPS bearer is assigned to the user. Once the user registers with the network, it transitions to EMM-REGISTERED and the serving MME/S-GW allocate the IP address and establish a dedicated EPS bearer.

Users registered with the network can either be in ECM-IDLE or ECM-CONNECTED state from a connection point of view. Users are in ECM-IDLE state when they have no active connections, but they are able to perform TA updates, and receive any incoming service requests. Users transition to ECM-CONNECTED when they initiate or receive incoming traffic, in which case the network knows the eNB serving the user and has established all the bearers.

Figure 48. LTE RRC management state diagram

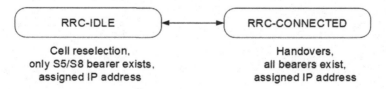

Figure 49. LTE RRC connection establishment

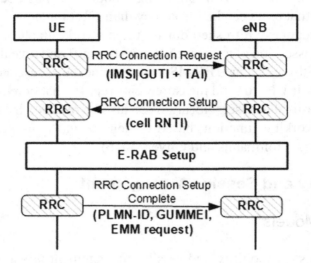

Figure 50. LTE Attach procedure

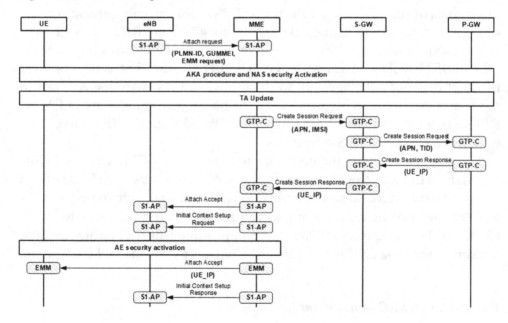

Figure 51. LTE tracking area update procedure

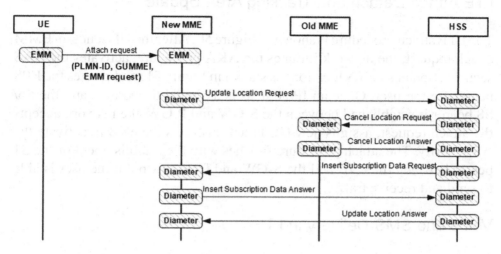

Similarly, the RRC-IDLE users have no E-RAB established with the network, but can perform cell reselection and are available to receive any incoming service requests. Users in RRC-CONNECTED have a dedicate E-RAB and can actively exchange traffic and perform handovers.

Cell Selection and RRC Connection Establishment

To register with the network, LTE users first select a camping cell and establish a RRC connection as shown in Figure 49. The UE acquires the system information from the eNB, starts the contention-based random access procedure (acquires a Cell RNTI - C-RNTI), selects the camping cell using the updated S1 algorithm (the most suitable cell per the measured RSRQ), and sends a RRC Connection request using its P-TMSI (or IMSI if this is a first-time registration). To move the UE from RRC-IDLE to RRC-CONNECTED, the eNB configures the connections in the RLC and MAC layers to establish the E-RAB with the UE. Upon completion, the UE sends a message with the PLMN_ID of the network it wants to register with, the last GUMMEI, and a request for either network attach/detach, service activation, or TA update.

LTE Attach/Detach and Tracking Area Update

The LTE attach procedure is shown in Figure 50. After the UE sends an EMM attach request, the network initiates the AKA procedure, activates the NAS security, updates its TA location (as shown in Figure 51) and creates the EPS bearer for the user. Once an IP address is assigned to the user and the S5/S8 bearer is established between the S-GW and P-GW, the network accepts the attach request, assigns new GUTI and instructs the eNB to activate the AS security. The attach procedure finishes with the establishment of the S1 bearer between the eNB and the S-GW and from this point the user is able to send and receive traffic.

Voice and SMS Delivery in LTE

As an all-IP based network, LTE has no build-in capabilities for delivery of the voice and SMS traffic. To realize this traffic, LTE can employ two basic approaches referred to as Voice over LTE (VoLTE) and CS fallback. The first one is to support VoIP and messaging service with either a third-party VoIP/messaging provider (e.g. Skype) or by its own IMS network segment. VoLTE is considered as another service of the LTE network so the implementation depends on operators' preferences. A complete description for a VoLTE support in given in (Poikselkä *et al.*, 2012).

The second approach is to connect the LTE to the CS domains of UMTS or GSM and to use their existing capabilities for realization of voice calls and delivery of SMS messages. The interconnection between the LTE and UTMS/GSM can be realized mainly in three ways (Sauter, 2010):

1. Cell reselection from LTE to UMTS or GSM (for users in RRC-IDLE)
2. RRC connection release with redirect from LTE to UMTS or GSM (for users in RRC-CONNECTED)
3. Inter-Radio Access Technology (Inter-RAT) handover from LTE to UMTS or GSM (for users in RRC-CONNECTED)

The RRC-IDLE users can initiate voice call and SMS as normal UMTS/GSM users as described earlier in this chapter and in Chapter 4. For the RRC-CONNECTED users, the MME initiates the Inter-RAT handover in coordination with the new MSCS/MSC so the users can proceed with realization of their voice and/or SMS traffic (for originating calls; for terminating calls

Figure 52. LTE X2-based handover

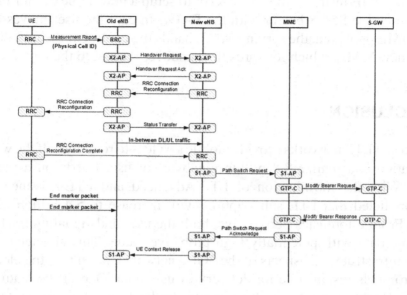

the MSCS/MSC notifies the MME about an incoming call so it can page the user before it initiates the Inter-RAT procedure).

LTE Handovers

Unlike UMTS, LTE supports only hard handovers. The most common handover type in LTE is the inter-eNB handover or the *X2-based handover*, shown in Figure 52. To initiate the handover, the serving NB instructs the UE to send a measurement report of the surrounding cells and their signal quality. Based on this report, the serving eNB selects the most suitable cell to hand the UE and sends a handover request to the new eNB. This request includes the GUMMEI, the security key K_{eNB}, and the configuration of the E-RAB currently assigned to the UE. Following the new eNB acceptance of the handover request, the serving eNB instructs the UE to start the contention-based random access procedure with the new eNB and sends the status of the sent/received packets in the UL/DL to the new eNB. Once the UE is handed over, the new eNB instructs the UE to release the connection with the old eNB, and proceeds to deliver the in-between UE traffic by switching the S1 bearer path with the S-GW.

In case the user moves between eNBs that are served by different S-GW, the MME instructs the serving S-GW to tear down the S1 bearer. In the same time the MME instructs the new S-GW to setup a new S1 bearer for the UE and switch the S5/S8 bearer with the P-GW. In case the user moves into a new MME pool area, the serving MME hands the control of the mobile over to the new MME, which forwards the handover request to the new eNB.

CONCLUSION

UMTS and LTE networks provide mobile services to roughly half the world's population and realize 8.8 billion gigabytes of user traffic on a monthly basis. With the introduction of LTE-Advanced and LTE-Advanced-Pro, it is predicted that LTE subscriptions will increase to 5.4 billion to year 2023. From a forensics perspective, both the user and signaling traffic are valuable data with potentially high probative value. This chapter focused on the infrastructural aspects of the 3GPP networks, accenting the elements and protocols responsible for delivery of user data. One of the features of the 3GPP networks is the built-in support for lawful interception and lawful user localization, that is, support for identification, acquisition and delivery of mobile network related data for forensics analysis. Because the lawful interception and the lawful user localization are essential for conducting mobile network forensics investigations, the next three chapters provide detailed explanation on the architectural and evidence-related aspects of these two mobile network forensics mechanisms.

REFERENCES

3rd Generation Partnership Project. (2005). *3GPP TS 23.060 V5.10.0 - Technical Specification Group Services and System Aspects; General Packet Radio Service (GPRS); Service description; Stage 2*. Sophia Antipolis, France: 3GPP.

3rd Generation Partnership Project. (2007a). *TS 23.107 V7.1.0 - Technical Specification Group Services and System Aspects; Quality of Service (QoS) concept and architecture (Release 7)*. Sophia Antipolis, France: 3GPP.

3rd Generation Partnership Project. (2007b). *TS 25.111 V7.1.0 - Technical Specification Group Radio Access Network; Location Measurement Unit (LMU) performance specification; User Equipment (UE) positioning in UTRAN (Release 7)*. Sophia Antipolis, France: 3GPP.

3rd Generation Partnership Project. (2007c). *TS 25.305 V7.4.0 - Technical Specification Group Radio Access Network; Stage 2 functional specification of User Equipment (UE) positioning in UTRAN (Release 7).* Sophia Antipolis, France: 3GPP.

3rd Generation Partnership Project. (2007d). *TS 25.922 V7.1.0 - Technical Specification Group Radio Access Network; Radio resource management strategies (Release 7).* Sophia Antipolis, France: 3GPP.

3rd Generation Partnership Project. (2007e). *TS 25.931 V7.4.0 - Technical Specification Group RAN; UTRAN functions, examples on signalling procedures (Release 7).* Sophia Antipolis, France: 3GPP.

3rd Generation Partnership Project. (2008). *3GPP TS 23.002 V7.6.0 -- Technical Specification Group Services and Systems Aspects -- Network architecture (Release 7).* 3rd Generation Partnership Project. Available at: http://www.3gpp.org/

3rd Generation Partnership Project. (2009a). *TS 23.271 V.7.10.0 - Technical Specification Group Services and System Aspects; Functional stage 2 description of Location Services (LCS) (Release 7).* Sophia Antipolis, France: 3GPP.

3rd Generation Partnership Project. (2009b). *TS 25.304 V7.8.0 - Technical Specification Group Radio Access Network; User Equipment (UE) procedures in idle mode and procedures for cell reselection in connected mode (Release 7).* Sophia Antipolis, France: 3GPP.

3rd Generation Partnership Project. (2010). *TS 25.101 V7.18.0 - Technical Specification Group Radio Access Network; User Equipment (UE) radio transmission and reception (FDD) (Release 7).* Sophia Antipolis, France: 3GPP.

3rd Generation Partnership Project. (2011a). *TS 23.107 V10.2.0 - Technical Specification Group Services and System Aspects; Quality of Service (QoS) concept and architecture (Release 10).* Sophia Antipolis, France: 3GPP.

3rd Generation Partnership Project. (2011b). *TS 31.101- V7.2.2 - Technical Specification Group Core Network and Terminals; UICC-terminal interface; Physical and logical characteristics (Release 7).* Sophia Antipolis, France: 3GPP.

3rd Generation Partnership Project. (2011c). *TS 36.401 V9.2.1 - Technical Specification Group Radio Access Network; Evolved Universal Terrestrial Radio Access Network (E-UTRAN); Architecture description (Release 9)*. 3GPP.

3rd Generation Partnership Project. (2012). *TS 31.102 V7.17.0 - Technical Specification Group Core Network and Terminals; Characteristics of the Universal Subscriber Identity Module (USIM) application (Release 7)*. Sophia Antipolis, France: 3GPP.

3rd Generation Partnership Project. (2014a). *3GPP TS 23.002 V13.1.0 -- Technical Specification Group Services and Systems Aspects --Network architecture (Release 13)*. 3rd Generation Partnership Project. Available at: http://www.3gpp.org/ftp/Specs/html-info/23002.htm

3rd Generation Partnership Project. (2014b). *3GPP TS 23.003 -- Numbering, addressing and identification (Release 12)*. Available at: http://www.3gpp.org/

3rd Generation Partnership Project. (2014c). *3GPP TS 33.106 -- 3G security --Lawful Interception requirements (Release 12)*. 3GPP. Available at: http://www.3gpp.org/

3rd Generation Partnership Project. (2014e). *Specification of the 3GPP Confidentiality and Integrity Algorithms; Document 1: f8 and f9 Specification (Release 12)*. 3GPP.

3rd Generation Partnership Project. (2014f). *TS35.205 V.12.0.0 - Specification of the MILENAGE Algorithm Set: An example algorithm set for the 3GPP authentication and key generation functions f1*, f1*, f2, f3, f4, f5 and f5*; Document 1: General (Release 12)*. Sophia Antipolis, France: 3GPP.

3rd Generation Partnership Project. (2014g). *TS 25.331 V7.25.0 - Technical Specification Group Radio Access Network; Radio Resource Control (RRC); Protocol Specification (Release 7)*. Sophia Antipolis, France: 3GPP.

3rd Generation Partnership Project. (2015a). *3GPP TS.33.108 -- 3G security -- Handover interface for Lawful Interception (LI) (Release 12)*. Sophia Antipolis Cedex: 3GPP.

3rd Generation Partnership Project. (2015b). *3GPP TS 33.107 V13.0.0 --3G security -- Lawful interception architecture and functions (Release 13)*. Sophia Antipolis Cedex: 3GPP.

3rd Generation Partnership Project. (2015c). *3GPP TS 33.401 - 3GPP System Architecture Evolution (SAE); Security architecture (Release 12)*. 3GPP.

3rd Generation Partnership Project. (2016a). *TS 35.216 V13.0.0 - Technical Specification Group Services and System Aspects; Specification of the 3GPP Confidentiality and Integrity Algorithms UEA2 & UIA2; Document 2: SNOW 3G specification (Release 13)*. Sophia Antipolis, France: 3GPP.

3rd Generation Partnership Project. (2016b). *TS 35.221 - Technical Specification Group Services and System Aspects; Specification of the 3GPP Confidentiality and Integrity Algorithms EEA3 & EIA3; Document 1: EEA3 and EIA3 specifications (Release 13)*. Sophia Antipolis, France: 3GPP.

3rd Generation Partnership Project. (2017a). *3GPP Specifications Numbering, Technical Specifications*. Available at: http://www.3gpp.org/specifications/79-specification-numbering

3rd Generation Partnership Project. (2017b). *TS 36.101 V14.1.0 - Technical Specification Group Radio Access Network; Evolved Universal Terrestrial Radio Access (E-UTRA); User Equipment (UE) radio transmission and reception (Release 14)*. Sophia Antipolis, France: 3GPP.

3rd Generation Partnership Project. (2017c). *TS 36.104 V14.3.0 - Technical Specification Group Radio Access Network; Evolved Universal Terrestrial Radio Access (E-UTRA); Base Station (BS) radio transmission and reception*. Sophia Antipolis Cedex: 3GPP.

3rd Generation Partnership Project. (2017d). *TS 36.211 V14.1.0 - Technical Specification Group Radio Access Network; Evolved Universal Terrestrial Radio Access (E-UTRA); Physical channels and modulation (Release 14)*. Sophia Antipolis, France: 3GPP.

3rd Generation Partnership Project. (2017e). *TS 36.212 V14.1.0 - Technical Specification Group Radio Access Network; Evolved Universal Terrestrial Radio Access (E-UTRA); Multiplexing and channel coding (Release 14)*. Sophia Antipolis, France: 3GPP.

3rd Generation Partnership Project. (2017f). *TS 36.213 V14.1.0 - Technical Specification Group Radio Access Network; Evolved Universal Terrestrial Radio Access (E-UTRA); Physical layer procedures (Release 14)*. Sophia Antipolis, France: 3GPP.

3rd Generation Partnership Project. (2017g). *TS 36.300 V14.2.0 - Technical Specification Group Radio Access Network; Evolved Universal Terrestrial Radio Access (E-UTRA) and Evolved Universal Terrestrial Radio Access Network (E-UTRAN); Overall description; Stage 2.* Sophia Antipolis, France: 3GPP.

3rd Generation Partnership Project. (2017h). *TS 36.306 V14.3.0 - Technical Specification Group Radio Access Network; Evolved Universal Terrestrial Radio Access (E-UTRA); User Equipment (UE) radio access capabilities (Release 14).* Sophia Antipolis, France: 3GPP.

5G. Americas. (2017). *Wireless Technology Evolution Towards 5G: 3GPP Releases 13 to 15 and Beyond.* 5G Americas.

Cox, C. (2008). *Essentials of UMTS* (1st ed.). Cambridge, UK: Cambridge University Press. doi:10.1017/CBO9780511536731

Cox, C. (2014). *An Introduction to LTE: LTE, LTE-Advanced, SAE and 4G Mobile Communications.* New York, NY: Wiley. doi:10.1002/9781118818046

Dahlman, E., Parkvall, S., & Skold, J. (2014). 4G LTE/LTE-Advance for Mobile Broadband (2nd ed.). Academic Press.

Dunkelman, O., Keller, N., & Shamir, A. (2014). A Practical-Time Related-Key Attack on the KASUMI Cryptosystem Used in GSM and 3G Telephony. *Journal of Cryptology*, 27(4), 824–849. doi:10.100700145-013-9154-9

Ghosh, A., Zhang, J., Andrews, J., & Muhamed, R. (2010). *The Fundamentals of LTE* (1st ed.). Boston, MA: Prentice Hall.

Global Mobile Suppliers Association. (2017) *Evolution from LTE to 5G.* Academic Press.

Golde, N., Redon, K., & Borgaonkar, R. (2012). Weaponizing femtocells: The effect of rogue devices on mobile telecommunications. *Network and Distributed System Security Symposium.*

Gorbil, G., Abdelrahman, O., Pavloski, M., & Gelenbe, E. (2015). Modeling and Analysis of RRC-Based Signalling Storms in 3G Networks. *IEEE Transactions on Emerging Topics in Computing.*

Holma, H., & Toskala, A. (2007). *WCDMA FOR UMTS – HSPA Evolution and LTE* (4th ed.). West Sussex, UK: John Wiley & Sons. doi:10.1002/9780470512531

Holtmanns, S., & Oliver, I. (2016). User Location Tracking Attacks for LTE Networks Using the Interworking Functionality. IFIP Networking 2016, 315–322. doi:10.1109/IFIPNetworking.2016.7497239

Hoy, J. (2015). *Forensic Radio Survey Techniques for Cell Site Analysis.* West Sussex, UK: Wiley. doi:10.1002/9781118925768

International Telecommunication Union. (2017). *Minimum requirements related to technical performance for IMT-2020 radio interface(s).* Available at: https://www.itu.int/md/R15-SG05-C-0040/en

Kaaranen, H., Ahtiainen, A., Laitinen, L., Naghian, S., & Niemi, V. (2007). *UMTS networks architecture, mobility and services.* Helsinki, Finland: Wiley.

Kambourakis, G., Kolias, C., Gritzalis, S., & Park, J. H. (2011). DoS attacks exploiting signaling in UMTS and IMS. *Computer Communications. Elsevier B.*, *34*(3), 226–235.

Kreher, R., & Gaenger, K. (2010). *LTE Signaling.* Troubleshooting, and Optimization, LTE Signaling, Troubleshooting, and Optimization; doi:10.1002/9780470977729

Lichtman, M., Jover, R. P., Labib, M., Rao, R., Marojevic, V., & Reed, J. H. (2016). LTE/LTE-A Jamming, Spoofing, and Sniffing: Threat Assessment and Mitigation. *IEEE Communications Magazine*, *54*(April), 54–61. doi:10.1109/MCOM.2016.7452266

Lin, H. (2016). Forcing Targeted LTE Cellphone into Unsafe Network. HITBSecConf.

Mavoungou, S., Kaddoum, G., Taha, M., & Matar, G. (2016). Survey on Threats and Attacks on Mobile Networks. *IEEE Access - Security In Wireless Communications and Networking*, (4), 4543–4572.

Meyer, U., & Wetzel, S. (2004). A Man-in-the-Middle Attack on UMTS. *3rd ACM workshop on Wireless security*, 90–97.

Mjølsnes, S. F., & Olimid, R. F. (2017). *Easy 4G/LTE IMSI Catchers for Non-Programmers.* Academic Press.

Nokia. (2017). *LTE evolution for IoT connectivity.* Available at: www.nokia.com

Nokia Solutions and Networks. (2015). *LTE-Advanced Pro.* Espoo, Finland: Nokia.

Poikselkä, M., Holma, H., Hongisto, J., Kallio, J., & Toskala, A. (2012). *Voice over LTE (VoLTE)*. Espoo, Finland: Wiley. doi:10.1002/9781119944935

Ricciato, F., Coluccia, A., & D'Alconzo, A. (2010). A review of DoS attack models for 3G cellular networks from a system-design perspective. *Computer Communications. Elsevier B.*, *33*(5), 551–558. doi:10.1016/j.comcom.2009.11.015

Sauter, M. (2010). *From GSM to LTE, An Introduction to Mobile Networks and Mobile Broadband*. Wiley. doi:10.1002/9780470978238

Sesia, S. (2009). *The LTE Network Architecture. In LTE — The UMTS Long Term Evolution: From Theory to Practice* (pp. 23–50). Wiley; doi:10.1002/9780470742891

Sesia, S., Toufik, I., & Baker, M. (2011). *LTE - The UMTS Long Term Evolution; From Theory to Practice* (S. Sesia, I. Toufik, & M. Baker, Eds.). West Sussex, UK: John Wiley & Sons. doi:10.1002/9780470978504

Shaik, A., Borgaonkar, R., Asokan, N., Niemi, V., & Seifert, J. (2016). *Practical Attacks Against Privacy and Availability in 4G / LTE Mobile Communication Systems*. arXiv preprint.

3rd Generation Partnership Project. (2014d). *3GPP TS 35.202 -- 3G Security -- Specification of the 3GPP Confidentiality and Integrity Algorithms -- Document 2: Specification, K. A. S. U. M. I. (Release 12)*. 3GPP. Available at: http://www.3gpp.org/

Traynor, P., Lin, M., Ongtang, M., Rao, V., Jaeger, T., McDaniel, P., & LaPorta, T. (2009). On cellular botnets: measuring the impact of malicious devices on a cellular network core. ACM conference on Computer and communications security, 223–234. doi:10.1145/1653662.1653690

Wannstrom, J. (2013). *LTE-Advanced, LTE-Advanced*. Available at: http://www.3gpp.org/technologies/keywords-acronyms/97-lte-advanced

KEY TERMS AND DEFINITIONS

1G: 1nd generation of mobile networks.

2G: 2nd generation of mobile networks. The most dominant technology is the global system for mobility (GSM).

3G: 3rd generation of mobile networks. The most dominant technology is universal mobile telecommunication system (UMTS).

3GPP: 3rd generation partnership project.

4G: 4th generation of mobile networks. The 4G technologies are long term evolution (LTE) and the advanced version, LTE-advanced. Colloquially, the terms LTE/LTE-A are used as a synonym for 4G as they are the only global standard for mobile communication from the fourth generation.

5G: 5th generation of mobile networks. Still in standardization phase, the first 5G deployments are envisioned for 2020.

AES: Advanced encryption standard.

AICH: Acquisition indicator channel.

AK: Authentication key.

AKA: Authentication and key agreement.

ALCAP: Access link control application part.

AMF: Authenticated management field.

AMR: Adaptive multi rate.

ARFCN: Absolute radio frequency channel number.

ARQ: Automatic reply request.

AS: Access stratum.

ASME: Access security management entity.

ATM: Asynchronous transfer mode.

AuC: Authentication center.

BCCH: Broadcast control channel.

BCH: Broadcast channel.

BSC: Base station controller.

BTS: Base transceiver station.

C-RNTI: Cell RNTI.

CA: Carrier aggregation.

CC: Content-of-communication.

CCCH: Common control channel.

CK: Ciphering key.

CoMP: Coordinated multipoint.

CPICH: Common pilot channel.

CS: Circuit switched traffic.

CSI: Channel state information.

CTCH: Common traffic channel.

DCCH: Dedicated control channel.

DCH: Dedicated channel.

DL: Downlink direction of communication

DL-SCH: Downlink shared channel.

DPCCH: Dedicated physical control channel.

DPDCH: Dedicated physical data channel.

DPS: Dynamic point selection.

DRS: Demodulation reference signal.

DSSS: Direct sequence spread spectrum.

DTCH: Dedicated traffic channel.

E-AGCH: E-DCH absolute grant channel.

E-DCH: Enhanced dedicated channel.

E-DPCCH: E-DCH dedicated physical control channel.

E-DPDCH: E-DCH dedicated physical data channel.

E-HICH: E-DCH hybrid ARQ indicator channel.

E-RAB: Evolved-RAB.

E-RGCH: E-DCH relative grant channel.

EARFCN: Evolved ARFCN.

ECGI: EUTRAN global cell identity.

ECI: EUTRAN cell identity.

EEA: EPS encryption algorithm.

EIA: EPS integrity algorithm.

eLLA: Enhanced LLA.

EMM: Evolved mobility management.

eNB: Evolved NodeB.

EPC: Evolved packet core.

EPS: Evolved packet system.

ESM: Evolved session management protocols.

EUTRAN: Evolved UTRAN.

FACH: Forward access channel.

FD-MIMO: Full dimensional MIMO.

FDD: Frequency division duplex.

FDMA: Frequency division multiple access.

FFT: Fast Fourier transformation.

GBR: Guarantied bit rate.

GERAN: GPRS radio access network.

GMLC: Gateway mobile location center.

GPRS: General packet radio service.

GRE: Generic routing encapsulation.

GSM: Global system for mobile.

GTP-C: Gateway tunneling protocol control part.

GTP-U: GTP user part.

GUMMEI: Globally unique MME identity.
GUTI: Global unique temporal identity.
HE: Home environment.
HI1: Handover interface 1.
HI2: Handover interface 2.
HI3: Handover interface 3.
HLR: Home location register.
HPLMN: Home public land mobile network.
HS-DPCCH: High-speed dedicated physical control channel.
HS-DSCH: High-speed downlink shared channel.
HS-PDSCH: High-speed physical downlink shared channel.
HS-SCCH: High-speed shared control channel.
HSDPA: High-speed packet downlink access.
HSPA: High-speed packet access.
HSS: Home subscriber server.
HSUPA: High-speed uplink packet access.
IFFT: Inverse fast Fourier transformation.
IIF: Internal interception function.
IK: Integrity key.
IMEI: International mobile equipment identity.
IMS: Internet multimedia subsystem.
IMSI: International mobile subscriber identity.
IMT-2000: International mobile telecommunications-2000 requirements.
IN: Intelligent network.
IoT: Internet-of-things.
IP: Internet protocol.
IRI: Interception-related information.
ISDN: Integrated service digital network.
ITU: International Telecommunication Union.
IU-UP: Iu interface user part.
JT: Joint transmission.
LA: Location area.
LAA: Licensed assisted access.
LAC: Location area code.
LAI: Location area identity.
LALS: Lawful access location services.
LCS: Location services.
LEA: Law enforcement agencies.
LEMF: Law enforcement monitoring facility.

LI: Lawful interception.

LMU: Location measurement units.

LTE: Long-term evolution.

LWA: LTE-WLAN aggregation.

M-TMSI: MME TMSI.

MAC: Medium access control/message authentication code.

MBMS: Multimedia broadcast multicast services.

MCC: Mobile country code.

MCCH: Multicast control channel.

MCH: Multicast channel.

ME: Mobile equipment.

MGW: Media gateway.

MIB: Master information block.

MIMO: Multiple in multiple out radio transmission.

MM: Mobility management.

MME: Mobility management entity.

MMEC: MME code.

MMEGI: MME group identity.

MNC: Mobile network code.

MSCS: MSC-server.

MSISDN: Mobile subscriber ISDN number.

mMTC: Massive machine type communication.

MTCH: Multicast traffic channel.

MU-MIMO: Multi user MIMO.

NAS: Non-access stratum.

NB-IoT: Narrowband-IoT.

NBAP: NodeB application part (NBAP).

OFDM: Orthogonal frequency division multiplexing.

OFDMA: Orthogonal frequency division multiple access.

P-GW: Packet gateway.

P-TMSI: Packet TMSI.

PBCH: Physical broadcast channel.

PCCH: Paging control channel.

PCCPCH: Primary common control physical channel.

PCFICH: Physical control format indicator channel.

PCH: Paging channel.

PCI: Physical cell identity.

PCRF: Policy charging rules functions.

PCU: Packet control unit.

PDCCH: Physical downlink control channel.

PDCP: Packet data convergence protocol.

PDSCH: Physical downlink shared channel.

PHICH: Physical hybrid ARQ indicator channel.

PHY: Physical layer.

PICH: Paging indicator channel.

PLMN_ID: PLMN identifier.

PMCH: Physical multicast channel.

PMIP: Proxy mobile IP.

PRACH: Physical random access channel.

PS: Packet switched traffic.

PSC: Primary scrambling code.

PSS: Primary synchronization signal.

PUCCH: Physical uplink control channel.

PUSCH: Physical uplink shared channel.

QAM: Quadrature amplitude modulation.

QCI: QoS class identifier.

QoS: Quality-of-service.

QPSK: Quadrature phase shift keying.

R-PDCCH: Relay physical downlink control channel.

RA: Routing area.

RAB: Radio access bearer.

RACH: Random access channel.

RAI: Routing area identity.

RANAP: Radio access network application part.

RF: Radio frequency.

RLC: Radio link control.

RN: Relay nodes.

RNC: Radio network controller.

RNTI: Radio network temporary identifier.

RRC: Radio resource control.

RSCP: Received signal code power.

RSRP: Received signal received power.

RSRQ: Reference signal receive quality.

RSSI: Received signal strength indicator.

S-GW: Serving gateway.

S-TMSI: Service TMSI.

S1-AP: S1 application protocol.

SAC: Service area code.

SAE: System architecture evolution.

SAI: Service area identity.

SC-FDMA: Single carrier frequency division multiple access.

SCCPCH: Secondary common control physical channel.

SCH: Synchronization channel.

SCTP: Stream control transmission protocol.

SDH: Synchronous digital hierarchy.

SGSN: Serving GPRS support node.

SIB: System information block.

SM: Session management.

SMLC: Serving mobile location center.

SN: Serving network.

SQN: Sequence number.

SRB: Signaling radio bearers.

SRS: Sounding reference signal.

SS#7: Signaling system no. 7.

SSCF-UNI: Specific coordination function – user network interface protocol.

SSCOP: Service specific connection-oriented protocol.

SSS: Secondary synchronization signal.

SU-MIMO: Single user MIMO.

TA: Tracking area.

TAC: Tracking area code.

TAI: Tracking area identity.

TD-SCDMA: Time division synchronous code division multiple access.

TDD: Time division duplex.

TDMA: Time division multiple access.

TLLI: Temporary logical link identifier.

TMSI: Temporary IMSI.

U-NII: Unlicensed national information infrastructure.

UDP: User datagram protocol.

UE: User equipment.

UICC: Universal integrated circuit card.

UL: Uplink direction of communication.

UL-SCH: Uplink shared channel.

UMTS: Universal mobile telecommunication system.

URA: UTRAN registration areas.

USIM: Universal subscriber identity module.

UTRAN: UMTS terrestrial radio access network.
VLR: Visitor location register.
VoIP: Voice-over-IP.
VoLTE: Voice-over-LTE.
VPLMN: Visiting public land mobile network.
WCDMA: Wideband code division multiple access.
X2-AP: X2-application protocol.

Chapter 6

Mobile Network Forensics:
General Principles and Legal Aspects

ABSTRACT

The sensitive nature of mobile network forensics requires careful organization of the investigative processes and procedures to ensure legal compliance and adequate privacy protection. Investigations in mobile networking environments can be conducted for two main purposes: (1) to reconstruct criminal activities facilitated by a use of a mobile service and (2) to attribute malicious attacks targeting the normal operation of the mobile infrastructure. In both cases, investigators need to know the concepts introduced in the previous chapters to operationalize any mobile network related investigation. This chapter elaborates the legal framework, the general investigative principles, and evidence types characteristic for investigations in mobile network infrastructures.

INTRODUCTION

This chapter introduces the general principles of mobile network forensics together with the legal framework legislating investigations that aim to uncover mobile network evidence. Two main types of forensic investigations are covered, one concerning mobile network facilitated crime and other concerning mobile network targeted attacks. For the purpose of mobile facilitated crime reconstruction, the required architecture and necessary mechanisms for lawful interception and localization are described, together with the corresponding

DOI: 10.4018/978-1-5225-5855-2.ch006

sources of mobile network evidence. For attributing mobile network targeted attacks, the utilization of the network performance measurement architecture for forensic purposes is explained in reference to known attacks against mobile networks. A review of the legal framework including the main interception laws is provided to assist with operationalization of the investigative principles and products elaborated throughout the chapter.

MOBILE NETWORK FORENSICS

Definition

Mobile network forensics is a cross-discipline of digital forensics and mobile networks. Digital forensics is the application of scientific methods to investigate evidence from digital sources about security incidents or criminal activities (Palmer, 2001; Ruan *et al.*, 2011). Mobile networks are a rich source of digital evidence and as such can help reconstruct any criminal activities facilitated by or targeted towards the network infrastructure. Formally, *mobile network forensics* refer to the scientific methods for identification, collection, acquisition, and preservation of digital evidence from mobile network infrastructures for further analysis, interpretation, and presentation in investigating security incidents and criminal activities. Mobile network forensics can also be denoted as *cellular network forensics*, referring to the cellular organization of the radio network subsystems.

Purpose and Investigative Types

The goal of the mobile network forensics is to investigate *mobile network facilitated crimes* and *mobile network targeted attacks* for the purpose of crime reconstruction or attack attribution, respectively. Mobile network facilitated crimes refer to any crimes carried out with the direct support of the network (e.g. perpetrators using mobile phones to communicate with each other) or the network is incidental to the crime (e.g. the network can provide historical data about perpetrators' past movements or their subscription data). Mobile targeted attacks refer to any malicious or incidental activities aiming to disrupt the normal operation of the network (e.g. botnets of mobile users trying to saturate the network with large amount of bogus connection requests or traffic).

In general, the mobile network forensics investigations can be conducted in *real time*, *non-real* time, or the investigation can be combined. The real time mobile network forensics work with evidence created or exchanged over the network at the time of the investigation. When investigating mobile network facilitated crimes in real time, active telephone conversations, user browsing sessions, or chat or Short Message Service (SMS) messages may be warranted by a Law Enforcement Agency (LEA) to preserve any communication pertinent to suspected criminal activities. Also, the LEA might request the geographical coordinates of an active mobile user(s) or its serving cell so it can localize her/him in real time. On the other side, the focus of the real-time investigation of mobile network targeted attacks is on uncovering irregular and/or malicious or user traffic flows, together with localizing potentially affected cells or location/routing/tracking areas.

The non-real time mobile network forensics work with evidence stored in the network in relation to past user or infrastructural activities. Such evidence includes Charging Data Records (CDRs), Operations, Administration and Maintenance (OA&M) data like network performance measurements, administration logs, or data from forensic radio surveys of the access network. In practice, most of the mobile network forensic investigations combine real and non-real time data when reconstructing crimes or attributing attacks. For example, suspected criminal activities are reconstructed both with conversations and CDR/subscription data or network radio localization information and forensics radio surveys. Similarly, mobile network targeted attacks are attributed using captured irregular/malicious traffic flows compared to the normal network performance. Table 1 lists several examples of potential mobile network evidence for each type of investigation in both real and non-real time.

General Principles

The comparison between the traditional and mobile is shown in Table 2. The mechanisms for mobile network forensic processing are Lawful Interception (LI) and Lawful Access Location Services (LALS), with potential heuristic analysis of the network topology for localization or detection of irregular/malicious traffic patterns. Mobile network forensics extend the traditional analysis of packet related data to include the circuit-switched and infrastructural data. It must be noted that all data other than the actual user traffic is referred to as mobile network meta-data.

Table 1. Mobile network forensics – investigative types

	Time of investigation	
	Real time	**Non-real time**
Mobile network facilitated crimes	Conversations, internet sessions, SMS/chat messages, cell ID(s), estimated geolocation	CDRs, subscriber provisions, network elements' logs, O&M data, forensic radio surveys
Mobile network targeted attacks	Irregular and/or malicious or traffic flows, cell IDs, location/routing/tracking areas;	Subscriber provisions, traffic load information; network administration logs, network performance measurements, forensic radio surveys

The forensic processing is mainly centralized at the Law Enforcement Monitoring Facility (LEMF) (or accredited digital forensics laboratory) where the LEA has active evidence delivery interfaces with each operator that offers mobile services in its jurisdiction (this is the general case, but it may differ depending on the national/state regulations). There is a possibility for decentralized mobile network processing in cases where the evidence need to be collected from multiple infrastructures from different jurisdictions (e.g. user subjected of investigation connects to visiting networks in roaming) so multiple LEAs need to work on evidence acquisition and consolidation. As already mentioned, the investigation can be both in real and non-real time, with the purpose of attribution, crime reconstruction, or evidence validation.

Lawful Interception (LI)

Lawful Interception (LI) refers to the legally provisioned action performed by a mobile network operator to make the communication and communication related information available to one or more LEAs, as shown in Figure 1 and defined in the TS 33.106 technical specification (3rd Generation Partnership Project, 2017e). In mobile network forensics terms, this refers to the identification, collection and acquisition, and preservation of the user and traffic, both in real and non-real time (sometimes referred to as *active interception* or *authorized surveillance* and *passive collection* of mobile network data, respectively).

To support mobile network forensics investigations, network operators and LEAs need to establish channels for administrative delivery of the interception requests and technical delivery of the intercepted evidence. The administrative requests containing information on the user and/or services subject of investigation are communicated over the Handover Interface 1 – HI1.

Table 2. Comparison between traditional network forensics and mobile network forensics

Category	Traditional Network Forensics	Mobile Network Forensics
Mechanism	Logging	Lawful Interception (LI) and Lawful Access Location Services (LALS)
	Packet Marking	
	Heuristic Base	Network infrastructural analysis, forensic radio surveys (e.g. traffic load/distribution, interference, weak coverage, high traffic/user cells areas)
Data Source	Traffic	User traffic, both circuit-switched and packet-switched
	Meta-data	traffic (communication-associated and location-associated control traffic), infrastructural information
	Traffic and meta-data	Combination of both
Data Instance	Traffic header	Investigation based only on mobile network meta-data
	Traffic payload	Investigation based only on mobile user traffic
	Traffic flow	Combination of both
	Network node	Analysis of the network elements and subsystems
Forensic Processing	Centralized	Law Enforcement Monitoring Facility (LEMF)
	Decentralized	Cross-jurisdictional LEA collaboration

The results of the interception are communicated over the HI2 interface for the mobile network meta-data and are referred to as the *Interception Related Information* (IRI). The intercepted user traffic as evidence is communicated over the HI3 interface and is referred to as the *Content of Communication* (CC).

The LI feature can be invoked for a particular user (e.g. user in her/his home network or when in roaming), or a mobile service (e.g. all calls from originating from a given cell) within a particular jurisdiction if that is legally permitted. 3GPP requires the LI to be *undetectable* to the subject(s) of interception or any involved communication parties, i.e. it must take place without their knowledge. Also, the invocation of the LI function must not affect the normal operation of the network. When the network provides the ciphering for the user and/or traffic (e.g. end-to-end encryption), it provides the respective ciphering keys to the LEA for the evidence decryption. In cases where the user traffic is ciphered by a third party (i.e. VoIP encryption), the third party needs to provide the decryption keys to the LEA (out of the scope for the mobile network operator).

Figure 1. General LI Architecture

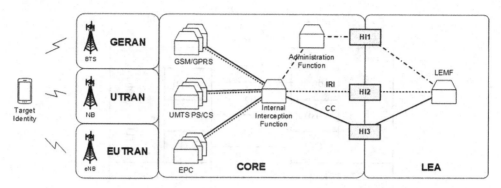

The protocol implementation of each of these interfaces is shown in Figure 2. The LI application layer is responsible for delivery of the administrative messages on the HI1 interface, the IRI records on the HI2 interface, and the CC on the HI3 interface. It is also responsible for encryption (using Advanced Encryption Standard - AES, Blowfish, or Triple Digital Encryption Standard - DES algorithms), integrity protection (using the SHA-1 algorithm), and periodic authentication checks (using Digital Signature Standard - DSS algorithm). The keys for the encryption and authentication algorithms are negotiated during the forensic readiness phase between the operators and the LEAs and implemented in the Internal Interception Function (IIF) on the operator side, and in the Law Enforcement Monitoring Facility (LEMF) on the LEA side. The specific implementation of the security algorithms is further described in the TS 102.232 technical specification (European Telecommunications Standards Institute, 2016).

For the LEMF to be able to delineate and distinguish between different LI application messages, a LI session layer is needed to encapsulate the IRI records and CC protocol data units before it sends them over a TCP/IP connection. The encapsulation is realized using the ISO Transport Service on top of TCP (ITOT) - also referred to as TPKT – and sent over port 106 (Pouffary and Young, 1997). The LI session layer is also responsible for implementing the "keep-alive" mechanism and buffering of the messages exchanged in a LI session between the Internal Interception Function (IIF) and LEMF. Since the LI protocol stack is implemented over Transmission Control Protocol/ Internet Protocol (TCP/IP), it is recommended that the operators and the LEA utilize IPSec for transportation level security protection.

Figure 2. LI protocol stack

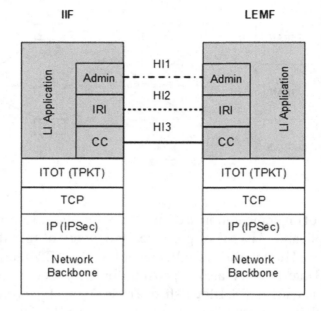

The LI is invoked based on a lawfully authorized *interception configuration information* that specifies the *target identity* (e.g. Mobile Subscriber ISDN number - MSISDN, International Mobile Subscriber Identity - IMSI, or International Mobile Equipment Identify - IMEI) and the *target service* for interception (i.e. voice calls, SMS messages, etc.). Every target identity is assigned a Lawful Interception Identifier (LIID) and used for both circuit-switched and packet-switched mobile services so the LEA can consolidate different evidence data for a given target identity of interest. The LIID for US operators is 25 alphanumeric string denoted as *CaseIdentity* (i.e. FBI-12345, CPD-12345) as specified in the J-STD-25 Technical Specification for North America (Alliance for Telecommunications Industry Solutions, 2003). For LI of circuit-switched services, 3GPP defines these identifiers:

1. **Communication Identifier (CID):** Used to distinguish between different user activities (i.e. receiving an SMS while web browsing). It consists of the Network Element Identifier (NEID) and the Communication Identity Number (CIN)
2. **Network Element Identifier (NEID):** The IP addresses and/or E.164 address of the network elements (see the Addressing and Network Identifiers sections in Chapter 4 and Chapter 5)

3. **Communication Identity Number (CIN):** Temporary identifier, operator specific
4. **CC Link Identifier (CCID):** Used to distinguish between interception information for active calls
5. **Network Identifier (NID):** Uniquely identifies the mobile network that provides the LI feature i.e. PLMN-ID (MCC+MNC). Optionally, this identifier can contain the NEID
6. **Correlation Number:** Unique number per user connection, session, bearer, or Gateway Tunneling Protocol (GTP) tunnel. Used to correlate CC with IRI, different IRI in a same session/bearer/tunnel, or correlate LALS reports with IRI records for localization proposes when both the location and the service of the user are intercepted.

For LI of packet-switched services, 3GPP defines these additional identifiers:

1. Network Element Identifier (NEID)
2. **Correlation Number:** This is a unique number identifying one or more concurrent user sessions (e.g. PDP context)

The administrative messages sent on the HI1 every time the LI is activated/ modified/deactivated for all target identities have a form of a special IRI-REPORT record (see Table 5 and 6) that includes:

1. **Lawful Interception Identifier (LIID):** Unique identifier for the target identity subject of LI
2. **Network Identifier (NID):** Unique identifier of the operator that provides the LI feature
3. **Broadcast Area Identifier (BID):** Identifier used to identify to which geographical/logical area the LI is applied. It can be also used to distinguish between the network type where the LI is invoked, i.e. GSM, UMTS, LTE, CS only, PS only, etc.
4. **Delivery Information:** IP addresses of Handover Interface 2 (HI2) and Handover Interfaces 3 (HI3)
5. **LI Activated Time (generalized UTC format):** Time the LI is activated
6. **LI Deactivated Time (generalized UTC format):** Time the LI is deactivated
7. **LI Setup Time (generalized UTC Format):** Time the LI warrant is administered in the Administration Function and LEMF

8.   **Type of Interception:** Voice IRI and CC, voice IRI only, data IRI and CC, data IRI only, voice and data IRI and CC, voice and data IRI only

Lawful Access Location Services (LALS)

Lawful Access Location Services (LALS) refers to the legally provisioned action performed by a mobile network operator to make the location information available to one or more LEAs. Mobile networks provide so-called Location Services (LCS) that utilize the geographical location of the user (e.g. emergency calls, recommendation of social events or places, advertising, sales promotions, location dependent billing, lawful localization, etc.). For this purpose, mobile networks need to have capabilities to position a mobile user in space and time based on signal measurements in the radio access network with certain precision, accuracy, and timing (e.g. three-dimensional coordinates within a range of 100 meters for 80% of the localizations and time-to-first-fix or TTFF of less than 30 seconds). The lawfully provisioned positioning is also referred to as *location interception.*

The general LCS architecture for all generations of mobile networks is shown in Figure 3 as specified in the TS 22.071 technical specification (3rd Generation Partnership Project, 2015). Each of the radio access networks have implemented so-called Location Measurement Units (LMU) in the respective base stations. LMUs communicate with their respective Service Mobile Location Centers (SMLC) using either the Radio Resource LCS protocol (RRLP), Mobile Location Protocol (MLP), or LTE Positioning Protocol (LPP) protocols. All SMLCs are connected to a central Gateway Mobile Location Center (GMLC). The GMLC delivers the location information to external LCS clients. In case of LALS, the client is one or more LEAs, so the localization information can be used for forensic purposes.

The location information for a given target identity is derived using various positioning methods, described in the TS 36.305 technical specification (3rd Generation Partnership Project, 2017g):

1.   **Cell-based positioning (Enhanced Cell ID - ECID):** In this positioning method, the coordinates of the mobile devices are derived from the coordinates of the serving cell by measuring either the Round-Trip Time (RTT) or the Angle-of-Arrival (AoA) of a reference signal between one or three base stations and the mobile device (known also as *triangulation*). The precision of the cell coverage positioning is between 50 m and 1 km, but the TTFF is less than a few seconds for more than 90% accuracy.

Figure 3. General LCS Architecture

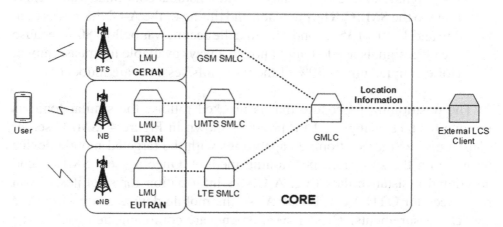

2. **Observed Time Difference of Arrival (OTDOA):** In this positioning method, the mobile device measures the Time-of-Arrival (TOA) for the downlink reference signals received from multiple base stations (at least three) and subtracts it from a reference TOA from it serving station (known also as *multilateration*). The measurements are known as Received Signal Time Difference (RSTD) and are described in TS 36.214 technical specification (3rd Generation Partnership Project, 2017f). Each of the RSTD describe a hyperbola or ellipsoid so intersection of their focus lines provides the 2 or 3 dimensional coordinates of the mobile device. The precision of the OTDOA is less than 50 m with a TTFF of around 10 seconds, but less than 70% accuracy.

3. **Uplink Time Difference of Arrival (UTDOA):** This is a similar positioning method as OTDOA in which the LMUs measure the time difference of arrival of the uplink reference signals from the mobile device. The advantage of the UTDOA is that it requires minimum mobile device involvement, so it improves the accuracy to more than 90% while retaining the same precision and timing as OTDOA.

4. **Assisted Global Navigation Satellite Systems (A-GNSS):** The standalone navigation based on Global Positioning Systems (GPS) requires unobstructed line-of-sight between the mobile user and at least four satellites. Given that most of the time users are indoor and cannot satisfy this requirement, mobile networks assist the users by suppling information about the availability and configuration of GPS satellites to the user. The user then uses this information to measure the available

GPS signals so it can calculate its 3 dimensional coordinates and report them to the SMLC. The precision and timing of the A-GNSS is less than 1 m and TTFF of 35 seconds, though the accuracy is bellow 80% because the GPS signals needed might not be always available for measurement (for example, almost 50% of the user calls/sessions are indoor).

The positioning procedure that is invoked follows the similar logic as the one for LTE using the LPP protocol shown in Figure 4. SMLC server communicates the positioning capabilities with the targeted mobile device to agree on the supported positioning method. Once agreed, SMLC send additional assistance data (e.g. A-GNSS information for satellites, signal references for OTDOA or UTDOA) so the mobile device can perform the RSTD measurements. These measurements are communicated back to the SLMC and depending on the localization method provide the information on mobile device's latitude sign, latitude, longitude, altitude, altitude direction, and optionally, its relative velocity. The details of the reporting parameters and their formatting is specified in the TS 36.355 technical specification (3rd Generation Partnership Project, 2017h).

Figure 4. LTE LCS positioning procedure

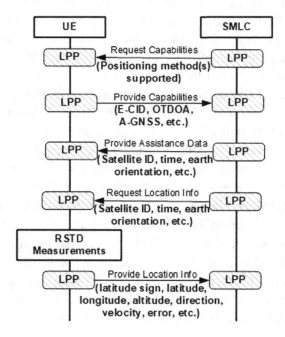

As a GMLS client, LEA can use the LALS by invoking the LCS function for two specific interception-related applications, *target positioning* and *enhanced location for IRI*. The target positioning is used to determine the target's location independently of the services used by the target and can be invoked in two modes, for an *immediate* localization or *periodic* localization. The immediate localization is invoked when LEA needs to determine the real-time location of the target, while the periodic localization is used in non-real time cases where LEA can track the movement of the target over a longer period of time. As such, it can specify the reporting interval and the number of reports it needs from the SMLC depending on the tracking granularity needed. In cases where the LEA needs to localize a target when she/he uses a specific service, for example receives an incoming call, the enhanced location for IRI application is used. Both location-based interception applications are discussed in more detail in Chapter 7.

Network Infrastructure Analysis

The network topology analysis refers to the analysis of malicious or irregular user or traffic behavior on a network level. As discussed in Chapter 5 and summarized in Table 3, there are various types of mobile-network targeted attacks (Mavoungou *et al.*, 2016). The network infrastructure analysis helps in reconstruction of the security mechanisms attacks by providing a proof-of-concept that demonstrates the feasibility of the attack in the real networking environment. The proof-of-concept can be used in conjunction with the information on the user subscriber provisions (e.g. HLR profile, historical CDR data) or network configuration (security architecture setup, key management) to demonstrate the existence of the vulnerability and the potential exploit in a given related to a particular user.

The analysis of /user traffic trends (peak busy hours, cells/areas with high load, percentage of dropped traffic/ channels and similar key performance indicators) are used in investigating abnormal behavior experienced by the network, including radio jamming. Although rare, cases of insider threats and installation of malicious network software exists (Androulidakis, 2016). For these types of mobile network targeted attacks, the network infrastructure analysis aids the investigation by retrieving and analyzing network performance data as well as administration logs. The details on how the network infrastructure analysis is operationalized for mobile network targeted attacks are provided in Chapter 9.

Table 3. Attacks against mobile networks

Category	Attack Types	Attack Objectives
Security mechanisms attacks	Man-in-the-middle attacks	Compromise confidentiality and/or integrity of the user/ traffic; eavesdropping traffic modification; user targeted Denial-of-Service (DoS)
	IMSI catchers and user location tracking	Capturing of IMSI, luring users to rogue base stations (downgrading to GSM from UMTS/LTE); tracking their location in time/space with a cell level precision
Traffic attacks	Traffic modification	Abuse assigned Quality-of-Service (QoS), undercharging, overcharging
	Traffic based DoS	Network traffic capacity overflow, inaccessibility of user services (access to internet, ability to make /receive calls)
	Signaling Based DoS	Network capacity overflow, inaccessibility of network services (mobility support, security and authentication, roaming support)
Jamming Attacks	Targeted jamming	Jamming of uplink/downlink channels, selective jamming
	Jamming DoS	Jamming an entire GSM/UMTS/LTE band
Network administration attacks	Insider threat	Leaking confidential network/user information (topology, setups, user profiles, billing records)
	Infrastructure-targeted malware	Installing malware for unauthorized traffic handling (i.e. interception)

Types of Mobile Network Evidence

Table 4 lists the general evidence types that can be obtained from mobile network infrastructures from any generation. The content of communication represents the data transported over the mobile network corresponding to any user service. The Interception Related Information (IRI) provides the so-called mobile network meta-data, i.e. the data that provides the service context and is used on the network side to transport and realize the user service. The location information evidence is the information about the location of a mobile user as positioned by the mobile network.

The Charging Data Records (CDRs) are another type of mobile network meta-data that are generated for charging and billing purposes for every user service. Each of the core network nodes that carry user data – Mobile Switching Centers (MSC), Serving GPRS Support Node (SGSN), or Serving Gateway (S-GW) – generate CDRs that are used for postpaid charging of the user services. The Intelligent Network (IN), Online Charging Function (OCS) and the Policy Charging Rules Function (PCRF) nodes also generate CDRs with the corresponding information for prepaid charging. Any other type of subscriber or infrastructure related logs, i.e. Home Subscriber System (HSS) logs, network performance measurements, or historical data about the traffic distribution in the network, are also sources of potential evidence.

Content of Communication (CC)

The intercepted content of communication data is a copy of the application level data exchanged as part of any CS or PS user services, i.e. calls, SMS texts, browsing sessions, chats, conferences, streaming, gaming, etc. For Circuit Switched (CS) services, the CC data is the conversational stream Integrated Services Digital Network (ISDN). For Packet Switched (PS) services, the CC data is the actual user IP packet stream transported between the User Equipment (UE) and the GPRS Gateway Support Node (GGSN) or the Packet Gateway (GW). The forensic analysis of the PS CC data can be performed using the traditional network forensics tools and procedures

Table 4. Types of mobile network evidence

Type	Description	Examples
Content of Communication (CC)	Information exchanged between two or more users of a mobile service, or between users and remote servers/hosts.	User Traffic: conversations (circuit or packet switched traffic), Internet sessions, streaming video, video conferencing, gaming, SMS/chat messages, email messages, voice mail messages
Intercept Related Information (IRI)	Communication associated information. This is the mobile network meta-data; it can also include location information.	traffic: calling and called party (MSISDN, IMSI, IMEI, Cell Global Identity - CGI, Location/Routing/ Tracking Area Codes – LAC/RAC/ TAC)
Location Information	Information relating to the geographic, physical or logical location of a mobile user	cell ID(s), estimated geolocation (degrees longitude, degrees latitude, altitude and altitude direction, speed); location/routing/ tracking areas
Charging Data Records (CDR)	Formatted collection of information about a chargeable event for use in billing, generated by the nodes serving user traffic in the network	Listings of user activity including information like calling/called party, time/duration of the call source/ destination IP address, data volume, serving node address, etc.
Infrastructural Information	considered as network meta-data	Network performance measurements, network element records and logs administration logs (patching),

elaborated in Chapter 2. It must be noted that in case of an encrypted PS CC data (nowadays an increased number of applications are using end-to-end encryption), the LEA need to obtain decryption keys in accordance with the federal and/legal framework discussed later in this Chapter.

Intercept Related Information (IRI)

3GPP standardizes four types of IRI records that the network can provide to LEAs:

1. **IRI-BEGIN:** The first event of a communication attempt of the target identity; opening the IRI transaction. For example, it can be the establishment call or a notification for an incoming SMS message for CS services or a Packet Data Protocol (PDP) context activation for PS services

2. **IRI-END:** The end of a communication attempt; closing the IRI transaction for the targeted identity and/or service. For example, it can be the termination of a call for CS services or PDP Context deactivation for PS services.

3. **IRI-CONTINUE:** Intermediary record at any time during a communication within the IRI transaction. For example, this type of record is used to inform the LEA for intermediary actions like activation of call hold for CS services or change of destination addresses for users with an already active PDP context

4. **IRI-REPORT Record:** Used for non-communication related events. For example, this can be a USSD request or unsuccessful communication attempts. It is also used to deliver location information in form of LALS reports back to the LEA.

There are different types of communication events that can be reported as interception related information for CS and PS services, as listed in Table 5 and Table 6, respectively (see Appendix). All of these events represent the one or more steps of the network procedures described in Chapter 3 and Chapter 4. The IRI records are often correlated with the CC, for example an IRI-CONTINUE record for Answer (ANS message in Figure 17 in Chapter 4) is correlated with the CC record for a given CS call. Similarly, an IRI-BEGIN record for PDP context activation (Activate PDP Context Request message in Figure 20 in Chapter 5) is correlated with a CC for a packet session.

Table 7 list the parameters used with different types of CS IRI records (see Appendix). All of the service related identifiers are described in Chapter 4 and Chapter 5 in the respective User Data sections and used in the mobility management and call control of CS procedures. For example, if LEA is interested in intercepting all the incoming calls of a target identity, the associated IRI records detail the calling party, the IMEI of the device currently used by the target identity, the CGI and the location area where the call was received, the serving MSC(S) address, and the release cause at the end of the call. For SMS messaging, the IRI records contain both the SMS content and the associated communication information like the sender, receiver, the SMSC number, and the number of SMS segments, if the SMS is longer than 160 characters.

In case the HLR records for the target identity are updated, for example if the user changes the MSISDN but keeps the IMSI or keeps the MSISDN but gets a new (Universal) Subscriber Identity Module (U)SIM card with new IMSI, the IRI record contains the new MSISDN/IMSI together with the old ones. If the LEA is interested in receiving IRI records when the target identity cancels and/or updates its location, the IRI records contain the last (old) and optionally the new serving system id, for example the MSC number or the SGSN IP address.

Tables 8 list the parameters used with different types of PS IRI records corresponding to the ones used in the GSM and UMTS mobility and session management procedures (see Appendix). For example, if LEA is interested in intercepting all the browsing sessions of target identity with a particular destination IP address, the associated IRI records detail the PDP address of the target as the source IP address, the serving SGSN, the transport protocol (e.g. TCP), the source and destination ports, the packet count in the session as well as the packet sizes and their sum. In case there is a PDP context modification, for example the user changes its IP address, the IRI records contain both the old and the new address assigned by the GGSN.

Tables 9 list the parameters used with the IRI records corresponding to the ones used in the LTE mobility and session management procedures (see Appendix). Most of the parameters are similar as ones listed in Table 8, with additional parameters supporting novel mobility and session management functions (e.g. maximum bitrate for an Access Point Name (APN), lifetime of a connection, or Closed Subscriber Group (CSG) home base stations. There are multiple redundant parameters such as home address, care address, or UE address, but this are provided to support interception in cases where the user is served by difference core network subsystems, i.e. relocated between different P-GWs.

Location Information

The location information is communicated with the LEA as a IRI REPORT record that specifies the target MSISDN/IMSI, NID, LIID, and the localization type. For target positioning, the SMLC delivers records shown in Table 10 in the appendix of this chapter. For the enhanced location for IRI positioning, the SMLC delivers the same records with an addition of the CIN so they can be correlated with the associated CC and/IRI used by the target identity for a given communication (i.e. localization of a user on a specific floor in a building while sending a SMS message).

Charging Data Records (CDR)

The billing for the mobile services can be realized in two variants: *offline charging* (postpaid) - where the network elements involved in the service realization generate so called Charging Data Records (CDR) for later processing; and *online charging* (prepaid) where the service is charged in real time by an Online Charging System (IN, PCRF). The OCS also generates CDRs, which together with the offline CDRs are one of the most valuable sources of mobile network evidence. The Attribute-Value Pairs (AVP) for each of the parameters of the CDRs are further specified in the TS 32.299 technical specification (3rd Generation Partnership Project, 2014b). These parameters are prescribed by 3GPP for the purpose of standardized charging, however, different vendors have different implementation, and the configuration differs from operator to operator, which affects the consolidation and time lining during a forensic analysis and interpretation as discussed in Chapter 2.

Every CDR contains the following generic parameters, specified in the TS 32.298 technical specification(3rd Generation Partnership Project, 2014a):

1. **Service Network Identity:** The PLMN ID (Mobile Country Code - MCC + Mobile Network Code - MNC)
2. **Service Content ID:** Used to indicate weather Diameter charging was used
3. **Subscription ID:** The E.164 number of the charged party, i.e. its MSISDN
4. **Subscriber Equipment Number:** The IMEI of the charged party

Table 11 lists the common parameters for CDRs generated in the CS domain of the network, Table 12 lists the CDR parameters for an SMS service as specified in the TS 32.274 technical specification (3rd Generation Partnership Project, 2017c), while Table 13 lists the common parameters for generated in the PS domain of the mobile networks (see Appendix).

Table 14 in the appendix lists a generic set of parameters used by the OCS for the purpose of online charging. The online charging is implemented using the Diameter protocol, so these parameters correspond to the AVPs included in the Diameter protocol messages exchanged between the OCS and the core network nodes, i.e. SGSN, MME, MCSS, S/P-GW. The CDRs generated by OCS include these parameters in terms of log records for the online charging (OCS can also generate CS, SMS, and PS standard CDRs if configured by the network for unified charging purposes). More details in the implementation of the OCS charging are provided in the TS 32.296 technical specification (3rd Generation Partnership Project, 2017d).

Infrastructural Information

3GPP has standardized the network performance measurement under the Operations, Administration, and Maintenance (OA&M) function. Every practical network deployment consists of elements, segments, and logical implementations that are specific to a given operator (3rd Generation Partnership Project, 2016, 2017a, 2017b, 2017c, 2017d, 2017e). Moreover, every operator has a unique set of subscriber base, coverage, traffic demands, and set of mobile services offered that change over time. The initial idea of the OA&M function is to provide a set of Key Performance Indicators (KPI) and procedures for their measurements so the operators can aid their network planning and traffic engineering or troubleshoot for any degradation of performance, for example traffic bottle necks, loss of coverage, or inefficient network capacity utilization.

These KPIs are highly useful for investigating mobile network targeted attacks because they can help detect, identify, and collect any potential evidence about irregular or malicious traffic behavior as registered by the network performance management monitoring systems. Table 15 summarizes the KPI categories per mobile network domains with their respective technical specifications. The complete list of GSM/GPRS, UMTS, and LTE KPIs are valuable instruments in mobile network forensic terms, and investigators can work with different combinations of values, thresholds, or historic data to produce evidence and attribute mobile network targeted attacks.

For GSM/GPRS, the KPIs are further grouped by a network element, so information can be retrieved from the performance as seen by the radio access or core network. For example, the Base Station Controller (BSC) measures the number of channel requests (Chapter 4 - Figure 12) for mobile originating calls (Chapter 4 – Figure 16), the successful channel assignments, and the mean inter-arrival time for mobile originating call attempts between consecutive requests. If there is a difference between the number of channel requests and successful channel assignments in a short time period (e.g. 10 minutes, 30 minutes, 1 hour), that may suggest irregular network behavior. The number of available/busy SDCCH/TCH/PDTCH channels (Chapter 4 – Figure 12 and Figure 25) and/or number of lost radio links while using TCH/PDTCH at the Base Transceiver Station (BTS) can warn of potential degradation due to selective radio jamming or user initiated DoS.

Similarly, the total number of attempted and successful mobile originating/ terminating calls or paging requests at the MSC and insert subscriber data/ location updates at the HLR (Chapter 4 - Figure 15 and Figure 27) can provide similar indicators for network-level targeted attacks. The number of attempted and successful PDP context activations per user per hour (Chapter 4 – Figure 27), the mean and maximum number of active PDP context in the SGSN, and the mean and maximum number of active PDP contexts per APN in the GGSN are good indicators to monitor for traffic based DoS. The Equipment Identify Register (EIR) measurements may also indicated potential abnormal behavior, for example if the number of black IMEI answers considerably increases above the average number of service attempts made with blacklisted equipment.

Table 5. Mobile Network Performance KPI Domains

Domain	Technical Specifications
GSM/GPRS	TS 52.402
UTRAN	TS 32.405
Packet Switched	TS 32.406
Circuit Switched	TS 32.407
E-UTRAN	TS 32.425
Evolved Packet Core	TS 32.426

The performance measurements for UMTS are organized per domain – UTRAN, PS, CS, and IMS – and further grouped by the respective network elements. If the number of the Radio Access Bearer (RAB) or Radio Resource Control (RRC) connection establishment attempts/successes/releases for both PS and CS services (Chapter 5 – Figure 19) increases and in the same time the mean/maximum time for RRC connection usage decreases, there is a possibility for a signaling storm in the UTRAN (Gorbil *et al.*, 2015). If the number of failed radio link setups on the *Iub/Iur* interfaces increases (Chapter 5 – Tables 3 and 4) or there are spikes in the RSCP measurements (i.e. disproportionate balance between uplink and downlink or drop in quality – see Chapter 4 for the relative values), that can also be an indicator of potential malicious interference of selective jamming in the radio segment.

The traffic related attacks can also be monitored, detected, and responded to with the network level KPIs in the PS and CS domains. For example, the number of attempted and successful standalone or combined GPRS/IMSI attached procedures (Chapter 5 – Figure 20), the mean and maximum number of subscribers in PMM-CONNECTED/PMM-IDLE states (Chapter 5 – Figure 17) or the mean and maximum PDP context setup time (Chapter 5 – Figure 22) can be used for this purpose. The GTP traffic load as of number of incoming/outgoing GTP packets, active GTP tunnels and the peak number or simultaneous sessions per APN can indicate a potential DoS attack from a mobile botnet (Traynor *et al.*, 2009). There are a series of KPIs monitoring the security in the network like the number of attempted/successful Authentication and Key Agreement (AKA) procedure invocations and authentications (Chapter 5 – Figure 10, 11, and 12) and attempted/successful ciphering procedures (Chapter 5 – Figure 13) providing the possibility for close monitoring for any AKA/security related attacks targeted towards UMTS (Beekman and Thompson, 2013; Gaml, Elattar and Badawy, 2014).

The LTE KPIs are also organized by domain, one set for the EUTRAN and one for the EPC. The monitoring of Evolved-RAB (ERAB) attempts/successes (Chapter 5 – Figure 49), the Received Signal Received Signal Power (RSRP) and Received Signal Received Quality (RSRQ measurements), Packet Data Convergence (PDCP) volume measurements per cell per hour, and changes in uplink/downlink throughput can help early detection, prevention, and investigation of jamming attacks targeting the EUTRAN (Lichtman *et al.*, 2016). In response to EPC related attacks, the monitoring for overload of the network nodes (traffic and) like the mean and peak processor usage or the mean and maximum number of EPS bearers provide the necessary capability for DoS detection, prevention, and investigation on a network level (Shaik *et al.*, 2016).

LEGAL ASPECTS

In the United States, the LI and LALS are covered by the following laws:

1. Title III of the Omnibus Crime Control and Safe Streets Act (OCCSSA)
2. Electronic Communications Privacy Act (ECPA)
3. The Foreign Intelligence Surveillance Act (FISA)
4. The Communications Assistance for Law Enforcement Act (CALEA)
5. Title II of the USA Patriot Act

The Federal Bureau of Investigation (FBI) is the main LEA that works with both *facilities-based operators* and *Mobile Network Virtual Operators* (MVNOs). The facilities-based operators are the ones that own their infrastructure, i.e. Verizon Wireless, AT&T, T-Mobile US, Sprint, or U.S. Cellular and may host one or more MVNOs. MVNOs provide retail mobile services by acquiring wholesale network access from the facility based operators, i.e. they are hosted on their infrastructure and use their (U) SIM cards. The interception related legislation for the rest of the world is summarized in (Miller, 2007).

Title III of the OCCSSA

The Title III of the OCCSSA legislates LI and use of LALS for domestic law enforcement purposes (Miller, 2007). It is also known as the "Wiretap Act", that was passed by the Congress in response to the extensive wiretapping by government agencies without the consent of the parties or legal sanction. As such, it prohibits unauthorized, nonconsensual interception of "wire, oral, or electronic communications" by government agencies as well as private parties, establishes procedures for obtaining warrants to authorize wiretapping by government officials, and regulates the disclosure and use of authorized intercepted communications by investigative and law enforcement officers (US Department of Justice, 2013b). Originally, the Title III of the OCCSSA included only wire and oral communication, but was amended with the Title I of the ECPA to include electronic communication. In terms of mobile communications, the interception refers to both the circuit-switched and packet-switched traffic exchanged of the network for all home subscribers (the CC, and the associated IRI and CDRs).

Title III of the OCCSSA establishes warrant procedures consistent with the Fourth Amendment for interception and prohibits the use of illegally obtained mobile user traffic as evidence. A judge may issue a warrant authorizing interception of mobile traffic for up to 30 days upon a showing of probable cause that the interception will reveal evidence that "an individual is committing, has committed, or is about to commit a particular offense" (US Department of Justice, 2013b). From a forensic perspective, the investigation of mobile network facilitated crimes always needs to be authorized by a judicial authority.

The same holds for mobile network targeted attacks, though, there is an exception for a warrantless interception if the attack threatens to disrupt the normal activity of the mobile network infrastructure, provided is considered a critical infrastructure of national interest. Warrantless interception is also possible if it is determined that an emergency situation exists involving: immediate danger of death or serious physical injury to any person, conspiratorial activities threatening the national security interest, or conspiratorial activities characteristic of organized crime. The responsible LEA in such a case needs to apply for an order approving the interception within 48 hours after the interception has occurred, or begins to occur.

Title III of the OCCSSA establishes the minimum protection privacy protections for mobile communications, however, states may impose greater privacy protection requirements. For example, some states may require all parties to a communication to consent to a recording of it, instead of only one of them as required by Title III of the OCCSSA. For practical mobile network investigations, the US department of Justice recommends that investigators consult the state interception laws (US Department of Justice, 2013b).

ECPA

ECPA also legislates the LI and use of LALS for domestic law enforcement purposes. Title I of ECPA is also referred to as the "Wiretap Act", amending the Title III of OCCSSA to include the electronic communication. As explained in the previous three chapters, all mobile communication is exchanged in electronic form so Title I ECPA is equally relevant for conducting mobile network forensics. Title II of ECPA, known as Stored Communications Act (SCA) protects the privacy of the contents of files stored by mobile operators and of records held about their subscribers. A warrant authorization is required for forensic investigators to obtain any stored information such as subscriber name, CDRs, billing records, network identifiers, IP addresses, voice mail, or subscriber provisions for supplementary services.

Title III of ECPA requires LEA or any other government entities to obtain a court order to install pen register (a device that captures the dialed numbers and related information to which outgoing calls or communications are made by the subject) and/or a trap and trace (a device that captures the numbers and related information from which incoming calls and communications coming to the subject have originated). This vocabulary is directly derived from the circuit switched nature of the early telecommunication networks, including GSM and UMTS. As briefly elaborated in Chapter 5, mobile network from the 3rd generation onwards provide these features with the built-in LI architecture for both circuit-switched and network-switched traffic (this feature was retroactively implemented in GSM). From a forensics perspective, Title III legislates the acquisition of service associated information or data (IRI and CDRs), but not the contents of the service (the associated CC) (US Department of Justice, 2013a).

FISA

While the Wiretap Act legislates the interception of communication for US citizens, the FISA covers the wiretapping for intelligence purposes where the subject could not be a US citizen, working as an agent on behalf of a foreign country (Miller, 2007). FISA establishes procedures for the authorization of electronic surveillance (interception), use of pen registers and trap and trace devices, physical searches, and business records for the purpose of gathering foreign intelligence (US Department of Justice, 2013). For mobile networks, the required forensics capabilities are the same, only the LI and LALS need to be available for all mobile subscribers, including the visiting ones.

To invoke the electronic surveillance, investigators need to obtain warrant from the special US Foreign Intelligence Surveillance Court (FISC) Federal court. Investigators need to demonstrate probable cause to believe that the "target of the surveillance is a foreign power or agent of a foreign power," that "a significant purpose" of the surveillance is to obtain "foreign intelligence information," and that appropriate safeguards for undetectable interception are in place (unlike Title III of OCCSSA, the investigators need not to demonstrate that commission of a crime is imminent).

CALEA

The CALEA was enacted in 1994 requiring mobile operators to assist LEAs in executing electronic surveillance pursuant to a court order for both LI and LALS types of interception. CALEA requires that the LEAs need to able to access CC, IRI, CDR, and infrastructure information as noted previously in this chapter with no degradation and interference to the subscriber service while protecting the privacy and security of subscribers and the respective intercepted material. In general, mobile operators are CALEA compliant if they have implemented the LI and LALS infrastructure shown in Figure 1 and Figure 2 (with the secure interface implementation as described in Chapter 7) and follow the standardized guidelines for formatting of the mobile network forensic evidence as elaborated throughout this chapter (Department of Homeland Security, 2006).

Title II of US Patriot Act

The Title II of US Patriot Act legislates enhanced surveillance procedures by amending the FISA and ECPA to add the terrorism, computer fraud, and abuse offences to the activities that can be subjected to an electronic surveillance (interception). It changed the primary probable cause under FISA (corresponding to the Fourth Amendment) to a "significant cause" so the electronic surveillance can be invoked in cases that involve not just foreign intelligence activities (e.g. criminal activities). The pen register and trap devices are allowed to be used for both CS and PS traffic passing through the mobile infrastructure under a broader approval where LEA can obtain authorization for LI or LALS invocation by demonstrating that the CC, IRI, and CDRs are "relevant" for an investigation, rather than the previous stricter requirement to demonstrate that the target identity is explicitly involved in unauthorized activities and terrorism. Title II of US Patriot act allows LEA to obtain CC for voice messages with a search warrant without the need to obtain wiretap order as it was required previously. It also allows for sharing any intercepted material among LEAs on a nationwide level for purpose of investigative cooperation (USA Patriot Act, 2001).

CONCLUSION

The investigation of mobile network facilitated crimes mainly includes lawful interception and lawful access localization targeting mobile network users or services. In both cases, the yielding evidence can be the content of communication (or the user traffic), the interception related information (or the traffic), or the service related information (or the CDRs). Depending on whether the users are home subscribers of the network under investigation and types of criminal activities, a legal authorization must precede any identification, collection, acquisition, and preservation of the respective evidentiary data as outlined in the provision of the OCCSSA, FISA, ECPA, or Title II of the US Patriot Act. For the investigation to be operationalized, the network operators need to have the capabilities required by CALEA, i.e. have a ready implemented LI and LALS architecture as elaborated in this chapter. The yielding evidence for investigations of the mobile network targeted attacks is mainly the network infrastructural information – or the performance measurement KPIs indicating malicious traffic content or other traffic abnormalities.

REFERENCES

3rd Generation Partnership Project. (2009). *TS 23.830 V9.0.0 - Technical Specification Group Services and System Aspects; Architecture aspects of Home NodeB and Home eNodeB (Release 9)*. Sophia Antipolis, France: 3GPP.

3rd Generation Partnership Project. (2014a). *3GPP TS 32.298 -- Telecommunication management -- Charging management -- Charging Data Record (CDR) parameter description (Release 12)*. 3rd Generation Partnership Project. Available at: http://www.3gpp.org/

3rd Generation Partnership Project. (2014b). *3GPP TS 32.299 -- Telecommunication management -- Charging management -- Diameter charging applications (Release 12)*. 3rd Generation Partnership Project. Available at: http://www.3gpp.org/

3rd Generation Partnership Project. (2015). *TS 22.071 V14.1.0 - Technical Specification Group Services and System Aspects; Location Services (LCS); Service description; Stage 1 (Release 14)*. Sophia Antipolis, France: 3GPP.

3rd Generation Partnership Project. (2016). *TS 32.425 V14.1.0 - Technical Specification Group Services and System Aspects; Telecommunication management; Performance Management (PM); Performance measurements Evolved Universal Terrestrial Radio Access Network (E-UTRAN) (Release 14).* Sophia Antipolis, France: 3GPP.

3rd Generation Partnership Project. (2017a). *TS 23.066 V14.0.0 - Technical Specification Group Core Network and Terminals; Support of Mobile Number Portability (MNP); Technical realization; Stage 2 (Release 14).* Sophia Antipolis, France: 3GPP.

3rd Generation Partnership Project. (2017b). *TS 32.274 V12.2.0 - Technical Specification Group Services and System Aspects; Telecommunication management; Charging management; Short Message Service (SMS) charging (Release 14).* Sophia Antipolis, France: 3GPP.

3rd Generation Partnership Project. (2017c). *TS 32.296 V.14.0.0 - Technical Specification Group Services and System Aspects; Telecommunication management; Charging management; Online Charging System (OCS): Applications and interfaces (Release 14).* Sophia Antipolis, France: 3GPP.

3rd Generation Partnership Project. (2017d). *TS 32.405 V.14.0.0 - Technical Specification Group Services and System Aspects; Telecommunication management; Performance Management (PM); Performance measurements; Universal Terrestrial Radio Access Network (UTRAN) (Release 14).* Sophia Antipolis, France: 3rd Generation Partnership Project.

3rd Generation Partnership Project. (2017e). *TS 32.406 V.14.0.0 - Technical Specification Group Services and System Aspects; Telecommunication management; Performance Management (PM); Performance measurements Core Network (CN) Packet Switched (PS) domain (Release 14).* Sophia Antipolis, France: 3GPP.

3rd Generation Partnership Project. (2017f). *TS 32.407 V14.0.0 - Technical Specification Group Services and System Aspects; Telecommunication management; Performance Management (PM); Performance measurements; Core Network (CN) Circuit Switched (CS) domain; UMTS and combined UMTS/GSM (Release 14).* Sophia Antipolis, France: 3GPP.

3rd Generation Partnership Project. (2017g). *TS 32.426 V.14.0.0 - Technical Specification Group Services and System Aspects; Telecommunication management; Performance Management (PM); Performance measurements Evolved Packet Core (EPC) network (Release 14)*. Sophia Antipolis, France: 3GPP.

3rd Generation Partnership Project. (2017h). *TS 33.106 V14.1.0 - Technical Specification Group Services and System Aspects; 3G security; Lawful interception requirements (Release 14)*. Sophia Antipolis, France: 3GPP.

3rd Generation Partnership Project. (2017i). *TS 36.214 V14.2.0 - Technical Specification Group Radio Access Network; Evolved Universal Terrestrial Radio Access (E-UTRA); Physical layer; Measurements (Release 14)*. Sophia Antipolis, France: 3GPP.

3rd Generation Partnership Project. (2017j). *TS 36.305 V14.2.0 - Technical Specification Group Radio Access Network; Evolved Universal Terrestrial Radio Access Network (E-UTRAN); Stage 2 functional specification of User Equipment (UE) positioning in E-UTRAN (Release 14)*. Sophia Antipolis, France: 3GPP.

3rd Generation Partnership Project. (2017k). *TS 36.355 V14.2.0 - Technical Specification Group Radio Access Network; Evolved Universal Terrestrial Radio Access (E-UTRA); LTE Positioning Protocol (LPP) (Release 14)*. Sophia Antipolis, France: 3GPP.

3rd Generation Partnership Project. (2017l). *TS 52.402 V14.0.0 - Technical Specification Group Services and System Aspects; Telecommunication management; Performance Management (PM); Performance measurements - GSM (Release 14)*. Author.

Alliance for Telecommunications Industry Solutions. (2003). *J-STD-025 - Lawfully Authorized Electronic Surveillance*. Author.

Androulidakis, I. I. (2016). *Mobile Phone Security and Forensics*. New York, NY: Springer Science and Business Media. doi:10.1007/978-3-319-29742-2

Beekman, J., & Thompson, C. (2013). Breaking Cell Phone Authentication: Vulnerabilities in AKA, IMS, and Android. *7th USENIX Workshop on Offensive Technologies*, 1–10.

Department of Homeland Security. (2006). *Communications Assistance for Law Enforcement Act (CALEA), CALEA.* Available at: http://transition.fcc. gov/pshs/services/calea/

El Gaml, E. F., Elattar, H., & El Badawy, H. M. (2014). Evaluation of Intrusion Prevention Technique in LTE Based Network. *International Journal of Scientific & Engineering Research, 5*(12), 1395–1400.

European Telecommunications Standards Institute. (2016). *Lawful Interception (LI); Service-Specific Details (SSD) for IP delivery.* Sophia Antipolis, France: ETSI.

Gorbil, G., Abdelrahman, O., Pavloski, M., & Gelenbe, E. (2015). Modeling and Analysis of RRC-Based Signalling Storms in 3G Networks. *IEEE Transactions on Emerging Topics in Computing, XX*(X), 1–1.

Lichtman, M., Jover, R. P., Labib, M., Rao, R., Marojevic, V., & Reed, J. H. (2016). LTE/LTE-A Jamming, Spoofing, and Sniffing : Threat Assessment and Mitigation. *IEEE Communications Magazine, 54*(April), 54–61. doi:10.1109/ MCOM.2016.7452266

Mavoungou, S., Kaddoum, G., Taha, M., & Matar, G. (2016). Survey on Threats and Attacks on Mobile Networks. *IEEE Access - Security In Wireless Communications and Networking,* (4), 4543–4572.

Miller, H. (2007). The Ready Guide for Intercept Legislation. Academic Press.

Palmer, G. (2001). *A Road Map for Digital Forensic Research.* Academic Press.

USA Patriot Act. (2001). *USA Patriot Act of 2001.*

Pouffary, Y., & Young, A. (1997). ISO Transport Service on top of TCP (ITOT). *IETF.* Available at: https://tools.ietf.org/html/rfc2126

Rajahalme, J., Conta, A., Carpenter, B., & Deering, S. (2004). RFC 3697 - IPv6 Flow Label Specification. *IETF.* Available at: https://www.ietf.org/ rfc/rfc3697.txt

Ruan, K., Carthy, J., Kechadi, T., & Crosbie, M. (2011). Cloud forensics. *Advances in Digital Forensics 7th IFIP WG 11.9 International Conference on Digital Forensics,* 35–46. 10.1007/978-3-642-24212-0_3

Shaik, A., Borgaonkar, R., Asokan, N., Niemi, V., & Seifert, J. (2016). *Practical Attacks Against Privacy and Availability in 4G/LTE Mobile Communication Systems.* arXiv preprint, 21–24.

Traynor, P., Lin, M., Ongtang, M., Rao, V., Jaeger, T., McDaniel, P., & La Porta, T. (2009). On cellular botnets: measuring the impact of malicious devices on a cellular network core. ACM conference on Computer and communications security, 223–234. doi:10.1145/1653662.1653690

US Department of Justice. (2013). *Electronic Communications Privacy Act of 1986 (ECPA), Federal Statues*. Available at: https://it.ojp.gov/PrivacyLiberty/authorities/statutes/1285#contentTop

US Department of Justice. (2013). *The Foreign Intelligence Surveillance Act (FISA) of 1978, Federal Statues*. Available at: https://it.ojp.gov/PrivacyLiberty/authorities/statutes/1286

US Department of Justice. (2013). *Title III of the Omnibus Crime Control and Safe Streets Act (OCCSSA), Federal Statues*. Available at: https://it.ojp.gov/PrivacyLiberty/authorities/statutes/1284

KEY TERMS AND DEFINITIONS

(E)RAB: (Evolved) radio access bearer.
(U)SIM: (Universal) subscriber identity module.
3GPP: 3rd generation partnership project.
A-GNSS: Assisted global navigation satellite systems.
AAA: Authentication, authorization, accounting.
AES: Advanced encryption standard.
AKA: Authentication and key agreement.
AMR: Adaptive multi rate.
AoA: Angle-of-arrival.
APN: Access point name.
AVP: Attribute-value pairs.
BID: Broadcast area identifier.
BSC: Base station controller.
BTS: Base transceiver station.
CALEA: Communications Assistance for Law Enforcement Act.
CAMEL: Customized applications for mobile enhanced logic.
CAN: Connectivity access network.
CC: Content-of-communication.
CCID: CC link identifier.
CDR: Charging data records.

CGI: Cell global identity.

CID: Communication identifier.

CIN: Communication identity number.

CLIR: Calling line identification restriction.

CS: Circuit switched traffic.

CSG: Closed subscriber group.

DES: Digital encryption standard.

DHCP: Dynamic host configuration protocol.

DoS: Denial of service attack.

DSS: Digital signature standard.

ECID: Enhanced cell ID.

ECPA: Electronic Communications Privacy Act.

EIR: Equipment identity register.

EPC: Evolved packet core.

EUTRAN: Evolved UTRAN.

FISA: Foreign Intelligence Surveillance Act.

GERAN: GPRS radio access network.

GGSN: GPRS gateway support node.

GMLC: Gateway mobile location center.

GPRS: General packet radio service.

GPS: Global positioning system.

GSM: Global system for mobile.

GTP: Gateway tunneling protocol.

HeNB: Home eNB.

HI1: Handover interface 1.

HI2: Handover interface 2.

HI3: Handover interface 3.

HLR: Home location register.

HPLMN: Home PLMN.

HSS: Home subscriber system.

IIF: Internal interception function.

IMEI: International mobile equipment identity.

IMEISV: IMEI software version.

IMS: Internet multimedia subsystem.

IMSI: International mobile subscriber identity.

IN: Intelligent network.

IP: Internet protocol.

IRI: Interception-related information.

ISDN: Integrated service digital network.

ITOT: ISO transport service on top of TCP (ITOT); also referred to as TPKT.

KPI: Key performance indicators.

LAC: Location area code.

LAI: Location area identity.

LALS: Lawful access location services.

LCS: Location services.

LEA: Law enforcement agency.

LEMF: Law enforcement monitoring facility.

LI: Lawful interception.

LIID: Lawful interception identifier.

LMU: Location measurement units.

LPP: LTE positioning protocol.

LTE: Long-term evolution.

MCC: Mobile country code.

MLP: Mobile location protocol.

MME: Mobility management entity.

MMS: Multimedia message service.

MNC: Mobile network code.

MSC: Mobile switching center.

MSCS: MSC server.

MSISDN: Mobile subscriber ISDN number.

MSRN: Mobile subscriber routing number.

MVNO: Mobile network virtual operators.

NEID: Network element identifier.

NID: Network identifier.

OA&M: Operations, administration, and maintenance.

OCCSSA: Omnibus Crime Control and Safe Streets Act.

OCS: Online charging function.

OTDOA: Observed time difference of arrival.

P-GW: Packet gateway.

PCRF: Policy charging rules function.

PDCP: Packet data convergence protocol.

PDP: Packet data protocol.

PDTCH: Packet data TCH.

PLMN: Public land mobile network.

PS: Packet switched traffic.

QCI: QoS class identifier.

QoS: Quality-of-service.

RAC: Routing area code.
RAI: Routing area identity.
RRC: Radio resource control.
RRLP: Radio resource LCS protocol (RRLP).
RSCP: Received signal code power.
RSRP: Received signal received signal power.
RSRQ: Received signal received quality.
RSTD: Received signal time difference.
RTT: Round-trip time.
S-GW: Serving gateway.
SAI: Service area identity.
SCCP: Signaling connection control part.
SDCCH: Standalone dedicated control channel.
SGSN: Serving GPRS support node.
SMLC: Service mobile location centers.
SMS: Short message service.
SMSC: SMS center.
TAC: Tracking area code.
TAI: Tracking area identity.
TCH: Traffic channel.
TCP: Transmission control protocol.
TOA: Time-of-arrival.
TTFF: Time-to-first-fix.
UE: User equipment.
UMTS: Universal mobile telecommunication system.
URL: Universal resource locator.
USSD: Unstructured supplementary service data.
UTDOA: Uplink time difference of arrival.
UTRAN: UMTS terrestrial radio access network.
VPLMN: Visiting PLMN.

APPENDIX

Intercept Related Information (IRI)

Table 6. IRI Record Types for CS communication events

Communication Event	IRI Record Type
Call establishment	BEGIN
Answer	CONTINUE
Supplementary service	CONTINUE
Handover	CONTINUE
Release	END
Location update	REPORT
Subscriber controlled input	
SMS / MMS	
Serving system	
HLR subscriber record change	
Update / Cancel location	
Location information request	

Table 7. IRI Record Types for PS communication events

Communication Event	IRI Record Type
GPRS / EUTRAN attach	REPORT
GPRS / EUTRAN detach	REPORT
PDP context / bearer activation (successful)	BEGIN
PDP context / bearer modification	CONTINUE
UE Requested bearer resource modification	REPORT
PDP context / bearer activation (unsuccessful)	REPORT
Start of interception with mobile station attached	REPORT
Start of interception with PDP context active / active bearer	BEGIN or optionally CONTINUE
PDP context / bearer deactivation	END
Routing / Tracking update	REPORT
SMS / MMS	
Serving System	
Packet Data Header Information	
HLR / HSS subscriber record change	
Cancel location	
Register location	
Location information request	
IMS Start of Conference (successful)	BEGIN
IMS Start of Intercept with Conference Active	BEGIN
IMS Conference Service Party Join/Leave/Modify	CONTINUE
IMS Conference Service End (unsuccessful)	CONTINUE
IMS Conference Service End (successful)	END
IMS Start of Conference (unsuccessful)	REPORT
IMS Conference Service Creation / Update	REPORT

Table 8. Parameters for CS related IRI Records

Parameters	Description
Observed MSISDN	MSISDN of the target identity
Observed IMSI	IMSI of the target identity
Observed IMEI	IMEI of the target identity
Event type	Description of which type of event is delivered (Table 5)
Event date/time	Date of the event generation in MSC/MSCS/SMSC or HLR
Dialed number	Dialed number
Connected number	Number of the answering party (e.g. MSISDN)
Other party address	Calling party for terminating calls
Call direction	Originating/terminating in or/out
NID	Network ID
CID	Communication ID
LIID	Lawful Interception ID
LAC	Location Area Code
Location Information	LALS location information
Serving system identifier	VPLMN ID of the serving system (e.g. MSC or SGSN)
Supplementary service	e.g. Call Forward - CF, Call Hold (see Chapter 4)
Forwarded to number	Forwarded to number at CF
Call release reason	Call release reason of the target call (e.g. busy)
SMS	The content of the SMS with the sender/receiver numbers
SCI	USSD (see Chapter 4)

Table 9. Parameters for PS related IRI Records (GSM and UMTS)

Parameters	Description
Observed MSISDN	MSISDN of the target identity
Observed IMSI	IMSI of the target identity
Observed IMEI	IMEI of the target identity
Observed PDP address	IP address of the target identity
Event type	Description of which type of event is delivered (Table 5b)
Event date/time	Date of the event generation in SGSN/S-GW/PGW or HLR
Access point name	See Chapter 4 Addressing and Network Identifiers section
Initiator	User or network initiated PDP context activation/deactivation
Correlation number	Unique number for each PDP context so LEA can correlate the IRI records for given target identity
LIID	Lawful Interception ID
SMS	Packet send/received SMS

continued on following page

Table 9. Continued

Parameters	Description
Failed context activation reason	(e.g. user not reachable)
Failed attach reason	(e.g. forbidden LAI)
Service center address	E.164 address of the MSCS/SMSC
QoS	QoS class (UMTS only, see Chapter 5)
Context deactivation reason	(e.g. closed session)
NID	Network Identifier
Serving system identifier	VPLMN ID of MSC/SMSC
IP assignment	Statically or dynamically assigned
SMS originating/terminating address	Identifies the originator/recipient of the SMS message.
SMS initiator	Originating/terminating/unspecified SMS
Serving SGSN number	E.164 number of the serving SGSN
Serving SGSN address	IP address of the serving SGSN.
NSAPI	See Chapter 5 Addressing and Network Identifiers section
ULI Timestamp	Indicates the time when the User Location Information was acquired.
Destination IP address	Identifies the destination IP address of a packet.
Destination port number	Identifies the destination port number of a packet
Source IP address	Identifies the source IP address of a packet.
Source port number	Identifies the source port number of a packet.
Transport protocol	Identifies the transport protocol (i.e., Protocol Field in IPv4 or Next Header Field in IPv6.
Flow label	The field in the IPv6 header that is used by a source to label packets of a flow (Rajahalme *et al.*, 2004)
Packet count	The number of packets detected and reported in a particular packet data summary report.
Packet size	The size of a packet (i.e., Total Length Field in IPv4 or Payload Length Field in IPv6)
Packet direction	Identifies the direction of the intercepted packet
Packet data header copy	Provides a copy of the packet headers including IP layer and next layer, and extensions, but excluding content.
Summary period	Provides the period of time during which the packets of the summary report were sent or received by the target.
Sum of packet sizes	Sum of values in Total Length Fields in IPv4 packets or Payload Length Field in IPv6 packets.
Packet data summary reason	Provides the reason for a summary report.
Packet data summary	For each particular packet flow, identifies pertinent reporting information (e.g., source IP address, destination IP address, source port, destination port, transport protocol, packet count, time interval, sum of packet sizes) associated with the particular packet flow.
Requesting network identifier	The requesting network identifier PLMN ID
Requesting node type	Type of requesting node such (e.g. GMLC)

Table 10. Parameters for PS related IRI Records (LTE)

Parameters	Description
Observed MSISDN	MSISDN of the target identity
Observed IMSI	IMSI of the target identity
Observed IMEI	IMEI of the target identity
Observed PDP address	IP address of the target identity
Event type	Description of which type of event is delivered (Table 6)
Event date/time	Date of the event generation in SGSN/S-GW/PGW or HLR
Access Point Name (APN)	See Chapter 4 Addressing and Network Identifiers section
APN-AMBR	Aggregate Maximum Bit Rate for the APN
PDN type	Indicated the used IP version (IPv4, IPv6, IPv4/IPv6)
PDN address allocation	Provides the IP version (IPv4, IPv6, IPv4/IPv6) and the IP address(es) allocated for the UE.
Protocol configuration options	Are used to transfer parameters between the UE and the PDN-GW (e.g. address allocation preference by DHCP)
RAT type	Radio Access Type (e.g. GERAN, UTRAN, EUTRAN)
Initiator	User or network initiated PDP context activation/deactivation
Handover indication	Provides information that the procedure is triggered as part of a handover
Procedure transaction identifier	Identifies a set of messages belonging to the same procedure; the parameter is dynamically allocated by the UE
EPS bearer identity	Identifies an EPS bearer for one UE accessing via EUTRAN. It is allocated by the MME.
Bearer activation/ deactivation type	Indicates the type of bearer being activated/deactivated, i.e. default or dedicated.
Linked EPS bearer identity	Indicates, in case of dedicated bearer, the EPS bearer identity of the default bearer.
Switch off indicator	Indicates whether a detach procedure is due to a switch off situation or not.
Detach type	Parameter sent by the network to the UE to indicate the type of detach.
Traffic Flow Template (TFT)	Collection of all packet filters associated with the EPS bearer.
Traffic Aggregate Description (TAD)	Consists of the description of the packet filter(s) for the traffic flow aggregate.
LLID	Lawful Interception ID
Failure reason	(e.g. forbidden TAI)
Failed bearer activation reason	Reason for a failed bearer activation of the target (e.g. QoS not allowed)
Failed attach reason	Reason for a failed attach attempt of the target.
Session modification failure reason	Reason for a failed session modification attempt of the target
EPS bearer QOS	Quality of Service associated with the EPS bearer procedure.
Bearer deactivation reason	Reason for bearer deactivation of the target
NID	Network Identifier
Failed bearer modification reason	Reason for failure of bearer modification
ULI Timestamp	Indicates the time when the User Location Information was acquired.
Lifetime	Lifetime of the tunnel; it is set to a nonzero value in case of registration or lifetime extension; is set to zero in case of deregistration.
UE address info	Includes one or more IP addresses allocated to the UE.

continued on following page

Table 10. Continued

Parameters	Description
Additional parameters	Protocol configuration options
Serving MME address	The IP address of the MME
Revocation trigger	Trigger for disconnecting the UE from the network.
Home Address	Contains the UE Home IP address
Requested IPv6 Home Prefix	The IPv6 Home Prefix requested by the UE.
Care of Address	The local IP address assigned to the UE by the Access Network.
HSS/AAA address	The address of the HSS/AAA triggering a P-GW reallocation.
Target PDN-GW address	The address of the PDN-GW which the UE will be reallocated to.
Foreign domain address	The relevant IP address in the foreign domain.
Visited network identifier	An identifier that allows the home network to identify the visited network inside the EPS Serving System
DHCP v4 Address Allocation Indication	Indicates that DHCPv4 is to be used to allocate the IPv4 address to the UE
Serving Network	(e.g. EPC, UMTS or GPRS core)
Request type	Provides the type of UE requested PDN connectivity
Failed reason	Provides the failure cause for UE requested PDN connectivity
Destination IP address	Identifies the destination IP address of a packet.
Destination port number	Identifies the destination port number of a packet
Source IP address	Identifies the source IP address of a packet.
Source port number	Identifies the source port number of a packet.
Transport protocol	Identifies the transport protocol (i.e., Protocol Field in IPv4 or Next Header Field in IPv6.
Flow label	The field in the IPv6 header that is used by a source to label packets of a flow (Rajahalme *et al.*, 2004)
Packet count	The number of packets detected and reported in a particular packet data summary report.
Packet size	The size of a packet (i.e., Total Length Field in IPv4 or Payload Length Field in IPv6)
Packet direction	Identifies the direction of the intercepted packet (from target or to target)
Packet data header copy	Provides a copy of the packet headers including IP layer and next layer, and extensions, but excluding content.
Summary period	Provides the period of time during which the packets of the summary report were sent or received by the target.
Sum of packet sizes	Sum of values in Total Length Fields in IPv4 packets or Payload Length Field in IPv6 packets.
Packet data summary reason	Provides the reason for a summary report.
Packet data summary	Reporting information (See Table 8)
CSG Information	Closed Service Group (CSG) service information – this is a service provided by a network for home base stations (HeNB) as specified in TS 23.830 technical specification (3rd Generation Partnership Project, 2009)
Requesting network identifier	The requesting network identifier PLMN ID
Requesting node type	Type of requesting node such (e.g. GMLC)

Location Information

Table 11. LALS Location Information IRI Records

Parameters	Description
Observed MSISDN	MSISDN of the target identity
Observed IMSI	IMSI of the target identity
Observed IMEI	IMEI of the target identity
Event type	Description of which type of event is delivered (Table 5 and 6)
Event date/time	Date of the event generation in MSC/MSCS/SMSC or HLR
NID	Network ID
LIID	Lawful Interception ID
CID*	Communication ID *only used for Enhanced Location for IRI REPORT records
Location Information	CGI, longitude, latitude, latitude sign, altitude, altitude direction, velocity (see TS 36.355 for formatting and options)
Extended Location Parameters	3D positioning, precision/accuracy of the positioning method
LALS Error code	Error code if the localization is not successful

Charging Data Records (CDRs)

Table 12. CS domain CDR parameters

Parameters	Description
Basic Service	Type of the service provided to the user, i.e. teleservice for establishing mobile originating calls
Call Duration (seconds/milliseconds)	For completed calls, this is the duration from answer to release of the call; for incomplete calls, this is the duration from allocation to the release of the traffic channel.
Call Reference	Unique identifier for the CS service in the generating element
Calling Number	MSISDN of the user initiating the call
Called Number	The number dialed by the user initiating the call
Connected Number	MSISDN of the user receiving the call, the actual party reached by the calling number (in case of call forwarding, this is the number to which the intendent call recipient has forwarded her/his calls)
Translated Number	The number used by the MSC to translate the number to a E.164 routable number (international calls, for example)
Called Party Number	This is the number of the call recipient of the CAMEL service is used during the call setup
Incoming/Outgoing Trunk	Indicates the trunks on which the calls are received/transmitted to and from the MSC, e.g. BSS trunk or fixed network trunk
IMEI Check Event	The type that caused the check for IMEI, i.e. mobile originating call

continued on following page

Table 12. Continued

Parameters	Description
IMEI Status	Whitelisted, Graylisted, Blacklisted (See Chapter 4)
Jurisdiction Information Parameter (JIP)	Used to indicate the geographical location of the originating exchange placing the IAM message (Chapter 4 – Figure 16; Chapter 5 – Figure 20). This used to support Mobile Number Portability (MNP) service where the users are allowed to keep their MSISDNs while changing their (U)SIM and IMSI. It is a 6 or 10-digit number in format NPA-XXXXXX (3rd Generation Partnership Project, 2017a)
JIP Query Indicator	Status of the query to the Number Portability Data Base (NPDB) containing the most recent mapping between the MSISDN and the corresponding IMSI
LCS Cause	Cause for optionally unsuccessful localization request
LCS Client Identity	The Identity of the LCS client, it can be LEA in case of LALS
LCS Priority	The priority of the location service (i.e. high priority for emergency localization)
Location Information	CGI, longitude, latitude, latitude sign, altitude, altitude direction, velocity (see TS 36.355 for formatting and options)
LCS QoS	The precision/accuracy/TTFF level (i.e. less than 5 meters, 50% of the LCS requests, and less than 30 seconds for TTFF)
Location/Change of Location	Location Area Code (LAC), Cell Identity (CI) and MCC+MNC of the cells serving the active call/session (See Chapter 4)
Location Routing Number	This the number used for the user the be reached in case it has ported to another mobile operator
MSC Address	The E.164 number of the MSC that generated the record
MSC Server Indicator	Indication whether a CAMEL service is used
Number of forwarding	The number of times a call has been forwarded before the HLR is interrogated for a MSRN
Positioning Data	CGI, longitude, latitude, latitude sign, altitude, altitude direction, velocity (see TS 36.355 for formatting and options)
Privacy Override	Indicates if the privacy of the user is overridden by the LCS client (i.e. this is the case for LALS so the LEA can link the location information with the MSISDN/IMSI/IME of interest)
Radio Channel	Full rate or hall rate channels for calls
Record type	Type of the CDR, i.e. Mobile Originating Call, Mobile Terminating Call, or Mobile Originating/Terminating SMS
Routing Number	The MSRN of the called party
Served IMEI	The IMEI/IMEISV of the calling party
Served IMSI	The IMSI of the calling party
Served MSISDN	The MSISDN of the calling party
Service Center Address	MSC or SMSC address
Speech version supported/used	Speech codec, i.e. GSM speech, Adaptive Multi Rate (AMR)
Supplementary services	Indicates the supplementary services used by the calling party, e.g. CLIR (to restrict presenting her/his number to the called party – "Caller Unknown")
System Type	GERAN or UTRAN
Update Result	Result of the location update procedure (Chapter 4 – Figure 15)

Table 13. SMS CDR parameters

Parameters	Description
Event Timestamp	Event triggering the SMS
Local Record Sequence Number	The sequence number of the CDR created by the serving node, e.g. SMSC
Message Class	e.g. personal, advertisement, information service
Message Reference	The identity of the entity that submitted the SMS
Message Size	Length of the SMS text part
Originator IMSI	The IMSI of the SMS sender
Originator MSISDN	The MSISDN of the SMS sender
Originator Info	Info of the entity sending the SMS if different than a mobile user (e.g. SMS gateway, email user) – E.164 address, SCCP address, email address
RAT Type	Type of access network used for the SMS transaction
Recipient IMSI	The IMSI of the SMS receiver
Recipient MSISDN	The MSISDN of the SMS receiver
Recipient Info	Info of the entity receiving the SMS if different than a mobile user (e.g. SMS gateway, email user) – E.164 address, SCCP address, email address
Served IMEI	IMEI/IMESV of the SMS sender
SM Data Coding Scheme	Bit encoding scheme for the SMS
SM Delivery Report Requested	Indicates whether the sender has requested a delivery report for the SMS
SM Serving Node	The MSC/SGSN/MME serving he user
SMS Node Address	E.164 number of the node that generated the CDR
SMS Result	e.g. submission or delivery
Submission Time	Timestamp when the submitted SMS arrived at the originating SMS node (e.g. MSC/SGSN/MME)
User Location Info	(E)CGI, LAI/SAI/RAI/TAI

Table 14. PS domain CDR parameters

Parameters	Description
APN Name/Operator Identifier	The APN name and PLMN-ID of the serving network (See section Addressing and Numbering for GPRS in Chapter 4)
APN Rate Control	i.e. the maximum allowed bitrate
Cause for Record Closing	e.g. SGSN change, S/P-GW change, intersystem handover between UMTS and GSM, or Radio Access Technology Change (UTRAN to EUTRAN)
Cell Identifier	Cell ID for GERAN; SAC for UTRAN
Duration	Duration of the PS service (Chapter 5 – Figure 21)
Dynamic Address Flag	i.e. wither the user has been assigned static or DHCP address
Enhanced Diagnostics	Set of causes for release of the connection, e.g. forbidden RA/TA
EPC QoS Information	APN-AMBR (see Table 10)
Event Timestamps	Minimum of date, hour, minute and second
GGSN Address Used	The current serving IP address of the GGSN/P-GW
IMSI Unauthenticated Flag	Used if the bearer is established for an emergency purposes without IMSI authentication
IP-CAN session type	Connectivity Access Network (CAN) type of session, i.e. IP for the control plane for the radio access network (E-RAB and S1 bearer)
IP-Edge Address	The IPv4 or IPv6 address used for the control plane
IP-Edge Address Type	Either IPv4 or IPv6
IP-Edge Operator Identifier	PLMN-ID (MCC+MNC) of the radio access network
Last MS Time Zone	Last time zone as provided by the SGSN/MME to the user
Last User Location Information	E(CGI) of the last cell when the IP-CAN session is deactivated
LCS cause	Cause for optionally unsuccessful localization request
LCS Client Identity	The Identity of the LCS client, it can be LEA in case of LALS
LCS Priority	The priority of the location service (i.e. high priority for emergency localization)
LCS QoS	The precision/accuracy/TTFF level (i.e. less than 5 meters, 50% of the LCS requests, and less than 30 seconds for TTFF)
List of Service Data	Data related to charging, e.g. data volume uplink/downlink, EPC QoS Information, time of first/last usage, radio access type, location information (see TS 32.298 for the complete list)
List of Traffic Data Volumes	Data Volume uplink/downlink, Change Condition/Time (e.g. closing the CDR), CGI/SAI, ECGI/TAI or RAI, QCI (Chapter 5 – Table 5) for each active PDP context/session
Local Record Sequence Number	The sequence number of the CDR created by the serving node
Location Estimate	CGI, longitude, latitude, latitude sign, altitude, altitude direction, velocity (see TS 36.355 for formatting and options)
Location Method	e.g. OTDOA, UTDOA, A-GNSS
Measurement Duration	Duration of the positioning measurement
MLC Number	The E-164 number of the GMLC
MME Name/Realm	Name/Realm of the serving MME – Diameter Identity
MS Time Zone	Time zone provided by the SGSN/MME when the IP-CAN session is created/ modified

continued on following page

Table 14. Continued

Parameters	Description
Node ID	The ID of the node generating the CDR, it can be the DNS name of the node e.g. MCCMNCS-PGW
P-GW Address IPv6	Indicates that P-GW uses IPv6 for control plane
P-GW Address Used	IPv4 or IPv6 of the P-GW
P-GW PLMN Identifier	PLMN ID (MCC and MNC)
PDN Connection Charging ID	EPS default bearer charging for GTP, unique charging ID for PMIP
PDP Type	e.g. IP session
Positioning Data	CGI, longitude, latitude, latitude sign, altitude, altitude direction, velocity (see TS 36.355 for formatting and options)
Privacy Override	Indicates if the privacy of the user is overridden by the LCS client (i.e. this is the case for LALS so the LEA can link the location information with the MSISDN/IMSI/IME of interest)
QoS Requested/QoS Negotiated	QCI/QoS Class (See Chapter 5)
RAT Type	e.g. GERAN/UTRAN/EUTRAN
Record Opening Time	Timestamp attached to the CDR (local time of the serving node)
Record Sequence Number	Sequence number for the CDR in an active user session
Record Type	e.g. SGSN-CDR, S/P-GW-CDR
Recording Entity Number	E.164 number of the node that generated the CDR
Routing Area Code/Location/Cell Identifier/Change of Location	RAC, LAC, CI as reported to the serving SGSN (See section Addressing and Network Identifiers in UMTS in Chapter 5)
S-GW Address IPv6	Indicates that P-GW uses IPv6 for control plane
S-GW Address Used	IPv4 or IPv6 of the S-GW
S-GW Change	Indicates this is the first record after an inter S-GW handover (See section mobility management in LTE in Chapter 5)
Served IMEI	The IMEI/IMEISV of the user
Served IMSI	The IMSI of the user
Served IP-CAN Session Address	The IP address of the user (LTE)
Service MSISDN	MSISDN of the user
Served PDP Address	The IP address of the user (UMTS)
Serving Node Address	IPv4 address of the SGSN, MME, S/P-GW
Serving Node IPv6 Address	IPv6 address of the SGSN, MME, S/P-GW
Serving Node PLMN Identifier	PLMN ID (MCC and MCC)
Serving PLMN Rate Control	Rate control for the IP connection to the P-GW
Start Time	Start time of the user session
Stop Time	Stop time of the user session
User Location Information	CGI, SAI, RAI (UMTS); TAI, ECGI (LTE)

Table 15. OCS prepaid CDR parameters

Parameters	Description
Session ID	ID of the online charging session
Actual Time	Timestamp of the online charging message
Subscription ID	ID of the subscriber, e.g. MSISDN or IMSI
Service Identifier	Type of service, e.g. packet session, mobile originating call, SMS
Destination ID	e.g. called party, destination IP address, APN, URL, email address
Service Information	e.g. service parameters like duration, calling party location (HLPMN or roaming),
Counter Information	Counter information for the rating messages for the session or the event subject of online charging.
Basic Price Timestamp	Basic Price, if applicable
Request Sub Type	Price request, tariff request
Price	Price per tariff if different than the basic price
Requested Units	Units requested by the serving node, e.g. 60 seconds, 1024 Kilobytes
Consumed Units	Total number of consumed units since the last request for charging
Consumed Units After Tariff Switch	In case tariff switch occurs (i.e. session passing midnight, user moves to another location), the number of consumed units after the tariff switch
Tariff Switch Time	Timestamp of the switched tariff
Current Tariff	Currently valid tariff
Next Tariff	Tariff after the Tariff Switch
Expiry Time	Time period in seconds from the time in Actual time set as expiration time of the charging information
Monetary Quota	Number of monetary units reserved for the service usage
Minimal Requested Units	Minimum number of units that can be requested for the service, i.e. not less than 10 kilobytes.
Allowed Units	Indicates how many units can be granted for the monetary quota

Chapter 7

Mobile Network Forensics:
Investigative Process and Procedures

ABSTRACT

A structured investigative approach is essential for an effective production of credible and admissible mobile network evidence. Chapter 2 discussed the ISO/ IEC SC27 digital forensic standardization as an effort that helps in developing a robust investigative process, procedures, and methodologies. This chapter applies the ISO/IEC SC27 family of standards for mobile network forensics investigations. Each of the standards is contextualized with the forensic aspects discussed in Chapter 6 together with examples of investigation scenarios, tools, and methods for forensic processing of the mobile network data. These contexts are of practical significance for investigators, elaborating on the approaches for investigative readiness, the techniques and tools for evidence processing from identification to interpretation, and the best practices in handling mobile network evidence data throughout an investigation.

INTRODUCTION

This chapter elaborates on the application of the ISO/IEC SC27 digital forensic standardization for mobile network forensic investigations. The investigative readiness recommended is discussed in terms of implementation of the interception and monitoring architecture discussed in chapter 6. The ISO/IEC 27037:2012 is explained in regards to the different types of mobile network evidence, while ISO/IEC 27042:2015 is exemplified with practical

DOI: 10.4018/978-1-5225-5855-2.ch007

investigative scenarios so investigators can recognize the critical elements needed for criminal activity reconstruction attack attribution. The ISO/IEC 27043:2015 is decomposed and elaborated for every set of investigative processes, focusing on the methods and tools used for potential mobile network evidence analysis, interpretation, presentation and reporting, and the practices maintained throughout every investigation. The chapter concludes discussing the suitability and adequacy of the LI, LALS, and network performance analysis as the main mobile network forensic investigation techniques.

APPLICATION OF ISO/IEC 27035:2016 FOR MOBILE NETWORK FORENSICS

The application of ISO/IEC 27035:2016 in mobile network forensic investigations is summarized in Table 1. The investigative readiness is established by implementing the LI and LALS architecture elaborated in Chapter 6, creating a secure channel for delivery of CDRs, and enabling the OA&M function on the network side. Investigators need to agree on the invocation details for LI and LALS and the protection of the delivery interfaces for IRI and CC between the Internal Interception Function (IIF) and the Law Enforcement Monitoring Facility (LEMF) for mobile network facilitated crimes.

For mobile network targeted attacks, the Key Performance Indicators (KPI) threshold definition need to be agreed upon before the detection, the assessment, and the attack response steps take place. For this purpose, a review of the regular traffic behavior is needed to establish a baseline when a certain KPI threshold is violated (see Chapter 6 – section *Infrastructural Information*).

With this in place, the investigation is initiated by either activating the LI and LALS, delivering the requested CDRs, or responding to an alarm for a KPI threshold violation. After the investigation is concluded, it is reviewed to learn if there are any points in the network requiring revision (e.g. redistribution of new keys, delivery of additional parameters in the IRI records, CDR records, customization for better time lining or correlation) or whether the KPI thresholds need to be adjusted (e.g. increase of the number of incoming/outgoing Gateway Tunneling Protocol (GTP) packets constituting

Table 1. Application of ISO/IEC 27035:2016 in mobile network forensic investigations

Investigative readiness phases		Mobile Network Facilitated Crime	Mobile Network Targeted Attacks
Plan and prepare	Investigative Capabilities	LI and LALS Architecture from Figure 1, 2, and 3 in Chapter 6; Delivery channels for CDRs	OA&M function
	Policies and Procedures	HI1, HI2, and HI3 interconnection; Exchange of ciphering keys; Exchange of LI and LALS invocation information (Lawful Interception Identifiers – LIID, correlation numbers, cell coordinates, localization procedures);	KPI threshold definitions for malicious and irregular traffic (user and signalization)
Detection and reporting		Activation of LI and LALS (see section *Mobile Network Forensic Procedures* below); CDR delivery	KPI threshold alarms
Assessment and decision			KPI historical information, known attacks, reported incidents
Responses			Network reconfiguration
Lessons Learned		LI/LALS architectural revision	KPI review, threshold adjustment

a DoS attack in response to a false alarm from an increase in regular GTP traffic due to a certain event – concerts, protests, breaking news, etc.).

APPLICATION OF ISO/IEC 27037:2012 FOR MOBILE NETWORK FORENSICS

The four phases of ISO/IEC 27035:2016 as applied to both mobile network facilitated crimes and mobile network targeted attacks are shown in Table 2. The search for, recognition, and documentation of potential mobile network evidence involves identification of the relevant IRI, CC, CDR, location, and infrastructural information needed for the investigation. Depending on the criminal activities, investigators need to identify the possible events listed in Tables 5a and 5b in Chapter 6 for circuit-switched and packet-switched traffic, respectively.

For example, in the interest of the investigation can be the IRI records indicating when the user answered a certain call together with the CC and the CDR of that call, or a Short Message Service (SMS) text received from a specific number. Investigators might need the information any time the target identity makes a location/routing/tracking area update or initiates a PDP context activation. For localization purposes, the potential mobile network evidence might need to be with the least Time-To-First-Fix (TTFF), so investigators need to look for Enhanced Cell ID (ECID) – Round Trip Time

Table 2. Application of ISO/IEC 27037:2012 in mobile network forensic investigations

Investigative phases	Mobile Network Facilitated Crime	Mobile Network Targeted Attacks
Identification	CC, IRI, Localization Information CDR (see Chapter 6 - Table 4)	CDRs, Infrastructural Information (see Chapter 6 - Table 4)
Collection & Acquisition	Delivery of IRI (HI2), CC(HI3) to LEMF; CDR over a secure channel	Secure channel (e.g. IPSec protected dedicated connection)
Preservation	Common forensic tools	

(RTT) localization IRI records (Chapter 6 - Table 10). For mobile network targeted attacks, investigators need to identify the critical KPIs related to the type of attack, for example Radio Access Bearer (RAB) or Radio Resource Control (RRC) connection establishment attempts/successes/failures for potential RRC-targeted signaling storms.

Once the evidence of interest is identified, the IRI and CC are transferred over the HI2 and HI3 interfaces to the LEA, while the CDRs and the infrastructural information over a secured channel for further analysis. The LEA and other responsible forensic laboratories responsible are required to have preservation mechanisms and chain-of-custody in place for the evidence. The IRI records and CDRs are delivered as textual files; the circuit-switched CC is delivered as speech AMR/WAV audio files; the packet-switched CC is delivered as *pcap* files; and the infrastructural information is delivered as a textual and/or graphical image files, so the integrity protection can be achieved using common digital forensic methods for this purpose (e.g. hashing or encrypting the material).

APPLICATION OF ISO/IEC 27042:2015 IN MOBILE NETWORK FORENSICS

Analysis

The two types of forensic analysis of mobile network evidence are shown in Table 3. In general, the mobile network forensic investigation can be conducted in real time – dealing with mobile network evidence in transit, and non-real time – dealing with stored mobile network evidence.

The analysis of the transient mobile network evidence is conducted in *live* in the following cases:

Table 3. Application of ISO/IEC 27042:2015 in mobile network forensic investigations

Analysis Type	Mobile Network Facilitated Crime	Mobile Network Targeted Attacks
Static	CC and IRI correlation; Forensic speaker recognition; Packet traffic validation IRI analysis; CDR analysis; Enhanced Location for IRI Target positioning – *periodic* localization;	Recorded KPI measurements; subscriber related data
Live	CC speaker spotting; CC application spotting; Target positioning – *immediate* localization	Real-time KPI measurements; subscriber related data

1. **Speaker Spotting for Telephony Service (CS or PS Calls):** Criminals often use multiple phones (known as "burner" phones) so a LI based on a Mobile Subscriber ISDN Number (MSISDN) or an International Mobile Subscriber Identity (IMSI) might not intercept the conversation of interest for the Law Enforcement Agency (LEA). In such a case, the LEA might invoke service and location dependent LI to intercept all the calls in a given period of time so it can automatically search for the speaker (voice) of interest, based on its distinctive speech (voice) features kept in a so-called "watch-list" of criminals (Ramasubramanian, 2012). This technique is called speaker spotting and is a form of a forensic speaker recognition, a forensic analysis method discussed later in this chapter. The similar application is also used for speech/keyword spotting, i.e. identifying keywords of interest from a set of calls.

2. **Application Spotting for Packet Service (CC of Packet Data Sessions):** In a similar way, the LEA might be interested in live analysis of given keywords, file types, IP addresses, or other packet content exchanged by one or more target identities used by the perpetrators.

3. **Target Positioning:** Immediate localization – This LALS service is invoked in emergency cases to provide the immediate location of a given target identity, for example users posting messages about suicides, terrorist attacks, life-threatening situations, or other events of investigative interests. It is of interest for LEA to have the live localization information (Chapter 6 - Table 10) so it can determine the physical position in real time and act upon it (e.g. 911 call, target identity about to cross a national/ jurisdictional border, etc.).

The static analysis is performed on the potential evidence data stored in the LEMF and includes:

1. **Correlation of CC and IRI for Reconstruction of Call Flows or Packet Sessions:** Figure 1 shows an example of correlation of CC and IRI for a mobile originated CS call (Chapter 4 - Figure 16). The LI is invoked for a target identity prior to the network registration, so once she or he registers with the network (Chapter 4 - Figure 15), the HLR generates an IRI that is later correlated with the CC and IRIs generated by the Mobile Switching Centers (MSCs) in the network for the call establishment, answer, handover, and call clearing. Figure 2 shows another example of CC and IRI correlation for a packet session (Chapter 4 - Figure 27). The General Packet Radio Service (GPRS) attach IRI report is correlated with the IP user session and the subsequent IRI records generated by the Serving GPRSs Support Node (SGSN) for the Packet Data Protocol (PDP) context activation/deactivation. For packet services, the LI service is invoked on IP level so every time the user initiates a session to a new destination IP address, a new Packet Data Header Information IRI is generated.

2. **Forensic Speaker Recognition (Recognition/Validation of the Conversational Parties):** Forensic speaker recognition is a process of determining if a specific individual (suspected speaker) is the source of the intercepted voice CC from any Circuit Switched (CS) or Packet Switched (PS) calls (Drygajlo, 2012). Multiple techniques can be used for this purpose, including aural/acoustic methods and automatic forensic speaker recognition to determine the voice features, dialect, speech errors, pathological speech problems, idiosyncrasies, or the foreign accent spoken (Eriksson, 2012). Usually, LEA produces a transcript of the intercepted conversations to aid the fact-finding process in parallel to the validation of the conversational parties.

3. **Packet Traffic Validation:** This is a traditional network forensics analysis of IP-based traffic for crime reconstruction as discussed in Chapter 2.

4. **Analysis of IRI, CDR, and Enhanced Location for IRI for Service Activity Reconstruction:** Figure 3 shows an example of forensics analysis of a Short Message Service (SMS) text exchange by two target identities to determine the context, the place, and the time when it occurred. The IRI report for location (triggered once each of the target identities sends a text message) is used in connection with the IRI SMS report and SMS CDRs to plot the location of the SMS originator/recipient (home/ work), the time, the size, and the content of the SMS message. Similar analysis is performed for calls, packet sessions, supplementary services or multimedia services realized over the mobile network.

5.   **Target Positioning:** Periodic localization – This LALS service is invoked for reconstruction of movement patterns over a longer period of time for the target identities. As shown in Figure 3, the Triggered Location IRI report enables for extended location parameters where the LEA can specify the reporting interval (e.g. minute, hour, day) or number of reports (e.g. 20 reports a day) together with the Quality-of-Service (QoS) of the localization in terms of accuracy, precision, and TTFF (e.g. hour-period for Observed Time Difference of Arrival - OTDOA localization).

For the mobile targeted attacks, the live and static analysis is performed on KPI measurements captured in real-time or stored by the mobile operator together with a subscriber related data (e.g. CDRs, service subscriptions),

Figure 1. Example correlation of CC and IRI for an intercepted CS call

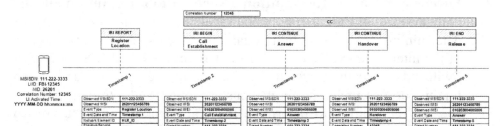

Figure 2. Example correlation of CC and IRI for an intercepted PS session

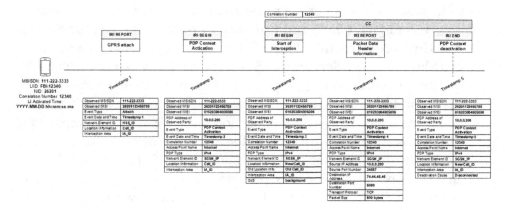

respectively. In both cases, the KPI measurements are analyzed to determine the nature of the mobile network-targeted attack (e.g. DoS, radio jamming, signaling storm) and attribute the initiators/involved mobile users. Figure 4 shows an example of increase in average Uplink (UL) Packet Data Convergence Protocol (PDCP) bitrate on a cell and user level that can indicate potential DoS originating form a given cell or location/routing/tracking area. This information can be benchmarked with the average UL PDCP bitrate or throughput per cell/area/user to determine the intensity of the attack, as well as with the information on the traffic elements' processing and traffic serving utilization (e.g. SGSN) to determine the overall impact of the network availability.

Figure 5 shows an example of decrease in total percentage of UL total Prioritized Bit Rate (PBR) usage that can indicate a potential worsening of the radio conditions due to selective jamming or interference with the UL signalization (Lichtman *et al.*, 2016). This information can be benchmarked with the average UL PBR usage to determine the severity of the attack, as well as with the information on the currently registered User Equipment (UE) with the NodeBs serving the cell to determine the number of affected users (in addition, the KPIs for cell unavailability and traffic utilization can be used).

Figure 6 shows an example of an increase in failed and a decrease in successful Radio Resource Control (RRC) connection establishment attempts

Figure 3. Service activity reconstruction for SMS interaction between two target identities

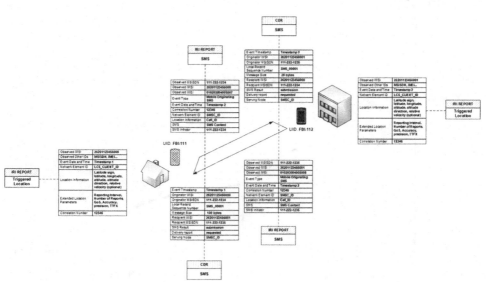

Figure 4. Average UL PDCP bitrate per cell and per user

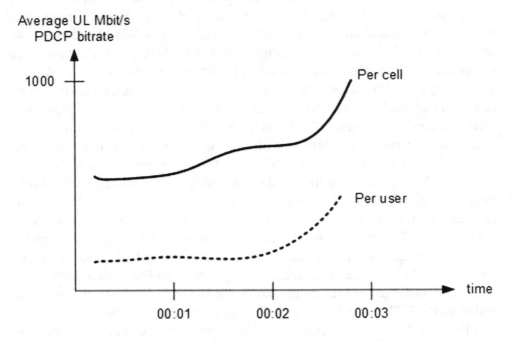

Figure 5. UL total PBR usage

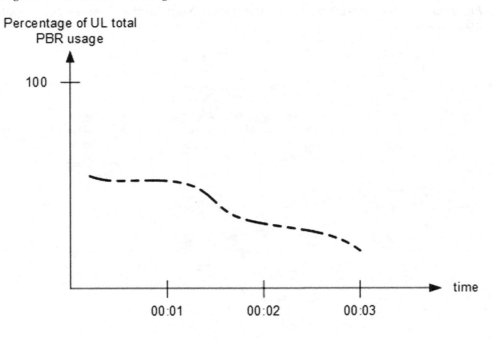

Figure 6. Number or RRC connection attempts

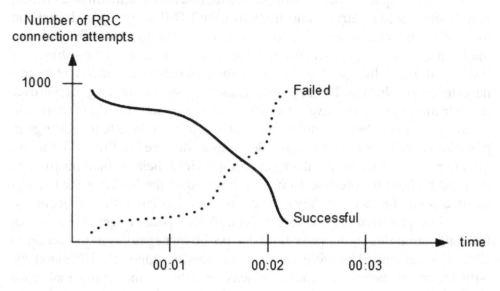

as an indicator of potential RRC signaling storm (Gorbil *et al.*, 2015). Here too, this information can be compared to the average RRC utilization over a longer period of time to infer the probability of a RRC signaling storms launched against the UMTS Radio Access Network (UTRAN) or the GPRS Radio Access Network (GERAN) segments in the network, as well as with the user identity to determine the UE attack set.

Interpretation

Following the analysis of the acquired mobile network evidence, investigators evaluate it to derive meaning in respect to the investigated criminal activity or security incident. The interpretation involves fact finding and validation/verification of results. For example, when investigating intercepted telephony conversations as depicted in Figure 1, investigators may request additional information from the mobile network on the time zone configuration/format of the network elements or the voice codecs used to be able to timeline the events and provide additional analytical input for the forensic speaker recognition. Similarly, operators can deliver information on the average network latency experienced for packet service users as depicted in Figure 3 so the investigators can interpret the browsing behavior captured in the packet CC and the respective IRIs.

When investigating localization related mobile network facilitated crimes, investigators need to retrieve information on the TTFF, accuracy, and precision of each of the techniques used so they can identify any inconsistencies in the localization evidence and other evidence used to localize the subjects of investigation. As discussed in Chapter 6, the different localization techniques have different values for TTFF, accuracy, and precision so the usage of one over another might affect the level of confidence in the facts found in the mobile network evidence. For example, when investigating a SMS text exchange in place and time between two target identities as depicted in Figure 3, the use of enhanced Cell ID for localization will not yield their vertical position so it might be hard to infer the floor in the house or the building for each of them, despite the fact that they can be pinpointed to 1m with 90% accuracy.

The interpretation of the evidence for mobile network targeted attacks can be challenging due to the potential false positives/negatives in the acquired KPI measurements. Therefore, investigators need to support the KPIs analysis with known instances of similar attacks or patterns indicating malicious traffic/behavior in the mobile network and indicate their level of confidence in the interpretation (Jover, 2013; Lichtman *et al.*, 2016). For example, the increase in the UL PDCP bitrate shown in Figure 4 might not be a result of a coordinated mobile botnet launching a DoS attack on the network, but a result of an increased user activity due to breaking news or other event of high public interest. The decrease in the PBR usage shown in Figure 5 and RRC connection attempts in Figure 6 may be an anomaly that occurred due to actual decrease in user activity and not due to selective jamming or signaling storms.

APPLICATION OF ISO/IEC 27043:2015 FOR MOBILE NETWORK FORENSICS

Readiness Processes

Following the ISO/IEC 27043:2015 harmonized model (Chapter 1 - Figure 2), the readiness processes of the mobile network forensic investigation model are shown in Figure 7. The readiness phase incorporates all the steps necessary for reconstruction of mobile network facilitated crimes and attribution of mobile network targeted attacks. Following the identification of the potential sources of digital evidence (Chapter 6 - Table 4) and the definition of the acquisition/analysis mechanisms, the LEA and the operators are required to define and implement the investigative architecture including: LI architecture (see Chapter 6 - Figure 1 and Figure 2), LALS architecture (Chapter 6 - Figure 3), and the OA&M function (this also includes a definition of a channel for offline delivery of CDRs).

The general LI/LALS architectures require implementation of an internal interception function that is comprised of multiple Interception Control Elements (ICE) and delivery functions as shown in Figure 8. The ICE elements are in fact the core and intelligent network elements responsible for realization of user and signalization traffic. The Administration Function (ADMF) needs to be configured with the HI1 X1_1/2/3 interfaces so the interception or localization can be automatically instantiated (with pre-negotiated security and authentication validation keys as discussed in Chapter 6) and the potential mobile network evidence delivered over the X2/X3 and HI2/HI3 interfaces to the LEMF. Once the interception, localization and the OA&M attack detection functions are implemented, the assessment phase is set in place to ensure that all the regulatory and technical requirements are met prior to instantiating any mobile network investigation.

Initialization and Acquisitive Processes

The initialization and acquisitive processes for mobile network forensic investigation are shown in Figure 9. The investigation for mobile network facilitated crimes is initiated with an invocation of LI/LALS while the detection and first response is initiated with selection of the KPIs indicating potential attack and network reconfiguration. During the planning and preparation, investigators assess the type, volume, and variety of the evidence material so they can dedicate sufficient storage capacity, setup the tools for later analysis, and organize secure transfer (LI ciphering key exchange, integrity protection, authorization, secure channel establishment, warrant presentation).

The identification, collection, and acquisition is realized by specifying the following parameters and communicating the with the mobile operator:

1. **Investigation Type:** LI (target identity or service-based interception), LALS (immediate or periodic localization, enhanced location for IRI), or mobile network targeted attack
2. **Time of Investigation**: Real-time, non-real time, combined
3. **Network ID and Broadcast Area ID: Mobile** County Code (MNC) +Mobile Network Code (MCC) and the network segment targeted with

Figure 7. Mobile network forensic investigation – readiness processes

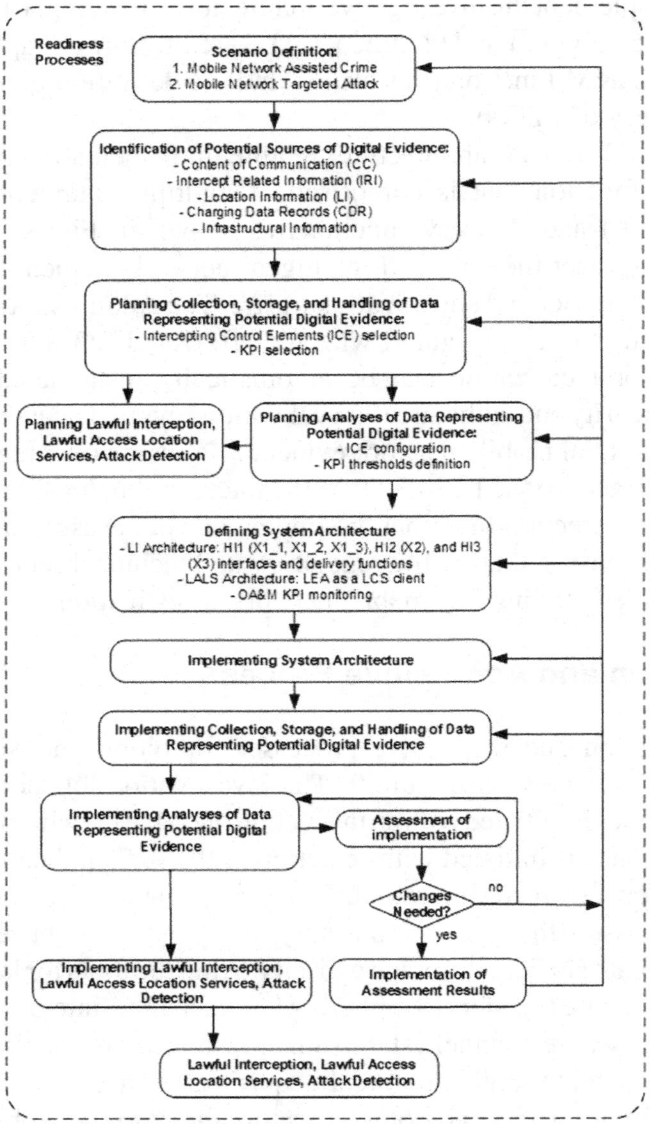

Figure 8. LI and LALS network configuration

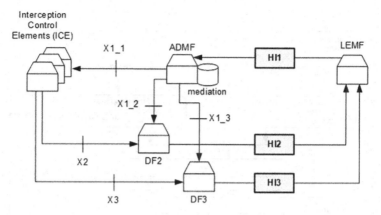

the investigation (geographical area, network generation, CS services only, PS services only)

4. Lawful Interception IDs and Correlation Numbers
5. **Target Identities and/or Target Services:** MSISDNs, IMSIs, IMEIs and/or service types (calls, texts, sessions, all CS user traffic, all PS user traffic)
6. **Specification of the Handover Interfaces and Delivery Channels:** HI2 and HI3 addresses/credentials, CDR, KPI secure channels' addresses/credentials
7. Investigation setup, activation, and deactivation time
8. Potential mobile network evidence of interest - IRI, CC, CDR, KPIs, other administrative data (billing, registration records, customer data, operator specific configuration)

The acquired potential mobile network evidence upon delivery is stored either in the LEMF or in an accredited digital forensics laboratory for further analysis and interpretation.

Investigative Processes: Potential Digital Evidence Examination and Analysis

The investigative processes encompass examination and analysis, interpretation, reporting, and presentation of the mobile network evidence as shown in Figure 10. When examining and analytically processing the acquired evidence material, investigators verify the authenticity and integrity of the data,

Figure 9. Mobile network forensic investigation – initialization and acquisitive processes

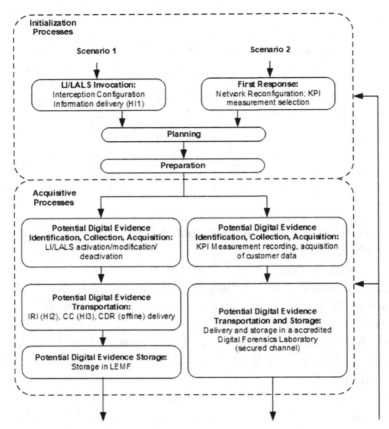

select the analytical methods appropriate for the investigation, and employ them to extract the evidentiary elements bearing the probative value for the investigated case. Table 4 maps the analytical methods for common mobile network evidence types with example processing tools facilitating the analysis.

Forensic Speaker Recognition and Speaker Spotting

The forensic speaker recognition is an analysis of the intercepted voice CC to determine whether the conversational parties are the ones subject to investigation. The speaker spotting is a variant of the forensic speaker recognition where the task is to determine whether a given speaker who is one of the conversational parties belongs to a given list of speakers of

Figure 10. Mobile network forensic investigation – investigative processes

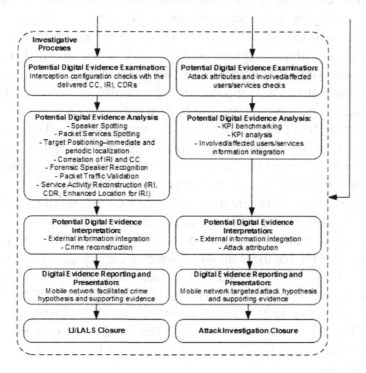

Table 4. Mobile network forensics – analytical method, evidence types, and processing tools

Analytical method	Evidence type	Forensic Processing Tool(s)
Forensic Speaker Recognition, Speaker Spotting	CC – voice/ conferencing traffic	Aural/Acoustic analysis, automatic forensic speaker recognition analyzers (i.e. ALIZE)
Correlation of IRI and CC	CC and IRI	LI analyzer (i.e. Stinga)
Packer Service Spotting, Packet Traffic Validation	CC – packet traffic	Protocol analyzer (i.e. Wireshark)
User/network tracing	Customer Data	Protocol analyzer (i.e. Wireshark)
KPI Benchmarking	KPI measurements	KPI aggregator (i.e. analysis and reporting), protocol/spectrum analyzers
Service Activity Reconstruction	IRI, CDRs, Enhanced Location for IRI	CDR aggregators (i.e. analysis and reporting), cell tower location mapper
Target Positioning – immediate and periodic localization	Localization Information (IRI)	Cell location/position mappers (i.e TraX)

interests. The common approaches for speaker recognition include aural/acoustic, auditory-instrumental, and automatic methods (Drygajlo, 2012). The aural/acoustic analytical approach relies on the experience and human perception in matching the intercepted voice CC and a recorded voice based on the phonetic similarity between the two sources.

The auditor-instrumental approach employs statistical analysis of common voice features like the average fundamental frequency, articulation rate, formant central frequencies, rhythm, and voice quality (Drygajlo, 2012; Eriksson, 2012). In the automatic forensic speaker recognition approach, the recognition system works by extracting voice features of a training set of speech data to model different speaker patterns that are later compared with the features extracted of the intercepted voice CC (test set of speech data) to yield a similarity score or detection of the speaker.

Most speaker recognition systems work with Mel-Frequency Cepstral Coefficients (MFCC) or the Relative or Spectral Perceptual Linear Prediction Coefficients (RASTA-PLP) as voice features used in the comparison. The MFFC feature extraction algorithm is specified in the ETSI 201.108 technical specification (European Telecommunications Standards Institute, 2003) and RASTA-PIP in (Hermansky *et al.*, 1991). The speaker patterns modeling can be text-dependent or text-independent based on the linguistic content subject of investigation.

In regards to the modeling approach, the speaker models can be: (1) *deterministic* – where the training and test voice features are directly compared to determine the degree of dissimilarity between them (vector quantitation for text-dependent and dynamic time wrapping for text-independent modeling, for example); or (2) *statistic* – where each speaker is modeled as a probabilistic source with unknown buy fixed probability density function and later evaluated to yield the similarity for a given ratio likelihood (Hidden Markov Model for text-dependent and Gaussian Mixture Models for text-independent modeling, for example).

The automatic forensic speaker recognition came to prominence with the proliferation of mobile networks as the main providers of telephony service and many proprietary software tools were developed and used for forensic analysis of an intercepted voice (Amino *et al.*, 2012; Greenberg *et al.*, 2012). Among the most prominent ones is the ALIZE open source tool for speaker recognition with a favorable performance in terms of *detection cost* - weighted sum of miss and false alarm error probabilities for speaker detection (Greenberg *et al.*, 2012; Larcher *et al.*, 2013; Laboratoire Informatique D'Avignon, 2017).

Correlation of IRI and CC

The correlation of IRI and CC is facilitated using LI analyzers, displaying the content of the IRI so to derive the call/session flow and the context of the captured CC. Among the most prominent tools for IRI and CC analysis is the STINGA LI Analyzer, developed by Utel Technologies as part of a complete LI LEMF soliton for LEAs. Figure 11 shows an example of an IRI REPORT for a EUTRAN attach event analogous to the IRI BEGIN depicted at timestamp 1 in Figure 3. Next to the LIID and the Correlation Numbers, the IMEI, IMSI, MSISDN, and IP address of the target identity are reported together with the location info consisting of TAI and eCGI (Chapter 5 - Figure 50 and Figure 51).

Figure 12 and Figure 13 show an example of a IRI-BEGIN record for a UMTS CS conference call party analogous to the IRI-BEGIN record depicted at timestamp 2 in Figure 3. The LI identifiers shown in Figure 10a include the Lawful Interception Identifier (LIID), the correlation numbers, the Communication Identifier (CID), the Network Identifier (NID), and the

Figure 11. STINGA LI analyzer output for a IRI-REPORT record for an LTE EUTRAN attach event

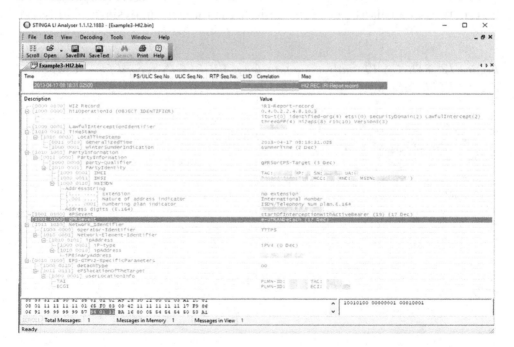

Network Element Identifier (NEID), accompanied with the type and the state of interception (call establishment, call setup in progress) and the location of the target identity at the beginning of the interception (Public Lang Mobile Network Identifier - PLMN_ID, Location Area Code - LAC, and Service Area Code - SAC).

The conference call parties' details shown in Figure 12 include the originating/terminating party and their MSISDNs, as wells as the target identity's IMEI and IMSI as the call initiator. An example of an IRI CONTINUE record is shown in Figure 14 for an ongoing interception of a GSM CS call, analogous to the IRI REPORT depicted at timestamp 3 and 4 in Figure 3. The IRI END record looks similar to the one depicted in Figure 12 with an addition of the release causes of the (conference) call, indicating the termination of the interception.

Packer Service Spotting, Traffic Validation, and Tracing

The analysis of the packet data in both cases of service spotting and traffic validation is facilitated with packet protocol analyzers, namely Wireshark (Bullock and Parker, 2017). For demonstration purposes, the tracing is performed on an Open Air Interface (OAI) implementation of a Long Term Evolution (LTE) network (Open Air Aliance, 2017). The OAI open-source LTE network can also be used to facilitate the forensic analysis, providing an

Figure 12. STINGA LI analyzer output for a IRI-BEGIN record for a UMTS CS event – LI identifiers

Figure 13. STINGA LI analyzer output for a IRI-BEGIN record for a UMTS CS event – parties' details

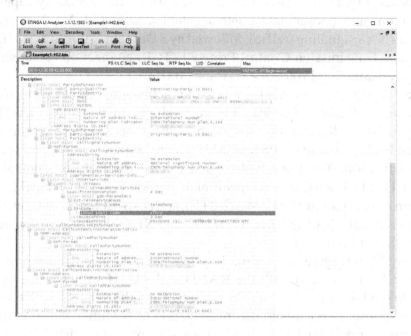

Figure 14. STINGA LI analyzer output for a IRI-CONTINUE record for a GSM CS event

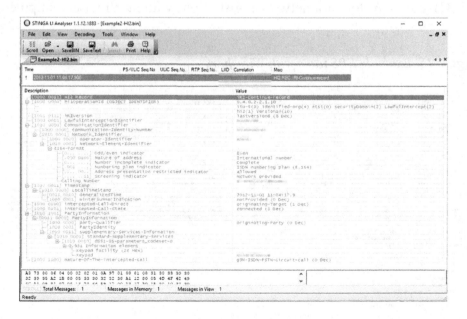

opportunity for the investigators to replicate or test certain attack or criminal hypotheses. Figure 15 shows a capture of a user attach, security capability negotiation, and packet data context establishment (S1-AP, Non-Access Stratum - NAS signaling traffic), followed by a Domain Name Service (DNS) query and Transmission Control Protocol (TCP) connection establishment (Gateway Tunneling Protocol - GTP user traffic).

The user/signalization tracing is also of practical importance for analyzing mobile network targeted attacks. Figure 16 shows an example of EUTRAN tracing including RRC connection establishment, network attach (combined Evolved Packet System – EPS and IMSI attach), authentication, and security mode activation. The trace is dissected for the Radio Link Control LTE (RLC-LTE), LTE RRC uplink/downlink Common Control Channel (CCH), Medium Access Control LTE (MAC-LTE), and NAS-EPS signaling, enabling standalone analysis of the *Uu, S1-MME,* and *S1-U* interfaces (Chapter 5 - Figure 28 and Figure 29).

Figure 17 and Figure 18 show the details of the LTE authentication procedure (Chapter 5 - Figure 33) with the RAND and AUTH values sent from the MME to the UE as part of the EPS challenge and the value of RES returned in the response. In regards to the investigation of potential abnormalities in the user/network behavior, Figure 19 shows an example of RRC connection re-establishment reject (similar to the failed RRC connection attempts shown in Figure 6) while Figure 20 shows an example of Tracking Area Update (TAU) request (efforts for network registrations with invalid user equipment

Figure 15. Example EPS trace with Wireshark

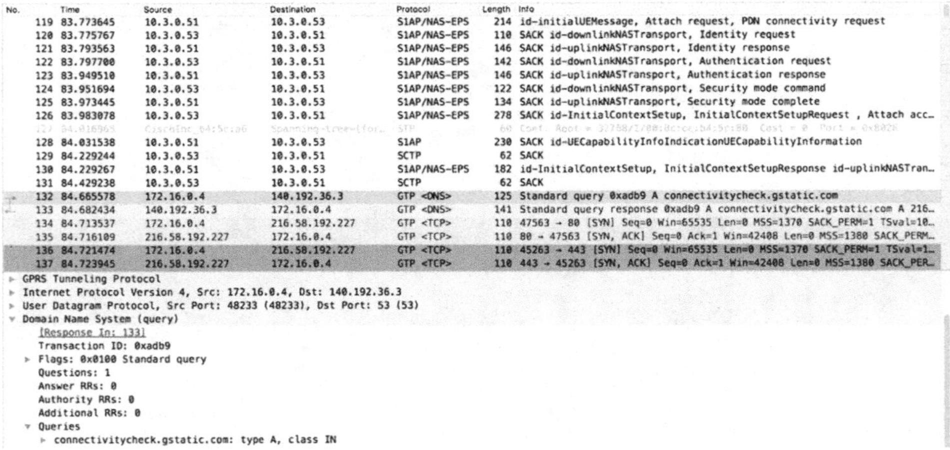

Figure 16. Example EUTRAN trace with Wireshark

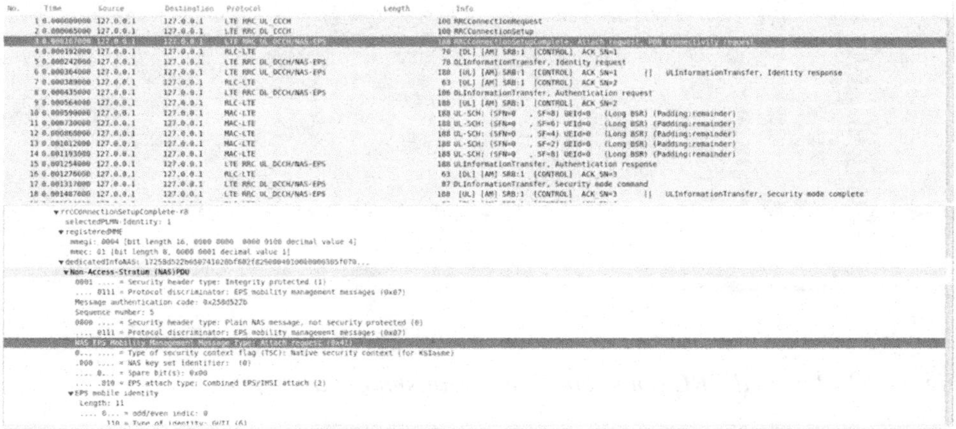

of Subscriber Module Identification – SIM cards to increase the signalization and/or deplete the Home Subscriber System - HSS resources).

KPI Measurements

In addition to the user/network tracing, investigators refer to the KPI measurements for detection, response, and analysis of mobile targeted network attacks, as previously discussed. Figure 21 shows an example of measurements performed on the MAC level at the EUTRAN (using the Open Air Interface LTE deployment), including measurements for uplink (UL)/downlink (DL) throughput, the Channel Quality Indicator (CQI), and the error/attempts per

Figure 17. LTE authentication procedure – Authentication request

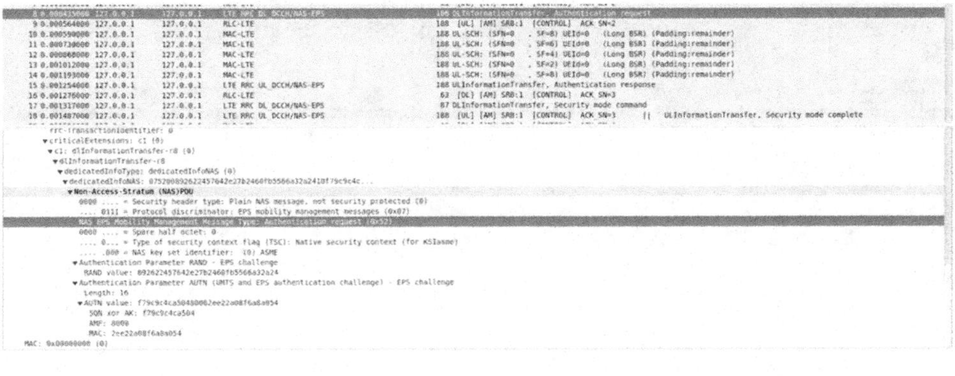

Figure 18. LTE authentication procedure – Authentication response

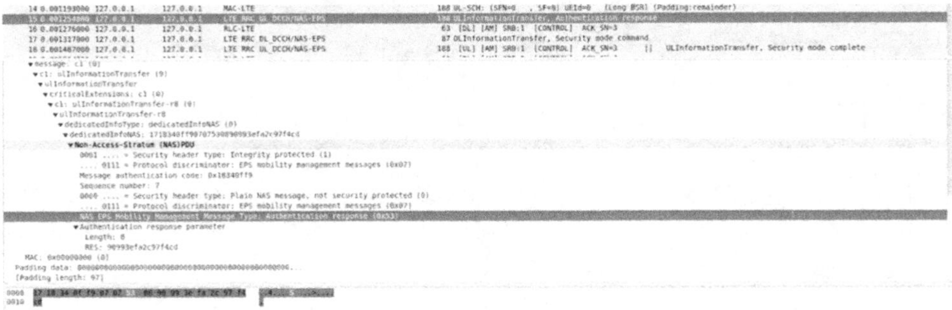

Figure 19. Rejected RRC connection re-establishment attempt

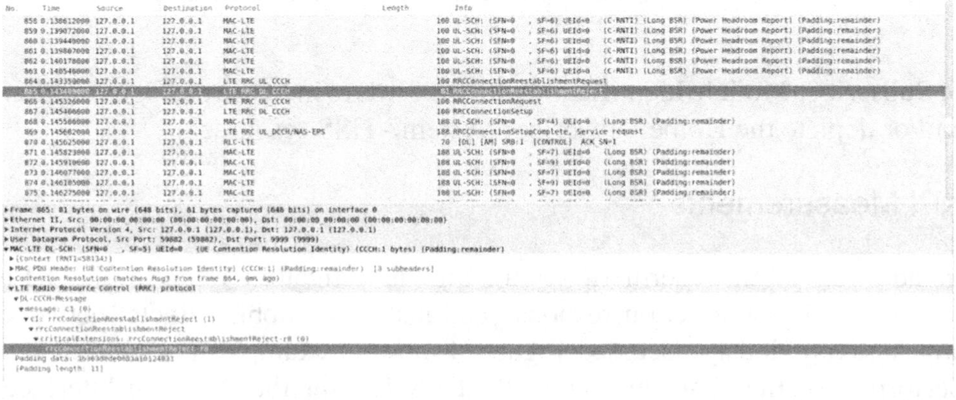

Figure 20. Rejected Tracking Area Update attempt

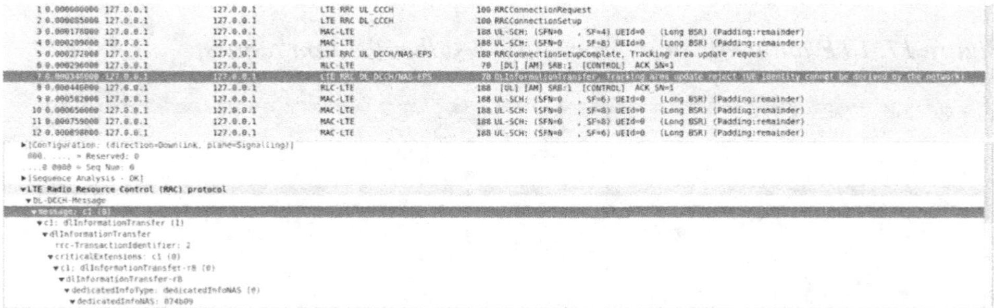

hybrid ARQ (HARQ) (Open Air Aliance, 2017). Any deterioration in these measurements, for example increase of the HARQ error/attempts ratio for the UL or drop of the CQI, can indicate potential malicious behavior like smart jamming.

Figure 22 shows an output of a software-based spectrum analyzer for a normal operation of an evolved Node B (eNB) (Open Air Aliance, 2017). The red plots show the LTE physical signals (Chapter 5 - Table 8), namely the received signal strength, Sounding Reference Signal (SRS) response, and channel frequency response. The yellow plots show the LTE Physical Uplink Shared Channel (PUSCH) and the Physical Uplink Control Channel (PUCCH) for transport of user and control traffic in the uplink direction, respectively (Chapter 5 - Table 6 and Table 7). Corresponding to the example in Figure 5, investigators can verify or obtain further insights about the increase in PDCP bitrate in the uplink by analyzing the PUSCH bitrate (throughput), given that the PDCP traffic carries the user data.

Service Activity Reconstruction and Target Positioning

The service activity reconstruction and target positioning analysis is realized by tools for CDR aggregation and so-called cell location/activity mappers. Among the most prominent tools for CDR aggregation and cell location/activity mapping is TraX, developed by the ZetX as part of a complete CDR analysis and cell phone investigation soliton for LEAs (ZetX, 2017). Figure 23 shows and example output of a Google Earth Pro location mapping of a SMS CDR for a target identity corresponding to the scenario for SMS interaction reconstruction depicted in Figure 3 (Google, 2017). The TraX

Figure 21. EUTRAN MAC-level KPIs

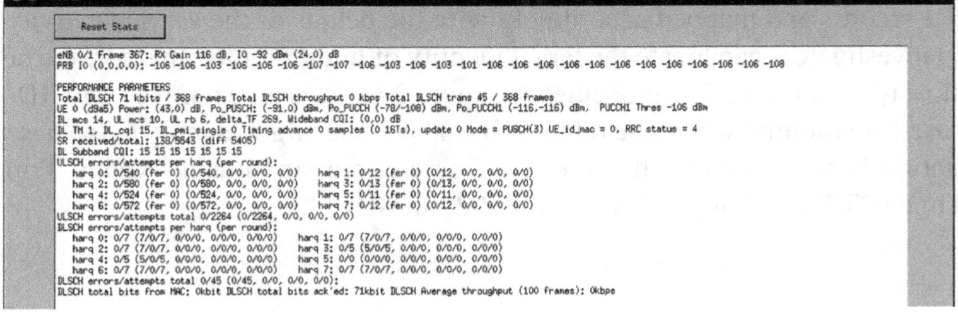
```
stats
Reset Stats
eNB 0/1 Frame 367: RX Gain 116 dB, I0 -92 dBm (24,0) dB
PRB I0 (0,0,0,0): -106 -106 -103 -106 -106 -106 -107 -107 -106 -103 -106 -103 -101 -106 -106 -106 -106 -106 -106 -106 -106 -106 -106 -106 -108

PERFORMANCE PARAMETERS
Total DLSCH 71 kbits / 368 frames Total DLSCH throughput 0 kbps Total DLSCH trans 45 / 368 frames
UE 0 (d9a5) Power: (43,0) dB, Po_PUSCH: (-91,0) dBm, Po_PUCCH (-78/-108) dBm, Po_PUCCH1 (-116,-116) dBm,  PUCCH1 Thres -106 dBm
DL mcs 14, UL mcs 10, UL rb 6, delta_TF 269, Wideband CQI: (0,0) dB
DL TM 1, DL_cqi 15, DL_pmi_single 0 Timing advance 0 samples (0 16Ts), update 0 Mode = PUSCH(3) UE_id_mac = 0, RRC status = 4
SR received/total: 138/5543 (diff 5405)
DL Subband CQI: 15 15 15 15 15 15 15
ULSCH errors/attempts per harq (per round):
   harq 0: 0/540 (fer 0) (0/540, 0/0, 0/0, 0/0)    harq 1: 0/12 (fer 0) (0/12, 0/0, 0/0, 0/0)
   harq 2: 0/580 (fer 0) (0/580, 0/0, 0/0, 0/0)    harq 3: 0/13 (fer 0) (0/13, 0/0, 0/0, 0/0)
   harq 4: 0/524 (fer 0) (0/524, 0/0, 0/0, 0/0)    harq 5: 0/11 (fer 0) (0/11, 0/0, 0/0, 0/0)
   harq 6: 0/572 (fer 0) (0/572, 0/0, 0/0, 0/0)    harq 7: 0/12 (fer 0) (0/12, 0/0, 0/0, 0/0)
ULSCH errors/attempts total 0/2264 (0/2264, 0/0, 0/0, 0/0)
DLSCH errors/attempts per harq (per round):
   harq 0: 0/7 (7/0/7, 0/0/0, 0/0/0, 0/0/0)    harq 1: 0/7 (7/0/7, 0/0/0, 0/0/0, 0/0/0)
   harq 2: 0/7 (7/0/7, 0/0/0, 0/0/0, 0/0/0)    harq 3: 0/5 (5/0/5, 0/0/0, 0/0/0, 0/0/0)
   harq 4: 0/5 (5/0/5, 0/0/0, 0/0/0, 0/0/0)    harq 5: 0/0 (0/0/0, 0/0/0, 0/0/0, 0/0/0)
   harq 6: 0/7 (7/0/7, 0/0/0, 0/0/0, 0/0/0)    harq 7: 0/7 (7/0/7, 0/0/0, 0/0/0, 0/0/0)
DLSCH errors/attempts total 0/45 (0/45, 0/0, 0/0, 0/0):
DLSCH total bits from MAC: 0kbit DLSCH total bits ack'ed: 71kbit DLSCH Average throughput (100 frames): 0kbps
```

Figure 22. EUTRAN PHY-level KPIs

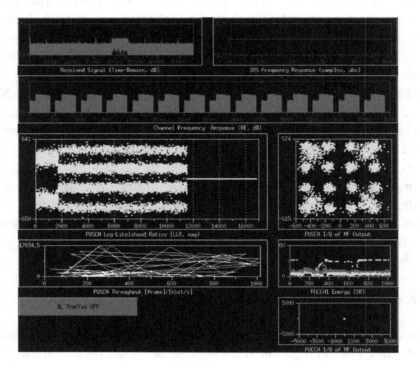

tool provides the estimated representation of the coverage footprint of the reported physical location of the cells in the CDRs of the user service activity. The CDR shows the sender (Target Number), the receiver (Connected to), SMS type (outgoing), the IMSI of the sender, the LAC/Cell ID (CID), and the date/time in Universal Coordinated Time (UTC) format.

Similar technique is used for both immediate and periodic target positioning. The LAC/(e)CID and optionally the longitude, latitude, altitude, and velocity (depending on the positioning method, see Chapter 6 – section *Lawfully Authorized Location Services*) are extracted from the Enhanced Location for IRI records and mapped accordingly with the details of the service activity so investigators can locate the target identity of interest either in real-time or closely monitor her/his movements. Figure 24 shows an example of ECID-based positioning where the relative distance of the target identity to the base station in the direction shown in the figure is measured using Round Trip Time (RTT), yielding a distance of 0.93 miles.

Figure 23. CDR analysis and map plotting for SMS reconstruction

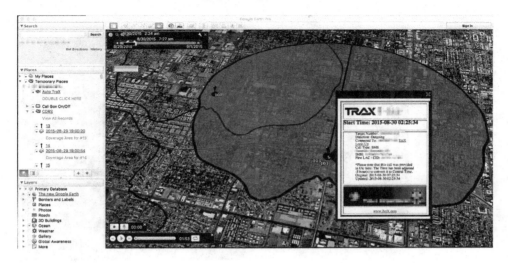

Figure 24. Example ECID target positioning with RTT

Figure 25 shows a Google Earth Pro location mapping of a voice call reconstruction in time and place for a target identity. The locations indicated on the map are all the cell where the target identity has initiated/received calls in the timeframe indicated in the CDRs. The particular CDR shown in Figure 25 details the calling party (Target Number), the called party (Connected to), the duration of the call-in seconds, and the LTE eCID where the call was initiated (the cell where the call is terminated might be different if the target identity moves between cells and as such is terminated in the last CDR

Figure 25. CDR analysis and map plotting for voice reconstruction

of that particular call). For both the SMS and voice CDRs, as well as for packet services, the TraX tool also enables animated representation of the service activity in place/time, which is a great feature for both the analysis/ interpretation and courtroom evidence presentation.

Examples of CDR aggregation for analysis with TraX is shown in Figure 26, Figure 27, and Figure 28. Figure 26 shows the number of contacts including any SMS, voice or other service data originated/terminated from/to the target identity of interest. Figure 27 shows the frequency by hour/day and type of service for the target identity of interest. Figure 28 shows a comparison between the two sets of CDRs to identify the relative proximity of the two target identities subject of investigation as a measure of the distance of their serving cells, with the distance in the first CDR record being 0.833 miles and in the second one 1.133 miles.

Investigative Processes: Potential Digital Evidence Interpretation

The interpretation of the potential mobile network evidence follows the analysis to form possible explanations about the facts, patterns, and specific details observed in the evidence in light of the criminal or attack context. Investigators use their expertise, experience and external information (e.g. mobile device forensic reports, floor plans, online browsing behaviors, information from

Figure 26. CDR aggregation analysis – number of contacts per day per target identity (subscriber)

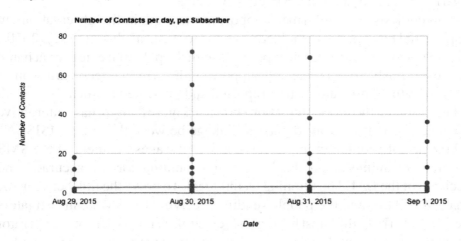

Figure 27. CDR aggregation analysis – service activity frequency

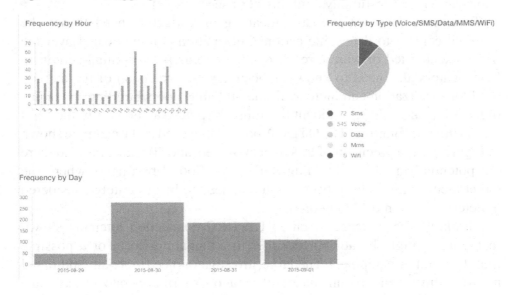

Figure 28. CDR aggregation analysis – proximity calculation

277

related cases) for a criminal/attack alternative hypotheses that are supported to variable degrees with the extracted evidence.

A hypothesis is an informed supposition to explain the observations in the potential evidence data yielded from the forensic analysis (Casey, 2010). After extensive testing of each hypothesis with the potential evidence at hand, the most probable one is selected supporting the criminal reconstruction or the attack attribution and further reported and presented as such.

For example, the SMS interaction shown in Figure 3 might have alternative explanations on the involved parties (linkage between the target MSISDNs and the actual people sending/receiving the messages), content of the SMS (different meanings), and the location (accounting for the accuracy and precision of the LALS positioning techniques). To prove the link between the target MSISDNs and the people sending/receiving the SMSs, investigators need to obtain both the latest billing and registration records from the operator and gather additional data to place them at the same places as indicated in the Enhanced Location for IRI records (video camera surveillance feeds, doorman witness testimony, building card access logs).

To extract the most probable meaning, investigators need to use the criminal context to determine actions/information communicated over the SMS text that led or were a result of the ongoing/past criminal activities. Investigators also need to know the accuracy and precision of the method used for localization and include all the probable floors/buildings or radius of location where the target identities might be placed at the time of the SMS interactions accounting. The OTDOA positioning used in the example shown in Figure 3 has a precision of less than 50 meters and 70% accuracy, so there are potentially multiple buildings/houses or floors/apartments where the target identity might have been (each one need to be separately considered to determine the most likely one).

Similarly, the increase in failed UL RRC connection attempts shown in Figure 6 might be attributed either to a signaling storm or a possible multifunctioning equipment. Therefore, investigators need to acquire additional network configuration/maintenance information from the operator to determine whether there was any indication of outage in the equipment, whether there was a scheduled maintenance during the time the KPI measurements were taken, or change of configuration to support or refute a hypothesis about the detected abnormal network activity.

Investigative Processes: Potential Digital Evidence Reporting, Presentation, and Investigation Closure

The resulting outcome of the investigative process is the criminal reconstruction or attack attribution that either confirms, rejects, or provides insufficient information to a criminal/attack hypothesis together with supporting evidence. The investigative phase concludes with a report summarizing the findings that is either presented in court or to the mobile network operator management. Depending on the investigation type, the report has to include at least these elements:

1. **Case Description:** The first section of Table 5 provides an example of a case description for a mobile network investigation including interception identifiers, target identities, evidence types, and the investigation structure.

2. **Criminal Hypotheses / Attack Hypotheses:** Thorough description of the criminal/attack supposition and the supporting evidence. The mobile network evidence data can be confusing for jurors, attorneys, even mobile operator executives, so the reconstruction/attribution must be conveyed in clear terms. For example, the terms Base Transceiver Station (BTS), NodeB, eNB are rarely used in common parlance, so they can be referred according to their main function, i.e. cell towers or radio towers, which are more frequent and more relatable terms.

3. **Confidence in the Interpretation and Conclusions**: The evidence can support/reject the criminal/attack hypothesis to a variable degree, so investigators need to clearly state the likelihood that the crime and the attack has occurred, has not occurred, or the evidence is inconclusive. Various scales exist for this purpose, for example: (1) almost definitely, (2) most probably, (3) probably, (4) very possibly, and (5) possibly (Casey, 2010).

4. **Tools Used:** The tools used for mobile network evidence analysis need to also be stated in the report so their reliability to produce consistent results can be objectively established, i.e. with a function driven tool testing methodology (NIST, 2014). For example, the performance of the forensic speaker recognition tool used to analyze voice CC in terms of false positives/missed detections need to be stated together with a validation proof of the testing.

After the investigation is closed, the intercepted/acquired mobile network evidence is kept in the LEMF or in forensic custody for the period required by the federal and local laws.

Concurrent Processes

The concurrent processes are a set of actions followed throughout the entire mobile network forensic investigation and include:

1. **Authorization:** Prior to any interception of attack detection, the investigation must be authorized by the mobile operator providing services to the target identiti(es) of interest.

2. **Documentation:** Information for all steps taken during the investigation should be kept, including the information on the personnel involved in setup, activation, modification, and deactivation of the LI/LALS services, acquisition of KPI measurements and CDRs, anonymization measures used for protection of target identities' privacy, external information included in the interpretation (e.g. watch-list, mobile device forensics report, floor plans, etc.), and any other contextual information (e.g, network outages during the interception, reasons for missing IRI, CDR, CC or KPIs, etc.).

3. **Information Flow Definition:** Because mobile network forensic investigations are sensitive in nature, any information flow needs to be defined detailing when, how and by who the LI/LALS is invoked, procedures for acquisition and delivery of CDRs and infrastructural information, and all the responsibilities for evidence, analysis, interpretation, reporting, presentation, and the overall investigation management on both the operator side and the LEA/forensics laboratory side.

4. **Chain-of-Custody and Network Evidence Preservation:** Table 5 shows an example of a chain-of-custody form for mobile network investigations. The case description provides the information used to invoked LI/LALS, the type and time of investigation and the structure in terms of potential sources of mobile network evidence. The evidence description lists the evidence acquired form the mobile operator, while the chain-of-custody provides with a trail on the current evidence custodian at any point of time from the invocation to the closure and archiving of the investigation.

The mobile network evidence is sensitive in nature bearing private information about the target identities and the network configuration, so the chain-of-custody and the evidence material must be preserved to prevent form privacy infringement (unauthorized access) or any other evidence spoliation, alternation, or destruction.

Table 5. Example chain-of-custody form for mobile network forensic investigations

Case Description				
Investigation Type	o LI o LALS o Mobile network targeted attack		**Time of Investigation**	o Real time o Non-real time o Combined
Network ID (NID)	o MCC+MCC	**Broadcast Area ID (BID)**	o Geo Area o GSM o UMTS	o LTE o CS/PS Only o IMS
Lawful Interception IDs	o Case Identity	**Correlation Numbers**	o MCC+MCC	
Target Identities	o MSISDNs o IMSIs o IMEIs	**Target Service**	o CS, PS, SMS, calls, sessions,	
Delivery Information (HI2)	o IP address o Login ID	**Delivery Information (HI3)**	o IP address o Login ID	
Other delivery channels	o IP address o Login ID o File types	**LI Setup Time**	o LI Setup Time	
LI Activated Time	o UTC format	**LI Deactivated Time**	o UTC format	
Type of Interception	o IRI only o CC only o IRI + CC	**Type of Localization**	o Target Positioning – immediate localization o Target Positioning – periodic o Enhanced Location for IRI	
Type of CDRs	o Postpaid o Prepaid	**Type of KPIs**	o List of KPIs o Thresholds o Normative Values	
Auxiliary Information	o Billing Records o Operator specific configurations		o Registration records o Other	
Evidence Description				
Item#	**Type of Evidence**	**Quantity**	**Description**	
Chain-of-Custody				
Item#	**Date/Time**	**Released by**	**Received by**	**Reason for Change**
		o Signature o Name and ID	o Signature o Name and ID	

APPLICATION OF ISO/IEC 27041:2015 FOR MOBILE NETWORK FORENSICS

To assure the LI, LALS, and network performance analysis as suitable and adequate methods for mobile network forensic investigation, the regulators, LEAs, and mobile operators need to agree on the architecture and the investigative processes for their realization. Chapter 6 and this chapter extensively elaborate on a 3GPP-based mobile network investigation architecture and ISO/IEC SC27-based investigative processes so they provide sufficient information to assure that the LI, LALS, and network performance analysis methods are suitable, adequate, and based on globally agreed standards for mobile network infrastructures and digital forensic investigations.

CONCLUSION

Presuming investigative readiness with the LI, LALS and the OA&M function in place, the mobile network evidence data is delivered to the LEA or other forensics laboratories either over the secured H12 and H13 interfaces or over a previously negotiated secure channel. Once in forensic/LEA custody, the examination and analysis takes place to ensure that the potential evidence data is adequate for testing the criminal/attack hypotheses supposed by the investigators. Depending on the type of analysis, investigators can use different tools to extract the actual evidentiary data, i.e. identifying speakers, correlating CC and IRI records, spotting packets, validating traffic, tracing user's network and service activity, reconstructing CDRs, target positioning, or KPI analysis. The extracted evidentiary data is interpreted so the investigative hypothesis can be supported, rejected, or in case there are no data with sufficient probative value to reach a definitive conclusion, rendered inconclusive. After the mobile network facilitated crime is reconstructed or the mobile network targeted attack attributed, investigators conclude by reporting the findings, presenting the evidence, and storing the evidence and the case documentation.

REFERENCES

Amino, K., Osnai, T., Kamada, T., Makinae, H., & Arai, T. (2012). Historical and Procedural Overview of Forensic Speaker Recognition as a Science. In A. Neustein & H. A. Patil (Eds.), *Forensic Speaker Recognition: Law Enforcement and Counter Terrorism* (pp. 3–20). New York: Springer International Publishing. doi:10.1007/978-1-4614-0263-3_1

Bullock, J., & Parker, J. T. (2017). *Wireshark for Security Professionals: Using Wireshark and the Metasploit Framework* (1st ed.). Indianapolis, IN: Wiley. doi:10.1002/9781119183457

Casey, E. (2010). *Handbook of Digital Forensics Investigations*. San Diego, CA: Elsevier Academic Press.

Drygajlo, A. (2012). Automatic Speaker Recoginiton for Forensic Case Assessment and Interpretation. In A. Neustein & H. A. Patil (Eds.), *Forensic Speaker Recognition: Law Enforcement and Counter Terrorism* (pp. 3–20). New York: Springer International Publishing. doi:10.1007/978-1-4614-0263-3_2

Eriksson, A. (2012). Aural/Acoustic vs. Automatic Methods in Forensic Phonetic Case Work. In A. Neustein & H. A. Patil (Eds.), *Forensic Speaker Recognition: Law Enforcement and Counter Terrorism* (p. 539). New York: Springer International Publishing. doi:10.1007/978-1-4614-0263-3_3

European Telecommunications Standards Institute. (2003). *ETSI 201.108 V13.1.1 Speech Processing, Transmission and Quality Aspects (STQ); Distributed speech recognition; Front-end feature extraction algorithm; Compression algorithms*. Sophia Antipolis, France: ETSI.

Google. (2017). *Google Earth Pro Desktop*. Author.

Gorbil, G., Abdelrahman, O., Pavloski, M., & Gelenbe, E. (2015). Modeling and Analysis of RRC-Based Signalling Storms in 3G Networks. *IEEE Transactions on Emerging Topics in Computing, XX*(X), 1–1.

Greenberg, C., Stanford, V., Martin, A., Yadagiri, M., & Doddington, G. (2012). The 2012 NIST Speaker Recognition Evaluation. in NIST SRE12, Orlando, FL.

Hermansky, H., Morgan, N., Bayya, A., & Kohn, P. (1991). RASTA-PLP Speech. Acoustics, Speech, and Signal Processing, 1992. ICASSP-92, 121–124.

Jover, R. P. (2013). Security attacks against the availability of LTE mobility networks: Overview and research directions. *Wireless Personal Multimedia Communications (WPMC), 2013 16th International Symposium on*, 1–9.

Laboratoire Informatique D'Avignon. (2017). *ALIZE - Open Source Speaker Recognition*. Available at: http://mistral.univ-avignon.fr/#download

Larcher, A., Bonastre, J., Fauve, B., Lee, K. A., Christophe, L., Li, H., . . . Parfait, J. (2013). ALIZE 3.0 - Open Source Toolkit for State-of-the-Art Speaker Recognition. Interspeech, 2768–2772.

Lichtman, M., Jover, R. P., Labib, M., Rao, R., Marojevic, V., & Reed, J. H. (2016). LTE/LTE-A Jamming, Spoofing, and Sniffing : Threat Assessment and Mitigation. *IEEE Communications Magazine*, *54*(April), 54–61. doi:10.1109/MCOM.2016.7452266

NIST. (2014). *Computer Forensics Tool Testing (CFTT), Computer Forensics Tool Testing (CFTT) Project Website*. Available at: https://www.cftt.nist.gov

Open Air Alliance. (2017). *Open Air Interface, Home*. Available at: http://www.openairinterface.org (Accessed: 1 January 2017).

Ramasubramanian, V. (2012). Speaker Spotting: Automatic Telephony Surveillance for Homeland Security. In A. Neustein & H. A. Patil (Eds.), *Forensic Speaker Recognition: Law Enforcement and Counter Terrorism* (p. 539). New York: Springer International Publishing. doi:10.1007/978-1-4614-0263-3_15

Zet, X. (2017). *TraX Suite, Cell Phone Investigation*. Available at: http://zetx.com

KEY TERMS AND DEFINITIONS

(e)CID: (Evolved) cell ID.
AMR: Adaptive multi rate.
ARQ: Automatic repeat request.
BTS: Base transceiver station.
CC: Content-of-communication.
CCH: Common control channel.
CID: Communication identifier.
CQI: Channel quality indicator.

CS: Circuit switched traffic.

DL: Downlink direction of communication.

DNS: Domain name service.

DoS: Denial of service attack.

ECID: Enhanced cell ID.

eNB: Evolved node B.

EPC: Evolved packet core.

EPS: Evolved packet system.

EUTRAN: Evolved UTRAN.

GERAN: GPRS radio access network.

GPRS: General packet radio service.

GSM: Global system for mobile.

GTP: Gateway tunneling protocol.

HARQ: Hybrid ARQ.

HI1: Handover interface 1.

HI2: Handover interface 2.

HI3: Handover interface 3.

HSS: Home subscriber system.

IIF: Internal interception function.

IMEI: International mobile equipment identity.

IMS: Internet multimedia subsystem.

IMSI: International mobile subscriber identity.

IP: Internet protocol.

IRI: Interception-related information.

ISDN: Integrated service digital network.

ISO/IEC: International Standardization Organization/International Electrotechnical Commission.

KPI: Key performance indicators.

LAC: Location area code.

LALS: Lawful access location services.

LEMF: Law enforcement monitoring facility.

LI: Lawful interception.

LIID: Lawful interception identifiers.

LTE: Long-term evolution.

MAC: Medium access control.

MAC-LTE: Medium access control LTE.

MCC: Mobile country code.

MFCC: Mel-frequency cepstral coefficients.

MNC: Mobile network code.

MSC: Mobile switching center.
MSISDN: Mobile subscriber ISDN number.
NAS: Non-access stratum signaling.
NEID: Network element identifier.
NID: Network identifier.
OA&M: Operations, administration, and maintenance.
OAI: Open air interface.
OTDOA: Observed time difference of arrival.
PBR: Prioritized bit rate.
PDCP: Packet data convergence protocol.
PDP: Packet data protocol.
PLMN_ID: Public lang mobile network identifier.
PS: Packet switched traffic.
PUCCH: Physical uplink control channel.
PUSCH: Physical uplink shared channel.
QoS: Quality-of-service.
RAB: Radio access bearer.
RASTA-PLP: Relative or spectral perceptual linear prediction coefficients.
RLC-LTE: Radio link control LTE.
RRC: Radio resource control.
RTT: Round trip time.
SAC: Service area code.
SGSN: Serving GPRS support node.
SIM: Subscriber module identification.
SMS: Short message service.
SRS: Sounding reference signal.
TAU: Tracking area update.
TCP: Transmission control protocol.
TTFF: Time-to-first-fix.
UE: User equipment.
UL: Uplink direction of communication.
UMTS: Universal mobile telecommunication system.
UTC: Universal coordinated time.
UTRAN: UMTS radio access network.
WAV: Windows audio video.

Chapter 8

Mobile Network Forensics:
Emerging Challenges and Opportunities

ABSTRACT

Mobile networks are evolving towards the fifth generation, with radical changes in the delivery of user services. To take advantage of the new investigative opportunities, mobile network forensics need to address several technical, legal, and implementation challenges. The future mobile forensics need to adapt to the novelties in the network architecture, establish capabilities for investigation of transnational crimes, and combat clever anti-forensics methods. At the same time, legislation needs to create an investigative environment where strong privacy safeguards exist for all subjects of investigation. These are rather complex challenges, which, if addressed adequately, will ensure investigative continuity and keep the reputation of mobile network forensics as a highly effective discipline. In this context, this chapter elaborates the next-generation of mobile network forensics.

INTRODUCTION

This chapter discusses the future of mobile network forensics as of the emerging challenges and investigative opportunities. The complete redesign of the 5G network architecture with new deployment scenarios, control and user plane separation, and flexibility for network slicing bring a whole new layer of complexity for implementation of the mobile network forensics mechanisms. The cross-border investigations are also discussed as a unique challenge

DOI: 10.4018/978-1-5225-5855-2.ch008

that warrants joint utilization of interception mechanisms from operators belonging to different jurisdictions. Mobile network forensic investigations are effective in yielding evidence with high probative value that criminals and attackers are trying to diminish or eliminate completely. The anti-forensics challenges and opportunities for detection are also discussed as of the types, tools, and common actions taken to preserve the normal acquisition, analysis and interpretation of potential mobile network evidence. Lastly, the privacy protection by design for LI and LALS is discussed to prevent illicit and unauthorized use of mobile network data.

5G Mobile Network Forensics

5G Deployment Scenarios

To meet the International Telecommunication Union (ITU) IMT-2020 requirements, the 3rd Generation Partnership Project (3GPP) envisions a fifth generation (5G) with a support for new radio access technologies, control and user plane separation, network slicing, and network sharing. The new 5G air interface is required to provide a marked improvement in the Quality-of-Experience (QoE) as of 20 Gb/s for downlink and 10 Gb/s for uplink peak data rates, 4 milliseconds latency for user traffic and 10 milliseconds latency for control traffic, and continuous service support for one million users per km^2 connection density.

The 5G radio access is also required to support internetworking with satellite networks next to the LTE-WLAN Aggregation (LWA) and LTE WLAN Radio Level Integration with IPsec Tunnel (LWIP) introduced with LTE-Advanced. 3GPP introduces new deployment scenarios that include: indoor hotspots, high urban density, high speed vehicles and trains, extreme long distance coverage in low density areas, urban coverage for massive Machine Type Communication (mMTC), connected cars, commercial air-to-ground service, and service for light aircraft/helicopters (3rd Generation Partnership Project, 2017b).

From a forensics perspective, the 5G access is required to extend the support for LALS and enable definition/measurement of the scenario-specific KPIs so investigators are able to use target positioning and predict any smart attacks in the radio networks. For LALS, 3GPP retains the current positioning techniques explained in Chapter 6 but also enables for new positioning based on Bluetooth, WLAN, Terrestrial Beacon Systems (TBS), or sensors (3rd

Generation Partnership Project, 2017b). While external positioning techniques will potentially improve the precision, accuracy, and Time-To-First-Fix (TTFF), they will also require adaptations in the forensic processing of the localization information. Investigators have to consolidate multiple (RSTD) measurements or localization Intercept Related Information (IRI) records received for a given target identity (e.g. eliminate/report discrepancies in coordinates, velocity, or timestamps).

As of interpretation, investigators have to contextualize the case under investigation as of the new deployment scenarios too. The velocity and altitude reported in the RSTD are of critical forensic significance in investigating users traveling on a high-speed train or light aircraft/helicopter or using an indoor hotspot, respectively. Similarly, the precision and accuracy expressed as errors in the RSTD measurements for the longitude and latitude are critical for the interpretation of the localization data received for investigated users/ device in dense urban areas, or in extreme long-distance coverage.

The new deployment scenarios will warrant reconsideration of the attack vectors targeting the mobile network infrastructure. One of the largest DDoS attack in Internet history was launched by an Internet-of-Things (IoT) botnet that generated more than 600 Gb/s traffic (Herzberg, Bekerman and Zifman, 2016). The mMTC opens the possibility for similar attacks to be launched to saturate the network capacity and decrease the QoE level. Investigators have to process new Key Performance Indicators (KPI) specific to the new radio access technologies, WLAN, and satellite networks to determine if there is any irregular/malicious traffic behavior that might not be detected with the present radio access KPIs discussed in Chapter 6 and Chapter 7.

Control and User Plane Separation

By separating the control and user planes, operators can independently scale the network, optimize the costs for deployment, and improve the quality of the mobile service as of speeds and latency. The Control and User Plane Separation (CUPS) is enabled by Network Function Virtualization (NFV) and Software Defined Networking (SDN) – two novel technologies allow operators to virtualize main components of the network and use network programming to configure the delivery of the mobile network service (Costa-Requena *et al.*, 2015; Nguyen, Member and Brunstrom, 2017; Schmitt, Landais and Yang, 2017).

Figure 1 shows an example 5G CUPS network architecture where the control and user plane of the Serving Gateway (S-GW), Packet Gateway (P-GW) and the TDF are separated (TDF – Traffic Detection Function is a network function that enables implementation of different charging and traffic policies in the Policy Charging Rules Function – PCRF, based on the application layer traffic exchanged on the *SGi* interface). Three new SDN interfaces are introduced – *Sxa*, *Sxb*, and *Sxc*, all of which implement the Packet Forwarding Control Plane (PFCP) protocol shown in Figure 2 in order to support:

1. Serving users by single control plane node, but more than one user plane
2. Allocation of Gateway Tunneling Protocol (GTP) Tunnel Endpoint Identifier (TEID)
3. Rules delegation - Packet inspection, packet forwarding, QoS enforcement, and traffic and performance measurement (3rd Generation Partnership Project, 2016)

To allow mobile network forensics investigations, CUPS requires adaptations in the LI configuration, as well as in the OA&M function. While the Handover Interface 1 (HI1) can basically remain unchanged as in the current LI/LALS configuration (see Chapter 7 - Figure 8), the S-GW-Control (S-GW-C) and P-GW- Control (P-GW-C) are the ones that deliver the IRIs over the Delivery Function 2 (DF2) and Handover Interface 2 (HI2) to the Law Enforcement Monitoring Facility (LEMF) and the S-GW-User

Figure 1. Conceptual CUPS architecture of the 5G network

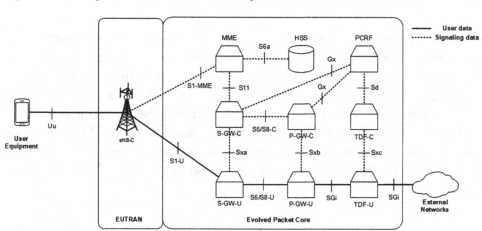

Figure 2. CUPS Sx protocol interface

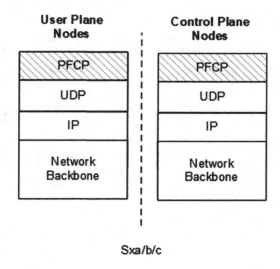

(S-GW-U) and P-GW-User (P-GW-U) are the ones that deliver the Content-of-Communication over Delivery Function 3 (DF3) and Handover Interface 2 (HI3) to LEMF as shown in Figure 3. Adaptation is also required in the IRI parameters to enable for correlation of IRIs produced from different user plane nodes that handle the same target/service subject of interception in the same time (see Chapter 6 - Table 6b). A possible parameter that can be used for this purpose is either the PCFP or Sx user session identifier.

With the separation, the KPIs used for detecting malicious or abnormal network behavior have to reflect the rule/flow based traffic handling in addition to the standalone user/ traffic. As discussed in Chapter 2, potential mobile network evidence can be extracted from the PDCP traffic and traffic flow graphs derived from user plane nodes. Given that CUPS is an SDN-based implementation, investigators can utilize some of the forensic processing techniques and tools developed for investigating standalone SDN environments, for example the *SDN interpreter* or *ForCon*, with modification to support PDCP as the SDN control protocol (Khan *et al.*, 2016; Spiekermann, Eggendorfer and Keller, 2017).

Network Slicing

Network slicing is a 5G feature that allows a creation of customized network partitions per traffic category, network performance, and subscriber type

Figure 3. Conceptual LI architecture of the 5G network

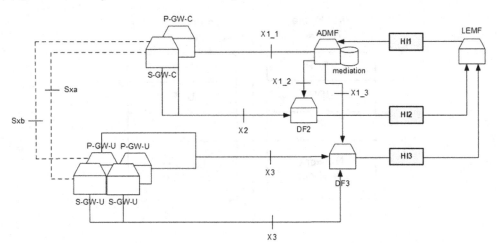

(3rd Generation Partnership Project, 2017a). For example, operators can create a slice for mMTC or slices for capacity/coverage on demand out of the available network capacity (Ericsson, 2017b). Each of these is a Network Slice Instance (NSI) that contains one or more Network Slice Subnet Instances (NSSI), which further contains network functions belonging to the core and/ or the radio access network elements as shown in Figure 4. NSI can share NSSI and each NSSI can belong to a different Network Operator (NOP) so Communication Service Providers (CSPs) can offer:

1. **Business-to-Consumer (B2C) Services:** E.g. web browsing, VoLTE, video streaming
2. **Business-to-Business (B2B) Services:** E.g. Internet access, instant messaging
3. **Business-to-Business-to-Business/Customer (B2B2X) Services:** e.g. services offered to other CSP (e.g. international/national roaming or radio access network sharing) or to NOPs (e.g. mobile broadband) offering themselves communication services to their own customers.

Each communication service can be a bundle of these service, meaning that it can include data (streaming), voice (VoLTE), and roaming (via rich communication services) offered and fulfilled by different packet data network functions (e.g. S-GW-U and P-GW-U can be from one operator and the serving evolved Node Bs - eNBs from another).

Figure 4. 5G network slicing concept

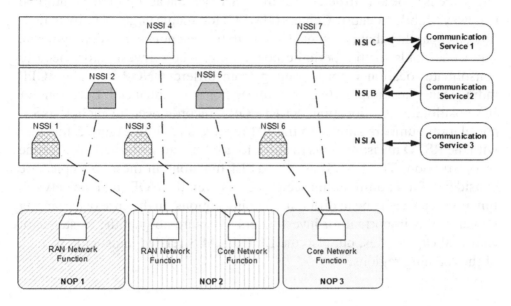

The network slicing feature poses several challenges for the mobile network forensics. For example, if the Law Enforcement Agency (LEA) wants to activate LI for a target identity using communication service 1 (e.g. VoLTE) and communication service 2 (e.g. web browsing) from different CSPs, it needs to simultaneously submit a LI activation request on all HI1 interfaces established with different NOPs as shown in Figure 5. Each NOP will have to deliver IRI and CCs with NSSI-correlation numbers in addition to the IRI-CC correlation numbers, so the LEA can consolidate all the records for a given Lawful Interception Identifier (LIID).

The tools for correlation of IRI and CC or service activity reconstruction described in Chapter 7 then have to be updated so investigators can work with multiple IR and CC sources. Further, the Charging Data Records (CDR) need also to reflect the NSSI and NSI information in order to extract the service details (e.g. receiving a VoLTE call while having an active browsing session) and location information (e.g. when on a high-speed train) so the service activity can be mapped and analyzed properly without missing service segments.

The LALS function for network slicing shown in Figure 6 requires adaptations to enable continuous support for target positioning and Enhanced Location for IRI. For the immediate target positioning, LEA as the LCS client needs to be able to determine the exact location as reported by multiple Gateway Mobile Location Centers (GMLC) for a same target identity in real-time, a capability that is not available with the recent network deployments. The same holds for the periodic positioning, where investigators need to consolidate location reports coming from different NOP and non-3GPP radio access techniques (e.g. satellite). For the Enhanced Location for IRI positioning, the location IRI-REPORT records need to include NSSI correlation numbers similar to the IRI records shown in Figure 5 together with the RSTD measurements to allow for a complete spatio-temporal crime reconstruction. The LALS, as well as LI functions in these examples are considered for a non-roaming scenario, however, the NOPs and the network functions can easily be in different roaming regions. In the case of a roaming scenario, it is important for investigators to ensure not just the existence of technical capabilities, but also the LI and LALS related legislation in each of the roaming regions.

Figure 5. LI function for network slicing

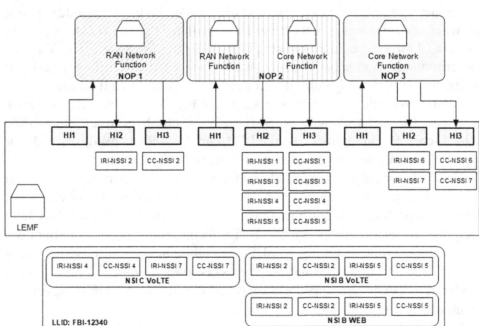

Figure 6. LALS function for network slicing

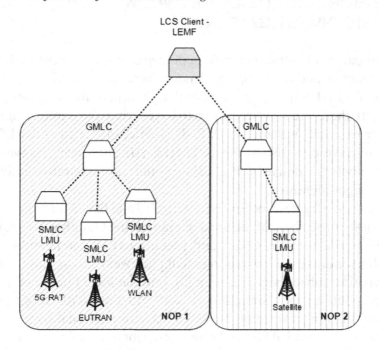

The communication services can also be attacked, targeting a particular NSI, NSSI, or a network function. Smart jamming of a Radio Access Network (RAN function in NOP 1 and signaling storm against the core function in NOP 2 can be coordinated to affect the NSI B (NNSI 2 and NSSI 5) and with that degrade the communication service 1 and 2. Different NOPs have differently configured KPIs both for their network functions and NSSIs so it is essential for investigators to be prepared to examine, analyze, and interpret KPI measurements from different NOPs, especially in responding to real-time attacks where the service outages times need to be in accordance with the service level agreement between the NOPs and the CSPs.

Traditionally, the affected mobile operator is in a possession of both the OA&M and the network functions, so the service attacks are considered as mobile targeted attacks. With the network slicing, there is a distinction between mobile service targeted and mobile network targeted attacks in that a mobile service attack can be accomplished with multiple network targeted attacks, and a single mobile network targeted attack can affect multiple communication services. The investigation of the suspected abnormalities in the and user traffic from different slices must reflect this distinction.

CROSS-BORDER MOBILE NETWORK FORENSIC INVESTIGAITONS

The investigations of mobile network facilitated crimes assumes that the mobile network operator and LEAs operate under the same regulation covering the use of LI and LALS in the geographical areas where the operator provides coverage. If there are multiple operators covering the same geographical areas - for example Verizon, AT&T, T-Mobile, or Sprint – the LEAs are assumed to have established the HI1, HI2, HI3 interfaces, as well as the secure channels for delivery of CDRs or other administrative information about the target identities.

The legislative framework covers the use of LI and LALS for target identities that are home subscribers of the local operators (the Omnibus Crime Control and Safe Streets Act - OCCSSA and Electronic Communications Privacy Act - ECPA for domestic law enforcement purposes) and for target identities that are visiting subscribers, i.e. roaming into the local operators' networks (the Foreign Intelligence Surveillance Act - FISA and Title II of the Patriot Act for investigating suspected foreigner activities on local soil).

The use of LI and LALS for home subscribers roaming to operators in other countries and jurisdictions is not regulated and depends on whether the local and visiting LEAs have previously established any formal agreement for delivery of cross-border intercepted materials. There are several challenges of LI/LALS authorization for such an investigation scenario (e.g. investigating organized crime or terrorism):

1. **Lack of Global LI/LALS Legal Framework:** LEAs need to make formal agreements with each country/jurisdiction to be able to obtain IRI, CC, or periodic location of the target identities investigated. Although most of the countries are willing collaborate on a reciprocal basis, there might be countries rejecting LI/LALS requests because their national laws prohibit the sharing of respective information with non-domestic LEAs. Without globally agreed LI/LALS legal authorizations, cross-border mobile network forensic investigations are hard to yield useful evidence and results. The development of such a framework is not an easy task, considering that it shall incorporate strong safeguards for privacy and harmonization of the investigative contexts. A similar effort for cross-border collaboration between the European LEAs was the objective of the MACACO project, but the focus was on satellite positioning and

push-to-talk radio communications for pursuit of criminals crossing a border, close support of vehicles going through a border, and disaster relief operations (Rajamäki and Kämppi, 2013).

2. **Lack of Global LI/LALS Architecture:** Even if there is an agreement between cross-border LEAs for collaboration, there exists no global LI/LALS architecture to realize any cross-border investigation. The implementation will require adaptations in the HI1 interface to either enable other LEAs to submit LI/LALS requests or have a centralized, global authority responsible for brokerage of these requests to contact the domestic LEA and submit the request on the behalf of a non-domestic agency. The similar architectural requirements hold for HI2 and HI3 so the delivery can be realized either in a distributed or a centralized manner. Currently, there are no technical guidelines or standardization on how such a global LI/LALS architecture can be realized for the current mobile network deployments. As already mentioned, the 5G networks will add additional complexity in realization of such an architecture with the CUPS and network slicing features.

3. **Lack of Globally Harmonized LI/LALS Investigation Processes and Procedures:** Chapter 7 proposes and elaborates on standardized processes and procedures for mobile network forensic investigation, but the investigative practice is far from being harmonized across different LEAs, even within the same country. For example, in some legal systems it is sufficient to provide a service reconstruction based only on CDRs, while in other legal systems warrant full reconstruction with the associated IRI and CC records, if such exist. The lack of common forensic language between different LEAs humpers the investigation and may introduce critical delays that can affect the timely acquisition, analysis, and interpretation of mobile network evidence.

MOBILE APPLICATION ENCRYPTION

The objective of the lawful interception is to extract potential mobile network evidence from both the content of communication and the intercepted related information. Historically, the content of communication was a Circuit Switched (CS) telephone service provided and encrypted by the mobile operator so the decryption for investigation purposes is easily negotiated during the readiness phase by delivering the decryption keys to the LEA. The same principle applies when the LI is invoked for network encrypted Packet Switched (PS) services. Nowadays, most of the mobile PS traffic is third-party encrypted, i.e. users' web sessions are Secure Socket Layer (SSL) protected and the Voice-over-Internet Protocol (VoIP) or interactive messaging chats are application-level protected, so the LEA needs to obtain the decryption keys from the third-party application providers to be able to decrypt and process the content of communication delivered by the mobile operators.

In practice, the analysis of the application-protected mobile traffic is not straightforward and investigators need to closely work with information produced either from a forensic analysis of the mobile devices used by the target identities (which might not be always available, especially in real-time investigations) or by application-specific analysis. Throughout the book, the forensic analysis of mobile devices was not explicitly addressed because it is a separate subfield of digital forensics that deals with the information stored on the mobile device itself, rather than the communication or transient information exchanged with it, which is the main focus of the mobile network forensics. As such, it warrants special attention and a book of itself, so interested readers can refer to (Ayers, Brothers and Jansen, 2014; Lee, 2015; Androulidakis, 2016) for detailed guidelines and elaboration of the mobile forensics practice. However, some of the information extracted from the mobile devices – for example, International Mobile Subscriber Identity (IMSI), International Mobile Equipment Identity (IMEI) dialed numbers, and Short Message Service (SMS) - were implicitly regularly referred to when discussing various aspects of mobile network forensics. These findings are instrumental in investigations where additional network information is needed (usually CDRs) for the IMSI, IMEI or the dialed numbers extracted from seized mobile devices.

Most of the VoIP and interactive messaging applications incorporate proprietary application communication protocols combined with different authentication and encryption algorithms. For example, the *WhatsApp* application uses FunXMPP protocol for communication, two proprietary authentication handshakes, and RC4 stream cipher for encryption/decryption of the traffic. The forensic analysis of the WhatsApp's encryption, authentication, call flow, and voice codes detailed in (Karpisek, Baggili and Breitinger, 2015) is essential for the mobile network forensics to enable full interpretation of a CC containing WhatsApp encrypted traffic. In a similar application-specific analysis, authors in (Walnycky *et al.*, 2015) forensically processed the communication flows, authentication, and encryption of 20 of the most popular VoIP and interactive messaging applications for Android mobile operating system.

The interactive messaging applications using SSL protection yielded no information after an extensive traffic, network and application analysis, implying that the investigation of SSL protected CC traffic is critically depended of the decryption keys provided by the application provider (the procedures of obtaining these keys by the LEA and their application for lawful traffic decryption is out of the scope of this book). An interesting finding from the analysis is the transmission of Google Maps coordinates by most of the applications. Given that these are Global Positioning Service (GPS) coordinates and can be correlated with the internal application timestamps and the coordinates/time in associated Enhanced Location for IRI reports for a same target identity, investigators have the opportunity to test any localization related hypothesis with an additional, application-level localization information (see Chapter 7 – Figure 3).

ANTI-FORENSICS

Criminals and attackers relying on the mobile network to support their illegal activities are well aware of the Locard's principle for cross-transfer of evidence with the scene: every action leaves a trace for the user activity on the network side, for example in the CDRs or user administration records, even for a normal operation with no ongoing investigation. Knowing that mobile networks can yield potential evidence of high quality that is hard to eliminate, many of them attempt to compromise the availability or usefulness of it to the forensics process (Harris, 2006). These attempts are known as *anti-forensics* and the common anti-forensic methods are summarized in Table 1.

Table 1. Mobile network anti-forensics methods

Anti-forensics methods	Mobile Network Facilitated Crime	Mobile Network Targeted Attacks
Destroying of evidence	Unauthorized access to the network/LEA/forensics laboratory databases/ systems – deletion of user/network performance data and potential mobile network evidence	
Evidence hiding	Use of proprietary application encryption, steganography, or Tor; Use of speaker disguise tools; Use of tools to fake/interfere with the cellphone location	Unauthorized access to the network databases/systems – modification of network performance data
Eliminating evidence sources	Use of burner phones	
Counterfeiting evidence	Use of (U)SIM/network impersonation tools	

To destroy, hide, or eliminate evidence sources about a potential criminal act or mobile network targeted attack, criminals/attackers need to obtain unauthorized access to the network databases with CDRs, KPIs, the Administration Function (ADMF), the GMLC administering the LI and LALS requests, the LEMF database, or any protected evidence database/system with potential mobile network evidence in a forensics laboratory. This requires getting valid credentials the network engineers, network equipment vendors, and investigators use during their normal course of action, tampering with the databases/systems and eliminating any suspicious logs about the unauthorized access/data destruction. Although these are not easy tasks to do, they were the exact ones that have been carried out in the malicious misuse of the LI function of Vodafone Greece mobile operator during 2004 and 2005 (Prevelakis and Spinellis, 2005).

In this infamous case of unauthorized wiretapping, attackers have implanted undetectable malware in the Remote-control Equipment Subsystem (RES) of three Interception Control Elements (ICE) (Ericsson AXE Mobile Switching Center) to store a list of targeted numbers and covertly forward their traffic to 14 prepaid cell phones, controlled by the attackers. The attack was possible because Vodafone has not implemented the ADMF part of the LI architecture at all (named Interception Management System - IMS) that is responsible for keeping a warrant list of target identities and activation of the LI function on the RES without compromising the integrity of the system. Without the IMS, attackers were able to conceal their presence and the parallel malware running unauthorized interception as routinely installed "patches" on the RES correction memory space. It took one incorrectly installed malicious patch to cause interruption in the SMS delivery that raised alarms to the network engineers, which forwarded the measurements and the logs of the abnormal behavior to Ericsson asking for a solution.

After examination of the logs and the software/patch versions on the RES, the rogue software together with the list of targeted numbers were found. As part of a later investigation, it was found that the network engineers had noticed that several BTSs were constantly utilized with an abnormal amount of voice and SMS traffic. It turned out that those BTSs were serving the 14 shadow prepaid phones that accepted constant stream of duplicated user traffic from tens of targeted numbers (voice, SMSs) on the attacker side (Bamford, 2015). Back in 2004/2005 there were no means of investigation of mobile network targeted attacks, but this case emphasizes the importance of close KPI monitoring for detection of any abnormal behavior targeting the normal network operation.

On the user side, several methods for hiding evidence exists, namely by the use of proprietary protected applications for PS voice/data, use of speaker disguise tools for CS voice, use of steganography and anonymous routing client Tor, or tools to fake/interfere with the internal device calculations that report the location of the mobile device. As discussed previously, there are numerous mobile applications enabling end-to-end user encryption that criminals/attackers can utilize to hide their communication. Given the ease of application development, criminals/attackers can make a proprietary application with a strong encryption that provides no decryption keys to the LEA. Another evidence hiding applications at disposal are the so-called *IMSI-catcher detectors* (AIMSICD, 2015).

Due to the nature of the initial network registration, users need to send their IMSI in plaintext to the network before they are assigned a Temporary IMSI (T-IMSI) (Chapter 4 – Figure 15). This vulnerability together with the lack of mutual authentication in GSM enabled law enforcement agencies to catch the IMSI of suspects using fake BTSs known as *Stingrays.* To prevent from this, users that are redirected to register to GSM from an UMTS or LTE network users can get notified whether any attempt was made to capture their IMSI and evade potential tracking.

To hide or counterfeit evidence from a CS Voice CC (usually the identity of the speaker), criminals/attackers can employ techniques to change the voice tone by (1) mechanical way - pinching the nostrils, clenching the jaw, speaking with an object in mouth, etc.; or (2) electronic way – using editing software or voice changer applications to modify the frequency spectral properties of voice (Cao *et al.*, 2017). The objective is to deceive the aural/acoustic analysis or the automatic forensic speaker recognition systems used to determine the identity of the speaker in the intercepted CC. Applications are also used for spoofing GPS location, so investigators need to be aware of fake GPS coordinates in the user traffic from a voice or interactive messaging application as noted earlier in this chapter.

One of the common techniques for eliminating mobile network evidence is the use of so-called *burner phones*. To popularize the prepaid service, mobile operators used to offer cheap mobile devices and/or prepaid Subscriber Identification Module (SIM) cards requiring no registration at all. Criminals quickly recognized the anti-forensics opportunity these prepaid phones/SIM cards were offering: they can be bought with cash, use without registration to establish few calls or send couple of SMSs and then dispose them. Burner phones are still popular options for evading both real-time and non-real-time investigations. Nowadays, criminals/attackers can use similar applications like Burner, Hushed, or CoverMe that can allow for use of multiple IMEIs or subscriber numbers to place/receive VoIP calls or exchange interactive messaging from a single mobile device. Just like the fake numbers, there are ways to fake the information stored on the SIM cards and potentially counterfeit evidence. Using tools like Turbo Sim, Stealth Sim, or Yessim, criminals can tamper and fake details like IMSI or unlock mobile devices to be used with operators different than the one that exclusively sold the device.

On the investigative side, the lack of investigative experience/human error, forensic tool limitations, or physical/logical limitations are also considered contributing factors that increase the changes for successful anti-forensics (Harris, 2006). Investigators have varying degrees of alertness, real world experience, or willingness to inquire hypotheses involving anti-forensics, leaving the investigation short of valuable evidence that otherwise might have been acquired and processed. The tools used for evidence analysis are not immune to anti-forensics too; criminals/attackers can get a hold of a tool, analyze its internal logic, and come with methods to hide or counterfeit evidence.

For example, the automatic forensic speaker recognition systems have less than 100% accuracy for speaker spotting or speaker identification and might easily lead to a wrong conclusion on the conversational parties in an intercepted voice CC. Lastly, criminals/attackers can take advantage of the limited storage and processing capabilities of the LEAs or forensics laboratories. For prolonged investigations that acquire large volume of user traffic or service traffic from a given region, the potential evidence data can easily pile up to several hundred terabytes in a course of a few days. If the LEA or a forensics laboratory has insufficient capacity to store and preserve the acquired material, some of the critical evidence might not get acquired at all.

PRIVACY

By design, LI and LALS are means for the LEAs to obtain legally sanctioned access to private communications and as such are privacy intrusive to the mobile users. Therefore, the invocation of LI and LALS is strictly regulated and expected to be granted only by court and not the LEA or any mobile operator by themselves (Koien and Oleshchuk, 2013). As a highly desirable proposition, authorities have to ensure that any illicit interception must not take place so to protect the individual rights and expectation of privacy, justified in the national security context. However, on several occasions like during the Vodafone Greece wiretapping scandal or the governmental warrantless surveillance program, the invocation of the LI and LALS overstepped the legal privacy protections.

To have privacy-by-design in the LI and LALS architectures, the main challenge is to develop an acceptable scheme for deriving privacy preserving identifiers so to conceal long-term identifiers such as IMSI, subscriber numbers, or IMEI. On one side, these identifiers need to enable fast and exact identification of the user or control traffic without affecting the time sensitivity of the investigation (e.g. real-time immediate positioning) and the operation of the network. On-demand generation of temporal identifiers introduces delays that might prevent acquisition of critical potential mobile network evidence material, for example missing to get the precise 3 dimensional coordinates for a suspect about to commit a crime. In addition, they require a trusting entity to keep constant relationship between the long-term identifiers and the temporal ones. The implementation can possibly resemble the working T-IMSI feature, but requires additional safeguards to ensure redundancy of the trusted entity and more importantly, continuous legal and regulatory oversight.

On the other side, they have to eliminate the possibility for LEAs or an unauthorized attacker to take advantage of both the long-term and temporary identifiers. The intercepted material containing the privacy preserving identifiers needs to be of ephemeral nature, yet available for the investigators even after the conclusion of the investigation. In the same time, any unauthorized party must be prevented from making any useful inferences using the privacy preserving identifiers and target illicit acquisition of CC and IRI. These requirements are hard to achieve with the current LI/LALS implementations, demanding not just technical adaptations, but legal and regulatory reforms too.

CONCLUSION

The new 5G scenarios will broaden the scope of the mobile investigations, warranting additional investigative preparedness and capabilities. The CUPS and the network slicing features introduce fundamental changes that affect the LI, LALS, and OA&M architecture so investigators need also to adapt to the infrastructural redesign to continue working with the next generation of mobile networks. In parallel, the mobile anti-forensics methods and the complexity of the transnational crime are rapidly evolving, challenging the effectiveness of routine mobile network forensics investigations. To stay ahead, this chapter elaborates on the investigative opportunities and highlights the technical and legal issues requiring immediate attention to ensure smooth transition to the next generation of mobile network forensics.

REFERENCES

3rd Generation Partnership Project. (2016). *TR 23.799 V.14.2.0 - Technical Specification Group Services and System Aspects; Study on Architecture for Next Generation System (Release 14).* Sophia Antipolis, France: 3GPP.

3rd Generation Partnership Project. (2017a). *TR 28.801 V2.0.1 - Technical Specification Group Services and System Aspects; Telecommunication management; Study on management and orchestration of network slicing for next generation network (Release 15).* Sophia Antipolis, France: 3GPP.

3rd Generation Partnership Project. (2017b). *TR 38.913 V14.3.0 - Technical Specification Group Radio Access Network; Study on Scenarios and Requirements for Next Generation Access Technologies; (Release 14).* Sophia Antipolis, France: 3GPP.

AIMSICD. (2015). *Android IMSI Catcher, Cellular Privacy.* Available at: https://github.com/CellularPrivacy/Android-IMSI-Catcher-Detector/wiki/Development-Status

Androulidakis, I. I. (2016). *Mobile Phone Security and Forensics (2nd ed.).* New York: Springer. doi:10.1007/978-3-319-29742-2

Ayers, R., Brothers, S., & Jansen, W. (2014). Guidelines on mobile device forensics. Gaithersburg, MD: Academic Press. doi:10.6028/NIST.SP.800-101r1

Bamford, J. (2015). *A Death in Athens, The Intercept.* Available at: https://theintercept.com/2015/09/28/death-athens-rogue-nsa-operation/

Cao, W., Wang, H., Zhao, H., & Qian, Q. (2017). Identification of Electronic Disguised Voices in the Noisy Environment. *Digital Forensics and Watermarking - 15th International Workshop*, 75–87. 10.1007/978-3-319-53465-7_6

Costa-Requena, J., Kantola, R., Santos, J. L., Guasch, V. F., Kimmerlin, M., Mikola, A., & Manner, J. (2015). LTE Architecture Integration with SDN. In M. Liyanage, A. Gurtov, & M. Ylianttila (Eds.), *Software Defined Mobile Networks (SDMN)* (pp. 83–105). Chichester, UK: Beyond LTE Network Architecture. doi:10.1002/9781118900253.ch6

Ericsson. (2017a). *Ericsson Mobility Report, Ericsson Mobility Report.* Available at: https://www.ericsson.com/assets/local/mobility-report/documents/2016/ericsson-mobility-report-november-2016.pdf

Ericsson. (2017b). *Network Slicing, Future 5G networks.* Available at: https://www.ericsson.com/en/networks/topics/network-slicing

Harris, R. (2006). Arriving at an anti-forensics consensus: Examining how to define and control the anti-forensics problem. *Digital Investigation*, *3*(9), 44–49. doi:10.1016/j.diin.2006.06.005

Herzberg, B., Bekerman, D., & Zifman, I. (2016). *Breaking Down Mirai: An IoT DDoS Botnet Analysis, Blogs, Bots & DDOS Security.* Available at: https://www.incapsula.com/blog/malware-analysis-mirai-ddos-botnet.html

Karpisek, F., Baggili, I., & Breitinger, F. (2015). WhatsApp network forensics : Decrypting and understanding the WhatsApp call signaling messages. *Digital Investigation. Elsevier Ltd*, *15*, 110–118. doi:10.1016/j.diin.2015.09.002

Khan, S., Gani, A., Wahid, A., Wahab, A., Abdelaziz, A., Ko, K., ... Guizani, M. (2016). Software-Defined Network Forensics : Motivation, Potential Locations, Requirements, and Challenges. *IEEE Network*, *30*(December), 6–13. doi:10.1109/MNET.2016.1600051NM

Koien, G. M., & Oleshchuk, V. A. (2013). *Aspects of Personal Privacy in Communications - Problems, Technology and Solutions.* Wharton, TX: River Publishers.

Lee, R. (2015). *Mobile Forensic Investigations: A Guide to Evidence Collection, Analysis, and Presentation.* New York: McGraw-Hill Education.

Nguyen, V., Member, S., & Brunstrom, A. (2017). SDN / NFV-Based Mobile Packet Core Network Architectures : A Survey. *IEEE Communications Surveys and Tutorials*, *19*(3), 1567–1602. doi:10.1109/COMST.2017.2690823

Prevelakis, B. V., & Spinellis, D. (2005). The Athens Affair. *IEEE Spectrum*, *44*(7), 26–33. doi:10.1109/MSPEC.2007.376605

Rajamäki, J., & Kämppi, P. (2013). Mobile Communications Challenges to Cross-border Tracking Operations Carried out by Law Enforcement Authorities. *Information Networking (ICOIN), 2013 International Conference on*, 560–565. 10.1109/ICOIN.2013.6496687

Schmitt, P., Landais, B., & Yang, F. Y. (2017). *Control and User Plane Separation of EPC nodes (CUPS), 3GPP next generation architecture.* Academic Press.

Spiekermann, D., Eggendorfer, T., & Keller, J. (2017). Network forensic investigation in OpenFlow networks with ForCon. DFRWS Europe, 66–74. doi:10.1016/j.diin.2017.01.007

Walnycky, D., Baggili, I., Marrington, A., Moore, J., & Breitinger, F. (2015). Network and device forensic analysis of Android social-messaging applications. *Digital Investigation*, *14*, S77–S84. doi:10.1016/j.diin.2015.05.009

KEY TERMS AND DEFINITIONS

3GPP: 3rd generation partnership project.

5G: 5th generation of mobile networks. Still in standardization phase, the first 5G deployments are envisioned for 2020.

AMDF: Administration function.

B2B: Business-to-business.

B2B2X: Business-to-business-to-business/customer.

B2C: Business-to-consumer.

CC: Content-of-communication.

CDR: Charging data record.

CS: Circuit switched traffic.

CSP: Communication service providers.

CUPS: Control and user plane separation.

DF2: Delivery function 2.

DF3: Delivery function 3.

ECPA: Electronic Communications Privacy Act.
eNB: Evolved node B.
EUTRAN: Evolved UMTS terrestrial radio access network.
FISA: Foreign Intelligence Surveillance Act.
GMLC: Gateway mobile location centers.
GPS: Global positioning service.
GTP: Gateway tunneling protocol.
HI1: Handover interface 1.
HI2: Handover interface 2.
HI3: Handover interface 3.
ICE: Interception control element.
IMEI: International mobile equipment identity.
IMS: Interception management system.
IMSI: International mobile subscriber identity.
IMT-2020: International mobile telecommunications-2020 requirements.
IoT: Internet-of-things.
IP: Internet protocol.
IRI: Interception-related information.
ITU: International Telecommunication Union.
KPI: Key performance indicators.
LALS: Lawful access location services.
LCS: Location services.
LEA: Law enforcement agency.
LEMF: Law enforcement monitoring facility.
LI: Lawful interception.
LIID: Lawful interception identifier.
LMU: Location measurement units.
LTE: Long-term evolution.
LWA: LTE-WLAN aggregation.
LWIP: LTE WLAN radio level integration with IPsec tunnel.
mMTC: Massive machine type communication.
MSC: Mobile switching center.
NFV: Network function virtualization.
NOP: Network operator.
NSI: Network slice instance.
NSSI: Network slice subnet instance.
OA&M: Operations, administration, and maintenance.
OCCSSA: Omnibus Crime Control and Safe Streets Act.
P-GW: Packet gateway.

P-GW-C: Packet gateway-control.

P-GW-U: Packet gateway-user.

PCRF: Policy charging rules function.

PFCP: Packet forwarding control plane.

PS: Packet switched traffic.

QoE: Quality-of-experience.

RAN: Radio access network.

RAT: Ratio access type.

RES: Remote-control equipment subsystem.

RSTD: Received signal time difference.

S-GW: Serving gateway.

S-GW-C: Serving gateway-control.

S-GW-U: Serving gateway-user.

SDN: Software-defined networking.

SIM: Subscriber identification module.

SMS: Short message service.

SSL: Secure socket layer.

T-IMSI: Temporary IMSI.

TBS: Terrestrial beacon systems.

TDF: Traffic detection function.

TEID: Tunnel endpoint identifier.

TTFX: Time-to-first-fix.

UDP: User datagram protocol.

UMTS: Universal mobile telecommunication system.

VoIP: Voice-over-internet protocol.

VoLTE: Voice over LTE.

WLAN: Wireless local area network.

Related Readings

To continue IGI Global's long-standing tradition of advancing innovation through emerging research, please find below a compiled list of recommended IGI Global book chapters and journal articles in the areas of heterogeneous computing, complex network analysis, and high performance computing. These related readings will provide additional information and guidance to further enrich your knowledge and assist you with your own research.

Acharjya, D. P., & Mary, A. G. (2014). Privacy Preservation in Information System. In B. Tripathy & D. Acharjya (Eds.), *Advances in Secure Computing, Internet Services, and Applications* (pp. 49–72). Hershey, PA: IGI Global. doi:10.4018/978-1-4666-4940-8.ch003

Adhikari, M., Das, A., & Mukherjee, A. (2016). Utility Computing and Its Utilization. In G. Deka, G. Siddesh, K. Srinivasa, & L. Patnaik (Eds.), *Emerging Research Surrounding Power Consumption and Performance Issues in Utility Computing* (pp. 1–21). Hershey, PA: IGI Global. doi:10.4018/978-1-4666-8853-7.ch001

Adhikari, M., & Kar, S. (2016). Advanced Topics GPU Programming and CUDA Architecture. In G. Deka, G. Siddesh, K. Srinivasa, & L. Patnaik (Eds.), *Emerging Research Surrounding Power Consumption and Performance Issues in Utility Computing* (pp. 175–203). Hershey, PA: IGI Global. doi:10.4018/978-1-4666-8853-7.ch008

Adhikari, M., & Roy, D. (2016). Green Computing. In G. Deka, G. Siddesh, K. Srinivasa, & L. Patnaik (Eds.), *Emerging Research Surrounding Power Consumption and Performance Issues in Utility Computing* (pp. 84–108). Hershey, PA: IGI Global. doi:10.4018/978-1-4666-8853-7.ch005

Ahmad, K., Kumar, G., Wahid, A., & Kirmani, M. M. (2016). Software Performance Estimate using Fuzzy Based Backpropagation Learning. In G. Deka, G. Siddesh, K. Srinivasa, & L. Patnaik (Eds.), *Emerging Research Surrounding Power Consumption and Performance Issues in Utility Computing* (pp. 320–344). Hershey, PA: IGI Global. doi:10.4018/978-1-4666-8853-7.ch016

Ahmed, M. S., Houser, J., Hoque, M. A., Raju, R., & Pfeiffer, P. (2017). Reducing Inter-Process Communication Overhead in Parallel Sparse Matrix-Matrix Multiplication. *International Journal of Grid and High Performance Computing*, 9(3), 46–59. doi:10.4018/IJGHPC.2017070104

Akram, V. K., & Dagdeviren, O. (2016). On k-Connectivity Problems in Distributed Systems. In N. Meghanathan (Ed.), *Advanced Methods for Complex Network Analysis* (pp. 30–57). Hershey, PA: IGI Global. doi:10.4018/978-1-4666-9964-9.ch002

Alfredson, J., & Ohlander, U. (2015). Intelligent Fighter Pilot Support for Distributed Unmanned and Manned Decision Making. In K. Sarma, M. Sarma, & M. Sarma (Eds.), *Intelligent Applications for Heterogeneous System Modeling and Design* (pp. 1–22). Hershey, PA: IGI Global. doi:10.4018/978-1-4666-8493-5.ch001

Alling, A., Powers, N. R., & Soyata, T. (2016). Face Recognition: A Tutorial on Computational Aspects. In G. Deka, G. Siddesh, K. Srinivasa, & L. Patnaik (Eds.), *Emerging Research Surrounding Power Consumption and Performance Issues in Utility Computing* (pp. 405–425). Hershey, PA: IGI Global. doi:10.4018/978-1-4666-8853-7.ch020

Alsarhan, A., Abdallah, E. E., & Aljammal, A. H. (2017). Competitive Processors Allocation in 2D Mesh Connected Multicomputer Networks: A Dynamic Game Approach. *International Journal of Grid and High Performance Computing*, 9(2), 53–69. doi:10.4018/IJGHPC.2017040104

Amitab, K., Kandar, D., & Maji, A. K. (2016). Speckle Noise Filtering Using Back-Propagation Multi-Layer Perceptron Network in Synthetic Aperture Radar Image. In P. Mallick (Ed.), *Research Advances in the Integration of Big Data and Smart Computing* (pp. 280–301). Hershey, PA: IGI Global. doi:10.4018/978-1-4666-8737-0.ch016

Aslanpour, M. S., & Dashti, S. E. (2017). Proactive Auto-Scaling Algorithm (PASA) for Cloud Application. *International Journal of Grid and High Performance Computing*, *9*(3), 1–16. doi:10.4018/IJGHPC.2017070101

Balluff, S., Bendfeld, J., & Krauter, S. (2017). Meteorological Data Forecast using RNN. *International Journal of Grid and High Performance Computing*, *9*(1), 61–74. doi:10.4018/IJGHPC.2017010106

Baragi, S., & Iyer, N. C. (2016). Face Recognition using Fast Fourier Transform. In P. Mallick (Ed.), *Research Advances in the Integration of Big Data and Smart Computing* (pp. 302–322). Hershey, PA: IGI Global. doi:10.4018/978-1-4666-8737-0.ch017

Benson, I., Kaplan, A., Flynn, J., & Katz, S. (2017). Fault-Tolerant and Deterministic Flight-Software System For a High Performance CubeSat. *International Journal of Grid and High Performance Computing*, *9*(1), 92–104. doi:10.4018/IJGHPC.2017010108

Bhadoria, R. S. (2016). Performance of Enterprise Architecture in Utility Computing. In G. Deka, G. Siddesh, K. Srinivasa, & L. Patnaik (Eds.), *Emerging Research Surrounding Power Consumption and Performance Issues in Utility Computing* (pp. 44–68). Hershey, PA: IGI Global. doi:10.4018/978-1-4666-8853-7.ch003

Bhadoria, R. S., & Patil, C. (2016). Adaptive Mobile Architecture with Utility Computing. In G. Deka, G. Siddesh, K. Srinivasa, & L. Patnaik (Eds.), *Emerging Research Surrounding Power Consumption and Performance Issues in Utility Computing* (pp. 386–404). Hershey, PA: IGI Global. doi:10.4018/978-1-4666-8853-7.ch019

Bhargavi, K., & Babu, B. S. (2016). GPU Computation and Platforms. In G. Deka, G. Siddesh, K. Srinivasa, & L. Patnaik (Eds.), *Emerging Research Surrounding Power Consumption and Performance Issues in Utility Computing* (pp. 136–174). Hershey, PA: IGI Global. doi:10.4018/978-1-4666-8853-7.ch007

Bhat, C. G., & Kopparapu, S. K. (2017). Creating Sound Glyph Database for Video Subtitling. In M. S., & V. V. (Eds.), Multi-Core Computer Vision and Image Processing for Intelligent Applications (pp. 136-154). Hershey, PA: IGI Global. doi:10.4018/978-1-5225-0889-2.ch005

Bhoi, A. K., Sherpa, K. S., & Khandelwal, B. (2016). Baseline Drift Removal of ECG Signal: Comparative Analysis of Filtering Techniques. In P. Mallick (Ed.), *Research Advances in the Integration of Big Data and Smart Computing* (pp. 134–152). Hershey, PA: IGI Global. doi:10.4018/978-1-4666-8737-0.ch008

Bhura, M., Deshpande, P. H., & Chandrasekaran, K. (2016). CUDA or OpenCL: Which is Better? A Detailed Performance Analysis. In P. Mallick (Ed.), *Research Advances in the Integration of Big Data and Smart Computing* (pp. 267–279). Hershey, PA: IGI Global. doi:10.4018/978-1-4666-8737-0.ch015

Bisoy, S. K., & Pattnaik, P. K. (2016). Transmission Control Protocol for Mobile Ad Hoc Network. In P. Mallick (Ed.), *Research Advances in the Integration of Big Data and Smart Computing* (pp. 22–49). Hershey, PA: IGI Global. doi:10.4018/978-1-4666-8737-0.ch002

Borovikov, E., Vajda, S., Lingappa, G., & Bonifant, M. C. (2017). Parallel Computing in Face Image Retrieval: Practical Approach to the Real-World Image Search. In M. S., & V. V. (Eds.), *Multi-Core Computer Vision and Image Processing for Intelligent Applications* (pp. 155-189). Hershey, PA: IGI Global. doi:10.4018/978-1-5225-0889-2.ch006

Casillas, L., Daradoumis, T., & Caballe, S. (2016). A Network Analysis Method for Tailoring Academic Programs. In N. Meghanathan (Ed.), *Advanced Methods for Complex Network Analysis* (pp. 396–417). Hershey, PA: IGI Global. doi:10.4018/978-1-4666-9964-9.ch017

Chauhan, R., & Kaur, H. (2014). Predictive Analytics and Data Mining: A Framework for Optimizing Decisions with R Tool. In B. Tripathy & D. Acharjya (Eds.), *Advances in Secure Computing, Internet Services, and Applications* (pp. 73–88). Hershey, PA: IGI Global. doi:10.4018/978-1-4666-4940-8.ch004

Chen, G., Wang, E., Sun, X., & Lu, Y. (2016). An Intelligent Approval System for City Construction based on Cloud Computing and Big Data. *International Journal of Grid and High Performance Computing*, 8(3), 57–69. doi:10.4018/IJGHPC.2016070104

Chen, Z., Yang, S., Shang, Y., Liu, Y., Wang, F., Wang, L., & Fu, J. (2016). Fragment Re-Allocation Strategy Based on Hypergraph for NoSQL Database Systems. *International Journal of Grid and High Performance Computing*, 8(3), 1–23. doi:10.4018/IJGHPC.2016070101

Choudhury, A., Talukdar, A. K., & Sarma, K. K. (2015). A Review on Vision-Based Hand Gesture Recognition and Applications. In K. Sarma, M. Sarma, & M. Sarma (Eds.), *Intelligent Applications for Heterogeneous System Modeling and Design* (pp. 256–281). Hershey, PA: IGI Global. doi:10.4018/978-1-4666-8493-5.ch011

Coti, C. (2016). Fault Tolerance Techniques for Distributed, Parallel Applications. In Q. Hassan (Ed.), *Innovative Research and Applications in Next-Generation High Performance Computing* (pp. 221–252). Hershey, PA: IGI Global. doi:10.4018/978-1-5225-0287-6.ch009

Crespo, M. L., Cicuttin, A., Gazzano, J. D., & Rincon Calle, F. (2016). Reconfigurable Virtual Instrumentation Based on FPGA for Science and High-Education. In J. Gazzano, M. Crespo, A. Cicuttin, & F. Calle (Eds.), *Field-Programmable Gate Array (FPGA) Technologies for High Performance Instrumentation* (pp. 99–123). Hershey, PA: IGI Global. doi:10.4018/978-1-5225-0299-9.ch005

Daniel, D. K., & Bhandari, V. (2014). Neural Network Model to Estimate and Predict Cell Mass Concentration in Lipase Fermentation. In B. Tripathy & D. Acharjya (Eds.), *Advances in Secure Computing, Internet Services, and Applications* (pp. 303–316). Hershey, PA: IGI Global. doi:10.4018/978-1-4666-4940-8.ch015

Das, B., Sarma, M. P., & Sarma, K. K. (2015). Different Aspects of Interleaving Techniques in Wireless Communication. In K. Sarma, M. Sarma, & M. Sarma (Eds.), *Intelligent Applications for Heterogeneous System Modeling and Design* (pp. 335–374). Hershey, PA: IGI Global. doi:10.4018/978-1-4666-8493-5.ch015

Das, P. K. (2016). Comparative Study on XEN, KVM, VSphere, and Hyper-V. In G. Deka, G. Siddesh, K. Srinivasa, & L. Patnaik (Eds.), *Emerging Research Surrounding Power Consumption and Performance Issues in Utility Computing* (pp. 233–261). Hershey, PA: IGI Global. doi:10.4018/978-1-4666-8853-7.ch011

Das, P. K., & Deka, G. C. (2016). History and Evolution of GPU Architecture. In G. Deka, G. Siddesh, K. Srinivasa, & L. Patnaik (Eds.), *Emerging Research Surrounding Power Consumption and Performance Issues in Utility Computing* (pp. 109–135). Hershey, PA: IGI Global. doi:10.4018/978-1-4666-8853-7.ch006

Das, R., & Pradhan, M. K. (2014). Artificial Neural Network Modeling for Electrical Discharge Machining Parameters. In B. Tripathy & D. Acharjya (Eds.), *Advances in Secure Computing, Internet Services, and Applications* (pp. 281–302). Hershey, PA: IGI Global. doi:10.4018/978-1-4666-4940-8.ch014

Das, S., & Kalita, H. K. (2016). Advanced Dimensionality Reduction Method for Big Data. In P. Mallick (Ed.), *Research Advances in the Integration of Big Data and Smart Computing* (pp. 198–210). Hershey, PA: IGI Global. doi:10.4018/978-1-4666-8737-0.ch011

Das, S., & Kalita, H. K. (2016). Efficient Classification Rule Mining for Breast Cancer Detection. In P. Mallick (Ed.), *Research Advances in the Integration of Big Data and Smart Computing* (pp. 50–63). Hershey, PA: IGI Global. doi:10.4018/978-1-4666-8737-0.ch003

De Micco, L., & Larrondo, H. A. (2016). Methodology for FPGA Implementation of a Chaos-Based AWGN Generator. In J. Gazzano, M. Crespo, A. Cicuttin, & F. Calle (Eds.), *Field-Programmable Gate Array (FPGA) Technologies for High Performance Instrumentation* (pp. 43–58). Hershey, PA: IGI Global. doi:10.4018/978-1-5225-0299-9.ch003

de Souza, E. D., & Lima, E. J. II. (2017). Autonomic Computing in a Biomimetic Algorithm for Robots Dedicated to Rehabilitation of Ankle. *International Journal of Grid and High Performance Computing*, *9*(1), 48–60. doi:10.4018/IJGHPC.2017010105

Deepika, R., Prasad, M. R., Chetana, S., & Manjunath, T. C. (2016). Adoption of Dual Iris and Periocular Recognition for Human Identification. In P. Mallick (Ed.), *Research Advances in the Integration of Big Data and Smart Computing* (pp. 250–266). Hershey, PA: IGI Global. doi:10.4018/978-1-4666-8737-0.ch014

Dey, P., & Roy, S. (2016). Social Network Analysis. In N. Meghanathan (Ed.), *Advanced Methods for Complex Network Analysis* (pp. 237–265). Hershey, PA: IGI Global. doi:10.4018/978-1-4666-9964-9.ch010

Don Clark, A. (2016). A Theoretic Representation of the Effects of Targeted Failures in HPC Systems. In Q. Hassan (Ed.), *Innovative Research and Applications in Next-Generation High Performance Computing* (pp. 253–276). Hershey, PA: IGI Global. doi:10.4018/978-1-5225-0287-6.ch010

Dutta, P., & Ojha, V. K. (2014). Conjugate Gradient Trained Neural Network for Intelligent Sensing of Manhole Gases to Avoid Human Fatality. In B. Tripathy & D. Acharjya (Eds.), *Advances in Secure Computing, Internet Services, and Applications* (pp. 257–280). Hershey, PA: IGI Global. doi:10.4018/978-1-4666-4940-8.ch013

Elkhodr, M., Shahrestani, S., & Cheung, H. (2016). Internet of Things Applications: Current and Future Development. In Q. Hassan (Ed.), *Innovative Research and Applications in Next-Generation High Performance Computing* (pp. 397–427). Hershey, PA: IGI Global. doi:10.4018/978-1-5225-0287-6.ch016

Elkhodr, M., Shahrestani, S., & Cheung, H. (2016). Wireless Enabling Technologies for the Internet of Things. In Q. Hassan (Ed.), *Innovative Research and Applications in Next-Generation High Performance Computing* (pp. 368–396). Hershey, PA: IGI Global. doi:10.4018/978-1-5225-0287-6.ch015

Elmisery, A. M., & Sertovic, M. (2017). Privacy Enhanced Cloud-Based Recommendation Service for Implicit Discovery of Relevant Support Groups in Healthcare Social Networks. *International Journal of Grid and High Performance Computing*, 9(1), 75–91. doi:10.4018/IJGHPC.2017010107

Fazio, P., Tropea, M., Marano, S., & Curia, V. (2016). A Hybrid Complex Network Model for Wireless Sensor Networks and Performance Evaluation. In N. Meghanathan (Ed.), *Advanced Methods for Complex Network Analysis* (pp. 379–395). Hershey, PA: IGI Global. doi:10.4018/978-1-4666-9964-9.ch016

Fei, X., Li, K., Yang, W., & Li, K. (2016). CPU-GPU Computing: Overview, Optimization, and Applications. In Q. Hassan (Ed.), *Innovative Research and Applications in Next-Generation High Performance Computing* (pp. 159–193). Hershey, PA: IGI Global. doi:10.4018/978-1-5225-0287-6.ch007

Funes, M. A., Hadad, M. N., Donato, P. G., & Carrica, D. O. (2016). Optimization of Advanced Signal Processing Architectures for Detection of Signals Immersed in Noise. In J. Gazzano, M. Crespo, A. Cicuttin, & F. Calle (Eds.), *Field-Programmable Gate Array (FPGA) Technologies for High Performance Instrumentation* (pp. 171–212). Hershey, PA: IGI Global. doi:10.4018/978-1-5225-0299-9.ch008

Garcia-Robledo, A., Diaz-Perez, A., & Morales-Luna, G. (2016). Characterization and Coarsening of Autonomous System Networks: Measuring and Simplifying the Internet. In N. Meghanathan (Ed.), *Advanced Methods for Complex Network Analysis* (pp. 148–179). Hershey, PA: IGI Global. doi:10.4018/978-1-4666-9964-9.ch006

Garg, A., Biswas, A., & Biswas, B. (2016). Evolutionary Computation Techniques for Community Detection in Social Network Analysis. In N. Meghanathan (Ed.), *Advanced Methods for Complex Network Analysis* (pp. 266–284). Hershey, PA: IGI Global. doi:10.4018/978-1-4666-9964-9.ch011

Garg, P., & Gupta, A. (2016). Restoration Technique to Optimize Recovery Time for Efficient OSPF Network. In P. Mallick (Ed.), *Research Advances in the Integration of Big Data and Smart Computing* (pp. 64–88). Hershey, PA: IGI Global. doi:10.4018/978-1-4666-8737-0.ch004

Gazzano, J. D., Calle, F. R., Caba, J., de la Fuente, D., & Romero, J. B. (2016). Dynamic Reconfiguration for Internal Monitoring Services. In J. Gazzano, M. Crespo, A. Cicuttin, & F. Calle (Eds.), *Field-Programmable Gate Array (FPGA) Technologies for High Performance Instrumentation* (pp. 124–136). Hershey, PA: IGI Global. doi:10.4018/978-1-5225-0299-9.ch006

Geethanjali, P. (2014). Pattern Recognition and Robotics. In B. Tripathy & D. Acharjya (Eds.), *Advances in Secure Computing, Internet Services, and Applications* (pp. 35–48). Hershey, PA: IGI Global. doi:10.4018/978-1-4666-4940-8.ch002

Ghai, D., & Jain, N. (2016). Signal Processing: Iteration Bound and Loop Bound. In P. Mallick (Ed.), *Research Advances in the Integration of Big Data and Smart Computing* (pp. 153–177). Hershey, PA: IGI Global. doi:10.4018/978-1-4666-8737-0.ch009

Ghaiwat, S. N., & Arora, P. (2016). Cotton Leaf Disease Detection by Feature Extraction. In P. Mallick (Ed.), *Research Advances in the Integration of Big Data and Smart Computing* (pp. 89–104). Hershey, PA: IGI Global. doi:10.4018/978-1-4666-8737-0.ch005

Ghorpade-Aher, J., Pagare, R., Thengade, A., Ghorpade, S., & Kadam, M. (2016). Big Data: The Data Deluge. In P. Mallick (Ed.), *Research Advances in the Integration of Big Data and Smart Computing* (pp. 1–21). Hershey, PA: IGI Global. doi:10.4018/978-1-4666-8737-0.ch001

Gil-Costa, V., Molina, R. S., Petrino, R., Paez, C. F., Printista, A. M., & Gazzano, J. D. (2016). Hardware Acceleration of CBIR System with FPGA-Based Platform. In J. Gazzano, M. Crespo, A. Cicuttin, & F. Calle (Eds.), *Field-Programmable Gate Array (FPGA) Technologies for High Performance Instrumentation* (pp. 138–170). Hershey, PA: IGI Global. doi:10.4018/978-1-5225-0299-9.ch007

Goswami, S., Mehjabin, S., & Kashyap, P. A. (2015). Driverless Metro Train with Automatic Crowd Control System. In K. Sarma, M. Sarma, & M. Sarma (Eds.), *Intelligent Applications for Heterogeneous System Modeling and Design* (pp. 76–95). Hershey, PA: IGI Global. doi:10.4018/978-1-4666-8493-5.ch004

Guan, Q., DeBardeleben, N., Blanchard, S., Fu, S., Davis, C. H. IV, & Jones, W. M. (2016). Analyzing the Robustness of HPC Applications Using a Fine-Grained Soft Error Fault Injection Tool. In Q. Hassan (Ed.), *Innovative Research and Applications in Next-Generation High Performance Computing* (pp. 277–305). Hershey, PA: IGI Global. doi:10.4018/978-1-5225-0287-6.ch011

Guerrero, J. I., Monedero, Í., Biscarri, F., Biscarri, J., Millán, R., & León, C. (2014). Detection of Non-Technical Losses: The Project MIDAS. In B. Tripathy & D. Acharjya (Eds.), *Advances in Secure Computing, Internet Services, and Applications* (pp. 140–164). Hershey, PA: IGI Global. doi:10.4018/978-1-4666-4940-8.ch008

Habbal, A., Abdullah, S. A., Mkpojiogu, E. O., Hassan, S., & Benamar, N. (2017). Assessing Experimental Private Cloud Using Web of System Performance Model. *International Journal of Grid and High Performance Computing*, 9(2), 21–35. doi:10.4018/IJGHPC.2017040102

Habib, I., Islam, A., Chetia, S., & Saikia, S. J. (2015). A New Coding Scheme for Data Security in RF based Wireless Communication. In K. Sarma, M. Sarma, & M. Sarma (Eds.), *Intelligent Applications for Heterogeneous System Modeling and Design* (pp. 301–319). Hershey, PA: IGI Global. doi:10.4018/978-1-4666-8493-5.ch013

Hamilton, H., & Alasti, H. (2017). Controlled Intelligent Agents' Security Model for Multi-Tenant Cloud Computing Infrastructures. *International Journal of Grid and High Performance Computing*, 9(1), 1–13. doi:10.4018/IJGHPC.2017010101

Ileri, C. U., Ural, C. A., Dagdeviren, O., & Kavalci, V. (2016). On Vertex Cover Problems in Distributed Systems. In N. Meghanathan (Ed.), *Advanced Methods for Complex Network Analysis* (pp. 1–29). Hershey, PA: IGI Global. doi:10.4018/978-1-4666-9964-9.ch001

Ingale, A. G. (2014). Prediction of Structural and Functional Aspects of Protein: In-Silico Approach. In B. Tripathy & D. Acharjya (Eds.), *Advances in Secure Computing, Internet Services, and Applications* (pp. 317–333). Hershey, PA: IGI Global. doi:10.4018/978-1-4666-4940-8.ch016

Jadon, K. S., Mudgal, P., & Bhadoria, R. S. (2016). Optimization and Management of Resource in Utility Computing. In G. Deka, G. Siddesh, K. Srinivasa, & L. Patnaik (Eds.), *Emerging Research Surrounding Power Consumption and Performance Issues in Utility Computing* (pp. 22–43). Hershey, PA: IGI Global. doi:10.4018/978-1-4666-8853-7.ch002

K. G. S., G. M., S., Hiriyannaiah, S., Morappanavar, A., & Banerjee, A. (2016). A Novel Approach of Symmetric Key Cryptography using Genetic Algorithm Implemented on GPGPU. In G. Deka, G. Siddesh, K. Srinivasa, & L. Patnaik (Eds.), Emerging Research Surrounding Power Consumption and Performance Issues in Utility Computing (pp. 283-303). Hershey, PA: IGI Global. doi:10.4018/978-1-4666-8853-7.ch014

Kannan, R. (2014). Graphical Evaluation and Review Technique (GERT): The Panorama in the Computation and Visualization of Network-Based Project Management. In B. Tripathy & D. Acharjya (Eds.), *Advances in Secure Computing, Internet Services, and Applications* (pp. 165–179). Hershey, PA: IGI Global. doi:10.4018/978-1-4666-4940-8.ch009

Kasemsap, K. (2014). The Role of Knowledge Management on Job Satisfaction: A Systematic Framework. In B. Tripathy & D. Acharjya (Eds.), *Advances in Secure Computing, Internet Services, and Applications* (pp. 104–127). Hershey, PA: IGI Global. doi:10.4018/978-1-4666-4940-8.ch006

Khadtare, M. S. (2016). GPU Based Image Quality Assessment using Structural Similarity (SSIM) Index. In G. Deka, G. Siddesh, K. Srinivasa, & L. Patnaik (Eds.), *Emerging Research Surrounding Power Consumption and Performance Issues in Utility Computing* (pp. 276–282). Hershey, PA: IGI Global. doi:10.4018/978-1-4666-8853-7.ch013

Khan, A. U., & Khan, A. N. (2016). High Performance Computing on Mobile Devices. In Q. Hassan (Ed.), *Innovative Research and Applications in Next-Generation High Performance Computing* (pp. 334–348). Hershey, PA: IGI Global. doi:10.4018/978-1-5225-0287-6.ch013

Khan, M. S. (2016). A Study of Computer Virus Propagation on Scale Free Networks Using Differential Equations. In N. Meghanathan (Ed.), *Advanced Methods for Complex Network Analysis* (pp. 196–214). Hershey, PA: IGI Global. doi:10.4018/978-1-4666-9964-9.ch008

Khan, R. H. (2015). Utilizing UML, cTLA, and SRN: An Application to Distributed System Performance Modeling. In K. Sarma, M. Sarma, & M. Sarma (Eds.), *Intelligent Applications for Heterogeneous System Modeling and Design* (pp. 23–50). Hershey, PA: IGI Global. doi:10.4018/978-1-4666-8493-5.ch002

Konwar, P., & Bordoloi, H. (2015). An EOG Signal based Framework to Control a Wheel Chair. In K. Sarma, M. Sarma, & M. Sarma (Eds.), *Intelligent Applications for Heterogeneous System Modeling and Design* (pp. 51–75). Hershey, PA: IGI Global. doi:10.4018/978-1-4666-8493-5.ch003

Koppad, S. H., & Shwetha, T. M. (2016). Indic Language: Kannada to Braille Conversion Tool Using Client Server Architecture Model. In P. Mallick (Ed.), *Research Advances in the Integration of Big Data and Smart Computing* (pp. 120–133). Hershey, PA: IGI Global. doi:10.4018/978-1-4666-8737-0.ch007

Kumar, P. S., Pradhan, S. K., & Panda, S. (2016). The Pedagogy of English Teaching-Learning at Primary Level in Rural Government Schools: A Data Mining View. In P. Mallick (Ed.), *Research Advances in the Integration of Big Data and Smart Computing* (pp. 105–119). Hershey, PA: IGI Global. doi:10.4018/978-1-4666-8737-0.ch006

Kumar, S., Ranjan, P., Ramaswami, R., & Tripathy, M. R. (2017). Resource Efficient Clustering and Next Hop Knowledge Based Routing in Multiple Heterogeneous Wireless Sensor Networks. *International Journal of Grid and High Performance Computing*, 9(2), 1–20. doi:10.4018/IJGHPC.2017040101

Kunfang, S., & Lu, H. (2016). Efficient Querying Distributed Big-XML Data using MapReduce. *International Journal of Grid and High Performance Computing*, 8(3), 70–79. doi:10.4018/IJGHPC.2016070105

Li, Y., Zhai, J., & Li, K. (2016). Communication Analysis and Performance Prediction of Parallel Applications on Large-Scale Machines. In Q. Hassan (Ed.), *Innovative Research and Applications in Next-Generation High Performance Computing* (pp. 80–105). Hershey, PA: IGI Global. doi:10.4018/978-1-5225-0287-6.ch005

Lin, L., Li, S., Li, B., Zhan, J., & Zhao, Y. (2016). TVGuarder: A Trace-Enable Virtualization Protection Framework against Insider Threats for IaaS Environments. *International Journal of Grid and High Performance Computing*, 8(4), 1–20. doi:10.4018/IJGHPC.2016100101

López, M. B. (2017). Mobile Platform Challenges in Interactive Computer Vision. In M. S., & V. V. (Eds.), Multi-Core Computer Vision and Image Processing for Intelligent Applications (pp. 47-73). Hershey, PA: IGI Global. doi:10.4018/978-1-5225-0889-2.ch002

Maarouf, A., El Qacimy, B., Marzouk, A., & Haqiq, A. (2017). Defining and Evaluating A Novel Penalty Model for Managing Violations in the Cloud Computing. *International Journal of Grid and High Performance Computing*, 9(2), 36–52. doi:10.4018/IJGHPC.2017040103

Mahmoud, I. I. (2016). Implementation of Reactor Control Rod Position Sensing/Display Using a VLSI Chip. In J. Gazzano, M. Crespo, A. Cicuttin, & F. Calle (Eds.), *Field-Programmable Gate Array (FPGA) Technologies for High Performance Instrumentation* (pp. 1–16). Hershey, PA: IGI Global. doi:10.4018/978-1-5225-0299-9.ch001

Mahmoud, I. I., & El Tokhy, M. S. (2016). Development of Algorithms and Their Hardware Implementation for Gamma Radiation Spectrometry. In J. Gazzano, M. Crespo, A. Cicuttin, & F. Calle (Eds.), *Field-Programmable Gate Array (FPGA) Technologies for High Performance Instrumentation* (pp. 17–41). Hershey, PA: IGI Global. doi:10.4018/978-1-5225-0299-9.ch002

Mahmoud, I. I., Salama, M., & El Hamid, A. A. (2016). Hardware Implementation of a Genetic Algorithm for Motion Path Planning. In J. Gazzano, M. Crespo, A. Cicuttin, & F. Calle (Eds.), *Field-Programmable Gate Array (FPGA) Technologies for High Performance Instrumentation* (pp. 250–275). Hershey, PA: IGI Global. doi:10.4018/978-1-5225-0299-9.ch010

Maji, A. K., Rymbai, B., & Kandar, D. (2016). A Study on Different Facial Features Extraction Technique. In P. Mallick (Ed.), *Research Advances in the Integration of Big Data and Smart Computing* (pp. 224–249). Hershey, PA: IGI Global. doi:10.4018/978-1-4666-8737-0.ch013

Mallick, P. K., Mohanty, M. N., & Kumar, S. S. (2016). White Patch Detection in Brain MRI Image Using Evolutionary Clustering Algorithm. In P. Mallick (Ed.), *Research Advances in the Integration of Big Data and Smart Computing* (pp. 323–339). Hershey, PA: IGI Global. doi:10.4018/978-1-4666-8737-0.ch018

Mandal, B., Sarma, M. P., & Sarma, K. K. (2015). Design of a Power Aware Systolic Array based Support Vector Machine Classifier. In K. Sarma, M. Sarma, & M. Sarma (Eds.), *Intelligent Applications for Heterogeneous System Modeling and Design* (pp. 96–138). Hershey, PA: IGI Global. doi:10.4018/978-1-4666-8493-5.ch005

Manjaiah, D. H., & Payaswini, P. (2014). Design Issues of 4G-Network Mobility Management. In B. Tripathy & D. Acharjya (Eds.), *Advances in Secure Computing, Internet Services, and Applications* (pp. 210–238). Hershey, PA: IGI Global. doi:10.4018/978-1-4666-4940-8.ch011

Martinez-Gonzalez, R. F., Vazquez-Medina, R., Diaz-Mendez, J. A., & Lopez-Hernandez, J. (2016). FPGA Implementations for Chaotic Maps Using Fixed-Point and Floating-Point Representations. In J. Gazzano, M. Crespo, A. Cicuttin, & F. Calle (Eds.), *Field-Programmable Gate Array (FPGA) Technologies for High Performance Instrumentation* (pp. 59–97). Hershey, PA: IGI Global. doi:10.4018/978-1-5225-0299-9.ch004

Meddah, I. H., & Belkadi, K. (2017). Parallel Distributed Patterns Mining Using Hadoop MapReduce Framework. *International Journal of Grid and High Performance Computing*, *9*(2), 70–85. doi:10.4018/IJGHPC.2017040105

Medhi, J. P. (2015). An Approach for Automatic Detection and Grading of Macular Edema. In K. Sarma, M. Sarma, & M. Sarma (Eds.), *Intelligent Applications for Heterogeneous System Modeling and Design* (pp. 204–231). Hershey, PA: IGI Global. doi:10.4018/978-1-4666-8493-5.ch009

Mishra, B. K., & Sahoo, A. K. (2016). Application of Big Data in Economic Policy. In P. Mallick (Ed.), *Research Advances in the Integration of Big Data and Smart Computing* (pp. 178–197). Hershey, PA: IGI Global. doi:10.4018/978-1-4666-8737-0.ch010

Mohan Khilar, P. (2014). Genetic Algorithms: Application to Fault Diagnosis in Distributed Embedded Systems. In B. Tripathy & D. Acharjya (Eds.), *Advances in Secure Computing, Internet Services, and Applications* (pp. 239–255). Hershey, PA: IGI Global. doi:10.4018/978-1-4666-4940-8.ch012

Mohanty, R. P., Turuk, A. K., & Sahoo, B. (2016). Designing of High Performance Multicore Processor with Improved Cache Configuration and Interconnect. In G. Deka, G. Siddesh, K. Srinivasa, & L. Patnaik (Eds.), *Emerging Research Surrounding Power Consumption and Performance Issues in Utility Computing* (pp. 204–219). Hershey, PA: IGI Global. doi:10.4018/978-1-4666-8853-7.ch009

Mohanty, S., Patra, P. K., & Mohapatra, S. (2016). Dynamic Task Assignment with Load Balancing in Cloud Platform. In G. Deka, G. Siddesh, K. Srinivasa, & L. Patnaik (Eds.), *Emerging Research Surrounding Power Consumption and Performance Issues in Utility Computing* (pp. 363–385). Hershey, PA: IGI Global. doi:10.4018/978-1-4666-8853-7.ch018

Mukherjee, A., Chatterjee, A., Das, D., & Naskar, M. K. (2016). Design of Structural Controllability for Complex Network Architecture. In N. Meghanathan (Ed.), *Advanced Methods for Complex Network Analysis* (pp. 98–124). Hershey, PA: IGI Global. doi:10.4018/978-1-4666-9964-9.ch004

Mukherjee, M. Kamarujjaman, & Maitra, M. (2016). Application of Biomedical Image Processing in Blood Cell Counting using Hough Transform. In N. Meghanathan (Ed.), Advanced Methods for Complex Network Analysis (pp. 359-378). Hershey, PA: IGI Global. doi:10.4018/978-1-4666-9964-9.ch015

Naseera, S. (2016). Dynamic Job Scheduling Strategy for Unreliable Nodes in a Volunteer Desktop Grid. *International Journal of Grid and High Performance Computing, 8*(4), 21–33. doi:10.4018/IJGHPC.2016100102

Netake, A., & Katti, P. K. (2016). HTLS Conductors: A Novel Aspect for Energy Conservation in Transmission System. In P. Mallick (Ed.), *Research Advances in the Integration of Big Data and Smart Computing* (pp. 211–223). Hershey, PA: IGI Global. doi:10.4018/978-1-4666-8737-0.ch012

Nirmala, S. R., & Sarma, P. (2015). A Computer Based System for ECG Arrhythmia Classification. In K. Sarma, M. Sarma, & M. Sarma (Eds.), *Intelligent Applications for Heterogeneous System Modeling and Design* (pp. 160–185). Hershey, PA: IGI Global. doi:10.4018/978-1-4666-8493-5.ch007

Nirmala, S. R., & Sharma, P. (2015). Computer Assisted Methods for Retinal Image Classification. In K. Sarma, M. Sarma, & M. Sarma (Eds.), *Intelligent Applications for Heterogeneous System Modeling and Design* (pp. 232–255). Hershey, PA: IGI Global. doi:10.4018/978-1-4666-8493-5.ch010

Omar, M., Ahmad, K., & Rizvi, M. (2016). Content Based Image Retrieval System. In G. Deka, G. Siddesh, K. Srinivasa, & L. Patnaik (Eds.), *Emerging Research Surrounding Power Consumption and Performance Issues in Utility Computing* (pp. 345–362). Hershey, PA: IGI Global. doi:10.4018/978-1-4666-8853-7.ch017

Panda, M., & Patra, M. R. (2014). Characterizing Intelligent Intrusion Detection and Prevention Systems Using Data Mining. In B. Tripathy & D. Acharjya (Eds.), *Advances in Secure Computing, Internet Services, and Applications* (pp. 89–102). Hershey, PA: IGI Global. doi:10.4018/978-1-4666-4940-8.ch005

Pang, X., Wan, B., Li, H., & Lin, W. (2016). MR-LDA: An Efficient Topic Model for Classification of Short Text in Big Social Data. *International Journal of Grid and High Performance Computing*, 8(4), 100–113. doi:10.4018/IJGHPC.2016100106

Perera, D. R., Mannathunga, K. S., Dharmasiri, R. A., Meegama, R. G., & Jayananda, K. (2016). Implementation of a Smart Sensor Node for Wireless Sensor Network Applications Using FPGAs. In J. Gazzano, M. Crespo, A. Cicuttin, & F. Calle (Eds.), *Field-Programmable Gate Array (FPGA) Technologies for High Performance Instrumentation* (pp. 213–249). Hershey, PA: IGI Global. doi:10.4018/978-1-5225-0299-9.ch009

Perez, H., Hernandez, B., Rudomin, I., & Ayguade, E. (2016). Task-Based Crowd Simulation for Heterogeneous Architectures. In Q. Hassan (Ed.), *Innovative Research and Applications in Next-Generation High Performance Computing* (pp. 194–219). Hershey, PA: IGI Global. doi:10.4018/978-1-5225-0287-6.ch008

Pourqasem, J., & Edalatpanah, S. (2016). Verification of Super-Peer Model for Query Processing in Peer-to-Peer Networks. In Q. Hassan (Ed.), *Innovative Research and Applications in Next-Generation High Performance Computing* (pp. 306–332). Hershey, PA: IGI Global. doi:10.4018/978-1-5225-0287-6.ch012

Pujari, M., & Kanawati, R. (2016). Link Prediction in Complex Networks. In N. Meghanathan (Ed.), *Advanced Methods for Complex Network Analysis* (pp. 58–97). Hershey, PA: IGI Global. doi:10.4018/978-1-4666-9964-9.ch003

Qian, H., Yong, W., Jia, L., & Mengfei, C. (2016). Publish/Subscribe and JXTA based Cloud Service Management with QoS. *International Journal of Grid and High Performance Computing*, *8*(3), 24–37. doi:10.4018/IJGHPC.2016070102

Raigoza, J., & Karande, V. (2017). A Study and Implementation of a Movie Recommendation System in a Cloud-based Environment. *International Journal of Grid and High Performance Computing*, *9*(1), 25–36. doi:10.4018/IJGHPC.2017010103

Ramalingam, V. V. S., M., Sugumaran, V., V., V., & Vadhanam, B. R. (2017). Controlling Prosthetic Limb Movements Using EEG Signals. In M. S., & V. V. (Eds.), Multi-Core Computer Vision and Image Processing for Intelligent Applications (pp. 211-233). Hershey, PA: IGI Global. doi:10.4018/978-1-5225-0889-2.ch008

Rawat, D. B., & Bhattacharya, S. (2016). Wireless Body Area Network for Healthcare Applications. In N. Meghanathan (Ed.), *Advanced Methods for Complex Network Analysis* (pp. 343–358). Hershey, PA: IGI Global. doi:10.4018/978-1-4666-9964-9.ch014

Rehman, M. H., Khan, A. U., & Batool, A. (2016). Big Data Analytics in Mobile and Cloud Computing Environments. In Q. Hassan (Ed.), *Innovative Research and Applications in Next-Generation High Performance Computing* (pp. 349–367). Hershey, PA: IGI Global. doi:10.4018/978-1-5225-0287-6.ch014

Rico-Diaz, A. J., Rodriguez, A., Puertas, J., & Bermudez, M. (2017). Fish Monitoring, Sizing, and Detection Using Stereovision, Laser Technology, and Computer Vision. In M. S., & V. V. (Eds.), Multi-Core Computer Vision and Image Processing for Intelligent Applications (pp. 190-210). Hershey, PA: IGI Global. doi:10.4018/978-1-5225-0889-2.ch007

Rodriguez, A., Rico-Diaz, A. J., Rabuñal, J. R., & Gestal, M. (2017). Fish Tracking with Computer Vision Techniques: An Application to Vertical Slot Fishways. In M. S., & V. V. (Eds.), Multi-Core Computer Vision and Image Processing for Intelligent Applications (pp. 74-104). Hershey, PA: IGI Global. doi:10.4018/978-1-5225-0889-2.ch003

S., J. R., & Omman, B. (2017). A Technical Assessment on License Plate Detection System. In M. S., & V. V. (Eds.), *Multi-Core Computer Vision and Image Processing for Intelligent Applications* (pp. 234-258). Hershey, PA: IGI Global. doi:10.4018/978-1-5225-0889-2.ch009

Saadat, N., & Rahmani, A. M. (2016). A Two-Level Fuzzy Value-Based Replica Replacement Algorithm in Data Grids. *International Journal of Grid and High Performance Computing*, *8*(4), 78–99. doi:10.4018/IJGHPC.2016100105

Sah, P., & Sarma, K. K. (2015). Bloodless Technique to Detect Diabetes using Soft Computational Tool. In K. Sarma, M. Sarma, & M. Sarma (Eds.), *Intelligent Applications for Heterogeneous System Modeling and Design* (pp. 139–158). Hershey, PA: IGI Global. doi:10.4018/978-1-4666-8493-5.ch006

Sahoo, B., Jena, S. K., & Mahapatra, S. (2014). Heuristic Resource Allocation Algorithms for Dynamic Load Balancing in Heterogeneous Distributed Computing System. In B. Tripathy & D. Acharjya (Eds.), *Advances in Secure Computing, Internet Services, and Applications* (pp. 181–209). Hershey, PA: IGI Global. doi:10.4018/978-1-4666-4940-8.ch010

Sarma, M., & Sarma, K. K. (2015). Acoustic Modeling of Speech Signal using Artificial Neural Network: A Review of Techniques and Current Trends. In K. Sarma, M. Sarma, & M. Sarma (Eds.), *Intelligent Applications for Heterogeneous System Modeling and Design* (pp. 282–299). Hershey, PA: IGI Global. doi:10.4018/978-1-4666-8493-5.ch012

Shahid, A., Arif, S., Qadri, M. Y., & Munawar, S. (2016). Power Optimization Using Clock Gating and Power Gating: A Review. In Q. Hassan (Ed.), *Innovative Research and Applications in Next-Generation High Performance Computing* (pp. 1–20). Hershey, PA: IGI Global. doi:10.4018/978-1-5225-0287-6.ch001

Shahid, A., Khalid, B., Qadri, M. Y., Qadri, N. N., & Ahmed, J. (2016). Design Space Exploration Using Cycle Accurate Simulator. In Q. Hassan (Ed.), *Innovative Research and Applications in Next-Generation High Performance Computing* (pp. 66–79). Hershey, PA: IGI Global. doi:10.4018/978-1-5225-0287-6.ch004

Shahid, A., Murad, M., Qadri, M. Y., Qadri, N. N., & Ahmed, J. (2016). Hardware Transactional Memories: A Survey. In Q. Hassan (Ed.), *Innovative Research and Applications in Next-Generation High Performance Computing* (pp. 47–65). Hershey, PA: IGI Global. doi:10.4018/978-1-5225-0287-6.ch003

Sharma, O., & Saini, H. (2017). SLA and Performance Efficient Heuristics for Virtual Machines Placement in Cloud Data Centers. *International Journal of Grid and High Performance Computing*, *9*(3), 17–33. doi:10.4018/IJGHPC.2017070102

Sheikh, A. (2017). Utilizing an Augmented Reality System to Address Phantom Limb Syndrome in a Cloud-Based Environment. *International Journal of Grid and High Performance Computing*, *9*(1), 14–24. doi:10.4018/IJGHPC.2017010102

Shojafar, M., Cordeschi, N., & Baccarelli, E. (2016). Resource Scheduling for Energy-Aware Reconfigurable Internet Data Centers. In Q. Hassan (Ed.), *Innovative Research and Applications in Next-Generation High Performance Computing* (pp. 21–46). Hershey, PA: IGI Global. doi:10.4018/978-1-5225-0287-6.ch002

Singh, S., & Gond, S. (2016). Green Computing and Its Impact. In G. Deka, G. Siddesh, K. Srinivasa, & L. Patnaik (Eds.), *Emerging Research Surrounding Power Consumption and Performance Issues in Utility Computing* (pp. 69–83). Hershey, PA: IGI Global. doi:10.4018/978-1-4666-8853-7.ch004

Sirisha, D., & Vijayakumari, G. (2017). Towards Efficient Bounds on Completion Time and Resource Provisioning for Scheduling Workflows on Heterogeneous Processing Systems. *International Journal of Grid and High Performance Computing*, *9*(3), 60–82. doi:10.4018/IJGHPC.2017070105

Sk, K., Mukherjee, M., & Maitra, M. (2017). FPGA-Based Re-Configurable Architecture for Window-Based Image Processing. In M. S., & V. V. (Eds.), Multi-Core Computer Vision and Image Processing for Intelligent Applications (pp. 1-46). Hershey, PA: IGI Global. doi:10.4018/978-1-5225-0889-2.ch001

Skanderova, L., & Zelinka, I. (2016). Differential Evolution Dynamic Analysis in the Form of Complex Networks. In N. Meghanathan (Ed.), *Advanced Methods for Complex Network Analysis* (pp. 285–318). Hershey, PA: IGI Global. doi:10.4018/978-1-4666-9964-9.ch012

Sreekumar, & Patel, G. (2014). Assessment of Technical Efficiency of Indian B-Schools: A Comparison between the Cross-Sectional and Time-Series Analysis. In B. Tripathy, & D. Acharjya (Eds.), *Advances in Secure Computing, Internet Services, and Applications* (pp. 128-139). Hershey, PA: IGI Global. doi:10.4018/978-1-4666-4940-8.ch007

Srinivasa, K. G., Hegde, G., Sideesh, G. M., & Hiriyannaiah, S. (2016). A Viability Analysis of an Economical Private Cloud Storage Solution Powered by Raspberry Pi in the NSA Era: A Survey and Analysis of Cost and Security. In G. Deka, G. Siddesh, K. Srinivasa, & L. Patnaik (Eds.), *Emerging Research Surrounding Power Consumption and Performance Issues in Utility Computing* (pp. 220–232). Hershey, PA: IGI Global. doi:10.4018/978-1-4666-8853-7.ch010

Srinivasa, K. G., Siddesh, G. M., Hiriyannaiah, S., Mishra, K., Prajeeth, C. S., & Talha, A. M. (2016). GPU Implementation of Friend Recommendation System using CUDA for Social Networking Services. In G. Deka, G. Siddesh, K. Srinivasa, & L. Patnaik (Eds.), *Emerging Research Surrounding Power Consumption and Performance Issues in Utility Computing* (pp. 304–319). Hershey, PA: IGI Global. doi:10.4018/978-1-4666-8853-7.ch015

Swargiary, D., Paul, J., Amin, R., & Bordoloi, H. (2015). Eye Ball Detection Using Labview and Application for Design of Obstacle Detector. In K. Sarma, M. Sarma, & M. Sarma (Eds.), *Intelligent Applications for Heterogeneous System Modeling and Design* (pp. 186–203). Hershey, PA: IGI Global. doi:10.4018/978-1-4666-8493-5.ch008

Swarnkar, M., & Bhadoria, R. S. (2016). Security Aspects in Utility Computing. In G. Deka, G. Siddesh, K. Srinivasa, & L. Patnaik (Eds.), *Emerging Research Surrounding Power Consumption and Performance Issues in Utility Computing* (pp. 262–275). Hershey, PA: IGI Global. doi:10.4018/978-1-4666-8853-7.ch012

Tchendji, V. K., Myoupo, J. F., & Dequen, G. (2016). High Performance CGM-based Parallel Algorithms for the Optimal Binary Search Tree Problem. *International Journal of Grid and High Performance Computing, 8*(4), 55–77. doi:10.4018/IJGHPC.2016100104

Tian, J., & Zhang, H. (2016). A Credible Cloud Service Model based on Behavior Graphs and Tripartite Decision-Making Mechanism. *International Journal of Grid and High Performance Computing, 8*(3), 38–56. doi:10.4018/IJGHPC.2016070103

Tiru, B. (2015). Exploiting Power Line for Communication Purpose: Features and Prospects of Power Line Communication. In K. Sarma, M. Sarma, & M. Sarma (Eds.), *Intelligent Applications for Heterogeneous System Modeling and Design* (pp. 320–334). Hershey, PA: IGI Global. doi:10.4018/978-1-4666-8493-5.ch014

Tripathy, B. K. (2014). Multi-Granular Computing through Rough Sets. In B. Tripathy & D. Acharjya (Eds.), *Advances in Secure Computing, Internet Services, and Applications* (pp. 1–34). Hershey, PA: IGI Global. doi:10.4018/978-1-4666-4940-8.ch001

Vadhanam, B. R. S., M., Sugumaran, V., V., V., & Ramalingam, V. V. (2017). Computer Vision Based Classification on Commercial Videos. In M. S., & V. V. (Eds.), Multi-Core Computer Vision and Image Processing for Intelligent Applications (pp. 105-135). Hershey, PA: IGI Global. doi:10.4018/978-1-5225-0889-2.ch004

Valero-Lara, P., Paz-Gallardo, A., Foster, E. L., Prieto-Matías, M., Pinelli, A., & Jansson, J. (2016). Multicore and Manycore: Hybrid Computing Architectures and Applications. In Q. Hassan (Ed.), *Innovative Research and Applications in Next-Generation High Performance Computing* (pp. 107–158). Hershey, PA: IGI Global. doi:10.4018/978-1-5225-0287-6.ch006

Winkler, M. (2016). Triadic Substructures in Complex Networks. In N. Meghanathan (Ed.), *Advanced Methods for Complex Network Analysis* (pp. 125–147). Hershey, PA: IGI Global. doi:10.4018/978-1-4666-9964-9.ch005

Xu, H., Rong, H., Mao, R., Chen, G., & Shan, Z. (2016). Hilbert Index-based Outlier Detection Algorithm in Metric Space. *International Journal of Grid and High Performance Computing, 8*(4), 34–54. doi:10.4018/IJGHPC.2016100103

Xu, R., & Faragó, A. (2016). Connectivity and Structure in Large Networks. In N. Meghanathan (Ed.), *Advanced Methods for Complex Network Analysis* (pp. 180–195). Hershey, PA: IGI Global. doi:10.4018/978-1-4666-9964-9.ch007

Youssef, B., Midkiff, S. F., & Rizk, M. R. (2016). SNAM: A Heterogeneous Complex Networks Generation Model. In N. Meghanathan (Ed.), *Advanced Methods for Complex Network Analysis* (pp. 215–236). Hershey, PA: IGI Global. doi:10.4018/978-1-4666-9964-9.ch009

Zahera, H. M., & El-Sisi, A. B. (2017). Accelerating Training Process in Logistic Regression Model using OpenCL Framework. *International Journal of Grid and High Performance Computing, 9*(3), 34–45. doi:10.4018/IJGHPC.2017070103

Related Readings

Zelinka, I. (2016). On Mutual Relations amongst Evolutionary Algorithm Dynamics and Its Hidden Complex Network Structures: An Overview and Recent Advances. In N. Meghanathan (Ed.), *Advanced Methods for Complex Network Analysis* (pp. 319–342). Hershey, PA: IGI Global. doi:10.4018/978-1-4666-9964-9.ch013

Ziesche, S., & Yampolskiy, R. V. (2017). High Performance Computing of Possible Minds. *International Journal of Grid and High Performance Computing*, 9(1), 37–47. doi:10.4018/IJGHPC.2017010104

Index

Ensure Quality Research is Introduced to the Academic Community

Become an IGI Global Reviewer for Authored Book Projects

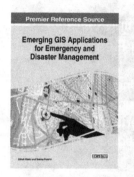
Premier Reference Source

Emerging GIS Applications for Emergency and Disaster Management

Premier Reference Source

Managerial Strategies and Green Solutions for Project Sustainability

Premier Reference Source

Comparative Approaches to Using R and Python for Statistical Data Analysis

Premier Reference Source

Solutions for High-Touch Communications in a High-Tech World

The overall success of an authored book project is dependent on quality and timely reviews.

In this competitive age of scholarly publishing, constructive and timely feedback significantly expedites the turnaround time of manuscripts from submission to acceptance, allowing the publication and discovery of forward-thinking research at a much more expeditious rate. Several IGI Global authored book projects are currently seeking highly qualified experts in the field to fill vacancies on their respective editorial review boards:

Applications may be sent to:
development@igi-global.com

Applicants must have a doctorate (or an equivalent degree) as well as publishing and reviewing experience. Reviewers are asked to write reviews in a timely, collegial, and constructive manner. All reviewers will begin their role on an ad-hoc basis for a period of one year, and upon successful completion of this term can be considered for full editorial review board status, with the potential for a subsequent promotion to Associate Editor.

If you have a colleague that may be interested in this opportunity, we encourage you to share this information with them.

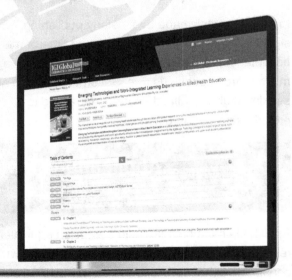